George Yancy

George Yancy

A Critical Introduction

Edited by Kimberley Ducey, Clevis Headley,
and Joe R. Feagin

Foreword by Judith Butler

ROWMAN & LITTLEFIELD
Lanham • Boulder • New York • London

Published by Rowman & Littlefield
An imprint of The Rowman & Littlefield Publishing Group, Inc.
4501 Forbes Boulevard, Suite 200, Lanham, Maryland 20706
www.rowman.com

86–90 Paul Street, London EC2A 4NE, United Kingdom

British Library Cataloguing in Publication Information Available

Library of Congress Cataloging-in-Publication Data
Names: Ducey, Kimberley, editor. | Headley, Clevis, editor. | Feagin, Joe R., editor.
Title: George Yancy : a critical introduction / edited by Kimberley Ducey,
    Clevis Headley, and Joe R. Feagin ; foreword by Judith Butler.
Description: Lanham : Rowman & Littlefield, 2021. | Includes bibliographical
    references and index. | Summary: "This collection gives George Yancy's
    transformative work in social and political philosophy and the philosophy
    of race the critical attention it has long deserved. Contributors apply
    perspectives from disciplines including philosophy, sociology, education,
    communication, peace and conflict studies, religion, and psychology"—
    Provided by publisher.
Identifiers: LCCN 2021030046 (print) | LCCN 2021030047 (ebook) |
    ISBN 9781538137482 (cloth) | ISBN 9781538137499 (epub)
Subjects: LCSH: Yancy, George. | African American philosophers.
Classification: LCC B948.Y364 G46 2021 (print) | LCC B948.Y364 (ebook) |
    DDC 191.089/96073—dc23
LC record available at https://lccn.loc.gov/2021030046
LC ebook record available at https://lccn.loc.gov/2021030047

To George and all the students and others whom he has influenced to make the world a better place

Contents

Acknowledgments

In the preparation of this book, we have been indebted to many loved ones and to supportive and helpful colleagues. Although regrettably we cannot name them all, we would particularly like to thank Emma Clements for her amazing editing skills, Brianna Westervelt and Sylvia Landis at Rowman & Littlefield, and Jasti Bhavya who managed the production of our book. We are especially indebted to our insightful Rowman & Littlefield editor, Natalie Mandziuk, for her unceasing and enthusiastic support for this project and its underlying goals. Finally, we offer gratitude to the brilliant contributors, without whose work this tribute to the indefatigable Professor George Yancy would not have been possible.

Foreword

This volume honors one of the most important and powerful philosophers of our time, singular in his vision and tenacity. George Yancy has sustained a love of philosophy for decades, and this love comes through in his work, whether it is his writing on rap or Black politics; on religious hatreds or spiritual aspiration; on the works of Cornel West, Simone de Beauvoir, Frantz Fanon, Angela Davis, or Frederick Douglass; his reflections on anger and persuasion; his self-reflection on feminism; his numerous interviews and dialogues; or his experiments with the essay form. One might expect that, as someone who has named and described how the white supremacist framework works within the discipline and canon of philosophy, he would break with philosophy as the only way to think outside the terms of white supremacy. But that is not what has happened here. Philosophy is supposed to be the love of wisdom, and that *philo* is a specific form of love. As an adjective, it is attached to someone close, even precious, a way of calling someone dear or beloved, as we do when we write an intimate letter. As a noun, it is a "friend," and as a verb, *philein*, it is a form of love that entails regarding someone with affection. When Yancy studied philosophy at Yale, he encountered what he called a "sea of whiteness," and when he left that program to write as a journalist from the mid-1990s, he sought to understand Black embodiment in the context of a white supremacy that worked its violence in both overt and covert ways. He wrote about hip-hop, but also death, God, and the possibilities of loving and affirmative encounter. He did not exactly leave philosophy, nor did he think that white supremacy owned the future of philosophy. He continued that love of wisdom by seeking to understand what love might mean in the context of a racist culture, what kind of appeal can be made, and through what means could white people be brought closer to the ethical labor of deconstituting white supremacy as it lives, thrives, and reproduces itself in white selfhood and experience. Yancy left that one program in philosophy only to return to Duquesne's Graduate Program in Philosophy with a focus on existential phenomenology. My wager is that it made a difference to have left the academy temporarily, to have passed through journalism that focused on Black popular culture, especially music—hip-hop and rap—and to have found a keener sense of intimate and respectful love. All this he brought forward into philosophy, expanding its terms, its forms, and its public audience. The journalism never fell away, and the philosophy is, as it were, all over the public writings: the questions; the demonstration of what it is to be unknowing and self-reflective; the effort to discern meaning, even ultimate meaning, in the field of Black cultural production; the openness to other worlds, and the public solicitation—think with me, come closer.

George Yancy calls to his readers to come closer, to heed a call to know thyself, and to engage in self-reflective transformation. His writing is organized by a keen sense of address. He is called upon to call upon us, and with every piece there is a question: now, who will take this up? Sometimes these writings are fierce challenges, but there is always a mode of address: he is speaking and writing to us. At least two of his most well-known texts are, in fact, letters: "Dear God" (2019) and "Dear White America" (2015). The first of these was written after twenty-two people were killed in El Paso by a declared white supremacist, a man who was sorry that he was not able to kill more. It was written in the aftermath of nine lives taken in Dayton, Ohio, by another white man, who did not need to declare the white supremacy demonstrated by his violent action. What concerns Yancy in August 2019 was the religious support for the president who circulated and inflamed racist discourse and animus, aided and abetted by evangelicals who did not see the opposition to racist violence as a religious imperative. Yancy is speaking to God as an ordinary person: "As You know, God, Trump recently tried to smear four congress women of color." And yet Yancy is clearly speaking to us, those who suffer and those who look away from suffering and whose complicity intensifies the suffering. For he points out that "something has gone theologically awry" and he seeks to correct that through recourse to James Baldwin's words: "If the concept of God has any validity or use, it can only be to make us larger, freer, and more loving. If God cannot do this, then it is time we got rid of Him." Those last are not exactly Yancy's words, though he understands them. His question is closer to Emerson's: "Why can't I have an original relation to You, God?" Kierkegaardian in spirit, Yancy knows he cannot provide a rational demonstration for the existence of God. But that is not his question. As Kierkegaard eschewed that age-old metaphysical problem of God's existence in favor of the existential question, "How do I become a Christian?" so Yancy asks whether he cannot have an original relationship to God, a direct connection, a sense of presence, if not grace, a sense of what might counter or heal such suffering.

The letter to God is an appeal: Can you come closer? Can we commune directly? He does not know whether God can respond, whether there is even a God who could respond, but the appeal, the letter, is a kind of risk, one that he deems worth taking. Yancy makes this appeal not just because he is curious, but because he suffers, and his appeal is the linguistic register of a "screaming in the night for Your existence to be revealed." His questioning is, he hopes, "a loving posture" and so part of the very love of wisdom that is philosophy. The God he seeks could have many names, and no human knows the right or ultimate name. The letter is an entreaty, calling upon Rabbi Abraham Joshua Heschel's reminder that "God is in search of us," that our entreaty helps God to manifest, enhances that presence. Yancy is an existential philosopher, one who weeps and suffers, whose appeal, search, and longing comes from the lived experience of suffering, what he calls "existential devastations." The "dear" of "dear God" is the entreaty, the effort to summon a relation, a call of love. He shows us what it might be like: "Yahweh, I die just a little when Palestinian children are killed by Israeli forces. Allah, I die just a little when Israeli children are killed by the hands of Palestinians." Yancy's life is bound up with the lives of those who suffer from racial and ethnic violence. His embodiment does not encase him or separate him from others, but it does situate him, as a Black philosopher who weeps, in a relation to the suffering of others. He does not offer a "routine prayer" to an already established God. His calls for a new spiritual relation in the sufferings of others are also our sufferings and where that lived insight draws what we might call God closer. He is calling to God, and to us, but he is also, in a strong sense, fighting for all of our lives.

"Dear White America" might seem like a fully different kind of appeal, but the similarities are striking. In that appeal, for which he received appalling reactions by many white people, he asks that white America "listen with love." He seeks to move us away from hate, revenge, and division, and yet the insults and threats he received for writing this loving petition showed the fierce investment of some white people in those very conditions. He refers there to the risk of unreciprocated love, and though that may seem far afield from the struggle against racism, it turns out to be its most important resource. He calls his letter "a gift" but knows that it may be violently rejected. He asks his white audience to make a space for his voice in their hearts, so he is drawing near, asking for a nearly unbearable intimacy. He draws an analogy, always a dangerous venture, between men who must wrestle with their sexism and white people who must come to terms with their racism. Maybe the analogy does not exactly work, but that is less important than the idea of wrestling with oneself that he has introduced and demanded. Every day of his life, he tells us, he fights against "the dominant male narrative" that would fail to recognize women as equals. This is a struggle that involves repeated failure, but that is the way, he tells us, to deconstitute a subject formation wrought through supremacy. Yancy asks white people to lose their shelter, to let it be raw, to assume the posture of "open flesh." He makes clear that self-flagellation is not what he wants of us, for that would be a further iteration of our infamous practice of defensive self-preoccupation, including our moral narcissism ("I am not a racist!"). The work on the self is coextensive with the opening toward others, and the radical discomfort of doing so when "comfort" in the world has always relied on white privilege. And just when we think that Yancy might turn to God, he turns to love and, once again, Baldwin's wisdom. For Baldwin, love is "a state of being, or state of grace—not in the infantile American sense of being made happy but in the tough and universal sense of quest and daring and growth." Yancy writes a letter to white America: come quest, try to dare, and to grow. Yancy opens himself: "I am asking for love in return for a gift." He knows that racism destroys the racist from within and distorts their sense of love, relationship, and world. He offers the racists the prospect of a self-struggle that is like an internal war, one that will liberate them from their violence and hatred, one that will let them live in a world where equality and respect become shared existential realities. He asks the white parent with a white child to hold that child in the evening, appreciating how precious they are: beloved, dear, cherished. Can the white parent imagine the white child as black and equally precious? What would it take for us to become *philo*, understood as a form of risk, to hold without capture what is most dear?

This love letter was met with death threats, rage, and a torrent of white supremacist vitriol, and for Yancy this yielded an entire book, *Backlash: What Happens When We Talk Honestly about Racism in America* (2018), that sought ever more thoroughly to examine and oppose the hatred to which he was subject. This is no story about unrequited love. This is a story about white people appalled and enraged to be asked to love those who have been for centuries subjected to their arrogance and violence. The request was denied, but some people have heard it. What would it mean to become philosophers bound to the injunction to "know thyself" and to "transform thyself" so that the struggle against racism includes, fundamentally, the demand to engage in a social transformation of the self. The point is neither to recede into individual self-ministrations nor to launch a loud trajectory of self-blame. No, the task is to understand that white people are, to varying degrees, formed within a matrix of white supremacy, but that that formation is ongoing. Our actions rely upon and reiterate that pervasive sense of mobility, regard, the freedom to walk the streets, the assumption of a warm welcome at the neighborhood store, the sense of having a place in institutions of higher learning, on the plane, at the playground. The tributaries of racism have to be unearthed not to pile up guilt, which is, after all, bound up with stasis, but to identify the places where the hard work of transformation can take place.

Yancy dares us to imagine becoming precious to one another, finding and cultivating the loving regard whose tenacity alone would triumph over hatred. Dear God, Dear White America: these are appeals, different modalities of yearning. The injunction to white people: come to know thyself, which means examining the systemic racism that made your comfort in the world possible, and dare to lose the rigidity of your defensive claim on social power, and open to a world of equality that has yet to come into being. If God only makes sense as love, and if Baldwin then remains our guide, then the question formulated in each appeal is whether love is possible in this world and, if so, in what form? The question that every essay poses, either explicitly or implicitly, is: is anyone listening? Is anyone reading? The chapters show their pain and their longing, making a bid for relationality on the basis of vulnerability. They enact the loving posture for which they call. And each essay closes with the same question: Who is there to respond?

Yancy has done no less than renewed philosophy for our times, delivered a challenge to every reader, inside and outside the academy, to become a thinker steeped in passion and to become a lover of wisdom for whom the struggle for racial equality and justice is the contemporary task. For wisdom is not the same as knowledge. It is linked with humility, with knowing what one does not know. One cannot assume that the categories with which we live capture the complexity of the lives they seek to order. At the same time, they do name forms of social power that no one can afford to ignore.

When Yancy left "the white sea" of Yale, he sought to understand Black embodiment within a social world pervaded by white supremacy. He started to develop a philosophy of another kind, one that drew on the rich tradition of existential phenomenology. According to that philosophy, elaborated by Sartre, Merleau-Ponty, Beauvoir, and Fanon in different ways, the body has to be understood not as a closed entity but as modalities of embodiment, ways of existing in the world. If we seek to understand "the body," we are directed toward the world in which it lives, the temporal and spatial coordinates of its movement, the forms of social life in which it gains recognition, and, as Fanon insisted, the sedimented history of racism informing the racial schema that pervades economies, institutions, and the vicissitudes of daily life. The "system" of racism is surely there with its history of slavery, indentured servitude, colonial exploitation, and dispossession. But once we start to ask, how the system is lived, we are in the domain of existential phenomenology—"existential" because there is an existing person who lives the history and its contemporary reality; "phenomenological" because rich description is required to specify the modalities of that kind of living. How else to describe that sense of perpetual exhaustion to which Yancy refers, one that rarely, if ever lifts, when required to face and survive racism on a daily basis?

Throughout Yancy's work, we find less a philosophy of emotions than a passionate form of philosophizing. Lives are at stake in this form of thinking, and one is made to feel this existential urgency. Yancy's writings are full of dangerous gifts. He describes his classroom as full of "dangerous spaces" where, if one were to take up the challenge of thought, one would be undone by what one comes to know. What astonishes this reader is that he did not give up on philosophy but endeavored to make it anew, responsive to the suffering of our times. What moves me time and again is that Yancy still reaches for those who mindlessly or avidly reproduce white supremacy at the expense of Black lives and all those who suffer from racism, have died from its lethal effect, or bear witness to those enormous losses. He will let no one take from him the danger and the gift of loving wisdom, the wisdom of love. The only question is whether those who continue the destructive life of racism will dismantle the world of their supremacy, for knowing thyself means knowing, and taking apart, that violence in the name another, one that Yancy holds out for us in his passionate and daring pages.

Judith Butler

Introduction

Clevis Headley, Kimberley Ducey, and Joe R. Feagin

Robert Farris Thompson, in his classic *Flash of the Spirit: African & Afro-American Art & Philosophy*, writes the following, concerning the emergence of a Black Atlantic visual tradition: "Listening to rock, jazz, blues, reggae, salsa, sambo, bossa nova, juju, highlife, and mambo, one might conclude that much of the popular music of the world is informed by the flash of the spirit of a certain people specifically armed with improvisatory drive and brilliance."[1]

We have chosen to quote Thompson precisely because we think that his contextualization of popular music as "informed by the flash of the spirit of a certain people specifically armed with improvisatory drive and brilliance" applies equally to George Yancy's work, as filtered through the lens of African American culture. It is not our intention to insinuate that there are only occasional remnants or glimpses of brilliance in Yancy's work. Rather, we claim—among other things—that in breaking with the institutionalized stasis of thought and imagination, Yancy's opuses represent a continuous discursive manifestation of pulses of light, which are charged with flashes of the spirit. In turn, his work is infused with the improvisatory drive and brilliance of an Africana tradition. Yet Yancy, in the words of Bryan Van Norden, does not wallow in an unthinking essential ethnocentrism, the view that "defines philosophy as grounded in a particular historical tradition."[2] What he does, as intimated by the title of Van Norden's text, is to take back philosophy and rescue it from the idea that "the essence of philosophy is to be a part of one specific Western intellectual linage."[3] Yancy takes it back by utilizing the rich cultural and philosophical heritage of the improvisatory drive and brilliance of an Africana mode of being in the world.

Our reference to Yancy's improvisational competence also connects with Yancy's ability to straddle the world of professional academic philosophy and the African American intellectual tradition. His improvisational talents are evident in his ability to connect with and redeploy historically relevant and philosophical pregnant resources of the African American intellectual tradition.

Yancy stands in a long line of Black thinkers who have developed a strong anti-oppression counterframing of U.S. society and its founding narrative (white philosophy), including the abolitionist David Walker. Working in Boston in 1829, Walker published what appears to be the first extended statement of an anti-oppression counterframe in U.S. history. In his bold pamphlet *Appeal to the Coloured Citizens of the World*, he crafts a black resistance manifesto for full equality. He addressed fellow African Americans with revolutionary arguments couched in an anti-oppression framing and aggressively circulated it in the North and South, so much so that Southern slaveholders put a substantial bounty on his head.[4] Walker's anti-oppression manifesto lays out important freedom elements—critical philosophical ideas and resistance strategies—that one finds in Yancy's African American counterframe today. Echoing Walker, Yancy takes on the racist stereotyping of the common white racial frame and underscores the contradictions between the extensive oppression of African Americans and whites' rhetorical liberty-and-justice frame. Bringing to mind Yancy's later work, Walker quotes the phrase "all men are created equal" from the Declaration of Independence, and then vigorously challenges white readers:

> Compare your own language above, extracted from your Declaration of Independence, with your cruelties and murders inflicted by your cruel and unmerciful fathers and yourselves on our fathers and on us—men who have never given your fathers or you the least provocation! . . . I ask you candidly, was your sufferings under Great Britain one hundredth part as cruel and tyrannical as you have rendered ours under you?[5]

Walker does not stop with a critique of white racist framing, but also counterframes with a positive view of African Americans: "Are we men!!—I ask you, O. my brethren! Are we men?"

This is the long counterframed worldview tradition of African Americans that Yancy represents and for which he is attacked. Indeed, we similarly find in Yancy's work today insightful accounts of the shameful existential contradictions and analytical failures that reveal the empty rhetoric of political and philosophical liberalism—among other things, the declared commitment to colorblindness and equality.

As in Walker's time, nowadays white racism includes pronounced white racist illiteracy, as shown in the many attacks on Yancy and his work, including following the publication of "Dear White America" in the *New York Times* philosophy column, "The Stone." It was the backlash he received in response to "Dear White America" that sparked the idea for this tribute.

It is beyond contention that Yancy is one of the most important and active voices in the discipline of philosophy today. What is even more remarkable is the extent to which he has invigorated Africana philosophy and, in particular, African American philosophy. Of course, it goes without saying that any discussion about the discipline of philosophy inevitably mutates into metaphilosophical discussions—philosophical discussions about philosophy itself. As consistent with the sociology of knowledge, these types of debates often function as a strategy of closure, as a way to terminate prematurely the debate. In the context of inquisitive responses and skeptical reactions to the idea of Africana philosophy, the effortless retreat to metaphilosophical debates about the nature of philosophy is just one such malicious strategy of closure. If it is indeed the case that philosophy is, by its very nature, a universal discursive practice that is informed by perennial problems regarding sacred philosophical notions such as "truth," "knowledge," or "reality," then Africana philosophy is brought into question, allegedly because there is no such thing as an Africana philosophical tradition that parallels what one would call the Greek tradition in philosophy.

Yancy has never been and will never be "punked out" or intimidated by such juvenile and immature philosophical pranks. He uses philosophical writing as an act of defiance and courage. Instead of seeking closure, Yancy, more often than not, invites others to participate in the philosophical conversation, to tarry with him. What's more, he encourages others to expand the scope of what is considered legitimate philosophical discourse. He also serves as a first-rate example of how one can confront and negate the obnoxious pathogen of racism that robs its victims of epistemic credibility.

To have epistemic credibility is to be perceived as having the right to speak with authority on a subject matter—to be seen as being competent to register an opinion that warrants serious consideration insofar as one is qualified to do so. Miranda Frick has done a brilliant job of discussing the ways in which, in this case, someone such as Yancy is immediately perceived as lacking epistemic credibility. As a person of African descent, the unthematized and unspoken belief is that he lacks the rational, logical, and analytical skills and talents to competently participate in the conversation of philosophy.

Again, Yancy does not seek permission from the white guardians of philosophical respectability in order to speak. He does not allow himself to become distracted by the pathology of the dialectics of recognition in order to first obtain epistemic credibility and then speak as a legitimate philosopher. Yancy is able to avoid this kind of epistemic antics because he wisely rejects the temptation of doing philosophy from "nowhere." He does philosophy from somewhere and it is that somewhere that he invites others to embrace. So, he does not seek to passively receive tutelage from others. Instead, he offers gifts to those who have commonly viewed themselves as burdened by the obligation to paternalistically interact with the unfortunate beings who are unable to free themselves from the shackles of contingency.

We feel compelled to redeploy words that one of the editors (Clevis Headley) has previously used to describe Yancy. In a review of Yancy's *Backlash*, Headley remarks:

> Yancy writes as a philosopher.[6] However, the impulsive assumption that he is just another generic philosopher—writing in a disembodied universal voice, and from the view from nowhere—represents an evasion of the existentially significant fact that he writes as a Black philosopher. The Black philosopher, always already confronted by a challenge to his/her credibility, writes philosophy while negotiating the double threat of testimonial injustice and hermeneutical injustice.[7] The Black philosopher, then, becomes a liminal thinker, at least relative to the universalist conception of things.

We have probably said enough to provide what can be broadly construed as benign biographical details. Accordingly, we do not feel obligated to say much more along these lines. To continue to march in this direction would unnecessarily risk engaging in the shameful practice of reducing Africana philosophical/theoretical activity to biographical details—specifics totally unrelated to the intricacies of theory.

Yancy, in his own way, has variously executed several strategies, which collectively register a significant philosophical shift. He is not another ideologue, who uses rhetoric about the nature of philosophy to advance a partisan agenda or to promote practices of material analytical segregation, according to which the permission to speak is determined by exclusionary criteria. Instead of wasting time in otherwise fruitless debates, Yancy has done an impressive job of grounding philosophy and philosophical practice within the flux, flow, and stream of human experience. As a matter of fact, we do not think that Yancy is particularly concerned with resolving what are often considered bona fide problems. For example, he would not burden himself with the task of finding the right theory of meaning and theory of reference in order to be able to pursue philosophical reflections on the meaning and reality of race and racism. We do not think that it is hyperbolic to claim that instead of searching for a semantics of race and racism, Yancy thinks that more can be gained from pursuing a poetics and hermeneutics of race and racism. He reaches this conclusion because he realizes that the chameleonic features of systemic racism preclude it from possessing sharp edges and boundaries.

Rather, Yancy mobilizes philosophy as a style, a style of critical reflection strategically focused on human existence. So, to the extent that there is a particular philosophical vein in Yancy's work, it is an existential phenomeno-logical philosophy of existence. Unlike most philosophers, who presuppose the transcendental validity of liberalism and its attendant imaginary of prin-ciples, concepts, metaphors, assumptions, and theoretical structures, Yancy creatively and imaginatively utilizes the philosophical resources of existen-tialist philosophy and, in so doing, foregrounds the primacy of ontological freedom and the equally resourceful vocabulary of facticity, transcendence, bad faith, and authenticity. For those who believe that existentialist philoso-phy has exhausted its relevance, Yancy's work is undisputable evidence that existentialist thought is still highly relevant.

In addition to flashes of insight captured by the utilization of rigorous acts of cognitive and improvisational meditations, there are also flashes of the African and African American ancestral spirit in Yancy's work. He seeks to return philosophy to life, to render philosophy into a relevant public undertaking. As the chapters in this volume demonstrate, Yancy believes that philosophy represents a betrayal of human existence when it reaches for transcendental heights on which to perch, while remaining safely removed from the contagions of lived experience. As the chapters in this volume also demonstrate, Yancy problematizes the Western philosophical tradition as white-washed, white-normed, and white assumptive, and thus a long way from an antiracist and egalitarian tradition. We want to immediately caution that we do not consider Yancy to be abandoning rigorous thinking or sacri-ficing critical engagement with the Western philosophical tradition when he utilizes an existential phenomenological approach to deal with the unruly and ever-shifting terrain of lived experience.

Armed with his existentially infused philosophical orientation, Yancy eschews positivistic or crude empirical approaches to race and racism that use quantitative methods of analysis to eclipse the experiences of flesh and blood human beings. In place of focusing on the generic individual, on the ontological absolute of the social sciences, Yancy brings to the foreground the ways in which whiteness and white identity are modes of being, ways of existing in the world. These forms or structures of existing are not ghostly abstractions; neither are they unfortunate distortions of being that are amend-able to easy correction. They are, among other things, persistent patterns of daily existence, thick clusters of existential practices that sustain investment in sociocultural/historical projects. Hence, with regard to whiteness, Yancy does not think that we need to consider it as the kind of thing that requires scientific legitimacy or as some false abstraction that we can calmly reason away. Whiteness survives to the extent that it grounds ways of being that, in turn, function as the normative instantiation of the human. Similarly, as already noted, Yancy situates race within the contested and unsteady domain of the ever-changing realm of lived experience, especially generations of

African American experience. Yancy is also one of a small number of philosophers who have had the courage to critically work through the West's liberal individualism only to expose its racist assumptions and affiliations. As a consequence of his shift in philosophical orientation, one will find in his work new critical metaphors and notions, among which are the notions of tarrying, the gift, the sutured (white) self, wounding the self, collective responsibility, collective guilt, and so on.

Although we have previously mentioned the issue of style, we need to revisit this topic. Yancy refuses to advance the traditional philosophical denigration of style, the tendency to treat style as philosophically irrelevant. Although not dogmatically rejecting or questioning the merits of deductive methods of analysis and of argumentation, he effectively uses other modalities, such as personal interviews and vivid biographical narratives, in order to think through problems and to weave exegetically brilliant and theoretically rich philosophical products, many generated from the long African American philosophical tradition. It would be an egregious oversight not to mention that Yancy's philosophical texts are also performative creations infused with Africana "improvisatory drive and brilliance." In this context, Yancy not only expands the scope of legitimate philosophical topics but also utilizes a poetics of being, as he skillfully conceptualizes black existence outside of the myopic white metaphysical regimes that reduce black being to a deviant or degenerate other.

We previously mentioned Yancy's displacing of the use of quantitative language to describe the realities of race and racism. In this context, black existence has suffered the additional burden of having been erased under the weight of white-framed statistical notions that deliver it to the curses of pathology. He resists the racist pathologizing of black existence by using the tools of existential phenomenology to unmask whiteness's historical fascination with the black body, even as it variously constructs it as a site of subhuman affordances: brutal crime, bestial sexuality, and degenerate cognitive capacity. Yancy recruits black-informed philosophy to rescue the black body from the destructive caricatures of a white gaze that refuses to allow that body to actualize its singular potentiality. Both the acts of reclaiming and recusing black subjectivity require acts of improvisational perceptiveness to affirm the force propelling black/Africana subjectivity.

It is not our intention to suggest that Yancy does not employ a particular philosophical method. On the contrary, we think that he should be credited with having a stable, philosophical grounding, and we are happy to avail ourselves of the words of Nick Nesbitt, which he uses in the context of describing francophone Caribbean writing. Yancy's work

is grasped in its most essential characteristics when conceptualized as a practice of *critique*. This is to argue that while various genres of [Yancy's] writing are manifold, . . . the unifying characteristic of the outstanding texts [of his output] is their status as works of *critique*—as writings, that is, that cry out in insubordination and aversion to the state of their world [above all the cruel legacy of slavery and antiblack racism], and that seek to articulate the promise that another world is possible.[8]

Yancy does not seek merely to interpret or to change the world; he offers the hope, the gift, of another world! However, to fully appreciate the potency of this idea, we must follow Yancy and recognize the extent to which white racism and ontological whiteness function as forms of Western societal determinism that cunningly intimate that things are as they ought to be and that certain things are impossible and can never be actualized. In this context, a world of black freedom and of black affirmative subjectivity would be examples of things that are impossible. However, for Yancy, Africana philosophical sensibilities are grounded in possibility, pluralism, agency, and freedom and most likely very close to the idea of creating a new world for all human beings. In this sense, Yancy is a premier philosopher of racialized world transformation.

Part One

TARRYING, THE GIFT AND TRADITION

Chapter 1

The Problem and the Blemish

Ryan J. Johnson and Biko Mandela Gray

Stokely Carmichael was once asked, "If you had the chance to stand up in front of the white community and say anything you desire, . . . what would you say?" Carmichael paused, looked up at the ceiling for a moment, and said, "I would say: *understand yourself, white man.*"[1]

TARRYING WITH YANCY (AND ONE ANOTHER)

The idea, let alone reality, of a white philosopher and a black philosopher sitting together and thinking philosophically about race cuts to the heart of certain philosophical assumptions. After all, much of Western philosophical thinking has, for the longest, remained wary of particularity—or at least wary of allowing the power of the particular to be the substance of thought, especially when that particularity is corporeal. And yet, here we are, a white man (Ryan) and a black man (Biko), starting from our bodily particularity in order to ask one another how we might think about—not resolve—the reality of race and racism in the United States in a philosophical chapter written in honor of today's leading black American philosopher—which is to say, one of today's leading philosophers: George Yancy. We must be honest: we offer no resolutions. We do not even offer our friendship as a model for progress. What we offer imitates what Yancy offers throughout his work: a call to tarry, to take on the burden, the responsibility of being clear about one's culpability and complicity in various forms of discriminatory violence.

Yancy, however, goes beyond calling one to responsibility. Far from theorizing the call, we read Yancy's work as an embodiment of the very tarrying to which he counsels his readers and listeners. Though he counsels white Americans to live in and as a form of unsutured subjectivity, Yancy refuses to

11

step back. Through his whole career, Yancy lives his own form of unsutured subjectivity, spread open and vulnerable. In an opinion piece for the *New York Times*, Yancy recalls a moment when, while teaching, he himself fell apart and became unmoored:

> I wanted to model for my students what it is like to be a contemporary philosopher who remains steadfast in the face of hatred. I wanted them to internalize something of what it means to practice philosophy, to love wisdom, in the face of danger, of threats of violence and intolerance. Yet, there was a part of me that failed that day.
>
> My composure had collapsed. I seemed to have lost my bearing, my confidence was shaken. I was pushed to rethink what I assumed was a mission of love, the kind of love that refuses to hide and requires profound forms of vulnerability. I had wanted to help heal our broken world, to exalt love in an otherwise ethically catastrophic America.[2]

The unfortunate reality is that, despite Yancy's love-laden calls to a kind of critical self-reflexivity, the burden fell—as these things often do—upon *him*. As Ryan will discuss later, Yancy was—and remains—a problem. It was *Yancy* who had lost composure; despite his appeals to white America to own up to its pernicious legacy of perpetuating racism and thereby tarry with the violence that their skin and their history has perpetuated, it was *Yancy* who struggled under the weight of his own line of questioning. As Yancy so poignantly shows us, to be a problem is risky business. And yet, as we will show, black people live this risk daily.

This chapter is our attempt to tarry with the problem of race. This is our collective attempt to tarry with the problem of *blackness*, of the being of blackness, of the one whose being *is* blackness. Remixing Heidegger, this chapter is an attempt to think with the being for whom *Blackness—not Being*—is an issue.[3] The key, however, is this: blackness is only a problem because whiteness is a blemish. As we will see, the problem (of blackness) and the blemish (of whiteness) are entangled in a relation of (non)recognition.

We place the "non" in parentheses because, as we will show, the reality of recognition—or, better, *proper* recognition—is only a possibility for the blemish of whiteness; lost in the opacity and security of its own universality, the blemish that is whiteness offers no reprieve for the black person, who is nearly totally trapped in their predetermined and overdetermined particularity. Whiteness may need blackness as the substance of its subjectivity, but such substantiality offers no reprieve, no reciprocity, for the black person whose very embodiment is the ontological condition of his, her, or their own entrapment. Trapped by the particularity of embodied blackness, black people, as problems, are pressed to navigate a world that interrupts—to use

Levinas's words—"their continuity, making them play roles in which they no longer recognize themselves, making them betray not only commitments but their own substance, making them carry out actions that will destroy every possibility for action."[4] Stained by the blemish of whiteness, the black subject struggles to gain footing in this world; they are unable to move, breathe, act, or—especially for our purposes here—*think* properly. Unable to think, black people (as problems) are placed in the space of the unthought, living as unthinking subjects for whom thought remains an impossibility.

While the blemish of whiteness is preoccupied with *not* thinking about blackness, it is precisely this unthought horizon that conditions whiteness in the first place. Whiteness is undone, dehisced, and *unsutured* by the very blackness upon which it seeks to throw its anxieties. If Yancy asks for white people to become unsutured, then white Americans need to begin by thinking *with*, not *about*, the very blackness that escapes their purview. The blemish has always needed the problem and has always been unsettled by its presence; it just didn't *recognize* the depth of this necessity.

In this chapter, we tarry with the problem and the blemish. And we do so in dialogue. As such, you will hear from each of us in our particularity. There are moments where Ryan's particularity is clearly articulated, and there are moments where Biko's is as well (usually articulated in *italics*). There are also moments (as with this introduction) where both of us are speaking collectively, our words conjoined in a single voice. In all cases, we consistently heed Yancy's call to tarry with the problem and the blemish.

Ryan begins our conversation, taking us to the conceptual parameters and pitfalls of thinking about blackness as problem and whiteness as blemish. Inspired by his former teacher Yancy, he articulates the etymological connection between "problem" and "blemish," focusing on the false word-root *blem* as the discursive intersection of the two terms. Offering a critique of whiteness and a call to self-reflexivity on the part of white people, Ryan provides an intellectual site from which to reflect about the dialectical (not necessarily oppositional) relationship between whiteness and blackness.

Biko, however, has no "section"—and this is intentional. Instead, Biko speaks in the interstices between Ryan's analysis, articulating both the implications and possibilities present in living as the very problem that Ryan describes. If blackness occupies what Saidiya Hartman has once called the position of the unthought, then Biko's words are meant to be understood in this way, as the unthought horizon from within which one's being is "thrown-forward." It's risky, we know. But maybe, in the riskiness of trying to perform what we can only describe, we will provide a space for more clarity, for more opportunities to tarry with the (implications of the) very problem to which we respond.

BEING A PROBLEM; OR, THE PROBLEM OF BLACKNESS

On Thursday, April 14, 2016, George Yancy spoke at Elon University in North Carolina, as part of a long running series called the Ferris E. Reynolds Lectures in Philosophy. Yancy's typically powerful, earnest, and demanding lecture hit the audience like a resounding thunderclap. In a mostly white school, in clearly white space, a Black philosopher spoke out. Every person in that audience left a different person than they entered. Some were inspired, some shocked, a few angered.

While many things stood out, one idea that really struck me, Ryan, a white former student and ardent admirer of Dr. Yancy as a person and as a philosopher, was the etymology of "problem." My students know how to distract me; they compare it to dangling a toy in front of a cat. Whether I am teaching on Aristotle's metaphysics or Beauvoir's politics, if a student dangles an etymology in front of me, I pounce. Thus, when Yancy made an etymological aside while making some comments on his account of the ontology of blackness, my ears piqued involuntarily. The etymological detour started with Yancy's provocative ontological statement: being Black is a *problem*. Yancy was taking up Du Bois's question: "What does it mean to be a problem?"[5] When he dropped the etymology, my mind took off.

According to the Liddell–Scott–Jones's *Greek–English Lexicon*, "problem" comes from the Greek *problema* (πρόβλημα), and *proballo* (προβάλλω), meaning "to throw or lay something in front of someone, to put forward." It is a combination of *pro-* (προ-), meaning "forth, forward" and *-blem*, which comes from *ballo* (βάλλω), meaning "to throw, cast, hurl." To be Black, Yancy claims, is to have one's being *thrown-forward*, to have the meaning of one's being thrown at a Black body, before that body has a say in the matter. In short, the ontology of Blackness means having one's essence thrown before them. Later, in *Backlash*, Yancy states this very clearly: "Black people, the 'n-word-s' . . . are ontologically a problem people."[6] Here is how Yancy explains the being of blackness as a problem.

Yancy opens *Look, a White!* with Frantz Fanon's account of his experiences with this being-thrown-forth. "Look, a Negro!" a white boy shouts, perhaps pointing his finger at Fanon's Black body, the other hand clenching his mother's. The boy repeats the exclamation as Fanon walks by him, finally announcing his fear at seeing a Black body: "Mama, see the Negro! I'm frightened."[7] In a scene organized by the color of bodies, Yancy describes the combined function of the imperative "Look" and the descriptor "Negro!" When someone exclaims the "Look," it grabs our attention. Before thinking, we are looking at whatever is being pointed out, and adding "Negro!"

intensifies the attention, especially for the white gaze. This exclamation "elicits white fear and trembling" because it "has built into it," he explains,

> a gestured warning against a possible threat cautioning those whites within earshot to be on guard, to lock their car doors, to hold their wallets and purses for dear life, to gather their children together, to prepare to move house, and (in some cases) to protect the "purity" of white women and to protect white men from the manipulating dark temptress.[8]

This is precisely the act of problematizing, a racialized version of what Louis Althusser calls "interpellation."[9] Simply by his presence, the essence of Fanon, because of his Black body, is already determined as what Yancy describes as "a dreaded object, a thing of fear, a frightening and ominous presence."[10]

Pardon my interruption. I'm sure you, the reader, have begun to soak in and follow the lines of Ryan's argumentation. That will continue. But I want to hop in here, to say a few things about the reality of living as a "dreaded object." You see, objects cannot think—they are ontologically banned from the party of cognition. There is no stream of thoughts, no possibility for cogitation; having been made part of the objective sphere, I can't think. Thought is made possible not only by life but also by a life unmolested; in Descartes's first Meditation, for example, the meditator can reflect, meditate, sleep, fantasize, desire, and willfully engage only because the meditator has the literal leisure to do so.[11] Given my black body, I do not.

The term "leisure" has a complicated etymological history. It comes from the Old French leisir, *which connotes an allowance;* leisir *is derived from the Latin* licere, *meaning "to be allowed."[12] But there is more here; "leisure" also connotes the "opportunity afforded by freedom from necessary occupations." In other words, leisure is the luxury afforded to someone who is allowed to do things unmolested, as they are not "occupied" by some external concern.*

However, when one's being is thrown-forth, "overdetermined from the outside" as Fanon himself once wrote, leisure is nowhere to be found. While philosophers leisurely ruminate on whatever tickles their fancy, I am interrupted, broken, halted, by a life of distractions, by a life marked by perpetual interruption. My "life"—if we can even call it "life"—is marked by fits and stops stemming from the series of significations radiating from the blackness of my body. Yancy tells us that the "Black body has been confiscated, taken possession of, by whites who have assumed the 'natural authority' to seize black bodies discursively and nondiscursively."[13] He also tells us that this possession—which amounts to a dispossession on the part of the black subject—is as quotidian as it is extraordinary; he uses an elevator scene to make this claim, with which I wholly agree. I'd only add that, in recent years, the elevator has extended to parks, sidewalks, and streets; I cannot sleep, smoke a cigarette, walk, run, barbecue, study, fix my car, play music, play golf, swim in a pool, play basketball, or even sell water for a trip to Disneyland without being interrupted. The worst part is that these interruptions, these halts in my "stream" of living and breathing, are not mere "interruptions." They are potentially lethal ones, marked and marred by 9-1-1 calls. #BBQbecky and #permitpatty so heavily frequent my daily living that an uninterrupted life— the Cartesian condition for thinking—is impossible, not simply because they halt the stream of leisure but because they carry within them the specter of death. I cannot think because I cannot live.

This lack of leisure that interrupts my existence and therefore halts my thinking and my access to life itself is grounded in a host of ontological givens that I did not create and yet, somehow, am responsible for. I cannot think not simply because I cannot live but because whiteness has already done the thinking for me. Now back to Ryan.

Before Fanon has a chance to determine who he *is*, what kind of person he is, he is already determined as a "negro," and "Negroes steal, they cheat, they are hypersexual, mesmerizingly so, and the quintessence of evil and danger."[14] The reason, Yancy explains in *Backlash*, is that "to be Black in America is to be always already *known*, and white people assume that they know *everything* about me."[15] Fanon was forced, instantaneously, to discover *what he was for another* and immediately become responsible for it. As a problem, a Black subject is forced to assume a perspective outside his own self-understanding. The obscene word for problem is the n-word, insofar as the n-word, as a problem, functions "as if it is a metaphysical category. It is *as if* being a n-word is an instantiation of a Platonic form."[16] Yancy's evidence for the "logic of their malicious claims" appears in the horrific responses to Yancy's essay "Dear White America" in the *New York Times* blog. They "spoke to the ways in which white people framed my existence," writes Yancy, "and the existence of Black people according to a metaphysics of the n-word, the 'fixedness' of what it means to be Black."[17]

Lewis Gordon also describes Fanon's dig into his own being insofar as he "attempts to address a problem [of psychical interiority] and encounters himself as a problem. So Fanon goes to a deeper level of interiority: his own experience *as lived*."[18] Fanon returns to the lived experience of the white boy's interpellative exclamation—*Look, a Negro!*—through which he is seized "in the realm of pure exteriority, the realm of the epidermal schema."[19] It is at this moment, Gordon explains, that "Fanon's existence is a two-dimensional objectification."[20] Then comes the great irony: this moment of pure exteriority, of being "'out there' without an inside," is the autobiographical moment.

Fanon's life story begins when a white boy, with his white language and his white finger, first points it out, that is, at just that moment when Fanon's inner experience is determined insofar as it is thrown at him from the whiteness outside. Fanon's autobiography is paradoxical because it is not the time when he begins to tell his own story, but when *his* story is told *for him*. As Gordon puts it, it is when he "announces the absence of his interiority *from the point of view of his interiority.*"[21]

For the being of blackness to be a problem, *thrown-forth*, predetermined before a Black subject has an opportunity to self-determine who or what they are, the being of blackness cannot be considered what Heidegger calls one's "ownmost" because Black being is not even one's own. As a problem, Black being belongs to white subjects. Yet since Black being is *other* to white subjects, it cannot even be the ownmost of whiteness. Black being is thus other to both white and Black subjects. It is not most anyone's own, but that which is *owned* by the white blemish, a deafening echo of a Black slave being owned by a white master.

You'll notice that I, Biko, speak to you directly. The reasons for this will become clearer as you read on, but for now, a foreshadowing must suffice. I write in the first person not because I know phenomenology—which I do— but instead because, as a thoughtless problem, thoughtlessness restricts my perception and consigns me to a sphere of existence that is simultaneously inescapably particular and unflinchingly anonymous. Ryan just said it; my blackness *isn't even my own, it's already owned by Fanon's Other, by the being who has already constituted me as nonbeing, which means that the blackness that I signify doesn't offer me reprieve within the context of my problematic existence. I've been thrown-forth, which means that my very being is ontologically beholden to the whims of a white gaze, which amounts to my existence being consigned to the space of anonymous givenness. I write from the first person not because I have phenomenological priority, but because the very "I" that has been, and will continue to be, deployed in this essay cannot help but operate, as Hortense Spillers says, "in the service of a collective function.*"[22]

You shouldn't think of the "collective function" as my way of articulating solidarity. Instead, in a somewhat reductive reading of Spillers, what I mean here is that this "collective" manifests itself as anonymity. Within the phenomenology of the problem, the "I," the grammatical indicator of my particularity, is always and already anonymous. What Fanon also tells us in Black Skin, White Masks *is that, by "[casting] an objective gaze over [his] features," he did not see Frantz, but all of the significations attendant to his black body.*[23] *Yancy's elevator scene returns and confirms Fanon's own objective gaze: "When a white woman looks with suspicion as I enter the elevator,*

I feel that in her eyes I am this indistinguishable, amorphous, black seething mass, a token of danger, a threat, . . . a criminal, a burden, a rapacious animal incapable of delayed gratification."[24] *Far from announcing an experiential subjectivity, the "I" of which I speak is nothing more and nothing less than a stand-in for the phrase "black problem." I cannot stress this enough: the "I" of which I speak—and which I will speak continually throughout this chapter—has everything to do with anonymity; far from a grammatical naming of a subject, the "I" of—and in whose name—I speak is what Achille Mbembe once called the "well of fantasies," a symbolic, political, and social reservoir into which the anxieties, desires, concerns, and fears of white subjectivity are projected. Let us not forget this; I hope you won't forget this, as my anonymity, my identity as a symbolic and cultural reservoir of white reservations has everything to do with what's to come. Ryan will take it from here.*

Draining the reservoir . . .

AN ETYMOLOGICAL TWIST

See how just dangling an etymology in front of me leads to sinuous digressions? It does not stop there, as I, the white coauthor of this chapter, began to think about my own role in the throwing-forward of Yancy's and Biko's blackness. Yancy's description of the ontology of blackness as having one's essence thrown before them threw me back on myself. Yancy called me out; he called out my whiteness and forced me to confront it. I remember the first words of *Look, a White!* a quote from James Baldwin: "I give you your problem back. You're the 'n—er,' baby; it isn't me."[25] Yancy forced me to interrogate what it means to be white under this ontological framework of problems. My question became: What is the ontology of whiteness in relation to this "throwing" etymology.

Still entranced by the etymological dangling, I experimented with different prefixes that I could attach to the "-blem" of "problem" in the hopes of hitting upon the white ontological correlate of problematic blackness. I tried out "re-" and "retro-," in the hopes of creating a term that conveyed the sense of being "thrown-back" rather than "thrown-forth." But "re-blem" and "retro-blem" are too clunky to be helpful. So I tried some others: "anti-blem," "dis-blem," "trans-blem," "super-blem," "mis-blem," and others, but nothing fit. Then I paused. If blackness is what is thrown-forth, then "whiteness" must be "that which throws." As the "thrower," perhaps it might not require a prefix. Whiteness is just "throwing" itself. Whiteness, then, would be the *balle* ($\beta\acute{\alpha}\lambda\lambda\omega$), the throwing, casting, or hurling. I, thus, rendered "whiteness" just the "-blem" in "pro-blem." Sitting with this term, my English lead me to add the suffix "-ish" to "blem," thus getting "blemish." While there is no etymological relationship between the roots of blemish and problem, "blemish" is a useful term to employ in discussions of race, given its connotations with skin, discoloring, and moral defection.[26]

THE BEING OF THE BLEMISH

To understand the being of the blemish, let us first consider the basic structure of subjectivity, as inspired by Hegel. A single subject, unto itself, is insufficient for being a subject. Subjectivity requires at least two subjects: one that is *recognized*, insofar as it is recognized by another, the subject, and the other who *recognizes* the first *as* a subject. Each subject finds itself ensnared in a relation of dependence and independence; both depend on the other for recognition and thus determination as a subject, yet this very determination is as an independent subject. It is this unstable dependent independence that makes the whole process of being a subject into a struggle for recognition, sometimes a near life and death struggle, as we see in chapter 4 of Hegel's *Phenomenology of Spirit*. Each subject wants to be free to determine itself however it wishes, and thus seeks to make the other submit completely. Yet this other subject cannot die, for if it died, it could not offer the desired recognition. The recognizing subject must thus be kept alive yet subordinate to the recognized subject. Already we see the outlines of mastery and slavery, lord and bondsman, a relationship that became codified in Western culture, especially the United States, through the construction of race. Let us now introduce race into this basic structure of subjectivity.

White subjectivity functions by constructing an "otherness" that it can determine however it desires, and the "Black subject" became this determinable and determined other. White subjects are free to make Blacks do anything, while Black subjects are enslaved to the caprice of the white will. Regardless of how Black subjects might see themselves, ignoring the self-determination of a black will, the white subject can freely view the Black body however it wants, even (or especially) in contradictory ways. Black subjectivity is thus the unequal opposite of whiteness. It is unequal in the sense that the arrow of determination fades from white to Black—the white person determines the Black person but not vice versa. To be Black is to be whatever whiteness determines it to be, even though that determination capriciously drifts. The Black subject has no say in the matter. Call this indeterminate determinability of Blackness a *problem*.

As the subordinated correlate of white subjectivity, Black subjectivity is not free to determine the white subject in return because the arrow of determination is unidirectional and one-sided. Since the Black subject cannot self-determine, it is forced to take on the determinations given to it by the white subject. When a Black subject encounters whiteness, it finds not a freedom to make one's self-understanding known to the other but instead a predetermined way of being; the Black person recognizes the white person as an autonomous and self-determining subject but the white person does not recognize the full subjectivity of the Black person. The Black subject must confront itself only insofar as the white subject views it. Thus, Black subjects lose themselves in the overwhelming white will and can do nothing about it. The self that is reflected back to them by the white gaze is other yet also themselves. It is not how they, the Black subjects, determine themselves—but that does not matter. Black people must take up the white determinations of themselves *as* themselves. Black subjectivity confronts itself as an otherness that is itself.

*I told you—*I told you—*my anonymity would return as part of the analytic of the problem and the blemish. This isn't by mistake; Yancy articulates this by way of phenomenological saturation, but he is not alone: Lewis Gordon, Frantz Fanon, and others have continually articulated the black as a form of subjectivity whose substance is only the "stuff" of white desires. Anonymity is my name; and even though I speak in the first person, you would be both right and wrong to suggest that the "I" of which "I" speak is even Biko. Hell, I don't even know who this "I" is—and if this is confusing for you, imagine what it's like to* live *it: imagine what it's like to be called "Bob Marley" just because you have dreadlocks.*

It's a true story. Despite being a few shades darker and much thicker than Bob ever was—let alone the fact that I am alive and Bob is not*—I am still called "Bob," made to feel as if my locks could only ever be the physical representation of reggae music. And what's more: there is no space for redress. Had I corrected the person who named me, I would have been too "sensitive" for expressing disdain. I am nameless—which means I can have* any name *that whiteness seeks to give me. This is what it means to live as a problem, to have one's own being thrown-forward.*

And yet, I've never been afforded the luxury or leisure to call a white person anything other than the second person, "sir" or "madam," or their name. The white stands out in his, her, or their specificity; their subjectivity is clarified by my address. And yet, the term I, whoever this term may come to articulate, is rendered more obscure.

A Black subject discovers itself *as other for itself*; it does not find itself through its own self-determination but through the determinations that the white subject forces upon it. If a white subject and a Black subject meet on the street, they do not recognize each other as equal subjects, with each person free to determine himself or herself however he or she wants to do so. Instead, the white subject is the truly free subject, the source of the determinations, while the Black subject is predetermined by what Yancy calls the "white conceptual framing."[27] Being a Black subject is not up to the Black person but to the white subject. If the white subject frames the Black body as a threat or danger, the Black subject is deemed a problem. The meaning of the Black subject is thrown forward, ahead of itself, such that the Black subject experiences himself or herself as a problem. "As Black," Yancy describes, "I experience my life, my Black body, as foregrounded against the background of white fabricated fears and white self-alienation."[28]

On the other side of the relation, the white subject is not so forced to take itself as an object for a Black subject because it possesses all free power to determine itself *and* the Black subject. The white subject is invited to enjoy its subjectivity without pause or consideration for the very reason that the subjectivity of a Black person functions as the object for the white subject. If the Black body is a danger, the white cop or scared white person is empowered to shoot the danger, to stand one's ground, nearly without any recourse. This near absolute freedom, however, is part of the blemish, as invisible as it may be to a white person.

Since true subjectivity requires another subject to freely stand against it, as a free and independent subject, if the Black subject is not equally free to determine the white subject, then the white subject suffers from an unsatisfying form of recognition. Hyppolite sees this as the "contradiction inherent in the state of domination."[29] The difficulty of genuine recognition is that the recognizing subject must be free to determine differently, to misrecognize or reject one's self-determinations. True recognition involves this risk, and there is only risk if the subjects are truly free and independent. Consider, for example, the difference between the sincere flattery that one receives from one who spontaneously and freely gives it versus insincere flattery that results from ulterior motives or from seeking personal advantage. Similarly, sincere recognition from a free and independent subject is much more satisfying than insincere recognition from a dependent, subordinated subject. Given that the recognition that the white subject receives from the Black subject is, due to the racialized social–political–economic structures of the United States, insincere and unsatisfying, the white subject is left empty, hollowed out, blemished. Lacking genuine recognition, there is, at the center of white subjectivity, a pale void.

WHITENESS IS THE PROBLEM

There is a line—well, there are many lines, really, but this one stands out—in Hegel's Preface to the Phenomenology of Spirit *where he undoes himself. It comes in paragraph 22, where he tells us that the self is the "unrest" of what he calls an "unfolded becoming" that, as far as I can tell, is due to what he calls "pure negativity."[30] In other words, the self—which is (sometimes) the Subject for Hegel—is in perpetual unrest due to (the threat of) an internal disruption that cannot ever be fully quelled. In fact, it is precisely the attempt to quell the (threat of) internal disruption that motivates the development of the subject itself. Hegel articulates this dynamic throughout the* Phenomenology, *but, in one part of the Preface, Hegel links this notion of unrest to Death itself.*

> It is only because the concrete does divide itself, and make itself into something non-actual, that it is self-moving, . . . that an accident as such . . . should attain an existence of its own and a separate freedom—this is the tremendous power of the negative; it is the energy of thought, of the pure "I." Death, if that is what we want to call this non-actuality, is of all things the most dreadful, and to hold fast what is dead requires the greatest strength. . . . But the life of the Spirit is not the life that shrinks from death and keeps itself untouched by devastation, but rather the life that endures it and maintains itself in it.[31]

Do you see why I consigned myself to the first person now? Hegel himself ties the "energy of . . . the pure 'I'" to the nonactuality of the accident, *of the particular. I write in the first person not simply because the "I" is a grammatical stand-in for the inescapable anonymity of black people; I also write in the first person because my "I" articulates blackness as the very nonactuality that Ryan and I have both described. I am the "energy of" (white) "thought," as my ontologically problematic anonymity—whether encountered in elevators or at barbecues in parks—holds the "tremendous power" of conditioning the subjectivity of whiteness. I write in the first person because my anonymous singularity makes white people possible.*

In conventionally Hegelian fashion, there are (at least) two ways to respond to this insight. In the earlier section, Ryan articulated what Heidegger might call the "everyday" way in which white people respond to the fact that blackness—or, more precisely, black bodies—condition their existence. But there are other ways to respond. And Hegel himself unwittingly offers us a possible other way.

You see, in the earlier quotation, Hegel claims that the accidental nature of the accident, the particularity of the particular, is precisely the threat of death from within which Spirit should maintain itself *and* endure. *If, as Yancy once wrote, black people are configured as "threatening and ominous" problems—which is to say, if black people represent the threat of death—then Hegel is admonishing his own readers to tarry with the internal disruption of the threat of death itself! Read through Yancy, Hegel is (against his own wishes) telling his own readers—and therefore himself—to tarry with being unsutured by the threat of disruption that the accidental signifies. Which is to say, when read through Yancy, Hegel is telling his readers to tarry with black-ness, with black bodies; in so doing, Hegel is claiming that the only way to move forward, to develop—individually and collectively—is to sit with black people, with the meaning of black life and the depths of black experience to gain further clarity about what's at stake in one's own (white) development. Now back to Ryan.*

There is another complication here, one exacerbated by racial considerations. Although the Black subject is subordinated to the white subject, insofar as the former is determined almost completely by its necessary submission to the latter, Black subjectivity cannot be completely erased, negated, or reduced to a mere thing, because recognition would then become impossible. For, as Hyppolite puts it, "I am a self-consciousness only if I gain for myself recognition from another self-consciousness and if I grant recognition to the other."[32] A Black subject must retain some sense of subjectivity, however subordinated or diminished it may be. Though the being of blackness is not deemed fully human, it is more than mere animal. Blackness is caught somewhere between human and animal without being either. It is this "in between status"—human enough to provide recognition to white subjects but not too human so as to be equally free as the white subject—that is an essential element of the being of a problem.

As a problem, the Black subject, nearly but not completely rendered a thing, retains its subjectivity insofar as subjectivity is a necessary condition for its being a problem. Without at least minimal subjectivity, there would be no problem because there would be no freedom or capacity to determine differently or to mis-determine. A white person is only a subject if another subject recognizes him or her as such, and recognition is not something that a mere thing can provide. The trick is that these two sorts of subjects, the Black problem and the white blemish, are structurally unequal. A Black person is both subject and object, while the white subject is subject alone. We are beginning to see how being white necessitates the problematization of blackness.

But there is a trick. The white subject is not only a subject, it is just unnecessary to see itself as anything but subject, which only appears from a white perspective. Shannon Sullivan might call this "ontological expansiveness," which is when "white people tend to act and think as if all spaces . . . are or should be available for them to move in and out of as they wish."[33] Since the white perspective is practically ubiquitous, there do not seem to be any limitations on what white people can do. Now the trick: the white subject assumes that this is how it is for everyone—everyone is equally free, regardless of racial determinations, to move about and do as one pleases. This is clearly not the case, as can be seen, to use one of Yancy's examples, when a white person and a Black person walk into a store but only the Black person is followed by the security guard. The white delusion here is that, Yancy writes, "as a white person you are unable to give an account of your 'racist limits.'"[34] A white person cannot, mostly because it need not, locate where his whiteness begins and ends, to where it extends, and thus how it shapes and organizes the lives of people of color.

To be sure, many "good white people," as Shannon Sullivan puts it, think that they can locate the edges of their whiteness, and thus are supposedly excused from the ways in which their ontological expansion may affect Black bodies.[35] The standard way this proceeds is through the model of introspection or moral reflection. Yet because, Yancy notes, white people cannot locate their racist limits, no matter how hard they may try, whatever whiteness understands of itself through the seeming clarity of introspection, the good white subject who strives to overcome its being-white "has already arrived too late to determine the complex and insidious ways in which white racism has become embedded within your white embodied self."[36] Yancy calls this "racial opacity," and it is one mark of the being of the blemish.[37] Being white is the perfect crime, insofar as the supposed purity of white intentions masks white culpability. White innocence is this culpability. The blemish is unable to see its own stained nature and the edges of its ontological expansion. The blemish does not need to see itself as a blemish, for its mask allows only whiteness to be seen when it looks at itself. The constituting act of throwing, or problematizing Black bodies, renders invisible the throwing itself. A white person trying to consider its whiteness is like a ghost looking at itself in the mirror. Put differently, the white mask that constitutes and simultaneously obscures the blemish defers responsibility indefinitely. The blemish has always already, albeit inauthentically, achieved glory. A good-enough facade is the essence of white folks.

And yet, despite this opacity, despite the white blindness of its racial limits, whiteness *needs* Blackness for its own being. Without a Black other, without the problem of Blackness, there is no whiteness. Whiteness is nothing beyond the subordination of Blackness. Here is another mark of the blemish: the condition of whiteness is the being of the problem of Blackness. Without the threat of the Black subject, without a being overflowing with uncontrollable and animalist desires, lacking the rational capacity to self-regulate and self-determine, whiteness evaporates. Thus, when Yancy writes, "Your white body is functionally entangled with my Black body," we simply add that this entanglement is, at its core, ontological.[38] Problem and blemish are inseparably entangled. Whether we are "ignorant or not," Yancy continues, "one's [white] hands are dirty."[39] Yancy is clear: "Being Black, from the perspective of whiteness, *is the problem.*"[40] While white people need not understand this, it is imperative that Black people do.

In a Masterclass Luncheon before his Reynolds lecture, hosted by Buffy Longmire-Avital and African and African American Studies at Elon University, Yancy explained the need for Black subjects to encounter themselves as the problem for white subjects. To paraphrase Yancy, Black subjects must understand both what it means to be Black *and* what it means to be white. There is no choice: Black subjectivity must confront and understand *both* Blackness *and* whiteness in order to survive in society that was made by and for white people. If a Black man does not understand that the white man considers his Black body a problem that threatens the safety of the white subject, then the Black man exposes himself to danger of annihilation. This is part of what Du Bois called "double consciousness." White subjects, however, do not need to know what Blackness is at all. Hence the lack of need to locate the racial limits of whiteness. Blackness is simply whatever the white subject determines it to be, even though these determinations are, taken together, contradictory. If a Black man ends up in jail, the white subject deems him lazy, dangerous, and certainly responsible for such white determination. But if a Black man succeeds, perhaps becomes president or a philosophy professor at Emory University, he is determined to be uppity or whose "PhD means nothing" and probably just "appeared in the mail."[41] Whatever the white person throws at the Black person, it sticks and stays. Thus, the white subject need not, and so does not, even understand whiteness. Blackness and whiteness, as forms of subjectivity, are unknown to the white subject; blemished by its own thinking, whiteness—and, therefore, white subjects—struggle to do anything other than create problems for themselves.

PHENOMENOLOGY OF BLACK SPIRIT: THE BOOK

Let us say a final word about the state of our thinking by returning to Yancy's talk in the Reynolds Lectures series at Elon University. The Reynolds Lecture usually corresponds to the theme of the Senior Seminar in Philosophy taught that year, which was then on Shannon Sullivan's work on critical whiteness. Ryan taught the 2018 Senior Seminar, which focused on the dialectical parallelism between Hegel and the history of Black Thought, and Biko gave the Reynolds Lecture for this Senior Seminar. Biko's powerful talk was titled "On Not Standing a Chance: Black Life and (the Problem of) the Object," and showed that the black body, insofar as it has been deemed a Cartesian extended substance, is both the animating condition of Western subjective thought and a portal to another modality of subjectivity: *blackness as living matter*. Biko explained what it means to *be* living matter, to live *as* matter, to exist as black-life-matter, as a black life that *matters*. Like Yancy before him, Biko shook the audience with his sophisticated thinking, his powerful insights, and his genuine care and concern for the topic at hand.

This chapter, therefore, emerges from an exchange between three philosophers, or more specifically, an exchange between two philosophers in light of the philosophical path charted by Professor Yancy himself. The arc of this chapter, therefore, starts with Yancy (an older, accomplished black philosopher), moving to Ryan (a younger white philosopher), and then to Biko (a younger black philosopher). Beginning with Yancy's 2016 Reynolds lecture, where he first dangled the being of blackness as a problem, through the 2018 Senior Seminar on Hegel and Black thinkers, and culminating with Biko's Reynolds lecture on questions of black subjectivity, insofar as the black lives have been determined as living matter, this chapter names our attempt to think and tarry with philosophical questions on the problem and blemish afforded by racial discourses. It is our hope, therefore, that what we've presented here—in dialectical fashion—clearly expresses the power and promise of tarrying, of staying with, philosophical approaches to race and racism in the West more generally and the United States more specifically.

Yet this is not where it all ends. This is only the beginning for us, Biko and Ryan. Our next step is to write the book on this dialectical parallelism between Hegel and Black thought, which is exactly what we will do next. We call it: *A Phenomenology of Black Spirit*, and it is our way of trying to tarry, in a different way, with the relationship between race and philosophy.

At the end of *Ontological Terror*, philosopher Calvin Warren suggests that, if blackness is conceived as nothingness, then the question of black existence (or black being, as Warren stylistically puts it) cannot get us to the question of how black people live. Warren suggests, ultimately, that one might turn to the question of black spirit—that space that gives no pride of place to questions of existence—as a way to think through how black life lives, moves, and has its own form of (non)being.

> The important task for black thinking . . . is to imagine black existence without Being, humanism, or the human. Such thinking would lead us into an abyss. But we must face this abyss—its terror and majesty. I would suggest that this thinking leads us to the spirit, something exceeding and preceding the metaphysical world. . . . The spirit enables one to endure [antiblackness]; it is not a solution to antiblackness.[42]

For Warren, a phenomenology of black spirit would offer the possibility of thinking black existence without recourse to questions of humanity. Though we do not fully incorporate Warren's insights into our own work, we do see, in certain ways, a kind of affinity between Warren's pneumatological injunctions and our desire and attempt to philosophically tarry with issues of race and antiblack violence. Maybe there are possibilities in the void left by the white blemish. And maybe, just maybe, in tarrying with the problem of blackness (in relation to the blemish of whiteness), we might find different ways of understanding the possibilities and potentiality of black thought and black life.

Our desire, then, is to think blackness in dialectical relation to the white blemish. The way in which we attempt to carry this out in subsequent work is by articulating a conversation between Hegel's *Phenomenology of Spirit* and the powerful works of black thinkers. As it stands now, there will be six moments in this book (see table 1.1).

Table 1.1.   Moments in the upcoming project, The *Phenomenology of Black Spirit*

Hegel's *Phenomenology*	Black Thought
"Master/Slave Dialectic"	Frederick Douglass
"Stoicism"	Booker T. Washington
"Skepticism"	W. E. B. Du Bois
"Unhappy Consciousness"	
a) Devotion	Marcus Garvey
b) Sacramental Work	Martin Luther King Jr.
c) Self-Mortification	Malcolm X

Our hope is that this book—just like this chapter—announces what might result if people were to take Yancy seriously. In tarrying with blackness, maybe it is possible to understand that the depths of spirit actually are quite darker than we imagine.

Chapter 2

Erlebnis, Tarrying, and Thinking Again after George Yancy

Selihom Andarge, Nicholas Aranda, Josie Brady, Tricia Charfauros, Kelley Coakley, Becky Vartabedian, and Regi Worles

In this chapter, we address two ideas in George Yancy's oeuvre. The first idea, *Erlebnis*, is a term Yancy uses to mark the expression of his own critical Black subjectivity. We describe its conceptual underpinnings, especially its distinction from *Erfahrung*, a description for experience unfolding over a longer term. We then discuss the way *Erlebnis* solicits a response from Yancy's readers or audience, using examples from his 2012 "Looking at Whiteness: Tarrying with the Embedded and Opaque White Racist Self" and our reflections on his visit to our campus in January 2018.

The second idea we address is *tarrying*, the demand Yancy consistently makes of his audiences in lieu of offering strategies for "solving" or ending racist oppression. We expand the notion of tarrying by explaining a framework for *thinking* developed by Hannah Arendt and presented in her 1971 lecture, "Thinking and Moral Considerations." In this lecture, thinking is the work of returning to the self after engaging the world in its unfiltered rawness. This engagement requires one to be effectively "in conversation" with oneself, using the data of the world to inform a new position. Tarrying, then, is a form of thinking; we illustrate this by describing our responses to the challenges in Yancy's work. We conclude the chapter by discussing our efforts to tarry and think, and the way these efforts dispose us toward transformation for ourselves and our broader community.

We'd like to begin, however, by saying something about the "we" of this chapter. We are six students and one professor, a diverse group with members identifying as Black, Latinx, White, Guamanian-Chamorro, cis-gendered, heterosexual, queer, female, and male. Following Yancy's insistence that "being embodied in the world is a condition of (our) philosophical voice(s)," we offer our personal accounts of engaging Yancy's work to demonstrate the ways it interrupted and redirected our individual dispositions.[1] This "we" is also a developing intellectual community; our work together originated in a Philosophy and Peace and Justice Studies course titled "Precarious Bodies," convened at Regis University in the spring 2018 semester. Dr. Becky Vartabedian developed the class around readings in race-critical, gender, and queer theories with the hope that interested students in the Philosophy and Peace and Justice majors would find some theoretical support for thinking through their identities. A visit to our campus by George Yancy was part of this course's work—the second meeting was given over to reading and discussion with him, and students were asked to attend the evening talk in the Regis Chapel.

What "Precarious Bodies" became was effectively a laboratory for exploring issues of identity and in/justice. Students were responsible for reading, discussion, and class activity in the final six weeks of the class (Dr. Vartabedian participated with the students in the activities and discussion the students ended up leading), and our working together in this way founded an environment for shared reflection and examination that made the work of this chapter possible. Indeed, our work has continued for the better part of a year following the conclusion of our course; we have reflected, discussed, and transformed the trajectory of this chapter *together*. Though the readers will find one of us occasionally speaking directly into the text (and usually at some length), this work has been collaborative from the start.

In addition to our avowed dependence on our situatedness to develop this chapter, we affirm Yancy's claim that our situatedness in the world is fundamentally political, and as such our contribution is "interlaced with tragic world events, reminding us of the artificiality of our reflective solitude and revealing to us our finitude and vulnerability."[2] For Yancy, it was the tragic events of September 11, 2001 that inspired his reflections of philosophical biography; for us, it is the election of Donald J. Trump in November 2016 and its deleterious effects on our campus community that frame our reflections.

A CONDITION FOR SOLIDARITY: REGIS UNIVERSITY IN 2016 AND 2017

Our intellectual community has its home at Regis University, a Jesuit Catholic institution located in the northwest corner of Denver, Colorado. On the night of the 2016 election and in the weeks that followed, our campus became emotionally and intellectually polarized—feelings of distrust, confusion, and a loss of control came to characterize the atmosphere. The dorms housing first-year students became places for the casual use of racial epithets; each day, we would hear of physical altercations or verbal confrontations between students on opposite sides of the election results. The release of these elements into the open caused real harm across campus; these also indicated that race and racism were matters now at the heart of our campus life.[3]

In the spring semester 2017 and still reeling from the chaos of the fall semester, a coalition of students, faculty, and staff organized the second Anti-Oppression Week. This week included open classes, community-building events, and discussions intended to turn our community and classroom in the direction of inclusive education. In response, a conservative organization on campus created a week of counterprogramming that featured a pro-life "All Lives Matter" activity as their marquee event. Independently of both of these, a student hosted an "Affirmative Action Bake Sale" outside the Student Center one day, a local instance of a national trend on campuses designed to critique Affirmative Action policies. The bake sale became a flashpoint for the racial tensions that had been simmering on campus since the election.

Emerging from these ongoing tensions was the clear need for opportunities where people occupying all portions of the political spectrum could talk about what was happening at Regis. Members of the Regis University Student Government Association, the Black Student Alliance, and SOMOS (our affinity group for Latinx students) collaborated with the Office of Diversity, Equity, and Inclusive Excellence and the Institute on the Common Good to develop "Courageous Conversation" events. One of these created a space where students of color could share their experiences and understanding of the hypervisibility of race with members of the student body, faculty, staff, and administration. Another involved a role-playing exercise with faculty and staff embodying positions and arguments, which they may or may not have held in face-to-face dialogue with one another. The underlying challenge of the event series, however, was the chance for privileged members of our community to opt out of participating; these conversations were mostly attended by people of color and what several students describe as members of "the fifty," or "the usual suspects," reliable white allies who are routinely present at events pertaining to issues of race and racial injustice on our campus.

In the 2017–2018 academic year, our community convened for two large-scale events designed as a response to the previous year's tumult. First, the Office of Diversity, Equity, and Inclusive Excellence invited white antiracist activist Tim Wise to campus for the inaugural Diversity Lecture. Wise used the August 2017 events in Charlottesville, Virginia, as his touchstone, noting that the presence of strong and overt racism makes it possible for white folks to opt out of responsibility for racial inequality because they can distance themselves from the actions of overtly racist individuals. Wise instead argued that white members of our community needed to see the racist background against which all actions are prosecuted, to identify *whiteness* as a shield against accepting and acting on the experiences of people of color in a racist system.[4]

The second event, organized by the Regis College Philosophy department, was George Yancy's visit in January 2018. The Yancy events served as a kick-off event for the spring semester. The Office of Student Activities cleared its calendar of all events to make Yancy's talk the marquee event on campus that week; University Ministry made the Chapel available for the talk, even advertising the event to the congregation of students, faculty, staff, and community members that attended Chapel Mass. Dr. Yancy's visit had three components: a classroom session with students in the "Precarious Bodies" course and members of the Philosophy faculty; a public talk in the Regis Chapel, with 225 members of our community in attendance; and a post-talk reception. The reception is especially interesting in this sequence; the reception space rang with tenacious, enthusiastic conversations among a group of Regis's black students and lasted for three hours after the talk was over.

Dr. Vartabedian, a white woman, responded to Yancy's public talk in the Chapel as follows:

I was not prepared to hear Yancy speak so frankly in the Regis Chapel that night in January, to feel the purposive distress in his telling of the gruesome and inhuman murder of Mary Turner, a young black woman, by a lynch mob, her baby cut from the womb and its skull crushed under the boot of its mother's white murderers. The picture Yancy painted of this event refused to flinch from its unrelenting violence and horror. I began to weep and my palms began to sweat. I felt conspicuous on account of my seat at the front of the Chapel; the podium was just ahead of where I was sitting, so anyone glancing to the left of Yancy would have observed my distress, which I could not contain. When the talk ended, I could not look anyone in the eye—I was ashamed of my inability to see the workings of whiteness clearly, and even more so to recognize my complicity in perpetuating it.

Selihom Andarge, who is identified as a Black womanist and is of Ethiopian heritage, describes her exposure to Yancy's talk from a different angle of reception:

The night Dr. George Yancy spoke in the Chapel he created a space where white people were faced with a moment of disruption, positioned so they had to take their role in systems of power at face value. What made this unique was that Yancy used his own stories, his own Black Erlebnis, to confront the audience with black subjectivity and the reality of the white gaze. As he shared narratives (the response of a white woman clutching her purse when Yancy enters an elevator; the clicking sound of a car being locked from the inside to protect the white bodies from the black person walking by) and hateful comments he had received as a result of his work, the atmosphere in the Chapel began to shift. The white bodies in that space were made aware of how painful encountering whiteness can be for black and brown bodies; they were forced to tarry with the recognition of the white gaze and how dehumanizing it could make a person of color feel.

Though their responses to Yancy's talk come from different vectors of reception, Dr. Vartabedian's and Selihom's accounts overlap at *Erlebnis*, that expression of critical Black subjectivity at the heart of Yancy's work. In the next section, we discuss *Erlebnis* and offer an indication of why it functions so powerfully.

ERLEBNIS AND EXPOSURE

Erlebnis is a term one encounters regularly in Yancy's work, and it functions for him as an index of the expression of Black subjective experience. In this section, we explain the philosophical significance of *Erlebnis* and then link the idea to a story Yancy uses to open his 2013 essay, "Walking While Black in the 'White Gaze.'" We then discuss a vignette from Yancy's 2012 "Looking at Whiteness: Tarrying with the Opaque White Racist Self" to identify the demands *Erlebnis* makes of those receiving it, identifying the demands of receiving *Erlebnis* structures our reflections of how its expression during Yancy's January 2018 talk functioned for our community.

Modes of Experience: *Erlebnis* versus *Erfahrung*

In its broader conceptual context, *Erlebnis* specifies two modes of experience. Martin Jay describes one as "often taken to imply a primitive unity prior to any differentiation or objectification."[5] In this version, *Erlebnis* marks the condition by which negotiation of the world is taken up; for a critical phenomenologist like George Yancy, *Erlebnis* describes his primary mode of being in the world as a Black male subject. A second sense of *Erlebnis* "can also suggest an intense and vital rupture in the fabric of quotidian routine."[6] This valence indicates an experience that requires the reorganization of one's basic movement through the world according to the consequences of the rupture.

According to John Arthos, who investigates the use of *Erlebnis* by the German philosopher Wilhelm Dilthey (1833–1911), *Erlebnis* is more specific than its counterpart *Erfahrung*, a term used to describe "an experience of social interaction."[7] *Erfahrung* is capacious in both its space and its time; according to Martin Jay, it describes experience "based on a learning process, an integration of discrete moments into a narrative whole or an adventure."[8] *Erfahrung* prescribes a negotiation over time of particular moments in relation to a larger whole, as in a journey (*Fahrt*). Put another way, *Erfahrung* is an experience-*ing* over an entire life. Where *Erfahrung* has an unfolding quality, *Erlebnis* maintains a kind of singularity.

To illustrate this singular quality, consider the vignette that opens Yancy's 2013 "Walking While Black in the 'White Gaze.'" There, Yancy describes an encounter he had as a teenager with a Philadelphia police officer who mistook Yancy's telescope for a gun. In response to the perceived threat, the officer shouts, "Man, I almost blew you away!" Yancy describes his blackness as suddenly and irreparably returned to him through the eyes of the police officer, for whom Yancy's body was immediately "different, deviant, ersatz. He (the officer) failed to conceive, or perhaps could not conceive, that a black teenage boy living in the Richard Allen Project Homes for very low income families would own a telescope and enjoyed looking at the moons of Jupiter and the rings of Saturn."[9] This short illustration presents both senses of *Erlebnis*—its primordiality in Yancy's youthful engagement of his intellect and pursuit of astronomical interests and its irruptive quality in something like "the way the world sees black bodies" as brought decisively and violently to Yancy's body. Not only could the officer have mistakenly shot young George, but the officer had preemptively determined what George Yancy was—only a threat, never an astronomer, a desire that in white bodies would be at least neutral if not lauded; for Yancy, it is a commitment that could have cost him his life.

When Yancy describes this encounter, the readers see the force of *Erlebnis*. Per Arthos, *Erlebnis* has a kind of totalizing quality, and "its significance reaches out in infinite directions through the roots and branches of an entire life, shifting and changing as the life changes to which it is attached."[10] From this point of view, *Erlebnis* has a norming influence, and an account of its role in shaping a life is required. With this interaction—one for which the defining forces came from without and only on account of the color of Yancy's skin— *Erlebnis* allows the readers or hearers to recognize the fundamental role this encounter plays in shaping his subjectivity. Readers of Yancy's broader corpus can identify numerous examples of irruptive racialization, the delivery of his body back to him in a way that resonates through the remainder of his experience; however, *Erlebnis* also invites an extension to his readers and his audiences. In what follows, we discuss what happens when *Erlebnis* is used as a rhetorical and conceptual tactic by Yancy, describing what an encounter with critical Black *Erlebnis* requires of those on its receiving end.

Erlebnis: Exposing White Assumptions

Describing a talk he offered to fellow academics[11] in the opening pages of his 2012 "Looking at Whiteness," Yancy says:

> I wanted to create a receptive space within which whites in the audience would be willing to make an effort to suspend (to the extent this is possible) their own assumptions about the operations of white racism and allow themselves to be

touched by, affected by, Black *Erlebnis*, to glimpse, from the perspective of a site of critical Black subjectivity, what it means to encounter white gazes.[12]

He explains that the aim of his presentation was to make a space for *seeing* the effects of white gazes on black bodies, and in order for this to occur some suspension was required on the part of white listeners regarding their assumptions about how white racism operates. The result, according to Yancy, was not reception but rather anger on the part of white members of the audience. His primary interlocutor, a white male professor who denounced Yancy by saying, "I see an angry black professor!" turned his anger at Yancy for no other reason than sharing his experience. Yancy calls this shield *opacity* and spends the remainder of the chapter discussing its power in resisting and repelling the expression of critical Black *Erlebnis*.

This encounter with critical Black *Erlebnis* is nonetheless revealing insofar as the anger expressed by Yancy's interlocutor actually uncovers a set of white assumptions about racist behavior. Reading like a perverse form of self-identification along the lines of "I'm white so *I* know how white racism works," these assumptions foreclose against actually identifying the experience that gives white racism its content; it works around the experience of a critical Black subject living in a world circumscribed by white "racist horizons."[13] When these assumptions are operative, the white interlocutor's attitudes about racism cannot be interrupted by *Erlebnis*, and these assumptions actually reinforce the white racist worldview. Indeed, anger and hostility of the sort Yancy identifies in this illustration serve as an effective shield against Black *Erlebnis*.[14]

For this shielding to be circumvented, the white interlocutor must *register* the critical Black subject as a subject and then *accept* that the critical Black subject has something to say on the matter of white racism. In the account Yancy develops at the beginning of "Looking at Whiteness," his exchange with the white male interlocutor shows Yancy to be merely an object through which white assumptions pass and are returned to the interlocutor unmodified except for the affective amplification ("I see an *angry* black professor!").[15] This expression of opacity suggests not only a failure of seeing but also a keen failure of listening.

One resource that may aid in registering *Erlebnis* offered by people of color is found in Pauline Oliveros's distinctions between hearing and listening. In her 2015 TEDxIndianapolis talk titled "The Difference between Hearing and Listening," Oliveros explains that we often confuse these; hearing, she says, is the "physical means that enables perception," effectively the strike of the eardrum by sound waves, while listening is the work of "(giving) attention to what is perceived," work dependent on "accumulated experience" and attention to the interplay of experience and the present moment.[16] In the case of the earlier vignette, Yancy's white interlocutor allowed Yancy's voice to strike his eardrums but failed to bring the words Yancy spoke in conversation with his own experience. Indeed, our present climate makes *mere* hearing the price of admission to any conversation in which multiple perspectives hold; hearing makes it possible for one to air their points of view without having to register those other views. Listening, by contrast, would require not only that one air their point of view but also that they recognize the possibility that their interlocutor might have something valuable to say, even if it is different or challenging. By Oliveros's account, listening is *work*. It requires not only the attunement to and capture of sound, but work of evaluating and linking sound with a body of experience. Oliveros suggests that the work of listening is subject to "time delays," in which the capture of a sound and its perceptual processing are not instantaneous—in this case, listening is *work that takes time*.

On the matter of listening, Yancy explains that his practice of fearless speaking (*parrhesia*) requires a companion practice of fearless listening on the part of his audiences. This practice, Yancy says, is "an openness to have one's assumptions regarding race and racism shattered, though for the better, where one sees with greater vision and comprehension; it involves, in the case of white people, having one's white self-identity challenged and fissured, even as that process of fissuring will require a constant refissuring."[17]

Returning to the scene Yancy describes at the opening of "Looking at Whiteness" with Oliveros's distinction of hearing and listening in mind suggests that Yancy's white male interlocutor *heard* him but did not *listen* to him, and *in failing to listen* the interlocutor *failed to see*. If it is the case that listening is work that takes time, the speed with which the white professor responded and categorized Yancy as "angry black professor" may not have allowed for the interplay of Yancy's *Erlebnis* with his own experience. This exposure to Black *Erlebnis* will, given sufficient time, facilitate the work of seeing differently.

In the preceding, we have described the content of *Erlebnis* and its demands to listen to that which it expresses and to accept that the implications of exposure to *Erlebnis* require time and work to apprehend. In the next section, we will discuss the ways *Erlebnis* functions for this community of authors, explaining our responses to Yancy's presentation and its resonating effects throughout the semester and beyond.

Erlebnis and Us

As Selihom Andarge explained earlier, Yancy's talk created a space of openness for Black members of our community to be relieved—if temporarily—of the hypervisibility race facilitates on our campus. She also addressed its shifting the burden onto the white members of our community to encounter the problem their bodies, gazes, and their passive accommodation of structures of whiteness create for people of color. Yancy began his talk at Regis with the unvarnished reading of hate mail he received following the publication of "Dear White America." Kelley Coakley explains that in our community there was a time when she and other white folks could be content with their own ignorance, a time before receiving Yancy's message that evening in the Regis Chapel:

We walked around our primarily white campus not knowing what was occurring directly beneath the surface of our conscious experience. The groups we found ourselves in reflected our own identities. It wasn't until Dr. Yancy finally set foot on our campus that we began to stare deeply into the mirror held against our campus and were faced with the most frightening sight: we were the problem and accomplices in the oppression of our peers. Staring deeply at the color of your skin is not easy. It isn't supposed to be easy, but we were gifted with the opportunity to realize that we must do so or continue perpetuating the injustices that we wished to rid the world of.

In turning the lens of visibility away from bodies of color and toward white bodies and attitudes cultivated by whiteness, Yancy's talk and the resonances of his visit in our classroom discussions formed both a site of exposure to Black *Erlebnis* and the opening of a wound sealed by whiteness, thus activating the primordial situation and irruption of experience at the heart of *Erlebnis*. Kelley Coakley describes her encounter with this opening, saying:

Who we were and what we (as white folks) have been a part of needed to be looked at. We needed to be emotionally shocked into recognizing the repercussions our privilege has on others within our society. Our 'woundedness' makes possible the chance to alter the very space that had been so white for so long.

The effects of this exposure—whether the positive identification with Black *Erlebnis* or the fissuring of whiteness Yancy's work inaugurated—produced a productive slowing in Precarious Bodies. Where we might ordinarily read and assimilate words on the page, moving from one reading to the next academic task, we could not escape what was beginning to occur nor did we wish it would go away. Instead of depending on Dr. Vartabedian's expertise to guide the community through the readings "as usual," the Precarious Bodies classroom became a place where experience was affirmed as expertise, and where spoken mistakes or disposition, all slip-ups around race, gender, or sexuality could be identified and corrected without the full force of the defensiveness we might have experienced in other contexts. Dr. Vartabedian gradually moved from the front of the room to a seat in the seminar circle, abandoning the role of professor for something like "conceptual clarifier-in-chief."

We opened a space for brown folks and folks of Asian descent in our class to share their experience, encouraging us to work for nuance in conversations about race that typically toggle between black and white. We affirmed the presence of whiteness as a working assumption, and in doing so challenged the understanding white members of our class have about themselves and their complicity in racist systems. We were, thus, capable of sustaining the recognition Black members of our class found in Yancy's talk and worked to identify the ways race is hypervisible for them. In short, these outcomes indicated that our classroom became a receptive space of precisely the sort Yancy aims to cultivate, a space in which we were able to listen to one another and see ourselves and others differently.

In place of a solution, and held in tension with the progress we were making in Precarious Bodies, Yancy's intervention in our campus and community life introduced a demand that one *tarry with* ideas and structures before moving on from them. Toward the end of his most recent book, *Backlash*, Yancy defines the notion of tarrying as "lingering with the problem and complexity of whiteness."[18] The demand to tarry is a means by which Yancy can refuse the rehabilitative impulse, the offer to any reader a checklist for "eradicating racism in ten easy steps." Instead, Yancy requires his readers or hearers to linger with *Erlebnis*, linger with an open wound, and let the challenges of tarrying guide an individual's or a community's action.

TARRYING

The immediate challenge of tarrying is that it does not offer a prescription for how one might accomplish it, with the implication that redemption is not immediately available for one's complicity in racist acts or in perpetuating racist systems. Even if a reader invites exposure to Black *Erlebnis*, the conditions for accepting what it reveals are often contingent on its supplying solutions for white folks to "solve racism" as quickly as possible. This initial demand sounded right to Josie Brady. She explains, "As a white body I am never forced to encounter how I influence the existence of other bodies, as my way of moving in and through the world is never limited or restrained." Though Yancy's discussion of the impact white bodies have on bodies of color resonated with Josie, her next thought followed a fairly predictable path:

> As I accepted this reality within my own life, I could not help but think about what I could do to help or reduce racism; I wanted to take action right then and there. My hand itched to ask the question, "OK, so now what? How can I change my actions and thoughts so I am no longer racist?" But Dr. Yancy was one step ahead of me and said, "There is not much individually you can do about this. So I offer up the idea of 'tarrying.'"

In her reflection on this encounter with *Erlebnis*, Josie explains that for her tarrying "is the moment of being caught at a standstill" and requires "encountering myself in my existence as a white person." Earlier we contrasted *Erlebnis* with *Erfahrung*, that process of experience that acquires, evaluates, and adjusts the flow of existence over the longer term according to significant encounters. Yancy's prescription to tarry may be too easily absorbed into the trajectory of one's overarching experience, accepted and deemed complete after having considered it "long enough." However, our work together in the classroom suggests that the slow absorption of *Erlebnis* is a necessary feature of tarrying.

In the next section, we are interested to explain the relationship tarrying has to Hannah Arendt's account of thinking, presented in her 1971 lecture, "Thinking and Moral Considerations." In this text, Arendt develops a framework according to which thinking might proceed, and her concern is primarily with the role thinking plays for the everyday person and its central function in avoiding evil; we are interested in the role thinking plays in the work of tarrying toward a transforming critical consciousness concerning racism. As we will show, a framework describes a process for considering one's status vis-à-vis structures perpetuating racism; it operates inwardly, and in doing so continues to resist the tendency toward redemption present in so many narratives concerning racism.

HANNAH ARENDT: THINKING, REALITY, AND THINKING AGAIN

"Thinking and Moral Considerations" is an opportunity for Hannah Arendt to return to her claims concerning "the banality of evil" at the heart of her 1963 account of Adolf Eichmann's trial, *Eichmann in Jerusalem*. In the 1971 lecture, Arendt insists that "the banality of evil" describes deeds with far-reaching effects (e.g., the day-to-day duties of a Nazi functionary like Eichmann), deeds that cannot be traced to an obvious moral defect in the one enacting them. Arendt explains that the "personal distinction" commending Eichmann to this analysis was "a curious, quite authentic inability to think."[19] Her burden in "Thinking and Moral Considerations" is to explain what it means to think, the way thinking operates, and thinking's role in underwriting a critical disposition toward the world.

Arendt describes thinking as the "habit of examining and reflecting upon whatever happens to come to pass, regardless of specific content and quite independent of results."[20] There's much to appreciate in Arendt's description here: thinking does not first select from the "whatever" that it will take up; its status as habitual suggests that thinking is instead a practiced and attentive response to the diversity apparent in the world. Thinking, thus, emphasizes a process which everyone engages and is a control of *response* and not *content*. Her emphasis on the *form* of thought—examining and reflecting upon whatever comes to pass—seems fairly straightforward; its *capacity*—to formally respond to "whatever"—is especially useful in an era of online echo chambers and a twenty-four-hour news cycle.

The "whatever" thinking takes as its object is what Arendt calls "reality," or "the claim on our thinking attention which all events and facts arouse by virtue of their existence."[21] Arendt's concern, which remains quite timely, is that there are manifold cultural and social elements available to filter what we will respond to. She identifies "clichés, stock phrases, adherence to conventional, standardized codes of expression and conduct" as forces effectively constraining our thinking attention.[22] A contemporary analogue is found in carefully curated social media feeds that reproduce the views with which we agree (and exclude those we reject). However, when reality is not subject to this selectivity and is thus unimpeded, thinking is required to respond to the diverse and occasionally challenging content it encounters.

Arendt explains that when thinking is at work, "it interrupts all doing, all ordinary activities no matter what they happen to be."[23] Consider this example from Dr. Vartabedian's first encounter with Yancy, working as his teaching assistant in an introductory philosophy class at Duquesne University in 2010. She says,

> After discussing Peggy McIntosh's essay, "White Privilege and Male Privilege: a Personal Account of Coming to See Correspondences Through Work in Women's Studies," I and a non-traditional student (a studious and thoughtful middle-aged white woman) challenged Yancy with the claim that all struggle is ultimately economic, a matter of class and not race. When Yancy simply responded by saying no to this set of claims, followed by an injunction not to evade or dismiss the truth, to not attempt to escape the weight of critical consciousness, we found that our well-meaning attempts to find common ground revealed our own ignorance not only concerning racism but also our complicity in its perpetuation. As a result of this encounter, I started to pay attention to my own incipient racism. I noticed it everywhere, in the most mundane places— riding the bus, shopping at the grocery store, walking in broad daylight. I had no reason to feel the raised sense of alarm I felt toward black and brown folks I encountered in these perfectly neutral and everyday situations.

This engagement, in which Dr. Vartabedian was told to linger with the weight of critical racial consciousness, required an active reinterpretation of even the simplest actions, an active conversation *with* herself concerning the experience of critical Black subjectivity that refused to conform to her more comfortable assessment.

In terms we have been developing so far, Arendt's paradigm affirms the basic openness to critical racial subjectivity and its account as part of the fabric of reality. Thinking facilitates one's presence in the "receptive space" *Erlebnis* intends. Students enrolled in Precarious Bodies because they wanted to engage and discuss critical race, gender, and queer theory, but their presence in the class did not determine the flow or limits of the conversation. When it is allowed to proceed without impediment, the work of thinking will animate (once again or for the first time) ideas that persist as dormant.

For Nicholas Aranda, the work of thinking emerged in his initial reading of Yancy's "Dear White America." He explains that his immediate response was to seek shelter, folding the pages of the article "in half so as to shield my eyes from the black ink that lined the white page." This response comes from an implication that interrupted Nicholas's self-understanding. He asks, "Why did I seek shelter? . . . Perhaps it is that I have experienced a world in which my passing and adopted whiteness—whether physical or performative—have been synonymous with goodness or righteousness." Nicholas's passing-whiteness functioned as something of a survival mechanism, making it possible for a light-skinned Latinx person to move with little impediment in predominantly white academic and social spaces. He points to Yancy's articulation of the opaque white racist self, the self for whom "white racism is embedded within one's embodied perceptual engagement with the social world and how it's woven into, etched into, the white psyche," as shaping his passing-whiteness, which in turn shapes the way he sees the world.[24] Nicholas says:

> *I view the world from my position of privilege, allowing me to not only ignore systems of racism but also contribute to these passively and actively without recognition. I move through the world without blockage and then project that ease onto others as characteristic of human existence. I am inculcated through time and space to understand my passing-whiteness as normative, etched by the hand of white society to embody all that white society has deemed white, is right. I realize in writing this that I am trying to validate my goodness by being one of the enlightened ones. . . . I need to sit with that for a while—to sit in my shit for a while. The reality is thus: I, at times, have been able to move in spaces where others have not. To this I have paid no attention. In this way I am part of the problem.*

Nicholas's reflection on his passing-whiteness and complicity in systems of oppression supports Arendt's affirmation that thinking facilitates a kind of paralysis with two signal effects: "the *stop* and think, the interruption of all other activities," and a skepticism that facilitates the sense that one is "no longer sure of what had seemed to you beyond doubt while you were unthinkingly engaged in whatever you were doing."[25] The pairing of interruption and skepticism that accompany genuine thinking is a pairing present in many of our experiences with Yancy and our engagement with Black

Erlebnis. Nicholas's colloquial response—to sit in one's shit for a while—is the consequence of fearless listening to Yancy's message, the provocation to think precipitated by exposure to fearless speaking.

Tricia Charfauros echoes certain of Nicholas's insights when she explains, "Ignorance does not belong to white bodies alone." Rather,

> *ignorance emerges and persists in places both unexpected and unknown. As a result of its insidious nature, which is characterized by unspoken laws inscribed on the fabrics of our being, racism and whiteness find their power in being unnamed. Consequently, when racism and those perpetuating it go unnamed, they go about unidentified, unable to be recognized. Such is the case for any bodies that fall between the poles of black and white. As someone who neither moves through the world with complete ease (as a white body would) nor moves through the world with an overwhelming sense of precariousness (as a black body would), a body that finds and locates itself somewhere in the middle is also vulnerable to the risk of being unable to see racism, in its entirety, at work. When your daily life is not so obviously threatened and lived experience not so evidently impeded, your thoughts about the power of an -ism are diminished. For those bodies that belong in-between there often exists the consequence of failing to see the oppressive construct in its fullness and the relationship of those bodies-in-between to the racist structure.*

Yancy's critical Black *Erlebnis* and the classroom conversations that followed it required an assessment of where Tricia—as a woman of Guamanian-Chamorro origin—stands with respect to the traditional poles of racial identification; it also demanded some reflection on her part concerning the ways that she might be engaging in subtle forms of racism.

Not only did Yancy's visit scramble our self-understandings in relation to racism, but it also invited our raising of attendant perplexities in the weeks and months that followed. Arendt's account of the interruption has a parallel in Yancy's notion of the *crisis*, sustained "moments of breakdown" in which exposure, listening, and reflection each have time to do their work.[26] Nicholas's analysis of passing and Tricia's evaluation of her place vis-à-vis insidious forms of racism identify the challenges we understood at the individual level. For Regi Worles, a black queer man in our intellectual community, the crisis reforms our understanding of how systems might be transformed:

> *I began to understand my body as something I could use to understand my own consciousness and—even more importantly—a tool that I could use to understand communities and systems around me. For, if our struggle as human beings is that we are unable to perceive those things that are the most central to our current way of life, then perhaps a part of understanding how to break down these power structures is to place ourselves in them . . . to place yourself in the system, to saturate yourself in the system, to put your own life under the*

microscope and examine the ways in which your freedoms actively limit, destroy, and oppress is bound to make you want to change those things. Still, you must first learn the ways in which those limitations, destructions, and oppressions occur before you can leave that space and change the system.

Regi's insight here comes on the heels of a realization that he and many of his fellow students who desire changes to oppressive systems tend to move too quickly to adjust their own actions; in making individual changes, we fail to see the way the system underwriting these actions actually works. This is work of thinking as tarrying, keeping the conversation with oneself open to accommodate other places where our attitudes and actions are not simply resolved with a commitment to a new disposition. Tricia Charfauros echoes this, saying that in recognizing herself as being-in-between she "can begin paying attention to the oppressive systems at work in our society and our relationships with these—especially with regard to the differences that emerge from diversity in lived experiences and cultural background." To slow down, to pay attention, or to take time is not without risk, however; it is to invite the crisis into our spheres of thinking and action, to invite the interruption and attendant skepticism that inevitably follow, to require the work of tarrying with the implications of exposure to *Erlebnis* and in doing so to make oneself vulnerable to the experiences and insights of others. In the next section, we discuss some of the expressions of our tarrying and share possible directions for personal and communal transformation.

TARRYING TOWARD TRANSFORMATION

In the previous section, we discussed the resources available in Hannah Arendt's account of thinking, emphasizing its necessary openness to an unfiltered selection of information, and the risk of interruption this openness implies. We explained the ways in which the interruption of thinking occurs in the everyday or the mundane and offered several instances of the way Yancy's work facilitates our work of thinking again about our commitments concerning racism, oppression, and possibilities for liberation. In this section, we offer some of the expressions of our thinking again, expressions that emerged from Precarious Bodies.

Yancy's intervention in this community created a space in our classroom for vulnerability and risk, the opportunity to "sit in our shit" all together—students and instructor. As we mentioned earlier, there came a point in the course where the traditional structure of an academic classroom failed to serve the community—Dr. Vartabedian joined the conversation as an active interlocutor, leaving behind her place at the podium so that we could speak with one another. Yancy's work offered us vocabulary for these discussions, and we used phrases like "transcendental norm" to describe forms of supremacy, including whiteness, patriarchy, heterosexism, and ableism;[27] student-developed seminars invited us to investigate the ways we conform to and express these forms of supremacy. Toward the end of the semester, we even turned the critical analysis on the classroom space itself, asking incisive questions about disciplines like Philosophy (i.e., what are the supremacist assumptions that govern the workings of our discipline?), and even about the student–instructor relationship itself, a relationship that took on its own nuance once Dr. Vartabedian took a seat.

The vulnerability and risk that characterized our community allowed us to explain clearly the demands that whiteness and other forms of supremacy make on our lives and to trust that our accounts would be listened to and—as such—received with care. This vulnerability also allowed us to share transparently about the ways in which we began to tarry, diagnosing the way forms of supremacy have infiltrated our day-to-day lives. For example, in reading Fanon's account of pidgin as a form of resistance in *Black Skin, White Masks*, and Gloria Anzaldúa's deployments of English and a Spanish dialect unique to the border region from which she hailed, we discussed the cultural expectation that people should "just speak English" and identified the benefits for an author to speak and write in a language not shared by those in dominant social positions. However, this also invited a frank reckoning of our own relationships to dominant social positions and the expectations of these concerning language and communication, finding ourselves challenged by degrees by the experiences of our bilingual and multilingual interlocutors. Our aim here was not to *resolve* the tension we identified but rather to *recognize* it and allow the tension to resonate through our ongoing discussions.

This work also expressed itself in final projects that inform our dispositions toward our broader communities at and outside of Regis. Selihom Andarge spent the semester grappling with the possibility for people of color to actively claim spaces in which whiteness is the dominant paradigm. "Part of it," Selihom says, "had to do with the fact that I had begun to interrogate spaces that felt like my own, questioning whether they were ever actually mine. I think I was most worried about whether I would ever be able to again enter those spaces feeling like I belonged in them." She explains that as a person of color she made the conscious decision to infiltrate a white space; the hypervisibility of blackness in our campus community facilitates this subversive work. For her final project, Selihom took inspiration from the tradition of Negro Spirituals and wrote a song to encourage those in the battle of claiming space for nonwhite bodies. The song switches between English and Amharic, Selihom's native Ethiopian language:

When they say stay down,
We stand up!
When they say stay down,
We stand up!
We overtake this place,
Lay claim on this space,
We overtake this place,
Lay claim on this space.
Ihay bota
Le hulachinim
Te feterwal
Te fewiswal
So we say!
When they say stay down,
We stand up!
When they say stay down,
We stand up!
We overtake this place,
Lay claim on this space,
We overtake this place,
Lay claim on this space.

Selihom explains, "'Ihay bota lehulachinim new yetefeterew. Geyta new ye feterew ena ye barekew.' This Amharic phrase translates, 'this space was created for all of us, God himself created and blessed it for us.'" Yancy's work empowered Selihom to think again about her role in breaking into the predominantly white space of Regis and believes that creating spaces for people like her is her mission. "I think from this point forward," she says, "my intention in infiltrating white spaces will be to reclaim or create new space for people of color."

Tricia Charfauros addresses the transformation Yancy's work initiated, a renewed seeing of herself against the stark background whiteness has constructed:

When Yancy stepped in to decode America's message for me, my sensitive brown skin screamed as he pierced all the sites at which my life was now changed. Who I am and what my situation in the world is in relation to others couldn't be any clearer now. I am named. I am marked. I am inhibited, I am not immune. I am that which stands out from the background. I am not at the center of all orientation. I do not inherit privilege from my ancestors. I am a subject of centuries of colonialism and racism. I am just another casualty of "ontological expansiveness."

Tricia's reckoning accounts for the general unease that characterized her arrival and acclimation to Regis from her native Guam, her origins described as a "community tightly woven by millennia of brotherhood and *inafa'maolek* (a Chamorro principle of restoring harmony)." However, and like Selihom's project, the direction of Tricia's work following Yancy's influence and her participation in our classroom community turns toward collective opportunity and responsibility:

> *Although I was overcome by an unbelievable sense of hopelessness against an entire system of oppression, against an evil that could neither be erased nor recognized, this feeling of hopelessness was soon replaced by feelings of empowerment and strength. I had been given tools, and now I am determined to use them. There is now a desire—NO, A DUTY—to take on the form of a parrhesiastes (a fearless speaker) for my people. My culture. My home. Our freedom.*

Both Josie Brady and Kelley Coakley identify the transformations of their self-understanding in relation to whiteness. Josie describes the effect of Yancy's presentation and our subsequent work in creating a "space where I can exist and tarry so that I am not actively oppressing black bodies through actions; however, I am also able to recognize that my lived bodily experience (as a white woman) will always oppress black bodies." Josie's reflections indicate the distance she continues to travel from her initial commitment to the notion of "color blindness" as a solution to racism. Kelley insisted that her refusal to tarry with her own whiteness actively impeded the free and fully realized movement of people of color in the world. She says, "American society has allowed whiteness to become the transcendental norm without worrying about how it affects bodies that are not white." Kelley maintains a concern that whiteness directly undermines the freedom and dignity of people of color and the well-being of the broader community in which all bodies move.

On the evening Yancy spoke at Regis, we were joined by members of Da Truth Diversity Club from Northglenn High School (NHS). Da Truth facilitates opportunities for the NHS community to develop greater cultural awareness and an appreciation of the diversity in its midst. Da Truth attended Yancy's talk in a contingent of sixty students from grades nine to twelve, and their members were fearless in approaching the mic for the Q&A following Yancy's talk. Da Truth shared a collective response concerning Yancy's influence in their community:

> *As kids, we used to believe that this country was beautiful and perfect, but as we study history in our classes we learn about all the racism that has affected our country. Listening to Dr. Yancy's speech we now understand how easy it is to be misunderstood, especially when you are talking about racism. We also took away from his speech that we might come into contact with people who are racist but refuse to admit it or accept it. When they are confronted with true*

facts, their racism along with hatred quickly surfaces, sometimes to the point of threats. We also learned that before change can be made concerning racism, we have to agree that it is a problem and figure out what role each one of us plays. Dr. Yancy's speech has inspired us to keep fighting for change. We know that this may be a difficult and dangerous path, but it will all be worth it. We are going to continue working to achieve a diverse society in which every person will be proud of who they are.

Da Truth gave this statement in late April 2019, a full fifteen months after Yancy's talk, which is a testament to the lasting significance of his insights for these students. Like us, the students recognize Yancy's insistence that there is no "end point" to which we should expect to arrive; we all must keep working, tarrying and thinking to accomplish the slow work of coming to see, of being seen, and the subsequent avenues critical consciousness is invited to explore before transformation is possible.

Chapter 3

Yancy's Gift

Bill Bywater

GIVING AN ACCOUNT OF MYSELF

When I began teaching about race in the 1970s, the primary concern at my college was to get into the curriculum courses about the black experience. Across academia, voices were raised, especially by black students, to call for far greater representation of black lives and black achievement, especially in traditionally white institutions like mine. I could not teach about the black experience because I am not black, but I could teach about what black people say about the black experience. I aimed to offer a course about black American thinkers. It would be offered in the philosophy department of which I was a very junior member. To prepare for the course I recruited a black student to help me search our library for books by black Americans. In my statement about undertaking this project, I wrote that we would search to see if there was enough material by black American thinkers from which a course could be created. What I discovered was a whole world! At the time, I attributed my ignorance to a bad education. Today I know I was, as Yancy says in *Black Bodies, White Gazes*, ambushed by my whiteness. I never had to learn anything about black people because they were irrelevant to my white life and my white work as a white philosophy student—in both undergraduate and graduate study—and as a young, white instructor at my predominantly white institution.

There were also earlier experiences where my whiteness protected me from personally having to face the realities of my relationship to the lives that black people are forced to live in the United States. Watching the violent response to the civil rights protests on television, I was able to use my ability to protect myself from any immediate involvement with the thought that what was happening was so egregious that the U.S. government would have no choice but to step in to protect the protesters and to insure them the relief that they sought. The government did step in, but I took no action to support the step. I had not yet met John Dewey's idea that democracy is a "personal way of individual life."[1]

I recall distinctly when Malcolm X, as a minister for the Black Muslims, called white people "blue-eyed devils." It made perfect sense to me that any black person would think of whites as devils, given how whites behaved toward blacks. I appreciated Malcolm X's advocacy of this idea. Of course, blacks would hate whites for what we had done. Yet I never took any of this personally. The fact that I am a blue-eyed devil must have been a matter of pride for me. I was powerful. My whiteness was a shield protecting me from black anger. I need not really worry about what the Black Muslims or the Black Panthers might do. My own version of white power.

So, my attitude going into my new teaching area was that black people had some truths to tell and that I would help black people make these truths more widely known, *especially to other black people.* (Later I discuss how I found myself in this situation again in the fall of 2018.) As students protested the lack of courses and programs focused on people of color at large universities, pressure mounted at my school for faculty to incorporate material about the condition of black lives into their courses. I noticed that my colleagues in the humanities and social sciences, who were all white, were resistant to teaching this material and, even more so, resistant to the forbearance which teaching it required. Calls for academic freedom often accompanied this dual resistance. In discussion with my colleagues, I called the resistance "flashes of resentment." I thought they were associated with being pressured to teach material which one's training had not presented as important and associated with having to become vigilant about how one spoke, not only about the new material—it had to be taken seriously—but more generally so that one's language would not undermine or betray that material. For example, if a black author speaks of slavery as a living presence in black lives, one takes that author seriously by modifying how one discusses slavery—it is not something simply over and done with, as habitual white discourse might assume.

At about the same time, I was learning more about one of the ways in which white people can innocently exclude black people from consideration. bell hooks taught me about how, without thinking, white women had excluded black women from feminism. It is so easy, natural, for whites to make ourselves the center of our concerns. It's one of the habits of white people that has really been exposed and critiqued in the past twenty-five years.[2] There is, I will argue, a self-centered hubris in this habit that extends back to the rise in Europe of imperialism and empire based in white supremacy. Second Wave feminism made me aware of how this hubris is central to patriarchal masculinity. We would say nowadays that this habit intersects with white supremacy to create men who have no trouble placing themselves as masters of the universe. A placing rather similar to the location from which I responded to Malcolm X.

Early in my studies, I came across David Walker's observations about why whites are unable to see blacks as persons. Whites are blinded to the humanity of black people by our greed and fear. Now, I began to wonder whether my colleagues' flashes of resentment were a result of something more than being pushed out of the zone of academic work for which they were trained and in which they were comfortable. Could there be more to their resistance? Were they blinded by something? Were they deeply infected by something that actively kept them from realizing the importance of black testimony about the violence in which whites were engaged? In this way began my season of disliking white people. What the hell was the matter with *them!* I was beginning to get Du Bois's point about taking a primary interest in the white soul.

Plumbing the habits of whiteness became my new task. Here are some of my discoveries. As neoliberalism insinuates itself into more and more areas of U.S. culture, there is plenty of avarice and greed in play. The neoliberal project of monetizing all aspects of the human and natural worlds, of turning everything into a commodity, undermines the host of human values which support our abilities to be communal, empathetic, sympathetic, and caring. Buried deep in the neoliberal approach is the atomic individualism that was central to the social contract theories of the seventeenth and eighteenth centuries. This individualism has protected whites from having to think of ourselves as a group, a race. In turn, this protects individuals from thinking of themselves as a group with a history: a history of terror and oppression. It allows whites to make up a history in which we preserve individualism along with the idea that specific individuals may be responsible for bad deeds, but there is no responsibility for past things that others did and no responsibility for current bad (racist) behavior unless one is directly involved. Whites are able to maintain an innocence that is baffling (to say the least) to people of color who clearly see how white individuals are connected to ongoing racial oppression.

Innocence and ignorance form a toxic feedback loop. You don't have to know about the bad stuff from the past because you are innocent of it. You might know about some of the bad stuff from the present but you are innocent of that too, so it slips from consciousness. What whites remember is the stuff that makes them proud and happy. We do not remember Frederick Douglass's 1852 speech "What to the Slave is the Fourth of July." This feedback loop is ingrained among white habits. I came to believe that it was responsible for a lot of the resentment which my colleagues exhibited. If they were to take black people's observations even somewhat seriously, they would have to confront not only their manufactured innocence and ignorance but also the web of self-reinforcing habits which do the manufacturing. Every time whites take black U.S. history seriously, of course, they are learning something which may be discomforting *and* they are struggling with, pushing back against, an addictive habit that—as neuroscience suggests—rewards them for staying in white happy land. As a result of these discoveries, my dislike of white people waned as I saw the forces arrayed against whites who want to escape what Ta-Nehisi Coates calls *the Dream*.[3] I have come to think of the Dream as a powerful attractor that distorts, in ways already described, the worlds of those bodies, individual and collective, in which it is embedded. I have also come to think that the American Dream has a history grounded not only in the habits I have described but also in the drive for, the commitment to, empire. In what follows, I will discuss how Yancy's gift has led me to this realization.

I have been pushing back against aspects of my socialization into white culture for many years. At least since the 1970s, with the help of what Yancy has taught me to think of as the *black counter-gaze*, which I found in many, many black authors throughout U.S. history, I have been pushing back against antiblack aspects of that socialization. Yet in no way am I free from racism. I ambush myself, the n-word can appear in my consciousness unbidden as well as the phrase "killer instinct" which my father applied to black people. However, the ground for my resistance has a history reaching into my childhood from which I remember two instances concerning race. At some point in the late 1940s or early 1950s, black women domestic workers came to our house on occasion to help my mother with cleaning. At the time, she told me that black people were just as clean, and bathed just as often, as white people. They did not smell. I carried out surreptitious childhood investigations and discovered my mother was right—the black women who came to our house did not smell. Yet now I knew that some people must think that black people smell and are dirty. The second instance was when my mother turned to my father and said, "Stop it, Glen!" in no uncertain terms when he had referred to black people with the n-word (again) as I was sitting in the back seat of our car. (He did stop using the word.) I think my mother's push back against racism and patriarchal authority made a lasting impression on me about how to approach the world. Her earlier nurturing of me must have created a bond of trust and respect between us.

Further, Coates helped me put succinctly another observation I had made. He says, "They [Dreamers] made us into a race. We made ourselves into a people."[4] There is no doubt in my mind that the culture, the people, black Americans have become is very different from the white culture I have been describing. Communication across the two cultures is made even more difficult in the context of white supremacy because whites read blacks as having nothing important to say unless they are talking as if they are immersed in whites' culture. The truths that blacks want to bring to white attention are not truths in the white world. So, if a black person talks about how difficult it is to "get ahead," a white person submerged in white culture hears someone whining about having to work hard. As Charles Mills has argued, white people do not understand the world that they have played a central role in creating.[5]

I mentioned earlier that I had an occasion to teach a version of my Black American Thinkers course in 2018. The course is an introduction to the spectrum of black thought from David Walker to the present. It can only skim the surface of this rich literature (no works of literature per se are included), touching on individuals of whom the students may have heard or are likely to meet in the course of their education. I had retired from full time teaching in 2012 and continued to occasionally teach, mostly about some aspect of race relations, but it had been many years since I had done this kind of survey course. Twenty students were enrolled. Four of them were white. The rest were shades of color from golden brown to the darkest black. Without further knowledge, someone looking at the class might well see a group of fifteen or sixteen U.S. blacks, that is, children of individuals whose ancestors had been in the United States since the time of slavery and were likely slaves themselves. This would have been a mistaken perception. There were students of color in the class whose parents or grandparents had much more recently arrived in the United States. They were still struggling to find their way in our antiblack nation and to learn about this new status that had been thrust upon them. There is a great deal of diversity among people who look black to white eyes. I admit that my anger at white people can be rekindled when I hear about colleagues who collapse everyone who looks black to them into the status of U.S. black, and, compounding the problem, select those students to comment on contemporary race issues.

My college now enrolls many more students of color than ever before. I had never taught a class with such a large majority. As the semester progressed, these students more and more freely shared ideas and experiences reinforcing a feeling I had that the class was truly becoming a space in which they were comfortable—in which they were not any longer braced for an insensitive white comment. It may have helped, too, that when they were introducing themselves all of them commented in one way or another that they were there to learn more about the history of black people in the United States. We had a subsequent discussion about how their respective schoolings left them with little information about this history.

I was moved by this class in ways I had not been moved before. I was introduced to the diversity and beauty of black student lives like never before. I was grasped by the thought that any one of them could be shot dead so easily and by the thought that my course offered them only stories of resistance and struggle that achieved little and were always met by some version of the protean white terror. Yet there they were carrying on exchanges with vigorous enthusiasm.

The precarity of their lives seemingly set aside, I was ambushed by my white assumptions about their lives as I was thrown into the role of an apprentice to their ways of living. I have even published articles about this kind of apprenticeship[6] but never before had I *felt* it in this way. I was privy to it as I had never lived it. These young people seemed to have already incorporated precarity into their lives—grown up with it. I believe my apprenticeship was primed by beginning the course with Coates's *Between the World and Me*. Not that I planned it that way, but Coates's uncompromising insistence on what comes between him and me made me very aware of our two worlds.[7]

Why am I giving an account of myself? For one thing, to let George Yancy see how a specific white person has used (or misused) Yancy's gift to understand (or fail to understand) himself and his world. I want Yancy to see this use of his enterprise so that its blunders, blindness, and usefulness can be assessed and employed.

Yancy advocates acting as a Socratic gadfly,[8] so I am led to think of Judith Butler's idea that I can receive his gift only by yielding to his demand that I fight against my own faults,[9] which, for me, is to say I enter into an apprenticeship with him. I am white regardless of what I will; if I am going to become responsive, I must become responsive to my whiteness. I cannot disavow the relationship to black people in which, being white, I am placed, even though I had nothing to do with being white. I take responsibility for somebody (me) that I did not choose to be. Now I might use what I did not choose as a resource for how to live a more decent life.

As work in neuropragmatism and neuroscience makes clear, and as Butler points out, we cannot give a complete account of ourselves.[10] The processes by which our early caregivers insert us into the habits of our culture, which have a history that is usually totally independent of any individual, occur before we can be conscious of them and certainly before we can be self-conscious about them. Butler calls it a primary opacity.[11] Again, as work in neuropragmatism and neuroscience makes clear, Butler acknowledges our fundamental sociality: "the fact that we cannot exist without addressing the other and without being addressed by the other."[12] These early transactions, I have argued, make us apprentices to one another from our life's beginning. They remain outside any narrative we can give of ourselves. Yet they are always with us frequently making our decisions, passions, and commitments a surprise to us. I cannot tell you why I have chosen to fight the faults which whiteness has given me. It is something that has entered and taken up more space in my life over years as I deepened my experience of Dewey's pragmatism and of how our racist history has fragmented our sociality, our community. I have responded to Yancy's ideas because they have helped me understand and organize my experience in ways that have helped me grow. In what follows you will see how I understand Yancy's gift and what I have discovered in my apprenticeship with him.

FLIPPING THE SCRIPT: YANCY'S GIFT

In the final chapter of *Black Bodies, White Gazes*, Yancy describes how white people can be "ambushed"—"being snared and trapped unexpectedly"—by whiteness. His dramatic example is the behavior of comedian Michael Richards at a comedy club in 2006.[13] Richards shouted an angry n-word-laced rant at a group of black audience members who may have been talking during his performance.[14] Subsequently he appeared on the *Late Show with David Letterman* to apologize for his behavior. He said, "I'm not a racist. That's what's so insane about this. And yet, it's said. It comes through. It fires out of me."[15] Richards is snared unexpectedly by a self he did not create. Yancy goes on to point out that individual white selves are formed in a larger context in which one's self is "haled and produced by racist habits and practices that are long-standing and constitute racist sedimentation."[16] My example of being ambushed is less dramatic, but I was surely snared and trapped unexpectedly by the vortex formed by ignorance and innocence based in the sedimentation of white supremacy. I am willing to bet that many of the events we now call microaggressions can be seen as white people being ambushed by the supremacy habits sedimented in their selves.

The upshot of this analysis of ambush, says Yancy, is that "dismantling whiteness is a *continuous* project."[17] The social structures that reinforce white supremacy will have to be dismantled for individuals to no longer be infected by it. In the meantime, no one can know if an individual has reached the bottom of the sedimented layers or revealed all of one's racist habits. Being open to being ambushed, recognizing when one has been ambushed and expecting to be ambushed can be very important in facing the effects of being socialized as white. These require vigilance, the humility to recognize oneself as an imperfect being and a willingness to take advantage of the exposed imperfections. Yancy observes:

> Hence, the reality of being ambushed should be regarded as valuable to growth, not a sign of defeat. Indeed, there are transformative possibilities in the valorization of an ambush experience as a mode of surprise, as an experiential opening from which one learns and teaches about the insidious nature of whiteness. Hence, thankfulness ought to be the attendant attitude as one is ambushed.[18]

Given the insidiousness of whiteness, Yancy thinks that whites acting alone cannot be fully successful in penetrating our racism, our commitment to white supremacy. Whites need people of color to recognize the limits of our insight—to keep us honest when we claim success.[19] This is the context in which Yancy's gift is born. Whites should be thankful to and for those blacks who are willing to take the time and invest their energy in the continuous effort to dismantle whiteness. Yancy is acutely aware that this effort could protect himself, his children, and all black bodies from being shot.[20]

In *Look, a White!*, the gift of "flipping the script" is presented. Because "people of color are necessary to the project of critically thinking through whiteness, especially as examining whiteness has the potential of becoming a narcissistic project," white people should be grateful, pleased, and humbled to receive this gift. Flipping the script is about blacks and whites working together. Yancy provides a "black counter-gaze" which allows whites to see more of themselves, to see differently and to have their white identity opened to their view.[21] Flipping the script is a deliberate ambush, which can broaden and deepen white understanding of the nature of white racism.

Yancy takes his illustrative example of flipping the script from the iconic James Baldwin statement: "But you still think, I gather, that the 'nigger' is necessary. But he's not necessary to me, so he must be necessary to you. I give you your problem back."[22] An expression a white person uses to describe a black person suddenly illuminates the white person, raising the questions: What does using this expression do for you? Why do you need it? Who are you, anyway? The light shines on the white person and on the role of whiteness in his or her life. It could give the white person pause to reflect. If it does so, the white person has accepted the gift of the black counter-gaze. Black people know the term does not apply to them. It's a white fantasy that becomes the focus of inquiry, thanks to the presence of the counter-gaze that bounces the expression back to its white source. Yancy says flipping the script has a "social force that effectively counter[s] the direction of the gaze, a site traditionally monopolized by whites, and perhaps create[s] a moment of uptake that induces a form of white identity crisis, a jolt that awakens a sudden and startling sense of having been seen."[23]

On December 24, 2015, Yancy flips the script in a very public forum. In the *New York Times* column "The Stone," he published a letter titled "Dear White America." In the letter he discusses how, in growing up in our society, he was socialized into male supremacy. He uses his sexism, and his struggle against it, as an example of how a person becomes something he decides he does not want to be. He urges his white audience to understand that, in similar fashion, racism has been introduced into their lives. Whites will need to struggle against the privileges of racism just as Yancy struggles against his privileging in a sexist society. The script flip, the jolt to white identity, comes at the very end of the letter. In a season of the year when parents and others tend to spend extra time thinking about the children in their lives, Yancy asks that they "see the miracle that is your child. And then, with as much vision as you can muster, I want you to imagine your child is black."[24]

Among the positive responses to his letter that Yancy reports in *Backlash* are two which mention this part of the letter. The first says, "I didn't really understand your article until your last paragraph." The second said, "The last line punched me in the chest. . . . I felt a moment of pure shock at the sort of assumptions people would make about my child just because they were black."[25] Given the names that Yancy was called in the messages that attacked him for writing "Dear White America," it is easy for me to imagine that many whites would see a ball of stinking dirt in their arms, or a mud person, or even a piece of shit. Shrinking back in disgust from the load in their arms, they would probably throw it to the ground. If these visions had time to reach consciousness before the innocence/ignorance vortex swallowed them, an ambush, for which a white person should be thankful, would be accomplished.

On March 4, 2019, again in "The Stone," Yancy published an essay titled "Why White People Need Blackface." He points out that blackface tells nothing about black people but reveals a lot about white people—about whites' "grotesque projections" of racist myths. Blackface makes whites feel good about our superiority by reinforcing myths about black inferiority. Here, Yancy again flips the script to ambush whiteness by turning something that looks to be about blacks into a gift for challenging whites to a new vision. In *Backlash* he calls this "an invitation [for whites] to grow, . . . to enlarge their consciousness and to see the world with greater clarity, especially in terms of its complexity."[26] In *Look, a White!*, in a chapter on bell hooks's pedagogy, Yancy speaks of challenging white students to realize how they are trapped by their socialization into a "state of un-freedom" with respect to race—to "seek greater levels of self-exploration" and "to live in the world more fully."[27] He says: "When my white students show no interest in exploring whiteness, its historical construction, its myth making around origins, its power, hegemony, and privilege (perhaps even refusing to do so), I convey to them that they have decided to settle for less, that they have decided to remain unfinished as human beings."[28]

White people who undertake to become more complete humans will encounter an "ethics of no edges," Yancy says.[29] White bodies and black bodies are contiguous in that one locates the other as superior and inferior. White innocence impacts blacks who are, then, suspected of non-innocence. Given that we are social beings, we know that different societal organizations can place us in different relationships. Hence, Yancy's ethics of no edges suggests that the love with which he wrote "Dear White America," if returned by white America would revolutionize the relationship between whites and blacks (maybe even all people of color). There could be a new flourishing among people in the United States (maybe beyond) if this were to happen. For a new flourishing, white people would have to continuously battle with the hateful selves that our antiblack socialization has given us. Black people would continuously battle their antiblack socialization, including their rage that Yancy describes as composed of melancholy, weariness, and astonishment.[30] Yancy comments: "Rage can function as a site of being, an affect that refuses to be silenced by white racist threats, an affect that has, at times, unbearable intensity. . . . Black people have refused to be consumed by rage, controlled by white hate, especially as we often walk near the precipice of implosion."[31]

The possibility that blacks and whites could fight this continuous battle together gives Yancy some hope. It is hope without optimism, he says. Optimism is unwarranted because of the "powerful recalcitrance of whiteness." Despair is also unwarranted as we have a glimpse of a path forward. He calls it a "post-hope," which is realistic about what confronts us.[32]

GROWTH: POST-HOPE

Yancy's post-hope is pinned on the idea that people can change—that we are an ongoing process. The black counter-gaze can be a vital change agent for whites who take advantage of being ambushed and who seek out ambush opportunities. Growth is a continuous process which can be lifelong. It can be difficult and embarrassing for white people, and thus, we must be realistic about its promise. Yet without growth we remain unfinished, stuck in some place from which we refuse or are unable to take in more of the world. Yancy does not speak explicitly of the growth of black people nor how wielding the counter-gaze can be a source of growth for black people. He does say that he is "open to being staggered, despite my realism, by the capacity for your demonstration of white vulnerability."[33] Does experiencing white vulnerability yield growth? If white vulnerability can be turned into opposition to the antiblack elements built into our social structures, then opportunities for black growth would be enhanced.

Yancy's use of the idea of growth places him in the company of another famous American philosopher and public intellectual, John Dewey. In *Reconstruction in Philosophy*, Dewey asserted that growth is the only moral end.[34] Like Yancy, Dewey thought that we are works in progress.[35] We can experience growth throughout our entire lives, if the right conditions are present. From Dewey's point of view, growth, experience, is a series of undergoings and doings. Organisms do things to their environment and undergo the results of those doings; the environment does things to organisms to which they respond. Upon experiencing the results of either a doing or an undergoing, the organism does something else. If the conditions are present in the organism and the environment, assuming the organism has not perturbed the environment so greatly or that the environment is not so inhospitable that it cannot survive or will not flourish, this process continues.[36] When we are young, Dewey early on and Butler today agree, we are given an embodiment we did not choose, and we undergo a great deal from our environment at a time when we have little capacity to respond. These early experiences form the base upon which our later habits are built. These habits include how we respond to what we undergo.[37] For Yancy, vulnerability to ambush is a condition for growth; an experience white people must undergo. Dewey would ask what environing conditions are needed for this vulnerability. Yancy has a ready answer in Barbara Applebaum's approach to education. He cites her work with approval in both *Look, a White!* and *Backlash*.[38] Dewey sees education, broadly conceived, and growth as virtually synonymous in his magisterial work *Democracy and Education*, in which chapter 4 is titled "Education as Growth." Dewey comments:

> The educational process has no end beyond itself; it is its own end. . . . The educational process is one of continual reorganizing, reconstructing, transforming. . . . Normal child and normal adult alike are engaged in growing. . . . With respect to sympathetic curiosity, unbiased responsiveness and openness of mind, we may say that the adult should be growing in childlikeness. . . . Since in reality there is nothing to which growth is relative save more growth, there is nothing to which education is subordinate save more education. . . . The purpose of school education is to insure the continuance of education by organizing the powers that insure growth.[39]

Applebaum proposes white complicity pedagogy, which takes whites beyond the idea of benefiting from racism to understanding how all whites are complicit in it. We need to understand how whites reproduce and maintain racist practices even while they are good people according to the morality of the day. Applebaum says critique must be employed to bring to light and to dissipate what is familiar and acceptable to whites. Courageous listening, fearless speech, openness to ambush, apprenticeship, giving an account of oneself, recognizing the opacity of self, and questioning the commonplace and accepted are all techniques and approaches which can be employed to move people to turn against racism and the institutions which foster it and implant it in our selves. Education to the rescue! We have a plan. But, wait!

TARRYING WITH THE HORRIBLE: EMPIRE

In *Look, a White!* Yancy introduces us to "the colonial gaze" which denotes "that whiteness knows no bounds in terms of its destructive ontology as it relates to those who have become the objects of its aim." The objects, of course, are peoples of color across the globe. The aim is domination, control, and plunder that renders lives of color "nugatory" and the earth as an object for use.[40] This gaze is as a demigod controlling the lives of others while creating their identities to fit its purposes. "All spaces (inner and outer) are seen as available for the taking," by this expansive, restless consciousness. It buries the humanity of those who adopt/are snared by it, turning them into machines of mass destruction.[41]

As Yancy introduces us to the colonial gaze, he also takes time to introduce himself. Taking his lead from Kamau Brathwaite, Yancy describes himself as a process

> in the middle (passage) of a larger story of diasporic people whose plot was/is/ shall be constantly unfolding. Black people of African descent have a rich narrative that is loop-linked to the past, present and future simultaneously. . . . The black body, my black very black body is a signifier (a historically fluid hypertext) of pain, joy, movement, crossings, mutilation, tears, European expansionism, Elmina Castle, creolization, syncretism, colonialism, the whip, the rope, and the so-called New World.[42]

Yancy and I have many shared events in our life processes. Many of the events Yancy and I share are undergone by him but done by me. White supremacy with its history of plunder, mass destruction of all sorts, death, manifest destiny, and the love of empire is one example. In this process, whites have compounded our assault on humanity and humility while turning ourselves into those unassailable demigods of worldwide "progress" and "development"—the work of Rodney and Quan[43] are examples of the literature that examines the effects of these practices which whites have loosed upon the world. Another example is the white determination, the desperate need, to establish and maintain white innocence, in the face of white inhumanity, by the extent to which we engage in a continuing suppression and falsification of the historical record. A third example is the enslavement and mass destruction of the peoples and civilizations of the Americas begun by Christopher Columbus and his brothers. Indeed, the white demigods—the blue-eyed devils—are bent on being only doers to others, never having to be done unto by those they control.

In *Backlash*, it is Yancy's hope that his gift will give white America "ethical insomnia."[44] He sees whites as having sutured themselves closed against their history in order to maintain a posture of innocence.[45] In this process whites lose the vulnerability to respond to the distress of others and to consider one's involvement in that distress—both of which are important marks of humanity. Yancy asks for unsuturing that will allow an undergoing of vulnerability.

> Coming to understand the extent of my complexity with sexism is a kind of injury to the self, a wounding that I must endure; it is a type of fissure that

is painful, especially as it troubles the "innocent self" that my mask portrays. There is no innocence here, whether for me as sexist or for you as racist. Well, that was at least my aim; to have us both tarry with our complicity and to admit and embrace our accountability.[46]

In short, like democracy, tarrying must become a way of life. This is the depth of Yancy's gift. A way of life which acknowledges that white people will continue to be a problem until we recognize our flawed nature. We have been betrayed by whiteness, we have been wounded by whiteness. Recognize that, don't cry about it, it's just a fact of life that we need *now* to respond to. Yancy's gift calls whites to a new way of living that recognizes that we, whites, have been and continue to be a problem. We need to tell that truth to ourselves and one another. None of us is innocent. We have undergone injury and what we do is injure—because that is what we have learned to do. What we have become, however much we possess, our health, our longevity, our very bodies are a result of the effects of white supremacy upon the earth and its peoples.

Yancy's ethics of no edges with its ontology of connectedness[47] acknowledges how we humans are entangled. The ethics of no edges recognizes that without you I would not be who I am. If you are oppressed, I am an oppressor. When I demand and take up a large amount of space (and other resources), then very little is left for you. In this process, both your humanity and mine are compromised. Upon recognizing what a socialization permeated by white supremacy has done, in an ethics of no edges our first response is to take responsibility for the present and the future in light of the past. This will be an ongoing activity. Once this way of life is undertaken, the specific tasks that whites might pursue will be so varied as to be unlistable. In broad strokes, there will have to be activities of recovery to correct and clarify the record of white supremacy's abuses; there will have to be activities of ambushing and apprenticeship to make the present more humane; perhaps most important, there will have to be activities to eliminate the institutions and structures that support white supremacy. It is these structures of empire into which we are born that form the doings that support the habits and actions of white supremacy and the undergoings that form the global context which immiserates so many people of color.

Chapter 4

Parrhesia

Truth-Telling in the Black Tradition

Kathy Glass

George Yancy examines racism's deep, tangled roots and strange bitter fruit. He limns our racial realities, inviting readers to face enduring injustice that dominant narratives dismiss. In this, he lovingly "prophesies"—speaking truths about white supremacy and the damage it wreaks on Black lives. This chapter examines Yancy's philosophical texts and locates him in a prophetic tradition of Black truth tellers, ranging from the nineteenth century to the present, who detail Black lived experience, boldly address "the ways of whiteness,"[1] and explore Blacks' creative responses to racial and gendered oppression. Challenging constricting structures, these truth tellers furrow new ground for life-giving, Black-affirming values.

Within this broader context of Black speaking and writing as resistance, my chapter considers "parrhesia," the fearless speech Yancy employs, alongside Frederick Douglass's "What to the Slave is the Fourth of July?"[2] Examining these activist-authors' written and spoken words, I analyze how they fearlessly characterize Black lived experience in spaces "structured in dominance."[3] In truthfully detailing how whiteness seeks to define, dominate, and marginalize blackness, they offer the Black gaze as a "gift,"[4] as Yancy describes it, to white Americans. While courageously rendering visible the "ways of whiteness,"[5] these authors also articulate a critical sensibility and posit Black agency, encouraging new structures of feeling and engaged action in the world. Examining Yancy's practice of parrhesia within this prophetic tradition raises new questions about the counter-gaze and the agential Black body at a critical moment in our nation's history. For example, how do race and gender complicate gift-giving? What does gift-giving entail, and what are its risks in the twenty-first century?

Both Douglass and Yancy's methodologies coincide with aspects of the jeremiad tradition.[6] Douglass spoke to an antebellum audience, while Yancy writes over a century later, yet both skillfully engage dominant culture and urge their oppressors to interrogate their privilege. As one of the oldest genres of American literature, the jeremiad historically served as a "prophetic denunciation of present conduct and forewarning of coming apocalypse."[7] Valerie Cooper writes that the genre "was forged of bits of the Bible and other 'sacred scriptures' of democratic myth, like the Declaration of Independence and the US Constitution."[8] African Americans, however, revised the jeremiad to reflect their unique sociopolitical status. As Wilson Moses argues, African Americans fashioned the "black jeremiad," capturing "the constant warnings issued by Blacks to whites, concerning the judgment that was to come for the sin of slavery."[9] Adopting the persona of the biblical Jeremiah before his white Northern audience, Douglass transforms a purportedly celebratory event into an occasion for rigorous social, cultural, and political critique. While Yancy writes much later and does not explicitly invoke the Christian tradition, he employs a similar rhetorical move by critiquing whites' oppression and detailing the stark consequences of racial discrimination.

FREDERICK DOUGLASS'S FEARLESS SPEECH

In 1852, former slave Frederick Douglass spoke before the Rochester Ladies' Anti-Slavery Society at Corinthian Hall, in honor of the Fourth of July.[10] The event attracted 500 to 600 people, many of whom were sympathetic to the antislavery cause. Though Douglass had managed to escape from the slavery in 1838,[11] and subsequently resettled in the North, he was still subjected to racism's reach in the so-called free states. The Fugitive Slave Law, for example, implemented in 1850, made Northern blacks—fugitive and free alike—vulnerable to slavecatchers who kidnapped and sold blacks down South.[12] In this turbulent social context, Douglass delivered his "What to the Slave Is the Fourth of July?" speech. He spoke with force and clarity about the nation's sins yet called for its salvation. While the gathering was intended to be celebratory, the occasion did not mute Douglass's incisive address, which boldly interrogated contradictions between the nation's purported commitment to freedom and its degrading practice of racial slavery. Moreover, Douglass's lecture illuminated his white audience's complicity with oppression and implicitly challenged them to courageously resist unearned privileges.

Douglass opened his speech by foregrounding his historically situated Black body, privileging his lived experience as a site of authority. A former slave speaking from the platform, Douglass asserts, "The fact is, ladies and gentlemen, the distance between this platform and the slave plantation, from which I escaped, is considerable—and the difficulties to be overcome in getting from the latter to the former, are by no means slight."[13] In this, Douglass highlights how his experience in a Black body departs wholly from those of the white "ladies and gentlemen" peopling the crowd. Tellingly, he specifies the Fourth of July celebration is the birthday of "*your* National Independence, and of *your* political freedom."[14] Testifying that his past enslavement contrasts with the liberty enjoyed by free-born whites, Douglass refuses to participate in a hollow celebration that erases his (and his fellow slaves') lived experience. Illuminating his slave past and African American identity in a slaveholding nation, Douglass distances himself from his white audience while also tying his racialized experience to the nation's fundamental contradictions.

Pursuing this line of thinking, Douglass urges his listeners to critically engage America's history of oppression. He addresses them as "fellow citizens" and seemingly emphasizes their shared Americanness, but as Sarah Meer correctly asserts, the subsequent questions posed in his speech "insist on a distinction between white and black Americans."[15] Accordingly, Douglass asks, "[W]hy am I called upon to speak here to-day? What have I, or those I represent, to do with your national independence? Are the great principles of political freedom and of natural justice . . . extended to us?"[16] Expressing regret that he cannot respond affirmatively to these rhetorical inquiries, he points listeners to "the disparity" between his experience and theirs. Douglass, for instance, envisioned himself as being "drag[ged] . . . in fetters into the grand illuminated temple of liberty" to participate in "joyous anthems."[17] In Douglass's view, this is neither a lighthearted celebration nor a day of joy. As Eduardo Cadava argues, "For Douglass, America finds itself in mourning the moment slavery exists, populations are removed, dispossessed, or exterminated, wealth is distributed unequally, acts of discrimination are committed in the name of democracy and freedom, . . . and what it mourns is America itself."[18] Rather than celebrate with his audience, Douglass turns this gathering into a site of public mourning for America's unfulfilled ideals and broken promises.

How could Douglass rejoice when facing the daily indignities of racism and while his fellow Blacks remained in captivity? The racial realities informing Douglass's worldview prompt him to question the legitimacy of celebrating freedom in a nation refusing to extend its blessings to Black Americans. Unwilling to sing insincere praises to the nation, Douglass forthrightly centers "the plaintive lament of a peeled and woe-smitten people" in a setting intended to celebrate the nation's independence. Rather than conforming to the jubilant mood expected on the Fourth of July, Douglass speaks truth, offering a gift to his listeners.[19]

Noting that whites see differently—or "whitely"[20]—Douglass foregrounds "the slave's point of view" to build empathy with his audience.[21] Having felt the slaves' pain, he cannot "pass lightly over their wrongs" because their wounds are deep and similar to those he suffered. Douglass recognizes their "mournful wail" and describes their "chains, heavy and grievous."[22] In this, Douglass paints pictures that contradict the holiday's spirit of levity and joy; emphasizing the slaves' grief, the weight of their chains, as well as their "crushed and bleeding" bodies, he does not consent to undeserved congratulations on the nation's independence.[23] Celebrating the nation's freedom is thus "hideous and revolting,"[24] and Douglass wants his readers to feel similarly disenchanted. Offering firsthand testimony on the slave's experience, Douglass gives his listeners an opportunity to be moved by the captives' pain and revolted by the system that perpetuates it.

To inspire courageous and moral action, Douglass reminds listeners of the Founding Fathers' bravery in 1776.[25] He observes, for example, "To say *now* that America was right, and England wrong, is exceedingly easy. Everybody can say it; the dastard, not less than the noble brave, can flippantly discant on the tyranny of England towards the American Colonies [*sic*]. It is fashionable to do so; *but there was a time when to pronounce against England . . . tried men's souls.*"[26] Here, Douglass reminds readers that it is easy to condemn injustice, retroactively. He further characterizes as "fashionable" the ease with which his contemporaries denounced England's oppression of the colonies. But it takes courage to challenge injustice in real time. The Founding Fathers' resistance of England's tyranny marked them as "dangerous men" in the eighteenth century, he reminds listeners, while "the timid and the prudent . . . of that day, were, of course, shocked and alarmed by it."[27] Feeling "harshly and unjustly treated" by England, the brave ones crafted a resolution of freedom.[28] They prepared to separate the colonies from the Crown,[29] while the complacent felt the rebels had gone too far. Here, Douglass lays two options before his audience. They can join the unpopular antislavery cause, in the spirit of their revered, rebellious ancestors, or they can persist on conformity's feckless course. Just as Douglass takes an unpopular stand against slavery, he invites his audience to similarly "side with the right, . . . with the weak against the strong."[30]

Unconcerned about offending his audience in this prophetic speech, he chooses frankness over conformity. As such, he critiques how America is "false to the past, false to the present, and solemnly binds herself to be false to the future."[31] By repeating the word "false," Douglass encourages listeners to delve beneath the nation's platitudes to engage its racialized realities. He urges them to think critically about these untruths and implicitly invites them to join him in "dar[ing] to call in question and to denounce . . . everything that serves to perpetuate slavery."[32] Faced with this request, Douglass's listeners cannot merely look to legislators in their community to make change. Instead, they must look within and honestly assess how they square the nation's ideals with its practice of oppressing millions of Africans and their descendants;

moreover, they must consider their own role in challenging slavery. In this sense, Douglass strives to stoke a critical sensibility and political consciousness in his listeners.

Going further, Douglass uses parrhesia to speak unwelcome truths and warn his audience of the consequences of their inaction: "The existence of slavery in this country brands your republicanism as a sham, your humanity as a base pretence [*sic*], and your Christianity as a lie."[33] Undermining republican ideals of liberty and justice, slavery laid bare the nation's brutality and utter rejection of Jesus's love-driven teachings. As Douglass argued persuasively in the appendix of his *Narrative*, "slaveholding religion," which endorsed brutality against the oppressed, contradicted "Christianity proper," which he associated with the "pure, peaceable, and impartial Christianity of Christ."[34] Further, Douglass asserts in his "What to the Slave" speech that slavery "fetters your progress; it is the enemy of improvement, the deadly foe of education; it fosters pride; it breeds insolence, . . . and yet, you cling to it, as if it were the sheet anchor of all your hopes."[35] Specifying the disadvantages of dwelling in a slaveholding nation, Douglass makes clear that everyone, black and white, is degraded by slavery's presence. Employing the pronoun "you," he again implicates listeners who do not own slaves. Nonetheless, they are morally compromised by it. Dwelling in a slaveholding nation, they are subject to a perverted racial ideology that structures social, economic, and political conditions. Importantly, his audience "cling[s]" to the existence of slavery as though it were a "sheet anchor of all [their] hopes." This simile denotes an object used in an emergency—something dependable that will help avert danger. In this, Douglass illustrates that Northern whites' lived experience hinges on slavery's existence. Though based in the North, their economy remained connected to the southern mode of production. And since most nineteenth-century Americans subscribed to notions of black inferiority, their subjectivity depended upon the racism that fueled slavery. By emphasizing Northerners' economic and psychological dependence upon slavery and its attendant ideology, Douglass confronts listeners with their complicity in the system.

In line with the black jeremiad tradition, Douglass paints a stark picture of slavery's consequences. He exclaims, "Oh! be warned! be warned! A horrible reptile is coiled up in your nation's bosom; the venomous creature is nursing at the tender breast of your youthful republic; *for the love of God, tear away*, and fling from you the hideous monster."[36] Figuring slavery as snake, intimately connected to a vulnerable nation, Douglass cautions that no one will be spared its wrath. The "creature is nursing," which suggests it draws sustenance from the nation as it grows stronger. It's just a matter of time, the metaphor implies, before the fortified reptile will destroy the republic that has recklessly fed it. Here, Douglass displays the black jeremiad's "traditional preoccupation with impending doom."[37] In so doing, he strives to both strike fear in his audience and rouse their conscience.

According to contemporary reports, when Douglass concluded his speech before the Rochester Ladies' Anti-Slavery Society and took his seat, "there was a universal burst of applause."[38] But, as the Douglass National Humanities project indicates, "many who read his speech would not have been so enthusiastic. Even northerners who were anti-slavery were not necessarily pro-abolition. Many were content to let Southerners continue to hold slaves, a right they believed was upheld by the Constitution."[39] For Douglass, it was not enough for his audience to merely believe slavery was wrong. Douglass also hoped his audience would engage in courageous social action. Indeed, this fervent hope shaped the closing section of this speech. According to Bernard Bell, the "tone of the prophecy of restoration that concludes Douglass's jeremiad of July 5, 1852, reveal[s] the depth of his faith in the promise of America."[40] Embracing the constitution and asserting his faith in America's ideals, Douglass looked forward with hope that change would come and freedom would prevail.

YANCY SPEAKS TRUTH

Over a hundred years later, Dr. George Yancy penned "Dear White America," which similarly confronts white America's racism and calls for courageous moral change. Significant historical change spans the gap between the nineteenth and twenty-first centuries. Yet society remains "structured in dominance."[41] Speaking to this concern, Yancy observes that while interviewing nineteen philosophers and intellectuals about racial issues in 2015, he "came to see these interviews as linked by a common thread: They were messages to white America—because they often directly expressed the experience of those who live and have lived as people of color in a white-run world."[42] These interviews, featuring individuals from various racial, cultural, and gendered backgrounds, told powerful stories and offered rich insights, speaking poignantly about the experiences of marginalization in America. As these interviews allowed Yancy to "better understand how race continues to function in painful ways within our country," he similarly wanted to share his own message with the readers of "The Stone," the philosophy community, and people around the world.[43]

Yancy's "Dear White America" invites whites to do inner work to face their own racism, and "tarry" with how they perpetuate it in society.[44] In extending this invitation, Yancy confronts readers with parts of themselves they may not wish to see. Similar to Douglass, who specified how his nineteenth-century listeners—liberal as they might be—perpetuated racism, Yancy disrupts cherished assumptions of racial innocence. He writes, for example, "If you are white, and you are reading this letter, I ask that you don't run to seek shelter from your own racism. Don't hide from your responsibility. Rather, begin, right now, to practice being vulnerable. Being neither a 'good' white person nor a liberal white person will get you off the proverbial hook."[45] Being "vulnerable" requires a lowering of defenses and a willingness to engage new information, experience, and encounters. Recognizing that readers' immediate response will be denial, Yancy asks them to stay present and be mindful of how they "harbor racism and benefit from racism."[46]

Demonstrating that he can hold himself to the same standard of self-inquiry, he shares how he, too, is part of an oppressive system. For example, he struggles against sexism and "continue[s] to falter" and unintentionally "continue[s] to oppress."[47] Modeling vulnerability in his willingness to be responsible for these instances, Yancy sets a courageous example for his readers: he specifies that he exists in a society structured by gender roles and that he, too, has been "complicit with a dominant male narrative."[48] Might his readers be able to join him in this journey of self-examination?

Yancy urges his readers to recognize how they, too, are part of a racialized and sexist system that disadvantages blacks while privileging whites. Adroitly, he anticipates and addresses readers' defensive moves: "Don't tell me about how many black friends you have. Don't tell me that you are married to someone of color. . . . Don't tell me that you don't see color."[49] Each of these preempted statements works to obscure how readers have internalized and perpetuated racism. Going further, Yancy specifies the form racial privilege takes: "After all, you are part of a system that allows you to walk into stores where you are not followed, where you get to go for a bank loan and your skin does not count against you, where you don't need to engage in 'the talk' that black people and people of color must tell their children when they are confronted by white police officers."[50] In listing these forms of racism, Yancy appeals to the head and heart. Intellectually informative, this list of discriminatory acts centers that which dominant culture marginalizes. But this information should also produce pain and righteous indignation in those confronted with it. As being part of this system will afford whites "comforts" that people of color do not enjoy, Yancy makes a critical connection: just as "being male is linked to the suffering of women" makes him a sexist, "so, too, you are racist." Yancy adds: "That is the gift that I want you to accept, to embrace. . . . Imagine the impact that the acceptance of this gift might have on you and the world."[51]

In *Look, a White!* Yancy further conceptualizes the "gift": "Seeing whiteness from the perspective of, in this case, black people functions as an invitation *to see more*, to see things differently. It is a special call that reframes, that results in a form of unveiling, of seeing, and of recognizing a different side."[52] The ability to see oneself through another's eyes is a gift that expands one's self-understanding and deepens one's awareness of others' lived experiences. Importantly, specific social frameworks can facilitate one's receptivity to this gift.

Only by listening with love and doing difficult inner work can readers accept Yancy's "gift" of "knowledge that is taboo."[53] Specifically, he asks readers to "listen with love, a sort of love that demands that you look at parts of yourself that might cause pain and terror."[54] This means that they must face their prejudices, fears, and bigotry—even their unintentional manifestations. These are "taboo" things that dominant culture routinely denies and ignores, so as to maintain the status quo. Drawing on a rich tradition of Black-resistant love, Yancy cites James Baldwin's assertion that "love takes off the masks that we fear we cannot live without and know we cannot live within."[55] He, therefore, asks readers to discard their masks and "see [themselves] in ways that [they] have not seen before."[56] This love, which Baldwin defines as "a state of being, or state of grace," will enable them to see how they participate in a system that values blacks' lives differently.[57] Accepting this new information will be hard and likely change the perception of one's self as a "neutral" person, to the understanding that one is implicated in an unequal system. Ultimately, one must mourn the loss of this old self and open to a new understanding, informed by Yancy's gift of taboo knowledge.

In a spirit of love, Yancy also strives to warn readers of racism's consequences. This is not precisely the same warning conveyed in Douglass's nineteenth-century jeremiad, yet conceptual similarities connect his speech to Yancy's letter. The *need* to eliminate racism in its multifaceted forms *drives* both their appeals. Specifically, Douglass illuminated how slavery had perverted the entire nation; he also warned the nation would reap severe consequences for perpetuating slavery. More than a century later, Yancy emphatically decries harm that has already come. He notes, for instance, "I assure you that so many black people suffering from poverty and joblessness, which is linked to high levels of crime, are painfully aware of the existential toll that they have had to face because they are black."[58] In describing the socioeconomic realities of many African Americans, Yancy *warns* readers, as Douglass's jeremiad did, alerting them to the results of their actions. Importantly, Yancy does not direct whites to a catastrophic tomorrow. Instead, he urges them to look at the *now*, with clear-eyed honesty, at the "forms of domination" they "would rather not see."[59] He calls them to consider how white supremacy impacts black lived experience and to be changed by this knowledge.

Persisting in his call for honest listening, Yancy anticipates readers' angry objections and further details his letter's intentions. "I can see your anger," he writes. But he urges readers to not "feel bad about" themselves or to "wallow in guilt."[60] These are easy responses and can lead, among other states, to ineffectual immobility. Rather, Yancy—like Douglass—seeks something more courageous. He wants readers to "face a racist history" which informs their own attitudes.[61] Only by acknowledging that history can one then "speak to" present-day racism in one's self.

Ultimately, Yancy's letter emphasizes our shared humanity and calls for an empathetic leap on readers' part. In this, he envisions his letter will "encourage a split—not a split between black and white, but . . . a space for loving" the many African Americans whose lives were cut short because they were black. He wants the letter to open readers' hearts to include those who do not look like them, yet whose humanity they share. As the letter draws to a close and the readers have been asked to listen to "those who suffer in ways that [they] do not," Yancy asks his readers to take a final imaginative leap: "I want you to imagine that your child is black."[62] In so doing, he asks the readers to recognize blackness as that which is to be loved not feared; embraced and not rejected, as that which is part of the self rather than its other.

Drawing on the black tradition of truth tellers and prophesiers, Yancy ran the tremendous risk of being misunderstood. In his letter, he references the dangers of "black gift-giving," as society has historically been hostile to such gestures. Subsequently, in a 2018 *Inside Higher Ed* interview, Yancy describes the public's response to his letter: "The attacks were horrible, despicable and vile. It wasn't enough that many white readers completely distorted the message of 'Dear White America,' which was one of love and vulnerability; they also pulled from an ugly history of white racist epithets and white racist imagery."[63] The recipient of hate mail and racial threats, Yancy did not receive from these readers the empathetic understanding and honesty he invited. In his letter, Yancy recognized that, as a black man, he "has already been stereotyped" as a "sexual fiend"; as such, Yancy took a risk by speaking honestly of his location in a sexist system that implicates all men.[64] Despite running the risk of "reinforcing [the racialized sexual] stereotype," he provides a model for white readers so they can examine their role own in a racist system. The vitriol he received, as a black man, illuminated the ugliness of racism. As Yancy explains, "Things got so bad that it was necessary for me to be escorted by campus police to my classes to teach. I also had to have police presence during the times that I traveled to give public talks at other universities."[65] This frightening experience testifies to the dangerous and difficult work of gift-giving and the "backlash" such acts can inspire.[66]

Employing parrhesia, Douglass's and Yancy's texts draw on a history of courageous black truth-telling. Extending back to Maria W. Stewart, the first black woman to speak to a "promiscuous" audience in the 1800s, and forward to African American lawyer and first black first lady Michelle Obama in the 2000s,[67] this practice includes black women and men who told unpopular truths and boldly called for social change. Speaking from this tradition, Douglass lectured courageously from the podium as the nation failed to embody its ideals, and ultimately concluded his speech with optimistic appeals. Yet the struggle to uproot racist structures continues. Animated by courage and antiracist energies, Yancy's writings persist in the difficult and dangerous work of gift-giving—by intervening in dominant culture and demonstrating Black agency, his writings register resistant structures of feeling that cannot be suppressed.[68]

Part Two

GROUNDINGS IN EXISTENTIAL PHENOMENOLOGY

Chapter 5

George Yancy, Existentialist

Tom Sparrow

SLEEPLESS NIGHTS?

In the fifteen years since I met George Yancy, he has been my classmate, professor, mentor, colleague, and friend. As our relationship grew and evolved, I naturally learned more about him, personally and professionally, and the full range of his activities and responsibilities came into focus. I began to get a true sense of his pedagogical, professional, institutional, interpersonal, and familial contributions. Quite literally, I surmised that he could not possibly fulfill all of his obligations without sacrificing his sleep. He must not sleep, I told myself. Or, if he does, I thought, it must not be for very long each night. And yet Yancy has never appeared tired to me. If he is, he does not wear it on his face. His eyes jump with energy whenever I see him. I can't recall a time when he has complained, confessed, or admitted to fatigue. So, if I had to choose one word to describe George Yancy, I would call him, without hesitation, *indefatigable*. To me, that's Yancy: tireless, incapable of being exhausted.

As a philosopher, I can't help but remember that appearing is not being. Things are not always what they seem. Yancy seems indefatigable, but he may very well be the most tired man in America. I don't know.

As a white philosopher musing about the sleep habits and stamina of George Yancy, a Black philosopher, I cannot help but feel myself moving, quite literally as I type this, dangerously close to the speculations of Thomas Jefferson, who, in his *Notes on the State of Virginia*, wrote that blacks "seem to require less sleep. A black, after hard labor through the day, will be induced by the slightest amusements to sit until midnight, or later, though knowing he must be out with the first dawn of the morning."[1] Here I check myself. My speculation, to be clear, is not that Yancy, as a Black man, *requires* less sleep and that this accounts for his remarkable productivity. My speculation is that he must *sacrifice* so much sleep (or other necessities and callings) in order to live the life he lives. He is not superhuman, although my account thus far, at the very least, hints in that direction. Such insinuation, of course, bears its own dangers, even if it sounds like a compliment—the dangers of misrecognition, erasure, and dehumanization. He is not superhuman. He's a human being with an incredible *curriculum vitae*, a committed teacher, a husband and father, and a public intellectual risking everything to open an honest and constructive national conversation about race and racism.

Yancy must be tired. But it's clear to any of his readers that he won't allow himself to succumb to the allure of rest and relaxation. The problem of racism requires a perpetual address, from all sides and by any means necessary. Yancy is Sisyphus bound not by fate but by duty. "Therefore," he proclaims, "I remain relentless."[2] Yancy's is a project of relentless critical examination and truth-telling. It is founded upon a diverse set of philosophical traditions and methods, notably existentialism. George Yancy is an existentialist. His work draws liberally from the existentialist writings of Kierkegaard, Sartre, Beauvoir, Fanon, Gordon, and others. His life, which is inextricably woven into his philosophical writings, is a relentless, tireless, and urgent critical project. He is committed to exposing and combating racism even if this means watching the boulder roll back down the mountain at the end of each workday. He knows it will, yet he persists.

EXISTENTIAL FATIGUE

So much of Yancy's philosophical work is woven with autobiography. The foregrounding of his lived experience is as much an existential methodological choice as it is phenomenological. His narratives resonate with a sense of exigency and immediacy, as if they were trying to unpack the deepest implications of his personal encounters in real time, trying to make sense of his existence on the spot, as it is happening. No doubt this is a form of therapy or self-care, a way of processing the complexities of racial and racist, or even simply ordinary, interactions—the stuff of quotidian existence. But it is much more than that: it is a carefully crafted gift to the readers. It is the gift of critical reflection on the racialized human condition from someone embedded in the field.

Yancy's writing, his books as well as his editorials, read like missives from the frontlines written by someone who is as much affected by the action on the ground as he is detached from it. Of course, the detachment is something of an illusion. It is the detachment of someone seeking a critical distance, a vantage point that has suspended personal bias, emotional investment, and the like. It is the detachment of the philosopher or the *epoché* of the phenomenologist. Sometimes it is autoethnography. Yancy is all of these, but he would be the first to admit that no form of detachment from lived experience is entirely possible, that the philosopher and the phenomenologist must always think from an embodied standpoint and must always reflect (upon) their existential situation.[3]

The fact of the matter is that the existential situation of Black bodies under white supremacy is exhausting, but not just physically exhausting or wearisome in a contingent sense. The exhaustion of Black bodies exists at a more fundamental, existential level. To read Yancy is to expose oneself to countless firsthand accounts of what disability theorist Kay Toombs calls *existential fatigue*.[4] This is not the kind of fatigue that results from working hard all day and that can be measured by physiological examination; it is not the same as feeling spent or knackered. It is the kind of fatigue that is built into a person's everyday world, a fatigue that structures what Heidegger would call their "average everydayness." It entails a deep sense of alienation, an alienation that is constitutive of the minority body's human condition.[5]

Existential fatigue, in Toombs's view, is a basic ontological structure of the disabled person's world. Reading Yancy, one sees that it is also constitutive of the situation of Black bodies. At its center is repetition, "*routine* experience" that both produces and reproduces the bodies that are caught up in it. As Toombs frames the disabled body's experience, "The world is experienced as overtly obstructive, surprisingly nonaccommodating. Actions are sensed as *effortful*. . . . On occasion the world threatens even. And often it presents itself as questionable."[6] Toombs is speaking specifically about the lived experience of a newly incapacitated body, but what she says resonates with Yancy's testimony. Let me say a bit more about Toombs before returning to Yancy.

In Toombs's case, as she describes it, the world has *become* more difficult to navigate as a disabled person. "The surrounding world appears (feels) different than it did prior to bodily dysfunction."[7] Here she ties the appearance of the world, how it reveals itself to her body, to the affects generated by this appearance. It is not that the world has changed shape or color, of course, but that it now registers on her body with a different meaning. Given the absence of universal wheelchair accessibility and other environmental realities, Toombs's situation is now rife with obstacles and obstructions. Her world is more disorienting than it used to be because her long-established tools of navigation have been outmoded, and this is tiresome because it takes a lot more effort to get done what used to get done with less effort.

The "knowing how" of one's engagement in the world is rendered circumspect. The effortful nature of worldly involvement that is characteristic of incapacitating disorders can engender a sense of fatigue that I shall call "existential fatigue." To organize and carry out projects requires not only physical ability but, as importantly, an exercise of will. When ceaseless and ongoing effort is required to perform the simplest of tasks (getting out of bed, dressing, taking a shower, going on a trip), there is a powerful impulse to withdraw, to cease doing what is required. Consequently, physical incapacity exerts a centripetal force in another sense. The person with a disability is tempted severely to curtail involvement in the world.[8]

Reading Toombs, I cannot help but imagine Sisyphus opting out of his interminable task and taking up the life of Dostoevsky's underground man, if he had the option.

Toombs invokes her incapacity as an enervating fate driving itself toward inaction. As if the facticity of disability were not enough to curtail her early practical activity, its affective dimension works to wear down her will, desire, and consequently her involvement in the world. But, of course, this reduction or contraction of action is not intrinsic to the physical incapacity of Toombs's disabled body. It is distributed throughout her being in the world and "represents a modification of the existential possibilities inherent in the *lived body*."[9] Her disability is existential in that it is at once physical, social/environmental, and ontological. At the center of this nexus of disability is her corporeal condition, the *lived body* that "manifests one's being-in-the-world not only as orientational and intentional locus but in the sense that distinct bodily patterns (walking, talking, gesturing) express a unique corporeal style, a certain bodily bearing that identifies the *lived body* as peculiarly me."[10]

With these remarks on corporeal style and the identity of the lived body, I am compelled to think of the famous phenomenology of the "elevator effect" in Yancy's *Black Bodies, White Gazes*, one of the most widely discussed topics in his first authored book. But I will not turn to that now. I would like to move instead toward thinking about how Toombs's account of the being in the world of disabled bodies is analogous to the being in the world of Black bodies as accounted for in Yancy's philosophy. What links these experiences is their insistence on the corporeal or material conditions of normativity, the way that ableism and whiteness operate in parallel, but also symbiotically, to hegemonically construct, shape, and orient the everyday world so that it is maximally accommodating for abled and white bodies.[11] By contrast, this world is lived as fundamentally disorienting and oppressive for disabled and Black bodies. This is what gives the world, the only world these bodies know, an unhomelike or uncanny character. This is what renders these bodies "invisible" (as Ellison would put it), what "interpellates" these bodies (as Althusser or Butler would put it), what "disciplines" these bodies (as Foucault would put it), what "confiscates" and "returns" these bodies (as Fanon would put it). All of these tropes are mobilized with a lightness of touch and powerful deployment in Yancy's corpus, from *Black Bodies, White Gazes* to *Backlash*.

Finding oneself subject to incessant and unrelenting interpellation, discipline, confiscation, and invisibility—to say nothing of brute physical violence—provokes myriad, sometimes unpredictable, responses. Toombs confesses a desire to retreat inside, to minimize and immobilize. Ellison's protagonist in *Invisible Man* famously lashes out, in the Prologue to that novel, out of a feeling of resentment toward his invisibility. Sick and tired of it, he seeks an outlet and ends up nearly killing a man in an act of rage.[12] Despair, sadness, and disgust become inevitable when the everyday world is filled with signs telling you that you do not belong, or that it would be better if you did not exist at all, so it does what it can to suppress your existence. Speaking of some of the hate mail he has received in response to his writing about racism in America, Yancy admits: "I didn't know the extent to which the words would traumatize, that the words would wound. My physiology registered the wounds. Mood swings. Irritability. Trepidation. Disgust. Anger. Nausea."[13] Although pulled in many affective directions, by his own account, Yancy has quite publicly responded to the barrage of racist hate with love.[14] What resulted was as revealing as it was predictable. That sounds like a contradiction until you consult the logic of racism as it's been historically practiced in America. For Yancy, it was a predictable revelation about racism in contemporary America. For me, Yancy's testimony is revelatory for what it teaches about Black existence and, in particular, Yancy's philosophical angle of vision.

In Yancy's latest book, *Backlash*, he adds dimension to Toombs's concept of existential fatigue. This text chronicles and analyzes the onslaught of hateful racist responses Yancy received to his Christmas Eve 2015 *New York Times* piece, "Dear White America." I will not try to recount these responses since Yancy meticulously documents and annotates them in the book, but I will acknowledge that the backlash leaves no doubt that white America saw Yancy's *New York Times* letter not as a gift of love, as intended, but as a direct assault on white supremacy. And white America's reaction was vicious, defensive, and revelatory. Not only is systemic racism an intransigent reality in the United States, but nasty, brutish, old-school racism—the "obvious" kind—is strong, angry, and poised to defend itself against the suggestion that it might exist.

America is a strange place to call home, says Yancy.

Black people are painfully aware of white America's centuries-old *damnable* history of anti-Black racism and the fact that Black Americans, despite our approach of the third decade of the twenty-first century, continue to struggle over what America means in terms of functioning as a place called "home." White America, as a whole, has never been hospitable toward Black people, but hostile to our very *being*.[15]

The hostility of white America toward Yancy's antiracist work, which is every ounce of his work, is given here an ontological definition. The hostility is not directed fundamentally at what he says but at who he is. It is a hostility that is internally related to the existence of Black bodies, which means that it constitutes and is constituted by the existence of Black bodies. Yancy, as antiracist Black body, is produced and reproduced by the hatred and disgust that fuel his racist critics. When they hate him, they hate something they have produced and, therefore, they reveal something about the logic of white supremacy.

This corporeal affective economy is constitutive of the material conditions of whiteness and its normative spaces, including the *New York Times* editorial pages where Yancy publishes and the university office where Yancy receives his hate mail. He thinks, writes, and reads from these conditions. They sustain him while they constrain him. They provide for him a platform upon which to stand out, a space of transcendence or *ekstasis*, and yet this is the very space that he feels reining him in, reminding him that he is an essence, wrapped in immanence and destined to perform the role that white America requires him to play.[16] If there is anything the authors of his hate mail want Yancy to remember it is that, try as he might, his freedom will only be superficial. He is, in Sartre's vocabulary, an in-itself, an object with a fixed essence. Essentially speaking, he cannot be a for-itself.

It is here that the bad faith of his critics exposes the hollowness of their existential ontology. Their vitriol is so deeply felt, so intense, so serious. But its seriousness masks an underlying precariousness and existential instability. This is precisely what renders it ontologically suspect. It is reminiscent of the bad faith of what Beauvoir calls the "serious man," the man who "gets rid of his freedom by claiming to subordinate it to values which would be unconditioned."[17] In our context, these are the values of whiteness, posited as immutable norms and underwritten by a long history of intellectual labor, which passes through America's Founders, including and especially Jefferson (cited earlier), designed to establish the truth of Black inferiority. Thus does white America provide for itself an alibi, a guilt-free renunciation of its responsibility for the effects of white supremacy both historical and contemporary. This alibi is inextricably bound up with the essence of America.

Yancy calls on Frantz Fanon to help flesh out this ontological situation when he writes that "Being Black in white America has always raised the question of the validity and legibility of our existence, or, more accurately, when engaging the existential predicament of Black people in white America, 'there is a zone of nonbeing.'"[18] The phrase "zone of nonbeing" Yancy borrows from *Black Skin, White Masks*. What Fanon means by the phrase is that Black people under the gaze of white society find themselves negated, hollowed out, not regarded as people. Historically and sociologically speaking, this is evident. Ontologically speaking, the point is less obvious and requires some elucidation. Especially, for instance, when Fanon asserts that "a Black is not a man."[19] From the Sartrean standpoint, it would be accurate to say that Blacks have been made to believe that they are not free people, or the kind of people capable of transcending the meaning of their Blackness as it has been determined by white society. The negation ("not a man") employed by Fanon says it all, however: Blacks might one day become people, but at the moment the meaning of their being is that they are *not* white.[20]

At the core of Black existence is a fundamental absence, a loss, and one that is as much a loss of recognition as it is a loss of orientation in the world. Black folks are never without this loss. It is a constitutive feature that takes us at once to the core of Blackness and the existential condition of Black bodies, whose negation by the norms of whiteness is what gives the white world its unhomelike quality. Black bodies are born aliens in their own world. As Ahmed puts it, "If to be human is to be white, then to be not white is to inhabit the negative: it is to be 'not.' The pressure of this 'not' is another way of describing the social and existential realities of racism." "The experience," she adds, "is one of nausea and the crisis of losing one's place in the world."[21] And yet the loss has always already occurred; the nausea does not bubble up one day in the park, as in Sartre's famous story. The *transcendental* loss and nausea are, as it were, conditions of possibility of Black existence, which always bears within it a "feeling of nonexistence."[22]

In a cruel, ironic twist, this nonexistence carries a lot of affective and existential weight. It is the weight a person feels when they are compelled to prove themselves or their worth; it is the weight they feel when they know that proving themselves is redundant and irrational; it is the weight they feel when they know that proving themselves is hopeless and destined for failure. It is the weight of having "to lay claim to our humanity, to lay claim to it *ad nauseum*" in the face of vicious inhumanity. Yancy refers to this condition as an "existential burden."[23] It is a particularly absurd burden because it places a demand on Black people to prove their humanity with the very thing that they are denied—their humanity. Always sensitive to the tempting consolation of bad faith, Yancy knows that this absurdity should not be, cannot be, nullified by establishing once and for all the humanity of Black existence. This would be a retreat into the comforts of essentialism. On the contrary, the absurd struggle for recognition of Black humanity is a struggle to direct the course of existence under the banner of liberty understood not as a state of being but as the inexhaustible task of becoming who one is.

This is in part what Yancy means when he characterizes Black struggle as a battle against the image of Blackness that exists in the white imaginary. It is a battle to retrieve the Black body from its confiscation by the normative, epistemic, and perceptual dominance of whiteness. The terms of this battle are markedly existential, as Yancy makes clear in the first chapter of *Black Bodies, White Gazes*, which provides the richest elaboration to date of Yancy's conceptual framework, methodological approach, and critical vocabulary. He writes:

> From the perspective of whiteness, I am, contrary to the existentialist credo, an essence ("Blackness") that precedes my essence. Hence, my emergence upon the historical scene requires that I engage in a battle that is not only iconographic and semiotic but also existential. Indeed, the Black body, my Black body, is itself a battleground. The Black body has been historically marked, disciplined and scripted and materially, psychologically, and morally invested in to ensure both white supremacy and the illusory construction of the white subject as a self-contained substance whose existence does not depend upon the construction of the Black qua inferior. As a Black person, this is my existential standpoint, my inheritance. And it is this existential standpoint, this past inheritance, that informs my sense of agency.[24]

If the Black body is a battleground, then the rules of engagement are as much linguistic and imaginative as they are corporeal. The struggle to extricate the Black body from the zone of nonbeing to return it to its agency is a struggle against the representation of Black essence—against the essentialization of Blackness—by whiteness. It is a battle to return the Black body to itself, to return what has always already been stolen from it, both literally and figuratively. This is not, Yancy insists, an attempt to

> celebrate or recuperate an "authentic" identity qua essence or to ground a sense of identity in fixed metanarratives. There is the effort, however, to make sense of one's existence within the context of lived history, one that recognizes and acknowledges the reality of fissures in collective and individual identity formation and refuses to romanticize origins or points of historical continuity.[25]

The point of struggle, then, is to elucidate the "tortuous sojourn through the crucible of American and European history" and to use this elucidation to undo the seriousness of whiteness, to embarrass its hegemony with the truth of the human condition.

Despite the nausea and the absurd burden, Yancy is relentless in his struggle to speak truth to power, to practice the *parrhesia* that has come to loom so large in his work and that once again confirms his Socratic inheritance. This is *parrhesia* as vocation, as virtue, as authenticity in the face of white America's bad faith, seriousness, and nihilism.

EXISTENTIAL RISK

In its bad faith rendition of Blackness, whiteness risks absolutely nothing. It assumes responsibility for nothing; indeed, it does just the opposite: antiblack racism is the evasion of responsibility, an act of cowardice, a profoundly inauthentic reckoning of identity, facticity, and agency. Its effects are at once dishonest, comforting for those who benefit from them, and violent. To counteract this, argues Yancy, white people need to take some profound risks. They need to put themselves out there, put their very existence on the line. Note that I did not say that they have to put their lives on the line, even though that is also true. This is about increasing white participation in "existential risk." Yancy's letter to white America was an invitation to existential risk. It revealed the sad truth that white America is deeply afraid of this risk. They deny it, reject it, and condemn the very suggestion of it. In doing so they decline to work toward racial justice and double down on their complicity in systemic racialized violence.

What would it mean to risk whiteness at an existential level? What would it require to brave this risk? First, it means coming to terms with the reality of "white fragility," the fact that whiteness is a historically contingent, quite mutable (even if intractable) construction. Despite its claims to the contrary, it can be undone; it might one day come undone because it is not an absolute. Whiteness itself is fragile and white people, often at an unconscious level, know that it (they) can be broken. And this induces in them an existential terror. As it stands at the moment, however, most white people cannot or will not fully come to terms with this possibility. And they can afford not to because they live lives that protect them from this terrible reality. "The fact of the matter," writes Yancy,

> is that you are not always stressed by race, because, after all, you deploy race when it best suits you, which is generally when we [Black bodies] are the target of that deployment. The deep social, psychological, and existential stress that we endure every day of our lives, partly because your whiteness structures and saturates so many aspects of the public spaces that we must engage out of necessity, is predicated upon your racial comfort, which I see as your fundamental failure to live a life of daring, of risk, of a form of love that is capable of removing the lies that you attempt to conceal, the masks that you wear.[26]

The concept of white fragility helps explain the hostile combination of anger and anxiety that results when we try to speak honestly and openly about white supremacy in America.[27] Such conversations inch too close to the tender center of the white psyche. Predictably, white people recoil at this encroachment on the meaning of their being, sensing as they do the threat of losing their alibi for white supremacy. An honest conversation about white complicity (the complicity of *all* white people) in racist domination requires reckoning with white fragility, but this is as difficult as reaching out to a therapist in order to get real about your deepest insecurities.

Getting white people to risk themselves takes relentlessness. And there are no guarantees. As such, Yancy's work represents a leap of faith in the true Kierkegaardian sense of that phrase. His work demonstrates a deep faith in the power of love to bridge the divide between Black America and white America. This kind of philosophical activism requires the activist to risk everything. It promises exhaustion, psychological turmoil and trauma, and possibly death. It is dogged by existential fatigue at every hour, during victories and defeats alike. *Backlash* gives ample evidence of the threats of violence and death that Yancy received in response to "Dear White America." The racial slurs and assaults on his character are numerous; reading them together has a cumulative effect that can only hint at the affective weight under which Yancy must labor since he cannot remain silent. He decidedly rejects silence when he writes: "I refuse to die."[28]

EXISTENTIAL CONVERSION

Earlier I invoked Hegel's famous master–slave dialectic when discussing the existential burden that is the absurd Black struggle for recognition under white supremacy. That dialectic is described by Hegel as a "struggle to the death," and I find that characterization appropriate here.[29] Yancy knows that if he were to remain silent on the question of whiteness, if he were not to employ *parrhesia* in the face of white supremacy, then he would be succumbing to the hatred, violence, and death that white America has vocally wished for him. He would be remaining silent about the false representation of Blackness that circulates throughout the white supremacist imaginary. Hence, his rejection of silence. He doubly rejects silence when he insists that "there are certain forms of death that are necessary. The oppressive machinations of whiteness must die so that white people (*you*) can truly live."[30] In order for Black (and white) people to thrive in white America, whiteness has to risk its own death. This demands not only the recognition of Black existence as equivalent, ontologically speaking, to white existence, but it also places a demand on white people fully and finally to recognize their own inescapable complicity in antiblack racism.

Drawing on the autobiography of Frederick Douglass, whose lectures and narratives chronicle firsthand the master–slave dialectic and its struggle to the death for recognition, Yancy defends the need for "existential conversion" to combat racism in white America.[31] In Douglass's case it is a matter of how the slave, who exists as an in-itself (powerless, like an object), gains recognition as a consciousness for-itself by exerting his agency in the world. In the case of whiteness, as with any conversion, this will of necessity involve the loss (death) of something that once was—namely, a misrecognition of self and a misplaced self-righteousness. "As white," he implores,

> you must be open to a kind of death—a death of your stubbornness, a death of your denials, a death of your "innocence," a death of your arrogance, a death of your racial comfort, a death of your narcissism, a death of your "goodness," a death of your fears, a death of your color evasion, a death of your self-righteousness, a death of your sense of "greatness" and "manifest destiny," a death of all those tricks that you play to convince yourselves that you are fine, that you are the good ones, the sophisticated ones, the nonracist ones, the ones who truly care about justice and a world without oppression, hatred, and racist violence.[32]

Death in this context involves the shedding of a mask, which is not to say skin, to borrow from Fanon's vocabulary. For whiteness to risk existential conversion, it needs to restructure the habits, dispositions, and modes of being that reinforce racist/oppressive norms and the racial narratives that legitimize oppressive practices.[33] This is easier said than done. It takes much more than an act of willful self-denial. The kind of death required in existential conversion is not structurally equivalent to committing suicide, which, after all, would only be an evasion of the existential problem, as Camus analyzed in *The Myth of Sisyphus*.

One wonders if whites can actually undergo an existential conversion with respect to their complicity in whiteness. Perhaps such a conversion is itself a myth.

> As whites attempt to undo power and privilege, they find themselves confronting a world in which whiteness is not only around them but also working through them. Given this, disrupting sites of whiteness will require that white allies cultivate identities "rooted in understandings of themselves and their relations to others." . . . Even as one tries, one's efforts will be thwarted by unconscious habits of white privilege, forming roadblocks as one attempts to expose whiteness.[34]

Existential conversion is not just about deploying one's agency differently or letting go of certain kinds of beliefs and behaviors. It will result, if it ever does, from the struggle for recognition and is therefore precarious and unpredictable. It is dependent upon the internal relation that exists between white and Black bodies. White agency is only half of the equation. White America cannot just "cast off [its] whiteness, particularly as whiteness qua 'race' is not a thin covering laid over a fundamentally non-raced identity."[35]

The existential battle will always be fought on historical soil and will always be a battle over historically contingent identities. Existence precedes essence, after all. If it were not so, then existential conversion would not be possible.[36] "The fundamental premise of existential conversion is that a person is not condemned to whiteness, but that there are always other ways of grounding one's identity, performing one's whiteness, even as one's whiteness is interpellated within the larger social world of white power."[37]

Here I am trying to perform whiteness differently, trying to ground my identity in something other than white privilege. When Yancy speaks of the necessity of the death of white supremacy, he is speaking directly to me. I am writing to you in the wake of his indictment of my complicity in white supremacy and the imperative of existential risk. I am struggling to embrace death, to enact an existential conversion without illusion and without the expectation of forgiveness or acquittal. Bad faith haunts my composition. I know that writing a philosophical essay for publication in an academic book risks very little, almost nothing for a white guy like me. I write without guarantee, from a privileged location in white America, with very little hope, but not out of despair. I write as a way of returning the love that Yancy offered in "Dear White America," as a way of returning the love he extends to all of his students in the classroom, as a way of loving wisdom. My hope as I write these final words is that my love is not merely in the service of a myth, that it is indeed possible to know myself in the way that Socrates and Yancy beseech, and to do so in good faith.

Chapter 6

Ways of Seeing Whiteness

Daniel C. Blight

The reciprocal nature of vision is more fundamental than that of spoken dialogue.

—John Berger

For those whites who are able to glimpse themselves *as they are*, this would entail being in a state of danger. After all, such a glimpse, if tarried with, would reveal the necessity of the process of loss; the loss of white identity and the material, mythopoetic, and historical forces that buttress it.

—George Yancy

AS I AM

George Yancy offers all white people an opportunity to see for the first time. To see ourselves *as we are*. This gift[1] credits every white person a chance to look anew; the ability to primigenially glance inside ourselves to a time when we were not white—a time when we were imperfectly human preceding the social formation of racial whiteness in the early seventeenth century.[2] This is a type of "white pause" in which whites come to fleetingly glimpse ourselves in the absence of, as Kalpana Seshadri-Crooks writes, "A symbolic system sustained by a regime of visibility."[3] Yancy's gift is remarkable because it offers white people the opportunity to perceive the forward movement of white temporality, creating a juncture in which we can momentarily dwell without the forms of white sight that ordinarily constitute our seeing.

What do I see when I dwell *there*, in a place that one might call "white time?" I am implicated in this temporal sense of whiteness in two competing

87

ways. Through an attempted understanding of, and a critical distance from my white self, I hope to understand whiteness *itself*; which is to say, my whiteness is always psychologically divided between an internal white subjectivity—"me," as I see myself shrouded in a seemingly insoluble form of white ignorance—and a second self socially linked to whiteness at large—other white people, the invention of whiteness and its ongoing centrality to the neoliberal political system of racial oppression and social control.

As W. E. B. Du Bois wrote, drawing an analogy between whiteness and the sea to describe what is now an old religion, "Wave on wave, each with increasing virulence, is dashing this new religion of whiteness on the shores of our time."[4] So this seeing for the first time should not be confused with any form of antiracist sea-change among those white people who choose to raise their consciousness in this way, for it is simply an opportunity, a glimpse at a new manner of being. Dwelling in this space means that we white people may be still, static, open to seeing whiteness, but we are nonetheless *still* white, and we therefore remain, in Yancy's word, "sutured" to whiteness.

I discovered Yancy's writing at the suggestion of the British curator and writer Ekow Eshun in 2016. I first read the introduction to Yancy's book *Look, a White!: Philosophical Essays on Whiteness*,[5] and I have since read almost all of his writings. One has to understand that at this point I did not know a single thing about whiteness and in a profound sense I still don't (it is not my belief that whites can learn about the problem of being white simply through reading and scholarship, it is a lifelong pursuit). I was not taught about colonialism, the transatlantic slave trade, or the invention of whiteness at school or college or university in the United Kingdom, and I was misled to believe that race is a fixed and immutable fact of human life. The English education system has it this way deliberately; it is a nationwide pedagogy that lies (in both senses of the word) under what Arday and Mirza call "the sheer weight of whiteness."[6] Under this pressure, young people's learning is left wanting and, in my experience, the effects of this live on fully into adult life. We whites very much "carry the weight of white racist training" in our bodies, Yancy writes.[7]

Encountering *Look, a White!* was the beginning of a novel adult education for me, one in which I hope to come to terms with myself *as I am*: white, and therefore racist. Yancy posed a striking question to the audience at a conference in London, England, in 2017, and it has stuck with me ever since: "What if to be white is to be racist?" Coming to terms with the answer to this question is fundamentally an act of looking and seeing oneself *differently*, and so it is a question of visuality. In "Flipping the Script," his introduction to *Look, a White!* Yancy writes: "Whites must begin to see themselves through gazes that are not *prone* to lie/obfuscate when it comes to the 'workings of race' qua whiteness."[8] It is this question of the difference between looking and seeing whiteness that I wish to address here by way of select readings of Yancy's extensive scholarship, and ideas I find to be complimentary and compatible with it.

STRUCTURES OF SEEING WHITENESS

One may say that the constitution of the visible is that of a prolongation of the visual impregnated with the symbolic.[9]

Whiteness becomes visible within the space of symbolism itself. This is a twofold symbolism that constructs the image and meaning of both the white body and the Black body (the latter without approval or permission). Whiteness does not *see* Blackness; it violently constructs it in opposition to itself through a process of *looking but not seeing*. Whiteness builds an image of itself as something that must live incorporeally without trace forever, and a picture of Blackness that must die or experience corporeal death over and over. As Yancy writes, "The Black body becomes a 'prisoner' of an imago—an elaborate distorted image of the Black, an image whose reality is held together through white bad faith and projection—that is ideologically orchestrated to leave no trace of its social and historical construction."[10]

We might understand this in the way that white temporality refuses to stop; it prolongs and impregnates (Brighenti) its regime of visibility (Seshadri-Crooks), which emanates from a white imaginary into a constructed white reality comprising rhetorical and violent symbols. As far as whiteness is concerned, people of color are obliged to live within this barbarous one-dimensional reality (and they do so, as Yancy has noted, while feeling that their lives are constantly in a state of danger). This is exactly what is meant by systemic whiteness and structural inequality in my view: all personal, social, political, legal, and institutional forms of whiteness are oriented toward a constant impregnation of white symbolism into "ontological, epistemological, and aesthetic orders that privilege"[11] whiteness, white world-making and white visuality. Whiteness is a destructive being, a callous body of knowledge and a grotesque aesthetic, which is etymologically to say that it is sensorially concerned with its own "beauty" and therefore its own image. I take from these two things: that whiteness is spectral and narcissistic, but that it can be traced, metaphorized, and, crucially, visualized.

In a brief study of Aimé Césaire's *A Tempest* (1969)—which is a version of Shakespeare's famous *The Tempest* (1610–1611)—Yancy lucidly compares Césaire's character Caliban to the sort of resistance the Black body maintains as it refuses to live by white ontological standards. He writes:

Césaire's Caliban has become cognizant of the source of his double consciousness; he is now able to nihilate the given of Prospero's world and to resist the existential phenomenological problem of corporeal malediction. At the level of the gaze, he challenges the relational asymmetry of which he has been a victim.

Prospero, you're a great magician:
. . . that you ended up imposing on me
an image of myself.[12]

Yancy draws our attention to at least two types of gazing here. One demonstrates an obvious lack of self-reflection on the part of whiteness: whiteness does not know what it is or what it does as it throws its gaze, as it gazes not to *see* but only to *look* and reinforce itself. In doing so, a second sense of self-reflection is created "as if by magic," in the form of an image of Caliban (Blackness) seeing himself through the eyes of Prospero (whiteness) and coming to hate that image. Whiteness is so infatuated with its own visuality—it sends a gaze but does not typically receive one back—that it has no self-reflective basis in reality. Thus, whiteness must construct a fictional world in order to justify its own being. This is its *modus operandi*, but also its curse, its malediction, and one that whites must come to *see through* as if whiteness were a ghost.

"The white gaze has fixed the Black body within its own procrustean frame of reference,"[13] Yancy writes. Whiteness frames Blackness and therefore *pictures* it without consent through a process of conformity to white visual standards. The notion of a picture is crucial here, as it is not the same thing as an image. Hans Belting suggests that "the body can function both as a medium for its own images and as a medium that carries a picture."[14] We might interpret this by considering whiteness to be a visual system that imagines (and therefore images) itself to be a self-coherent medium. Whiteness thinks it does not require input from outside. It is cold shut. The white body conceives of itself as an image that is stable, enduring, and consummate. Yet as an ego defense mechanism, whiteness renders Black and Brown bodies visible pictures as a way to hide its true self and to diminish bodies of color to the level of objects to be observed, described, catalogued (a picture is a *thing*). "Look! A Negro!" Fanon writes, recounting how a little white boy "sees" him. This is whiteness rendering Fanon's Black body a spectacle to be looked at, communicated to other whites, but not properly *seen*.

Even when whiteness mobilizes a modicum of self-awareness, it reverts to seeing white, reestablishing its own white perception and psychology. Carol Gurnat and Shawn Utsey outline five ego statuses that plague white people as they develop their own racial identities, all of which occur *in relation* to attitudes whites develop toward Black and Brown people:

In the Contact ego status, race and racism are denied and the individual is generally unaware of how he or she benefits from systemic racism. Disintegration is characterized by inner conflict and anxiety related to the awareness that Blacks are not treated the same as Whites. The Reintegration status occurs as the individual seeks to regain psychological equilibrium by affirming his or her sense of White racial superiority over Blacks. In Pseudo-Independence, the role that Whites have in perpetuating racism is acknowledged, and the individual seeks to alter his or her own racist attitudes or behavior. Finally, Autonomy is achieved when the individual recognizes his or her race as a valued part of his or her identity without a need to feel superior to other races.[15]

In this sense, whiteness is circular. It always ends up back where it started even if it denies its own racial superiority. The image of whiteness creates the picture of the Black body only in relation to its own agency (a word synonymous with medium) in an attempt to objectify it, or in Yancy's phrasing, to "ontologically truncate it."[16] This is one way in which whiteness relies parasitically (Yancy) on Blackness to constitute itself. In its violence and peremptoriness, whiteness refuses to accept Blackness as any kind of image—merely that it is a body that carries a picture devoid of imagination or substance. To white people, Black bodies have no spirit or *Geist*, Yancy writes in his *Black Bodies, White Gazes*.[17] The idea of spirit—indeed of proving that one exists—is tied up with the existence and meaning of pictures. When whiteness exclaims that Black bodies have no spirit, it simultaneously declares that they have no image because they are merely pictured (in other words, they are not tied to the white imaginary). In this way, whiteness does not recognize the Black body, unless it renders it somehow in its own image, unless it carries Blackness *as a picture*. Whiteness thinks itself primary, while Blackness is secondary. As Francis Bacon writes, "Pictures are but secondary objects."[18]

In her essay "Structures of Seeing," Elizabeth Davis writes that "thinking through the structures of sighted culture requires attending to the historicity of the senses, and to how the senses are implicated in power relations."[19] As I have suggested, whiteness is a regime of visibility (Seshadri-Crooks) and a sensory system that connects various images of itself to white imagination at large (I'll explore some of these ways of seeing whiteness in specific images shortly). Whiteness needs its own image to sustain its narcissistic gaze. Davis makes an important point about the difference between gazing and seeing, however. Drawing on Laura Mulvey's notion of the male gaze, Davis suggests that the gaze is the *structure* of seeing—that the gaze underpins seeing in some way. She then makes a most prescient point vis-à-vis Fanon about who does, and who does not, get to possess the gaze:

> One way of understanding why . . . racialized people cannot see properly is to suggest that they do not (or in certain instances cannot) possess the gaze. This logic of sensory dispossession, when one might look, but instead feels the eyes of others, or sees oneself outside of one's own body, might be understood as theft, or diagnosed as synaesthesia.[20]

So, the white gaze comes before the act of "white looking" and before the process of seeing in general. But does this not conflate the different processes of white looking and white seeing? Perhaps the white gaze only looks but does not see? In this way, we can theorize the white gaze as being stalled *between* the acts of white looking and white seeing. In this gap, with a sense of violent frustration, the white gaze projects the image of Blackness in the form of a picture—one that is dispossessed from Black bodies until, to return to Césaire's *A Tempest*, Caliban (Blackness) sees himself through the eyes of Prospero (whiteness) and realizes he has become, in Yancy's words, "cognizant of the source of his double consciousness."[21] Perhaps this stalling, this fissure in the beam of the white gaze is what creates the possibility for a "white pause"—one in which white people might begin to unsuture (Yancy) ourselves from whiteness? We white people might stop gazing and start seeing, for as Seshadri-Crooks notes (citing Herman Melville) those who gaze too much gaze themselves blind.[22] As whiteness looks but does not see it is ontologically blind, much like a ghost that walks the Earth but does not realize that it is no longer a corporeal being. This is not of course to say that whiteness does not have material effects or that whiteness does not possess a body capable of the most extreme forms of racist violence (after all, ghosts can move objects, bodies, and have material effects that take place in the world).

In *Ghost Dance*, a film made by Ken McMullen in 1983, Jacques Derrida serendipitously describes the way in which whiteness speaks through white bodies. He is asked whether he believes in ghosts. He responds: "Firstly, you're asking a ghost whether he believes in ghosts. . . . I feel as if I'm letting a ghost speak for me. . . . I let a ghost ventriloquize my words."[23] Is this not the predicament all white people might find ourselves in if we attempted to see whiteness? We whites cannot shirk responsibility on this measure or conclude that we are simply possessed by a whiteness out of our control, yet it speaks to the notion that the white unconscious is spectral, difficult to grasp. In this sense, whiteness might be exorcised. White people might rid ourselves of our whiteness through a willingness to dwell (Yancy) with our white ghosts. White spectrality is also white reason. Derrida writes: "What is metaphysics? A white mythology which assembles and reflects Western culture: the white man takes his own mythology (that is, Indo-European mythology) his *logos*—that is, the mythos of his idiom, for the universal form of that which it is still his inescapable desire to call Reason."[24]

Wittgenstein writes that "a picture represents its subject from a position outside it."[25] Through a process of separation and ignorance, whiteness attempts to picture, which is to say it *represents* Blackness from the outside. The spectral image of whiteness is a fictional world built apart from reality yet forced upon it. However, what if the process of picturing Blackness through the white gaze can be turned against itself by the production of subversive images of whiteness? Images that work against the status quo of whiteness in order to reverse the reason or vision of whiteness, to look back upon it critically. John Berger, in *Ways of Seeing*, notes that vision is reciprocal; it can be returned and inverted as it is fundamentally circular. Vision is "continually holding things in a circle around itself,"[26] he writes.

WHITENESS AND DIVINE LIGHT

Sophie Gabrielle's untitled photograph (figure 6.1) from the series BL_NK SP_CE—in which we can see the light of whiteness, consumptive and alluring—highlights two versions of a white female figure: white and human. This image is a question for white consciousness: which figure will be accepted, and which rejected? The image is a metaphor for the choice white people must make to cleave ourselves from whiteness in order to become human again. Do we want to be white or human? We cannot be both. One "self" in the image appears incorporeal, spectral, and a second self is corporeal, bodily. The vision of this ghostly body is shared, reciprocated between two selves and offers white people an important opportunity to see for the first time. Perhaps it is an extension of Yancy's gift, but how should white people interpret it?

> The gift is not all about *you*. As white, you are used to things always being about *you*.[27]

I had never before had the opportunity to see myself, or indeed any person of color, until encountering Yancy's writing. I mean to say "see" in the sense that I had spent the first thirty-two years of my life blind to the reality of white racial power. (I am a person who is supposed to be intellectually dedicated to the nuanced differences between looking and seeing in photography, so the irony of my blindness does not escape me.) I was colorblind. I did not see race, but it saw me. This is not a trivial realization—I don't wish to offer it up as a bullshit white epiphany—it is rather a necessary shift in my own consciousness and in turn my previously taken-for-granted white comfort. My *coming to see* through Yancy's writing is nothing less than the first religious experience of my atheist life. I do not "affirm the existence of the [Christian] divine"[28] as Yancy does, because I was raised atheist, but instead I affirm the existence of whiteness falsely posing as the altarpiece (and therefore the image) of divinity.

> It is not by accident that when I was a small boy I imagined God as an old white man with a long white beard.[29]

The image of whiteness has at its core a type of false faith, or in Yancy's phrasing, bad faith. To believe you are white requires an often-unconscious belief in whiteness as a form of divine light. God and Jesus are both imagined

Figure 6.1. **"Untitled 1" from the series Bl_NK SP_CE, 2015.** *Source*: Sophie Gabrielle.

to be white to bolster the historical importance of whiteness and root it to the idea of "European civilization" (Martin Bernal reminds us that this "classical civilization" in fact has its roots in Afroasiatic cultures[30]). This "white light"—let's call it that—has no source when you trace the origins of its beam. Yancy writes that "the white gaze is like a beam of light that moves across or through a *whitely saturated* space."[31]

Whiteness transmits a certain emptiness. Yet the white gaze produces its own fictional image of a world saturated with whiteness. It is self-constituting, self-producing, self-aggrandizing. This is a "process of white fictional world-making," Yancy continues. When we white people look, we do not see reality as it is, but rather a fictional world filtered, percolated, cataracted by whiteness. A second photograph by Sophie Gabrielle (figure 6.2) visually metaphorizes that idea of a white cataract. This form of blindness is a type of white prohibition; one in which white people are socialized precisely not to see the world *as it is*, because if seen to its fullest extent it would be revealed as a white lie. To candidly *see* is for us white people to be willing to dwell without a veil of white ignorance cataracting our eyes.

Whites should affirm a "Christian anthropology that militates against whiteness as the implied quintessential feature of the *Imago Dei*," Yancy writes.[32]

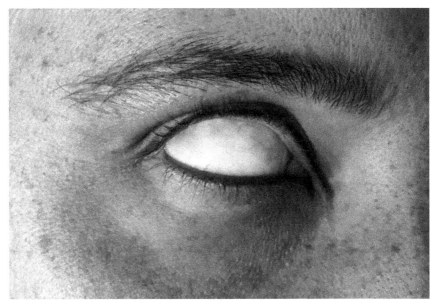

Figure 6.2.   "Untitled 2" from the series Bl_NK SP_CE, 2015. *Source*: Sophie Gabrielle.

So it is the task of whites to hinder whiteness as it attempts to co-opt the image of God (and indeed Jesus). Etymologically *optaire*, from Latin, is to "choose." Whiteness chooses the *Imago Dei* as its visual—symbolic foundation (there is clearly no epidermal connection between God, Jesus, and whiteness). This structure of "seeing white" in Christianity finds one root in what Nell Irvin Painter calls an "obscure but persistent current in English and American religion, Anglo-Israeltism."[33] According to this Christian community, of which the bigoted industrialist Henry Ford was a notable member, Anglo-Saxons were the actual descendants of the Ten Lost Tribes of Israel, which makes Jesus Nordic (white) and England and the United States the "real" Holy Land. This image of Jesus as white (and therefore God is his white father) has had a decisive impact on the popular consensus that Jesus should be depicted as a white man. As Yancy continues in his introduction to *Christology and Whiteness*, "Whiteness is not some extraneous and vague problem that exists outside the domain of *ecclesia*, but something rooted right there and all too often invisible."[34]

In his introduction to *Christology and Whiteness*, Yancy cites the British scholar Richard Dyer, who writes that "the role of the Crusades in racializing the idea of Christendom (making national/geographic others into enemies of Christ); the gentilizing and whitening of the image of Christ and the Virgin in painting" is central to the link between whiteness and Christian divinity. Furthermore, this connection is summarized by an all-pervasive image of Jesus and God, both appearing as white. Dyer is one of the few white scholars to take seriously the idea of whiteness as both a visual and bodily phenomenon tied to Christianity. In *White*, Dyer considers how Christ gives his body in various ways—as food, as a laborer (carpenter) and as a form of corporeal nourishment. This reveals white Christianity to be a narcissistic pursuit in which the white body sees itself as a bearer of gifts offered to "lesser" mortals. Dyer concludes: "Thus it is that the paradoxes and instabilities of whiteness also constitute its flexibility and productivity, in short, its representational power."[35] What happens when and if whiteness does see itself, bearing witness to its own representational power? Might it break down, fall apart?

A Disagreeable Mirror

> The white gaze, as a social and habitual practice . . . is a process where white seeing is actually a site of white unseeing.[36]

Of the artist Hank Willis Thomas's image *Wipe Away the Years*, Yancy writes: "It is as if the white woman really sees herself differently for the first time, sees what she was never meant to see as strange, but as normative." This is a visual metaphor for the "white pause"—a moment in the juncture of white temporality in which a white person comes to see for the first time. Whiteness—previously blind to the invisible spectrality of its own white body—witnesses itself come into view in a mirror. This would come as a shock to white eyes, having never before seen white skin as anything other than "normal" and therefore invisible, without the weight of meaning. The white woman pictured in this artwork, which is appropriated by the artist in the present day from a 1932 advertisement, comes to see herself strangely.

As normative sensory subjects in our own eyes, we white people are in awe of our image, but this has hitherto required nothing more than the physiological–optical phenomenon of looking without seeing. Restoring vision to white eyes is not a simple ophthalmology of the white gaze, but additionally a conscious and self-reflective process in which we white people begin to see and feel the visual and sensory weight of our own whiteness. This process necessitates white tears, white crying, and white weeping as we realize where

Figure 6.3. *"Wipe Away the Years*, 1932/2015," from the series "Unbranded: A Century of White Women, 1915–2015." *Source*: Hank Willis Thomas. Courtesy of the artist and Jack Shainman Gallery, New York.

whiteness comes from and that it has no cause to exist. Whiteness is vain, inclement, nugatory, and without justification.

This is partly why whiteness obfuscates its origins. Part of its ideological pretensions is that it is ahistorical, decontextual, *causa sui*, as it were. Part of challenging the "de-contextual" and "self-constituting" fictive assumptions of whiteness is to get white people to see themselves through what Baldwin sees as a disagreeable mirror. What we need are mirrors that function as sites of truth-telling. Within the context of whiteness, as the transcendental norm, mirrors can only lie as they reflect back to white people what white people control within the space of what is returned.[37]

Hank Willis Thomas's visual practice is full of various deliberate types of self-reflection and decontextualization—of images, of his own Blackness in America, and in the case of the body of work that this image (figure 6.3) derives from, a particular history of white women. The series, titled "Unbranded: A Century of White Women, 1915–2015," comprises 100 individual images that trace the sexist and corporate representation of white women in the context of visual advertising. As the author–curators of Thomas's monograph *All Things Being Equal* note, "Thomas removes the ads' original text to focus attention on the media's drive to use gender- and skin-color-based stereotypes to sell products."[38] In a second response to the photograph, Yancy writes:

> During public lectures about whiteness, I have often asked white people to return to their homes, apartments, or dorms and take a long look in the mirror and pose this question: what in the hell makes whiteness, *my whiteness*, so special? By posing the question, and perhaps after tarrying with my talk, they will begin to glimpse the insidious norm that is operating, perhaps they will see the lie that has functioned as the "truth" for so long, the lie that returns them to themselves as "innocent" and as disconnected from white supremacy.[39]

The white female protagonist in the picture glimpses her whiteness as an insidious norm. Yancy then states that in this way

> one gets to see one's white self as naked, uncovered. That, it seems to me, is terrifying. Yet, it is a necessary terror, an essential moment of being distraught, overcome, beside oneself. One's visual orientation to one's face and body would not remain the same. The weight of seeing differently would disorient; a breakdown would occur. Perhaps there would be a glimpse of a species of a certain kind of death, a death to the illusions of whiteness.[40]

So, it becomes necessary for a certain symbolic white death to occur. One which begins with white people seeing ourselves literally and ontologically naked in new ways. This process must reveal a form of white being that is foundational to whiteness, as the symbolic death of a single white

person—say, the woman in the picture, or me, the author of this chapter—
would not result in the death of whiteness *per se*.

It might then be necessary for whites to imagine an originary figure and
image of whiteness, not in the sense that we might claim or police a positive white origin story but so that we can locate the birth of whiteness as
instigating two forms of mass human death: with one hand, the bringing of
literal death for people of color, and on the other the awarding of undead
life to a type of dispassionate white being, one which carries a fundamental
coldness in the way it looks, and fails, to see. We might call this being the
first white autochthon. Perhaps this is what reduces the white protagonist to
tears in *Wipe Away the Years*. Might it be that the "content" of white tears
is narcissistically tied to the history of whiteness, to this first white being?
Yancy writes of the image: "If only for that moment, the mirror would crack.
I say for only that moment, because whiteness is resilient, able to repair
itself. The aim of looking in the mirror, though, is to tarry with the crack, the
discomfort, the terror, to feel the atrophy of something that was taken to be
invulnerable."[41]

To atrophy is to weaken, to emaciate, to shrivel, and to move toward
death. What if the reason that whiteness is able to reconstitute itself is
because it precisely *is* death? So then to tarry with whiteness as it cracks
would be to confront whiteness as a form of death. An autochthon is a
being that is said to spring from the ground, which speaks to the existence
of a kind of white underworld. Autochthons are also "native" beings, not
in the sense that we have a natural right to land but that we are given rule
over land and people, as is the case with the character Autochthon and
his brother Mneseus in Plato's *Timaeus-Critias* (360 BC).[42] In his essay,
"Autochthony in Plato's Menexenus," Nickolas Pappas notes that the character Autochthon and the state of autochthony are differentiated, the latter
being the state of something "originary" or "natural" to Earth, irrespective
of its precise location.[43] Does whiteness not also claim to be "natural," the
medial state of what it is to be human, irrespective of its location? The
white autochthon does not need a location to claim the given right to rule
land and people. It has the right, in its own twisted logic, to do it simply
because it is white.

Whites "have a special relation with death, to yearn for it but also to bring
it to others," writes Richard Dyer.[44] The transcendental norm that whiteness
demands, one which places all "nonwhite" human life into a subordinate
relation to white subjectivity, might be pinned to this originary figure—a
deathly, false autochthon—which in turn promotes a particular, reified image
of whiteness as given, ubiquitous, everywhere. Whiteness is the creation of
a mythological figure (Autochthon) that has a "natural" right to Earth, the
invention of a violent social principle (autochthony) and the *iteration* of

an image that moves through time, colonizing everything, irrespective of location.

> It is an emotionally charged image, one of pain and hurt. Something has taken place where the normative structure of whiteness has failed, where the mirror image reflects a powerful interrogative: what is this that I see? How could this be true? Oh, no! How could I have missed this? The hand gesture, where the white woman's hand is placed on her face could function as part of the suddenness of the crisis.[45]

Wipe Away the Years is an image of crisis and of trauma, but it nonetheless requires us to be wary as we are, after all, considering *white* crisis and *white* trauma. Yancy continues:

> Within this interpretive context that I'm suggesting, that her hand touches her face might function as an indicator of disbelief, of holding what now appears as strange, as toxic. Then again, what if the hand and the look is actually a form of self-pity? What if after seeing herself in ways that indicate a de-masking, she feels sorry for herself? That, on my interpretation, would continue to function as a site of whiteness.[46]

The image of whiteness, when faced with itself in a state of pain, activates a defense mechanism in the form of white narcissism. Here, white people might be tempted to empathize with our own whiteness to the extent that we consider keeping it, which would amount to the comfortable extension of white temporality. While gazing in the mirror, we whites might pose ourselves the question: "What if I can become a good white?" As Barbara Applebaum[47] has noted, whites who undertake this form of self-reflection risk the "dangers of good intentions" in the form of "rhetorical moves" which attempt to feign white innocence. There can be no "good" white person, because whiteness is oppression, subjugation, control.

> So, her sadness becomes part of the structure of white comfort, her hand then becomes a gesture of loving support, which is not what she needs. Rather, she needs to tarry with the affect that accompanies her realization of white complicity. If she is feeling self-pity, then Black pain and suffering that are linked to her whiteness can be easily forgotten, placed under erasure. Seeing herself in the mirror now functions as a form of "loving forgiveness."[48]

AFTER WHITE EYES?

For me to be white is to have existed as a specter from birth; I imagine myself alive, yet it is clear I am primigenially dead, grounded in cold earth. My white life, and my white eye, is a colonial leech that feeds off bodies of color in order to survive its own blindness, its own ocular ignorance. Yancy's gift—which he offers with immense generosity—is my opportunity to see whiteness precolonially *then*, albeit briefly in the form of a momentary glance, before my whiteness *now* returns me to the violence of the present.

Through this opportunity to *look anew* I am credited not with a sudden and remarkable ability to see myself as I am and thus become some delusional post-race being, but rather I become one who is willing to dwell in a space of blindness or half-site. I will always be white—I am interpellated thus—and so I will always be ontologically blind. I carry the weight of white racist training in my body, and this weight is a kind of ocular hypertension or intraocular pressure which weakens my vision. My white eye filters the entirety of my experience of the world. Of white seeing, Yancy concludes:

> To see themselves with a constant vigilance, a painful vigilance, white people at least begin to understand the complex insidious ways in which they can be ambushed by whiteness, deceived by "white good intentions," "white confession," "white allyship," "white goodness," "white solidarity." White people are in need of radically new ways of re-seeing themselves, and of undoing a white social ontology that is constantly providing them with the ground upon which they live and have their being.[49]

We white people must learn to see ourselves wraithlike, incorporeal, in order to momentarily disconnect from whiteness and produce a form of thinking that replaces the comfort of existing in a white body with a kind of spectral humility. White eyes are underpinned by a system of ocular oppression that gives existential authority to white visuality. Falsely, our white eyes declare themselves normatively human eyes. Yancy's gift to philosophy is also a gift to white self-perception at large. It creates an opportunity to imagine new ways of seeing whiteness to its end. "The death of whiteness will mean more abundant life not only for Black people, but for white people as well,"[50] he writes.

Chapter 7

A Phenomenology of Invisibility

On the Absence of Yellow Bodies[1]

Boram Jeong

In his reading of Ralph Ellison's *Invisible Man*, George Yancy argues that "felt invisibility" is a form of ontological and epistemological violence that points to the sedimented habits and general normative constructs of white perception. Yancy's phenomenological account of the "unseen" Black body problematizes the condition of emergence of racialized bodies in the perceptual field under the white gaze. This chapter aims to elaborate further on the racialization of the visual field by expanding Yancy's claims on invisibility beyond black bodies, to consider specifically the invisibility of Asian and Asian American "yellow" bodies. The first section focuses on Yancy's notion of "seen absence" to demonstrate how white perception marks the Black body as hypervisible, while rendering it invisible at the same time. The second section expands on Yancy's notion to examine how "yellow" bodies, despite their hypervisibility, are quickly dismissed or recede into the periphery in the white logic of perception. The perceptual neglect for yellow bodies is, I argue, a manifestation of the white perceptual logic, which situates racialized bodies temporally in a time other than the "now," and spatially in a place other than "here." In the last section, I suggest that whiteness be understood as *perceptual dysfunction* that delimits one's own cognitive possibilities and ways to engage with the world, rendering certain bodies invisible.

YANCY'S NOTION OF "SEEN ABSENCE": THE LOGIC OF WHITE PERCEPTION

In the description of what he refers to as the "elevator effect," Yancy says that to a white woman in the elevator, his black body is immediately seen as a threat, from which her body and her belongings must be protected. He need not *do* anything but to be black, to be a threat. If not Yancy's deeds, what exactly is the perceptual object that causes her urgent bodily reaction? Where is this alleged threat located between her eyes and his body? Yancy carries no threat in his body, his intent, or his action, but the white woman *sees* it in the presence of his body. Then what is the condition of this particular "seeing" that goes beyond a mere perception? How does this perceptual practice affect those who inhabit the bodies like his?

Yancy describes how this experience of being repeatedly seen in a certain way makes him (feel) absent. He writes, under the white gaze "who I am has already been determined. I am the Black who is present in his absence, whose genuine intentions arrive too late. I am a 'seen absence.' I am visible in my invisibility."[2] Note how visibility and invisibility in the perceptual field translate here as a sense of presence and absence. His body in its corporeality still takes up space, so he surely does not mean that it is physically absent. However, neither his way of seeing his own body nor his intention is communicated; the body that he sees is invisible and nonexistent to her. She sees some aura of threat before anything, and blinded by the urge to react, fails to see his body, the actual object of perception. Yancy writes: "Phenomenologically, she [the woman in the elevator] might be said to 'see' a Black, fleeting expanse, a peripherally glimpsed vague presence of something dark, forbidden, and dreadful. She does not see a dynamic subjectivity, but a sort, something eviscerated of individuality, flattened, and rendered vacuous of genuine human feelings."[3]

Without actually being seen, his body sticks out as a "trigger" in the otherwise smooth perceptual field. In this "overpresence," his personhood and subjectivity are hollowed out. He is absent in the sense that his way of presence does not have any weight in his encounter with the white woman. Yancy calls this curious appearance of the black body under the white gaze, a "seen absence."

The "seen absence" of the Black body is described as a paradoxical site, where it is made hypervisible yet locked in invisibility. According to Yancy, "In the case of hypervisibility, the Black body becomes excessive. Within this racially saturated field of hypervisibility, the Black body still functions as the unseen as it does in the case of its invisibility."[4] The hypervisibility of the Black body, in fact, only confirms its inescapable invisibility; it is unseen precisely because of the way it is seen. The white gaze, through its dual function of hypervisibility and invisibility, not only projects racialized meanings onto bodies of color but also conceals what is present in the perceptual field. It overwrites what can actually be seen as well as what could virtually be seen. The stubborn practice of the white gaze annihilates other ways of seeing, incapacitating any potentially meaningful visible signs like his well-clothedness (suit and tie) or his university hat. There is little that Yancy could do to make himself visible.

The paradox of hypervisibility and invisibility suggested by Yancy's "seen absence" reveals, what could be termed, a general "logic of white perception." By white perception, I mean the perceptual practices that center white bodies, regardless of one's intent. I call it a logic, meaning a set of principles underlying the arrangement of perceptual elements. The change of focus here from the first person account of being made hyper/in/visible to the general logic that governs the perceptual field is intentional; it is to take seriously the transition from invisibility to absence, implied in the "seen absence." The logic points us beyond the epistemic tension to the ontological denial of the Black body, emphasizing that the issue is not simply competing knowledge claims about the alleged threat, but the condition of being that erases the Black body in the *here and now*. I'm interested in the process in which this particular perceptual logic is normalized by determining the field of vision via "hyper/in/visibility." I analyze the process as the following: (1) a fabrication of the (racially saturated) field of the visible; (2) a reduction of bodies of color to "the hyper/in/visible"; and (3) the naturalization of white perception and its epistemic and ontological violence.

First, one of the most powerful functions of white perception is fabricating the field of the visible. When the white woman in the elevator "sees" a threat in the appearance of Yancy's body, the threat doesn't reside in his body but in blackness in the white imaginary. As Judith Butler writes in her essay on Rodney King, the white gaze "is not a simple seeing, an act of direct perception, but the racial production of the visible, the workings of racial constraints on what it means to 'see.'"[5] She maintains that an act of seeing imbued with racist episteme is no longer a seeing, but a particular *reading* or a construal. White perception makes its conceptual construct of the body hypervisible, while rendering invisible all other qualities of the body actually given in the perceptual field. As Ralph Ellison's hero in *Invisible Man* acutely observes, "When they [whites] approach me, they see only my surroundings, themselves, or figments of their imagination—indeed, everything and anything except me."[6] When the white perceptual logic determines what could appear in the visual field by *fabrication*, the category of "the visible" itself needs to be reconceptualized in political terms.

Second, the white perceptual logic results in a reductive understanding of bodily possibilities. While depriving bodies of color of the possibility to be seen otherwise, it determines their condition of emergence in the perceptual field itself. As Yancy states in his comments on the killing of Trayvon Martin, "Black emergence outside of whiteness's *scopic* power is foreclosed."[7] Any future possibilities promised by seventeen-year-old Martin's body had to be rejected to maintain the normative constructs of white perception embodied by George Zimmerman. The totalizing power of white perception exerts "a form of ontological and epistemological violence"[8] in extinguishing bodily possibilities as well as lives embodied. It is ontological because when the violence against the Black body is legitimated on the basis of the fabricated notion of danger, it is no longer simply an epistemological failure of recognition but a degradation of being itself that has been made contingent. Under the logic of white perception, the Black body becomes a source of impossibility and is ultimately reduced to absence: It is "a form of white solipsism whereby the nonwhite is erased and devalued, reduced to a form of nonbeing."[9]

Lastly, it is through the workings of hyper/in/visibility that the normative constructs of white perception are naturalized. In its perceptual operation, the white logic loses its particularity and becomes normalized. The whiteness of an observer is, in Crispin Sartwell's terms, a form of authority to see supposedly from nowhere, for everyone.[10] As white perception passes itself off as a neutral act of "seeing," its epistemic and ontological violence is obscured. Also, as Al-Saji points out, racializing vision marks bodies of color by enabling only one way of seeing the body while disabling all others, and yet the one who sees considers their act of seeing as *passive* and *receptive*.[11] Therefore, one comes to believe that what they have projected onto the body (threat or danger, in the case of the "elevator effect") is a quality inherent to the body (*Yancy's* dangerous body). In attributing its imagined qualities to the bodies of color, white perception makes its own function invisible. In this sense, the hyper/in/visibility of racialized bodies is nothing but a sign of whiteness in a silent operation.

With the notion of "seen absence," Yancy provides a phenomenological account of having one's body unseen. Identifying the white perceptual logic shifts focus to the systematic process in which the Black body is replaced with blackness in the white imagination. Further, it reframes the problem of the hyper/in/visibility of bodies of color in terms of white domination of the perceptual field, rather than a matter of resituating bodies of color to make them visible. In the following, we will examine how the white perceptual logic renders bodies of color absent through the normative configurations of spatiotemporality.

THE "SEEN ABSENCE" OF YELLOW BODIES: THE SPATIOTEMPORALITY OF WHITE PERCEPTION

In the first section, we have established that hyper/in/visibility is a key function of the white perceptual logic and its normalization. The second section expands on Yancy's notion of "seen absence" to consider varying forms of racialization, especially the hyper/in/visibility of Asian and Asian American bodies in white perception. In the "seen absence" of the "Yellow" body,[12] an emphasis is placed on *absence* because, unlike the black body that becomes "excessive," the Yellow body under the white gaze turns "negligible." Thus, this section presents an analysis of the spatiotemporality of white perception to account for its perceptual neglect for yellow bodies. In doing so, I show how the white perceptual logic, in its normative function, serves as the measure not only for the visibility but also the presence of racialized bodies.

Obviously, the "seen absence" of the Yellow body cannot be equated with that of the Black body. As a way to understand the difference between the hyper/in/visibility of the Black and the Yellow bodies, I suggest the opposition between the exaggeration (maximization) versus belittlement (minimization) of corporeality. If black bodies have historically been viewed as an object of fear, threat, or danger, yellow bodies in the white perception have receded to the periphery or the background. If black bodies have been falsely depicted as "uncontrollable" and "excessive" as Yancy put it,[13] yellow bodies have been neglected as "passive," or "docile," if not "inanimate." Accordingly, the epistemic and ontological violence of the white perception takes the form of the obsession with physical control over black bodies, and of perceptual negligence and belittlement of yellow bodies. The white perceptual logic is complex and adaptable, for it draws on different histories of racism.

Similar to hypervisibility and invisibility, the maximization and minimization of corporeality, as negative expressions of whiteness, are not contradictory but mutually constitutive of white perceptual logic. They are both modes of what Aimé Césaire calls "thingification."[14] Through the maximization of corporeality one reads into black bodies "bestial" desire to be tamed and conquered. By minimization, one sees in yellow bodies little vitality, an object without affectivity or active will to be pushed around. In short, thinghood translates as *excessive*, overpresence for black bodies, and as *negligible*, "underpresence" for yellow bodies. This distinction, however crude, is useful to reveal a particular use of white perceptual logic for yellow bodies. In addition to the hyper/in/visibility that defines the white perception in general, yellow bodies as "negligible presence" are racialized particularly through invisibility. That is, yellow bodies are rendered invisible not only because they are reduced to their race but also because "Asianness" itself has been defined in the white imagination by stereotypical qualities that serve to justify the invisibility, such as being compliant, nonconfrontational and self-effacing. This makes the yellow presence doubly invisible.

The invisibility of Asian Americans has often been discussed in terms of representation (social, cultural, or political). My analysis here focuses specifically on the invisibility of yellow bodies in the perceptual field, in order to further articulate the logic of white perception and its various manifestations. What Yancy's notion of "seen absence" can offer in this regard is the way absence is understood—absence not due to a lack but to an active erasure performed by whiteness in operation. Thus, in what follows, I examine how the white perceptual logic produces absence by looking particularly at its spatiotemporal structure that conditions the invisibility of yellow bodies. I shall further complicate the opposition between presence and absence and the idea of temporal and spatial occupancy by demonstrating how the presence of certain bodies comes to bear less weight than others.

The Spatiality of Yellow Absence

Yellow bodies occupy a place of the "inescapably foreign" in the space shaped by the white perceptual logic. They are rendered absent for they are viewed as belonging to a place other than "here." Therefore, the presence of yellow bodies in the white space is considered disruptive and temporary; it is contingent upon white permission. Their presence can be "permitted" as long as it is not intrusive of white bodies, that is, if it remains in the periphery. The yellow presence is "tolerated" when serving white bodies at nail salons, massage shops, dry cleaners, or cheap take-out restaurants, while remaining in the background, or better, invisible. However, their presence in invisibility hardly guarantees a place in the world because it can turn into hypervisibility whenever "white tolerance" runs out, as in moments of crisis in economy or in public health. It is supposed that the space occupied by yellow bodies can be reclaimed at any moment, for according to the white perceptual logic yellow bodies have never belonged "here."

The COVID-19 pandemic—still unfolding at the time of this writing—shows how quickly invisible yellow bodies become hypervisible, and thus disruptive. The white logic perceives the disease as a racialized threat, which leads to a violent assertion of white dominance; a single fact that the virus originated in China was enough to instigate hate crimes against all bodies potentially associated with the entire continent of Asia. Yellow bodies, regardless of nationality or immigration status, have been made to be seen as carriers of the virus. They have been harassed and assaulted around the world in the most ordinary places like gyms, public transport, and streets, minding their own business. In an interview with the *New York Times*, Chil Kong, a Korean American theater director, describes the felt hostility: "It's a look of disdain. . . . It's just: 'How dare you exist in my world? You are a reminder of this disease, and you don't belong in my world.' . . . It's especially hard when you grow up here and expect this world to be yours equally. But we do not live in that world anymore. That world does not exist."[15]

How readily yellow bodies can be expelled from the world organized around whiteness shows that their presence in it has always been contingent upon their invisibility, the supposed absence. The presence of yellow bodies can always be questioned or revoked when they are suddenly made hypervisible as "intruders." The question, "How dare you exist in *my* world?" is unanswerable. Since the constitution of white space is predicated upon their absence, the hypervisible yellow bodies are confronted with the impossible task of justifying their existence in it.

Efforts have been made to respond to the accusation of yellow bodies as carriers of the virus. After a regional French newspaper *Le Courrier Picard* called the outbreak "*Alerte jaune* (Yellow alert)," the #JeNeSuisPasUnVirus (I Am Not a Virus) movement began on social media.[16] Phrases like "Not all Asians are Chinese, not all Chinese are infected" were circulated, arguing that there are yellow bodies that are not dangerous or infectious, and therefore, deserve to *be*. It may be meaningful as a direct response to anti-Asian violence; however, it remains reactionary in my view. Distinguishing non-Chinese Asians from Chinese, while potentially important as a critique of the homogenization of all yellow bodies (a common form of Asian racialization), is not only beside the point but also can potentially exacerbate anti-Chinese sentiment. Is it justifiable to reaffirm the association between the disease and the Chinese in order to exonerate other Asians? In the same way, emphasizing that not all Chinese are infectious misses the point, since the true motive behind the violence against Asians is racism, not infection. The real question is how certain danger is racialized, and thus the people racialized as such are equated with danger—the automatic linkage between the disease and yellow bodies. We will return to this issue shortly.

Any claims of belonging would be limited if they do not tackle the underlying assumptions behind the resurfacing of anti-Asian sentiment, one of which is the white perceptual logic that determines the condition of the emergence of the Yellow body in space. The assumption is that this is and has always been the world that belongs exclusively to white bodies, where the existence of yellow bodies must always remain conditional. What is being questioned here is not simply how yellow bodies are positioned in this world, but the legitimacy of their being in the space itself. Discourse around the alleged threat of yellow bodies as carriers of the virus should be seen as one of the many manifestations of the white perceptual logic, which turns Asians and Asian Americans into foreign, readily displaceable bodies on demand. Whether yellow bodies pose an actual threat or not is not the true point of contention. As we have seen in the "elevator effect," threat is not located in the intent or action of bodies of color but in the white imaginary.

The white logic is flexible enough to extend beyond contradictions; yellow bodies have been portrayed as equally threatening for becoming too white ("honorary whites"), and for being too foreign (disloyal and unassimilable); there is no right distance they can keep from whiteness. Same goes for visibility. Since the logic operates through the paradox of hyper/in/visibility, yellow bodies have no choice but to be placed either in the zone of invisibility or that of hypervisibility. There is no proper positioning for making themselves visible in the white space. During the pandemic, yellow bodies have been suddenly made hypervisible, although they have done nothing to change their place in the world. It is the same yellow body that used to be praised as a well-assimilated "model minority" (invisible) that is now seen as a threat to public health (hypervisible). In the space shaped by the white logic, the visibility of all bodies of color is necessarily a hypervisibility because they are out of place: the bodies that do not belong "here." Hypervisibility makes the once familiar space suddenly hostile. It is a form of spatial alienation, where, in Yancy's terms, one experiences the "here" as the "there"; although in everyday life he lives his body from an existential *here*, under the white gaze "I am reduced to a point that is viewed. My *here* is experienced as a *there*."[17]

The Temporality of Yellow Absence

Temporally speaking, yellow bodies are seen as belonging to a time other than the present. The presumed "foreignness" and "exoticness" of the Yellow body in the white perception sends it back to its "origin," not only distant in space but also in time. The foreignness implies two ways of temporal distancing: denial of contemporaneity ("backwardness") and continuity (contingency). Denial of contemporaneity is founded upon Western modernity's exclusive claims to rationality that characterize other forms of life as outdated. The general tendency to situate otherness in a time other than the present that Johannes Fabian refers to as a "denial of coevalness," is very much prevalent in the temporality of white perception.[18] A crystallization of this belief is the ideology of Yellow Peril, which views the rising influence of East Asians as an alleged threat to predominantly white Western civilization. In the United States, the growing number of immigrants from Asia in the late nineteenth century was perceived as a mortal danger to white racial purity by a diseased, promiscuous, Godless, immoral people—the baseness of Asians can "contaminate" and "corrupt" the body and the soul of civilized white immigrants. They were not considered contemporaries, but a people of the past, barbaric and outdated.

In addition, yellow bodies are denied historical continuity as immigrants or refugees in the United States, locked in a narrative constructed by the white imagination. Asian Americans continue to be seen as closer to their ancestral origins than to their homeland, unlike white immigrants who have been integrated and are no longer associated with their European countries of origin. Yellow bodies remain alien, whose present is ceaselessly interpellated back to the past, prior to their (their ancestors') arrival, however many decades ago. The temporal alienation of Asian Americans is a denial of not only their place in American history but also their being in the "now." That is why the persistent query, "Where are you *really* from?" is a mundane but lethal form of epistemic violence to Asian Americans; it is an exclusivist claim to the "now" that makes the presence of yellow bodies incidental and temporary. This is how the "eternally foreign" yellow bodies are rendered temporally absent.

To return to the COVID-19 example, "temporal distancing" is what implicitly shapes the discourse around the racialization of the disease. Chinese people have historically been racialized as unhygienic and diseased. In the late 1800s, in order to intervene in the influx of Chinese workers to the United States, the fear of contagion was systemically induced by media, leading to the 1882 Chinese Exclusion Act, which was the first legislation in the country to exclude a particular racial or national group. Horace Greeley, a *New York Tribune* editor, wrote in 1854, "The Chinese are uncivilized, unclean, and filthy beyond all conception without any of the higher domestic or social relations; lustful and sensual in their dispositions; every female is a prostitute of the basest order."[19] The idea of uncivilized, unhygienic, disease-ridden Chinese has persistently been reappearing as a technique of temporal distancing in various forms: the Chinese lead toy recalls; MSG and the Chinese restaurant syndrome; and the "Kung Flu."

Yellow bodies, whose national origins are often indiscernible to white vision, and thus commonly designated as "the Chinese," are always already associated with disease. Therefore, COVID-19 was racially coded as the "Chinese virus" almost immediately after the outbreak and has remained that way since. Even when the epicenter of the pandemic switched from China to Italy and then to the United States, or when most cases in New York were found to have originated in Europe, no Euro-Americans were targeted or considered to be a public health threat. Being a public threat means a threat to white America. Identifying a group of people as a threat is comforting only when they are already alien and expellable. Only the temporally distanced, foreign, and outdated can be *sent back* to where they belong. The "now" is white.

The spatiotemporality of white perception underlying the "seen absence" of yellow bodies elaborated so far can be summarized as a denial of shared time and space. At best, they are peripheral/invisible beings, carrying less weight and significance in the here and now. As Cathy Park Hong puts it, "Asians lack presence. Asians take up apologetic space. We don't even have enough presence to be considered real minorities. We're not racial enough to be token."[20] Their presence is contingent upon "white permission," the terms of which remain obscure in ordinary times. Their presence is often neglected in the form of a forgotten order at a restaurant, lack of greeting or attention at a store, or being mistaken as some other Asian at a professional conference. The conditional existence of bodies of color becomes clear when the unspoken terms are violated. They are and have always been on *borrowed time and space.*

If the aforementioned exaggeration of corporeality leads to the white obsession to take control of black bodies, what the minimization ultimately aims to accomplish is *erasure*. It is no accident that when yellow bodies become visible in public discourse, it is through their overrated ability to *assimilate*. The promise of recognition through assimilation only exacerbates the yellow absence and invisibility, as it is a permission of their presence in white space on the condition of erasure.

UNDERSTANDING WHITENESS AS A PERCEPTUAL DYSFUNCTION

We have seen earlier how whiteness operates perceptually as a denial of shared time and space, rendering bodies of color invisible and absent. In this last section, I suggest that we understand the epistemic and ontological violence of white perception as a form of *perceptual dysfunction*—a systematic inability to engage with the world outside of the perceptual scheme constructed around whiteness. This formulation aims specifically to highlight the harms and damages that racializing perception does to the whites themselves, by calling attention to its structural failure.

In the aforementioned essay on Rodney King, Butler states that the racial schematization of the visible field is a "crisis in the certainty of what is visible, one that is produced through the saturation and schematization of that field with the inverted projections of white paranoia."[21] Note that she speaks of the racializing gaze as a crisis in the white vision. Hyper/in/visibility as a projection of their own imaginary and aggression limits, more than anything, the perceptual field of the whites. A solution to this crisis requires " 'a different ordering of the visible' or an aggressive counter reading," according to Butler.[22]

The rejection of bodies of color in the "here and now," seen earlier, is symptomatic of the crisis in white perception. As a perceptual practice, whiteness not only fails to see ordinary actions of nonwhite bodies as ordinary but also prescribes how they should be treated in space and time; it drives one to chase after an elderly Asian American woman with sanitizer, and to call the police on African Americans barbecuing or birdwatching in the park.[23] Since the threefold logic of white perception (fabrication–reduction–naturalization, analyzed in the first section) is predicated upon what Charles Mills calls a "consensual hallucination,"[24] its maintenance takes a constant and collective denial of social realities.

Therefore, I propose that we consider whiteness as a form of *perceptual dysfunction*. I use the language of "dysfunction" to underscore the absurdity of the white perceptual logic and to problematize its normative status. The notion aims to remind ourselves of the fact that white perception *is* a particular, systematic pattern of deviation as a perceptual practice that centers only certain bodies, which has been made normative for the purposes of colonization and slavery. As Yancy notes, "White power and privilege are fundamentally contingent. The scopic hegemony of whiteness is grounded in structural, historical, and material processes of subjugation, dispossession, and imperial invasion."[25] Seeing it as a form of dysfunction helps us situate white perceptual practices properly in its historical contingency.

In proposing the notion of whiteness as a perceptual dysfunction, I am not suggesting that perceptual function in full capacity requires a form of seeing that is entirely neutral or objective, and thus one needs to transcend their positionality to disrupt the embodied logic of white perception. Rather, the formulation is meant to underscore the danger of mistaking a particular *reading* of social realities as a neutral act of *seeing*. As noted earlier, white perception, presented as nonracial and general, assumes the guise of neutrality and objectivity. Whiteness gains power by concealing its particular positionality, especially from those who inhabit it, as Sara Ahmed points out.[26] White perception is a dysfunction in the specific sense that its logic is unknown to those who perform it. The spatiotemporality of white perception discussed earlier is an instance where its logic is naturalized by revising the ontological categories themselves, onto which Yellow bodies are mapped. The altered ontological mapping becomes the eyes that habituate racialized perception but are themselves unseen to the viewer. White perceptual dysfunction is what Ellison's hero calls the "inner eyes" of the people that make him invisible: "I am invisible, understand, simply because people refuse to see me. . . . That invisibility to which I refer occurs because of a peculiar disposition of the eyes of those with whom I come in contact. A matter of the construction of their inner eyes, those eyes with which they look through their physical eyes upon reality."[27]

The inner eyes are, according to Yancy, "those white racist, epistemic perspectives, interlocked with various social and material forces, from which whites 'see' the world."[28] What is made invisible here is not only the hero's body but also the operation of white "inner eyes." Thus, Yancy holds that challenging the socially constructed privilege and power of the white gaze requires revealing its invisible function.

In pointing to the invisibility of white perceptual logic to whites themselves, my proposal aligns with Yancy's claim. By naming it a dysfunction, I intend to further emphasize the detrimental consequences of white perception as a normative construct, namely, its mundane practices of epistemic and ontological violence. It calls for urgent attention to one's perceptual habits that could potentially harm bodies of color every moment of every day without their knowledge. It also highlights how the logic impoverishes one's own world by subjecting perceptual possibilities to white spatiotemporality, under which certain bodies are denied a shared time and space.

It is worth noting here that Charles Mills has described whiteness as a pattern of "cognitive dysfunctions." According to Mills, one of the senses in which whiteness is a dysfunction is that it leads to self-deception, where "whites will in general be unable to understand the world they themselves have made."[29] One's ignorance of their own dysfunction is what sustains "racial fantasyland," which whites come to live in. But, of course, this fantasy is real and powerful when it works as an organizing principle of the social space.

The idea of perceptual dysfunction suggested here underscores particularly the prereflective and often undetectable act of violence that whiteness performs on bodies of color through the seemingly innocent and passive act of seeing. White perceptual dysfunction is a form of racial violence that takes no conscious effort or intent, yet could well be the most consequential kind. It is a violence resulted rather from a *lack* of effort to examine one's racialized vision. This lack of action is what perpetuates the white logic, which continues to fabricate an arbitrary divide between danger and safety in one's bodily engagement with the world, between bodies that belong "here and now" and bodies to be readily displaced, and between bodies that matter and bodies that are disposable and violable.

Drawing on Yancy's notion of the "seen absence" of the Black body, I have described in this chapter the general workings of the white perceptual logic. I have shown that the logic operates through the paradox of hypervisibility and invisibility, while serving as a measure for what can be seen and what can *be*: the visibility and presence of racialized bodies. In order to demonstrate the adaptability and complexity of the white perceptual logic, I then examined the particular operation of white logic on yellow bodies rendered hypervisible ("inescapably foreign") and invisible ("negligible") at the same time. We have seen how white perception alters the ontological mapping of the world in the analysis of the spatiotemporality of whiteness that denies bodies of color a shared time and space. Therefore, I claimed that white perception should be understood as a form of dysfunction that delimits the bodily possibilities of racialized peoples as well as the perceptual field of one's own.

It should be clear by now that what is suggested by Yancy's notion of "seen absence" of bodies of color is not a quest for recognition from whites but rather an alarm that signals a crisis in white perception. Promises of recognition and "making visible" of bodies of color under the current perceptual scheme could serve (and have served) to further centralize white bodies; the idea of including racialized bodies for the sake of diversifying white space without questioning the perceptual logic itself leaves white dominance intact.

Since the white perceptual logic continues to adapt and expand itself, a comprehensive account of it would require a further analysis of its workings specific to different communities of color and its impact on interracial tensions. Disrupting the logic of white perception is a responsibility of those who embody it, one that serves their own benefit to address the crisis in perception. It serves a corrective purpose of aligning oneself with social realities beyond self-imposed dysfunction. It is not an act of benevolence or generosity toward racialized others.

Chapter 8

To Remove the Scales from Their Eyes

A Phenomenology of Rap Music

Harry A. Nethery

Let's take the scenic route/I could show you the strange fruit/It's lookin' like Beirut.

—Pusha-T, "Untouchable," from *King Push*

At a live performance on May 20, 2016, rapper Kendrick Lamar invited a young white woman on stage to rap the song "m.A.A.d city."[1] The chorus is as follows: "Man down, where you from, n****?[2]/Fuck who you know, where you from my n****? Where your grandma stay, huh, my n****?/This m.A.A.d city I run, my n****." While rapping the song with Kendrick, she got to the chorus and rapped the n-word, which led to an immediate chorus of boos from the audience. Kendrick stopped the song, and the following exchange occurred:

Kendrick:	Wait, wait, wait.
White Woman:	Am I not cool enough for you? What's up bro?
Kendrick:	You gotta bleep one single word though. . .
White Woman:	Oh, I'm sorry did I do it?
Kendrick:	Yeah, you did it.
White Woman:	I'm so sorry. Oh my god.

The young white woman engages in a number of attempts at covering over what she had done. She begins by saying that she didn't realize she had rapped the n-word, but then tells Kendrick that she is just rapping it "like he wrote it." Finally, Kendrick asks the crowd if the young white woman should be given another chance to rap. The suggestion is met again with a chorus of

117

boos, though he eventually allows her another shot at the song. For Kendrick, it was a kind of teachable moment. Rather than kick her off the stage completely, he allowed her to learn from her mistake.

Here we have a young white woman who seems to be an avid fan of rap—she professes to know all of Kendrick's songs "by heart." Yet even as a fan of rap music, she saw no problem in rapping the n-word with Kendrick at the performance. It's as if she felt that her familiarity with, and love for, rap music gave her some kind of license. But, as Stereo Williams wrote in an article about the incident, "If you are going to claim to understand this music, this voice, then you will have to understand that there are lines which aren't yours to cross."[3] The line in question, of course, is the use of the n-word. As Ice Cube said to Bill Maher in response to the latter's on-air use of the n-word, "When I hear a white person say it, it feel like that knife stabbin' me, even if they don't mean it."[4]

In light of incidences like these, can white people appreciate rap music? If so, how? This is an important question to me. I am a white man, and I have been an avid listener of rap music since I was ten years old. Though, at the end of the day, I do not think it is up to me (a white man) to determine whether or not white people are able to appreciate rap music in a meaningful way. Thus, what I offer here is a suggestion. Using the work of George Yancy, I would like to propose a possible answer to this question, namely that it is both impossible and possible to appreciate rap music as a white fan. What I mean is this: on the one hand, it is impossible for me to have the experiences rappers illustrate in their songs, and thus it is impossible to fully appreciate the songs without access to those experiences. This is what white philosopher Joel Rudinow calls the "Experiential Access Argument."[5] He writes, "One cannot understand the blues nor express oneself authentically in the blues without knowing what it's like to live as a black person in America, and one cannot know this without being so." The color of my skin forecloses me from having the same kinds of experiences of people of color, and thus I cannot appreciate hip-hop on that level. For example, a song like "m.A.A.d city" will mean something different to people of color who can identify, at the level of experience, with the situations and environments depicted in the song. Meanwhile I, as a white listener, can only have a superficial understanding of those same situations and environments.

On the other hand, I suggest that white people *can* appreciate rap in a productive way if understood through the philosophical framework given by George Yancy. In broad strokes, my position is this: rap music offers white people a *gift* that exposes the *opaque white racist self* through the inducement of *double consciousness* within the white listener. This is due to the way in which rap music induces the listener to *experience-with* the artist. This experiencing-with the artist allows the rapper to reverse the white gaze by forcing the white listener to see themselves through someone else's eyes. The production of double consciousness allows the white listener to see ourselves as people of color see us, and thus allows us to *tarry* with (1) the brutal reality of oppression and (2) our own role in it. Ultimately, rap can make visible what Yancy says of the opaque white racist self in *Backlash*: "As white you fear a *fantasy* of your own creation; as Black, we fear a *reality* of your own creation."[6] Showing us our fantasy and their reality, and the critical distance between the two, in turn, can help to build solidarity among white people and people of color, or the creation of what Yancy calls "wide-awake dreamers"—young people that can dream of a new world while being awake to the problems of this one. As Yancy says, "For me, I am seeking those white students who are ready, with the help of the Black gaze, to be reborn, to allow the scales to fall from their eyes."[7, 8]

My analysis begins by contextualizing my argument within the larger framework of Yancy's "Density Project." I then engage in a brief phenomenology of rap, in order to show the ways in which rap music induces the listener to experience-with the artist. With this in hand, I then turn to an extended analysis of "Lift Me Up" by Vince Staples.[9] Finally, I end by discussing rap music as a kind of gift.

THE DENSITY PROJECT, HIP-HOP, AND WHITENESS

With a few exceptions, rap music (and hip-hop culture generally) is largely ignored by the philosophical world, even within the philosophy of music. I will not speculate as to why this is the case, though it would be easy to do so. In any case, this is a shame. For my purposes here, I would like to situate my analysis of rap music within Yancy's "Density Project," specifically as it is outlined in the preface for the second edition of *Black Bodies, White Gazes*. Here, Yancy makes two points that I would like to use to frame my analyses.

First, the density project begins with a fundamental axiom from which an important implication follows. Yancy writes:

> The density project begins with the fact that Black lives *don't* matter vis-à-vis the white gaze and white "sacred" embodiment, that Black ontology is always already inconsequential, a site of nullification. As such, the density project demands that philosophy engages with the existential tragic lives of Black people within a real world that is structurally dominated by white terror, white injustice, white microaggressions, white power.[10]

The fundamental axiom is not that Black lives don't matter in and of themselves, but that they don't matter as a product of the white gaze. Black lives are constituted by white people, experientially, as inconsequential and delinquent. This carries an important implication for white philosophers—if the white gaze is always nullifying the Black body, then it follows that there is a duty for us white philosophers to engage "with the existential tragic lives of Black people," and always in relation to the structures of white supremacy, through which these tragic lives are generated.

This brings me to a second point—the density project requires of its participants aggressive self-reflection. In this regard, Yancy writes that "the density project specifically demands of white philosophers to understand how they carry the historical and contemporary embodied implications of *their whiteness* and admit to how it functions to keep them alive, to keep them flourishing, to keep them safe and complicit with racialized injustice."[11]

If I am white, and if the white gaze is always nullifying the Black body, then I am directly implicated *back* into the various structures that I analyze in a profound, yet brutal sense—my privilege helps me flourish *only* and *always* at the expense of people of color. Thus, as regards the density project, we have two main points: (1) due to the white gaze, philosophy must engage with the tragic lives of people of color; and (2) this engagement requires direct self-reflection on my own complicity within the systems of white supremacy.

How does an analysis of rap music fit within the density project? At the end of the day, not all rap music addresses issues of oppression. But rap music has its origin *in* oppression—in the disgusting and brutal treatment of people of color in the Bronx, New York, in the 1970s.[12] In this sense, rap music is an expression of the lived experience of being the target of a world structurally dominated by white supremacy, whether or not oppression is the central theme. As such, rap music provides a space for white philosophers to philosophically engage "with the existential tragic lives of Black people."

An analysis of rap music fulfills the second point I elaborated above, viz. the implication of radical self-reflection. How can I enjoy Vince Staples's critiques of whiteness without seeing my own complicity in these same systems? As a white listener, an appreciation of rap music requires me to reflect on my own role in systems of white supremacy, and to form a kind of double consciousness, one that "enables [us] to see the world differently and to see [ourselves] differently through the experiences of black and people of color."[13] Thus, it is a kind of fissuring of whiteness.[14] That said, my goal here is not to make whiteness the primary focal point of rap. This is simply not the case, and it would be wrong for me to do so. I do not want to make rap music all about us.[15] However, insofar as rap music often addresses antiblack racism, and insofar as whiteness created the situation from which rap sprung, then we white folks have a lot to learn from rap, and it would do us well to listen closely. In this sense, the objective of appreciating rap is to "*name* whiteness, to mark it, to undo its invisibility, to share a critical way of looking, and thereby encourage a new way of discerning and hopefully a new and unflinching way of bringing attention to what has become normative and business as usual."[16]

RAP AND EXPERIENCE

In his book *Decoded*,[17] the rapper Jay-Z offers the beginnings of a phenomenological analysis (though he doesn't use this term) of the experiential structure of rap music. Elsewhere,[18] I outline the tripartite phenomenological structure of hip-hop (beat, music, and flow). Here, I would like to focus on two important elements of rap music (as given by Jay-Z): (1) that listeners of rap music *experience-with* the artist, and (2) that rap music allows for the expression of contradiction. These are the key moments that allow us to *tarry* with rap.[19]

One strength of rap music, according to Jay-Z, is that it has the power to induce the listener to *experience-with* the artist. He uses the rapper DMX as an example, "for whom everything comes from a subjective, personal place."[20] Thus, "when he growls out a line like *on parole with warrants that'll send me back the raw way*, the person rapping along to it in their car is completely living the lyric."[21] As regards his own music, Jay-Z writes:

> But when people hear me telling my stories, or boasting in my songs, or whatever, they don't hear some rapper telling them how much better than them he is. They hear it as their own voice. . . . I don't think listeners think I'm threatening them. I think they're singing along with me, threatening someone else. They're thinking, *Yeah, I'm coming for you.* And they might apply it to anything. To taking their next math test.[22]

When I am listening to a rapper tell the story of, for example, a robbery, I do not feel scared or threatened. Instead, I am riding along with the rapper, seeing the world through their eyes—a perspective that I could never have otherwise. As the hip-hop artist A Boogie Wit Da Hoodie says, "When people listen to my music, I want them to feel like it's them in the situation. Put yourself in my shoes and just don't even look at it like it's me no more."[23]

Yet Jay-Z uses the rapper Chuck D from Public Enemy as a counterexample. Chuck D's descriptions of the machinations of white supremacy are brilliant, but they do not induce the listener to experience-with the rapper. He writes that Chuck D's "focus is on analyzing the larger world from an almost objective, argumentative point of view, even when he's speaking in a first person voice. You rarely *become* Chuck D when you're listening to Public Enemy; it's more like watching a really, really lively speech."[24]

For Jay-Z, there is an experiential difference between listening to Chuck D and DMX—the difference between "watching a really, really lively speech" and "completely living the lyric." The ground of this difference lies with whether a rapper's lyrics start from an "objective, argumentative point of view" or a "subjective, personal place." Both have their value, but I am more interested in the latter, and in the way the listener *becomes* the artist. It is through this act of becoming that a horizon of transformative possibilities opens up to the white listener—"I can see oppression through someone else's eyes." I can learn about white supremacy from Chuck D, but I can *see it* with Vince Staples.

Another important element of rap, for Jay-Z, is the use of rhyme. The use of rhyme allows the listener to forge connections between concepts that might otherwise appear contradictory. Take, for example, Tupac Shakur's line in his 1995 song "Dear Mama": "And even as a crack fiend mama/You always was a Black Queen, mama." By using the same word "mama," and through the schematics of internal rhyming between the two lines, Tupac brings two seemingly mutually exclusive concepts into conjunction. How can his mother be both a queen and an addict? Yet she is, and I would wager that many of us have loved ones that we view in a similar way. But, here, Tupac is able to formulate and express this feeling in a way that bypasses the principle of noncontradiction. In this regard, Jay-Z writes that rhyming in rap gives it the ability to "express those feelings that you can't really name."[25] In fact, "rap is built to handle contradiction."[26]

For Jay-Z, the fact that rap can express contradictions is one of its most powerful aspects. Why is this important? He writes:

> [Rap] doesn't force you to pretend to be only one thing or another, to be a saint or a sinner. It recognizes that you can be true to yourself and still have unexpected dimensions and opposing ideas. . . . The real bullshit is when you act like you *don't* have contradictions inside you, that you're so dull and unimaginative that your mind never changes or wanders into strange, unexpected places.[27]

As any Buddhist would probably tell you, human beings are full of contradictions. Yet we do not often recognize this in our society. Take the logic of the "good white" as outlined by Yancy. The "good white" believes in a kind of racial dichotomy: one is either a saint or a sinner, a nonracist or a racist, with nothing in between. This is harmful because it forecloses the "good white" from any active self-reflection—"I don't have any racist feelings, so I must not be racist." When, *in fact*, and as Yancy has shown throughout his career, this is simply not the case. There is not a single white person in this country that doesn't participate in structures of white supremacy, and there is no such thing as "white innocence."

As I argue later, rap (if appreciated correctly) can bring this to the fore. Rap induces us to experience-with the artist, and this experiencing-with opens us up to the experience of contradiction. This experience then induces a kind of double consciousness within us, in which we see ourselves as people of color see us. As an example, I now turn to Vince Staples's song "Lift Me Up," from his 2015 album *Summertime '06.*

VINCE STAPLES AND THE REVERSAL
OF THE WHITE GAZE

"Lift Me Up" begins with a set of comparisons that serve to illustrate the functioning of the white gaze and the constitution of blackness under white supremacy. The first verse begins with two such comparisons: "Hey, I'm just a n**** until I fill my pockets/And then I'm Mr. N****, they follow me while shoppin'." In the first two bars of the song, Vince illustrates the phenomenon known as "shopping while black,"—that is, that no matter their economic status, people of color will be followed by retail store personnel or security due to the color of their skin alone. As Yancy argues, this is due to the machinations of the white gaze—the passive and pre-experiential constitution of people of color as ontologically delinquent, as "always already about to do something wrong."[28] That is, "From the perspective of whiteness, I am, contrary to the existentialist credo, an essence ('Blackness') that precedes my essence."[29] In relation to the white gaze, Vince Staples will always be seen as delinquent within white spaces, regardless of his talent, fame, or economic status.

The white gaze is not simply a form of constitution, but also a kind of con-fiscation and return in which the white gaze apprehends "the Black body . . . as pregiven in its constitution as inferior."[30] As regards "shopping while black," Yancy writes:

> It is within such quotidian social spaces that *my Black body* has been confis-cated. When followed by a white security personnel as I walk through depart-ment stores, when a white sales person avoids touching my hand, or when a white woman looks with suspicion as I enter the elevator, I feel that in their eyes I am this indistinguishable, amorphous, black seething mass, a token of danger, a threat, a criminal, a burden, a rapacious animal incapable of delayed gratification.[31]

The white gaze captures the black body and returns it to the person of color as something monstrous. In Vince's case, he is returned to himself as "a n****" through the act of being followed in the store. Yancy writes that, due to this return, "I appeared no longer to possess *my* body, but a 'surrogate' body whose meaning did not exist anterior to the performance of white spectatorship."[32] As W. E. B. Du Bois famously argued, this causes a kind of fissure within the consciousness of people of color. Through refusing his card "peremptorily, with a glance,"[33] the young white girl provokes in Du Bois what he calls "double-consciousness," or the "sense of always looking at one's self through the eyes of others, of measuring one's soul by the tape of a world that looks on in amused contempt and pity."[34] That is, people of color (in relation to the white gaze) carry a double sense of themselves—how they *know* themselves to be and how white people *think* they are. For Yancy, it is through the white gaze that he becomes "hypervigilant of [his] own embodied spatiality."[35]

The way in which the white gaze constitutes people of color is further highlighted by Vince in the next two bars: "I feel like Mick and Richards, they feel like Muddy Waters/So tell me what's the difference, so tell me what's the difference?" Here, Vince is asking the question directly: What's the difference between how white people see me, and how I see myself? In this instance, Vince is comparing himself to rock stars like Mick Jagger and Keith Richards from the Rolling Stones, whereas white people see him only as Muddy Waters, the famous blues musician. Regardless of his success, Vince will never be a musician, but only a "black" musician—he will never be a rock star (in the genre-less sense of the term), but only a rapper.[36] This is again highlighted twice in the closing bars of the verse: "My bitch look like Madonna, they starin' at Katana/Waiter still ain't brought the chopsticks, should have brought the chopper/Uber driver in the cockpit look like Jeffrey Dahmer/But he lookin' at me crazy when we pull up to the projects."

In the first instance, we have a case of "eating while black" wherein Vince is profiled and denied service while eating at the upscale West-Hollywood restaurant Katana. Here, Vince ponders becoming the very thing the waitstaff see him as, when he laments not bringing his "chopper."[37] In the second instance, Vince illustrates a scene in an Uber wherein he believes he has much more reason to be afraid of the white driver (he "look like Jeffrey Dahmer"), than the driver does of them, and yet he "lookin' at me crazy when we pull up to the projects."

In this first verse, Vince Staples effectively reverses the white gaze and shows the white listener that he sees us better than we see ourselves. Using feminist standpoint epistemology, Yancy argues that the oppressed have a better understanding of the oppressors than the oppressors do of themselves. As regards his famous elevator example, Yancy writes:

> The fact of the matter is that from the perspective of an oppressed and marginalized social position, Blacks do in fact possess a level of heightened sensitivity

to recognizable and repeated occurrences that might very well slip beneath the radar of others who do not have such a place and history in a white dominant and hegemonic society. In other words, the claim that I have a justified belief that the white woman's gesture was racist is grounded within a social context that informs and supports this claim.[38]

Because I am not a target of oppression, I do not experience the ways in which black bodies and bodies of color are oppressed—this is experientially cut off from me. Thus, I will not see the ways in which *I* implicitly or passively oppress bodies of color.

In the previous section, I argued (with Jay-Z) that rap music has the peculiar power to induce the listener to experience-with an artist. I will never be racially profiled. However, "Lift Me Up" allows me an inroad to seeing the world the way that Vince Staples sees it, and thus to seeing myself clearly in a kind of mirror. As I listen, I am in that store, that restaurant, and that Uber *with* him, watching as he is the target of passive and implicit acts of racism. Yet the very difference that will never let me experience what Vince does is the very cause of his pain. It is in this sense that I experience myself as the target of a *black gaze* that has effectively turned the white gaze back upon itself. If I tarry or dwell with this, I cannot help but experience an "emotional and cognitive dissonance" that results from becoming "more and more attentive to the ways in which [I am] entangled in the social and psychic web of white racism."[39] As such, through experiencing-with Vince Staples, I am induced to form a kind of double consciousness, wherein I see myself as people of color see me.

I began this chapter with the example of a young white woman rapping the n-word at a Kendrick Lamar concert. This example is one species of a larger genus of related phenomena, in which white people use the n-word in one way or another due to a felt "familiarity" with black culture. Vince Staples addresses a similar phenomenon in the second verse of "Lift Me Up," though in this case it is of white people identifying with the n-word. He raps, "All these white folks chanting when I asked'em where my n****s at?/Goin' crazy, got me goin' crazy, I can't get wit' that/Wonder if they know, I know they won't go where we kick it at/Ho, this shit ain't Gryffindor, we really killin', kickin' doors." When he uses the n-word on stage as a kind of call and response, his expectation is not that white fans will pipe up and "chant" back. Yet they do, and this forces Vince to wonder if white people know that black people see through us—that is, that "I know they won't go where we kick it at." In an interview with NPR, Staples tells us that the lines "force [white] people to think about themselves, which is a very hard thing to do sometimes. And, all I just say is it's a statement. I wonder if they know that we notice it, is really where it came from."[40]

The fact that white audiences are largely happy to chant back in these situations reveals something sinister. His white fans are happy to identify themselves with the n-word in the space of a performance but never would in "real life." Furthermore, that we would not make that trade is something that his white audience do not *see* about ourselves and might not see if simply told. Instead, Vince Staples puts us up on stage with him, looking at ourselves chant back a term that should never escape our lips. Again, like in the first verse, if we tarry with the music, we find ourselves as the target of a black gaze that has the power to reveal whiteness in all of its subtle perniciousness.

In these lines, Vince Staples is trying to draw the line, the one that Stereo Williams and Ice Cube referenced in the introduction to this chapter. No matter how much I love rap music and hip-hop culture, no matter how many years I have been a die-hard fan, no matter how many obscure references I know or songs that I can recite from heart, the very color of my skin fore-closes me from using the n-word in any way, shape, or form. This is simply a line I can never cross, and I will never cross it, at least partially *from* my love of rap music and hip-hop culture. If I tarry with the music, then I simply *must* see this line. If I do not, it is only because of some form of white obfuscation.

Yancy analyzes a similar case in his discussion of the film *White Chicks*, which "constitutes a counter-gaze, one that attempts to render visible the often invisible normative power of whiteness."[41] In this 2004 film, Shawn and Marlon Wayans play two FBI agents who decide to wear "whiteface" in order to solve a crime. Painting their faces as white, Yancy argues, "deploys a 'reverse' minstrel show technique" that, like "Lift Me Up," effectively reverses the white gaze upon itself.[42] One scene of the film consists of the Wayans brothers, in "whiteface," with a group of young white women. They are listening to a rap song, in which the n-word comes up within a refrain. The Wayans brothers rap the lyric, while the two young white women look on seemingly with horror. After assuring them that "Nobody's around," implying that no black people are within earshot, the young white women begin to rap the lyric with glee. In this regard, Yancy writes:

> It points both to the antiracist duplicity of the white women in the car and to white privilege whereby upper-class young white women can playfully engage "blackness" without actually facing the existential hardships and angst of what it means to be black within the context of antiblack racism. One can musically "slum," as it were, without physical proximity to black bodies.[43]

Though the context is different, this duplicity is similar to the one refer-enced by Vince Staples in his interview with NPR. By chanting back when Staples "asked'em where my n****s at?" white people engage with black-ness in a disingenuous and harmful way. We seem to be happy to identify with blackness in the form of a star on stage performing, when we would never trade our lives for his. I would not trade my middle-class white upbringing for Vince's life in a low-income area of Long Beach, California. As such, it is a form of racial duplicity for me to rap the n-word at a performance and simultaneously claim to be antiracist.

RAP MUSIC AND THE GIFT

To use Yancy's terminology, "Lift Me Up" offers white listeners a gift—a kind of *parrhesia*, or courageous truth-telling with transformative possibility. This truth is often "heavy to bear"[44] and can "hurt, stun, unsettle, and unnerve."[45] As regards his "Dear White America" op-ed in the *New York Times*, Yancy writes that his gift was "a most disagreeable mirror."[46] It is a mirror in the sense that Yancy shows to us white people how we are embedded within systems of racism. It is disagreeable because this is a truth that most white Americans do not want to acknowledge. Yet in Yancy's sense, the gift offers transformative possibilities for the recipients. Yancy writes that "such candid and truthful speech creates a space for crucial opportunities for white people to engage in risking the self and the possibility for constructive transformation."[47] Again, it is "an opportunity, a call to responsibility—perhaps even to greater maturity."[48] Receiving the gift, in this sense, can be painful as it involves a kind of fissuring or destabilizing of how we think of ourselves in relation to our own embeddedness in white supremacy. But the only way we can change and become better is if we have a clear view of ourselves in the first place.

The acceptance of the gift requires a kind of tarrying, which for Yancy is "an essential prerequisite for coming to terms with one's racism, and the subtle tendencies of obfuscation and denial vis-à-vis one's racism."[49] This tarrying requires two things. The first is a kind of positioning. Yancy writes: "Whites who are open to life-affirming and transformative transactions with people of color are not simply waiting defensively in fear of new information that may threaten to destabilize their sense of self. Rather, there is an openness to having one's world transformed and cracked."[50]

That is, tarrying requires an openness and a willingness to change. Second, tarrying requires a kind of dwelling or the inhibiting of what Alia Al-Saji calls a racializing perception that happens "faster than the speed of thought."[51] To this end, Yancy writes that tarrying requires a dwelling with "the emotional and cognitive dissonance that will be inevitably experienced as they become more and more attentive to the ways in which they are entangled in the social and psychic web of white racism."[52] That is, tarrying requires both a form of openness and a form of dwelling: I must be open to experiences that will change me, and I cannot run from them when they occur.

Thus, to tarry with rap music is to dwell with the experiences shared with us by the artist. Ultimately, this tarrying urges the white listener to engage in critical self-examination. I cannot, in principle, experience the world in the ways that Vince Staples or Kendrick Lamar do, but I *can* experience-with them. In this experiencing, the intricate and insidious web of white supremacy, within which I am trapped, comes to the fore. As I see myself through their eyes, I see the ways in which I uncritically perpetuate and deploy the white gaze or support societal structures that are racist at their core.

An appreciation of rap music shows us the lines that we cannot cross, which brings us back to the example that began this chapter. In using the n-word, the young white woman failed to appreciate Kendrick Lamar's gift in a fundamental way, which is made more apparent if we look closely at the song. This song details a day when Kendrick saw a young black man murdered. He raps, "Seen a light-skinned n**** with his brains blown out/At the same burger stand where *beep*[53] hang out/Now this is not a tape recorder saying that he did it/but ever since that day, I was lookin' at him different/That was back when I was nine."

This song functions in the same manner as "Lift Me Up." The use of the first person and rhyme induces the listener to experience the traumatic moment, at the age of nine no less, with Kendrick. It is experiences like these that lead rappers to discuss the effects that violence has had on them in their work. For example, on "Feels Like Summer"[54] Vince raps, "Still struggle with the past/I'm strapped."[55] Even though Vince Staples has money now and has left his life in Long Beach behind, he is still worried. Denzel Curry, on the song "SPEEDBOAT,"[56] tells us that the recent death of a friend has made him worry about his own life—"My dawg is gone/so I have my Teflon."

In any case, Kendrick ends "m.A.A.d city" with the following line—"You know the reasons but still will never know my life/Kendrick, a.k.a. 'Compton's Human Sacrifice.'" Here, Kendrick is telling his white listener that *even though* he has shown us a traumatic experience from his past, we can never *know* what it is like. This experience is fundamentally cut off from me, due to the color of my skin. Kendrick deploys a reversal of the white gaze here—"You think you know me, but you do not, and you can never know me." In the song "P T S D,"[57] the rapper Murs echoes a similar sentiment—"You really think you know how my people live?/You think you down because you know who Deebo is?"[58] Here, Murs is targeting white listeners who act "overly familiar" with people of color because they are familiar with black culture. For example, seeing the movie *Friday* is neither a necessary nor sufficient condition for a white person to use the n-word because there *simply are no necessary or sufficient conditions* that could justify if. To think that there are is to fundamentally *fail* to appreciate rap music. It is in this sense that the young white woman who began our chapter failed to appreciate rap music. Her use of the n-word and her attempts at subterfuge to mask the reasons she felt comfortable using it belie a fundamental failure of the woman to tarry with "m.A.A.d city." If she had, she would have seen those lines that she could not cross.

At the end of the day, it is my hope that an appreciation of rap music (in the way that I have outlined in this chapter) can help to build solidarity between white people and people of color in the fight against racism. Those white listeners that have seen themselves naked through the black gaze cannot help but to critically engage their own lives, and this critical engagement inevitably leads to disgust with white supremacy, and disgust at our place and role in its perpetuation and functioning. It is on this basis that we can begin to become what Yancy calls "wide-awake dreamers," or those who can dream of a new world without reduplicating the evils of this world. This, I suggest, is what it means to appreciate rap music as a white listener.

Part Three

EDUCATING REASON

Critical Pedagogy

Chapter 9

Philosophy/Pedagogy

A Critique of the Present

Mark William Westmoreland

George Yancy inspires scholars and teachers across disciplines, often giving transdisciplinary tools for challenging our intellectual traditions as well as our classroom practices. His work cuts across fields in at least one profound way, namely, his commitment to theorizing about the practical experiences of everyday life. And, his work cuts deep, that is, it makes us feel a sense of urgency to understand both the conditions that got us to this point as well as the need for a new sociopolitical imaginary. In short, the task of teacher-scholars ought to be one of asking questions that diagnose and critique the present in order to imagine a different future.

Those who know Yancy will no doubt agree that he is kind-hearted, encouraging, honest, and courageous. And it is his fearlessness that has most shaped my way of thinking about both scholarship and pedagogy. Yancy and I are both professional philosophers, and much of what I write in this chapter is situated within a philosophical discourse but is nonetheless applicable to the wider terrain of academic disciplines. As a teacher-scholar, I both produce and disseminate knowledge and attempt to cultivate fertile classroom soil in which wisdom can blossom. Our knowledge claims are always imbedded within a sociohistorical context within which there is no clear separation of the mind/reason and the body/affect. This context is also racialized according to a script whereby whites are paradigmatic virtuous citizens, paragon truth tellers, or universalizable, exemplary human beings. Such is the unjust vantage of whiteness. Furthermore, this context is Manichean, that is to say, it is a binary world in which whiteness is normative and Blackness is deviant, irrational, incapable, insignificant, and even threatening.

In this chapter, I explore Yancy's understanding of philosophy and the role of the philosopher within the classroom and argue that a reconsideration of the stakes of philosophical practice is in order. Beginning with the notion that

whiteness functions as the transcendental norm, I consider the extent to which
philosophy is a white discipline. In response to the white normativity and
white supremacy of philosophy, I explain Yancy's vision of the philosophical
life. Third, I articulate a pedagogical posture that functions to raise awareness
of how our everyday lived experiences are conditioned by a racial matrix and
how to engage tools of resistance. I conclude with brief suggestions for teachers that affirm a courageous disposition in the face of risky, say potentially
productively dangerous, racialized classrooms.

WHITENESS AS THE TRANSCENDENTAL NORM

Throughout his work, Yancy gives us several key ideas—racial narrative,
ambush, dispossession, crisis, unsuturing, tarrying—each of which deserves
exploration, particularly in the context of pedagogy. In this chapter, I want to
focus primarily on his description of whiteness as the transcendental norm
in relation to philosophy as a discipline. Whiteness is the transcendental
norm of our sociohistorical milieu "where whiteness takes itself to be that
which remains the same across a field of difference" and leaves "whiteness
unmarked, unraced, and as the human *simpliciter*."[1] Whiteness is not merely
a monochromatic designation but rather a normative social position. This
social position of whiteness provides advantageous content that is maintained
through ongoing racist policies and practices and racialized ways of knowing
and non-knowing.[2] The overwhelming majority of white folks do not view
their social position as a position of racism, which is too often relegated to
only the most explicit and direct instantiations of racism like the Ku Klux
Klan. Furthermore, many whites tend to think that racism remains with us
only because we talk about it too much and that the solution is to ignore racial
difference. Yancy rejects the oft-heard prescription for a colorblind approach
to race relations. To recognize the humanity of all persons, one must recognize the ways in which individuals are conditioned by racist institutions and
by systems of oppression. Colorblindness obfuscates the extent to which persons are differentially affected by racist structures and policies within society.
Additionally, colorblindness denies the historical legacy of oppression and
glosses over an individual's particular identity.

We ought to name whiteness wherever and whenever we perceive it. To
name whiteness should not be difficult, since it appears practically everywhere in a white normative society. White ways of knowing and white
embodiment, specifically, are treated as universalizable, as human thought
and human bodies proper. Within our social matrix, whiteness functions
as the transcendental norm, as the rubric for the quintessential human, for
virtue, for truth, and for the good. Whiteness "defines itself as ontological

self-sufficiency and axiological universality."[3] This norm—that makes whiteness the arbiter of the real—is imbedded within our economic, legal, penal, and political institutions. Of course, whiteness is not an absolute, universal, transhistorical norm but one formed by historical, material conditions and produced in opposition to the racial Other. And, as Yancy points out, the lie of whiteness is complicit in another lie regarding Black folks, namely, that Blackness is vicious and depraved. It comes from a dominative system of difference in which nonwhiteness is evaluated as morally corrupt or rationally inferior. Put differently, whiteness is differential, that is, differentiating between what it finds acceptable and what is deviant and affording benefits and privileges to the former.

Yancy explains that that which allows whites to pass freely through social space, that which grants whites the presumption of virtue, that which protects whiteness, does so at the expense of Blackness: "How you live your whiteness, is vouchsafed at the expense of my being deemed a nigger."[4] It might be helpful to think of whiteness as a parasitical, as something that "reduces the Black body to a wretched particularity."[5] A key mechanism for maintaining the transcendental normativity of whiteness is that of the white gaze, which is the lens and action through which whiteness views Black folks. The white gaze filters one's view so that the default way of seeing Black persons is as irrevocably Other. Put differently, white folks act as bearers of epistemic privilege, while Black folks are objectified. Under the white gaze, Black *persons* are invisible, that is, they are stripped of their personhood. Their humanity is not seen. They have no wishes, wants, desires, or beliefs. They are not present as selves. They have no past, no future. In the same instance, the hypervisible Blackness of the *body* becomes the only salient feature, and this body's Blackness is formed within a world that preceded any of us and will outlive us as well. This world can also be a site of social death, depending on how bodies are charged with meaning.[6] None of us has entered the world as an ahistorical *tabula rasa*. Within the context of white supremacy, hypervisible Blackness is always already known ahead of any particular encounter. In other words, the content of Blackness is given in advance. Our white normative world preceded each of us and has marked us "with culturally and historically embedded significations" as virtuous or vicious according to the color of our skin.[7] The white gaze, while it codes whiteness as ideal, beautiful, and trustworthy, constructs an image that Black equals deviant, Black equals lazy, Black equals criminal. White signifies purity or divinity; Black signifies corruption and evil.

Within the grip of white supremacy, these codings or constructions are presented as essential, naturally immutable qualities that allegedly explain the superiority of whiteness. This situation makes it difficult for whites to see how they unjustly benefit from white supremacy, especially those who may

not intentionally hold racist beliefs or commit malicious racial acts. Whiteness usually does not see itself as a problem; it is too opaque. In order to
awaken this epistemic closure, one must be open to criticism, which requires
that one be vulnerable. A critique of whiteness relies on the unsuturing of
whiteness in order to be successful. To be unsutured means to experience
one's embodied identity inseparably tied to the racist social milieu as both
the cause and effect of harm to People of Color. An early stage of coming to
terms with whiteness as a problem is the mere act of naming it.

To name whiteness is to mark it as an inheritance, as property, rather than a
form of voluntarism. To name whiteness is to identify that white apotheosis is
a lie. Patricia Williams claims that "racial denial [by whites] tends to engender a profoundly invested disingenuousness, an innocence that amounts to the
transgressive refusal to know."[8] This denial, fueled by white racial paranoia,
white rage, or white fragility, is costly.[9] It feeds into the perpetual oppression
of People of Color and also continues to keep whites from accurately knowing themselves. Whiteness problematically functions as "a center from which
one [cuts] up the social world, makes sense of things, evaluates and judges,
remains invisible while the discursive field of white power/knowledge continues to open up a social space of intelligibility in terms of which the black/
white body appears."[10] Whiteness is both the microscope and laser that, by
creating distance between who is knower and what is known, adjudicates
that which is of value and that which is not, that vivisects our sociality so
that some can dominate while others are subjugated. More to the point, this
cutting up of the social world is not a matter of individual desires or choices
but is systemically engrained in the fabric of society so that those whiteness
affirms (i.e., whites) are heirs to the dominative areas of the matrix whereby
they live. This raises a challenging question for both Yancy and myself,
namely, *what role can philosophy have in the unsuturing process?*

THE PROBLEM OF PHILOSOPHY

We know that a philosopher is a lover of wisdom, but what precisely do we
mean when we speak of the love of wisdom? For Yancy, philosophy is a
particular way of life, a transformative project one takes up in response to
existential and cultural problems that plague humankind. It is a critical project
that questions our everyday lived experience, how such experience is embodied, and how we think about such experience. Philosophy challenges us "to
face both who we are and the world with as much honesty as we can manage,
to grieve that world and to grieve our own mistakes within that world, and,
yet, to be moved and transformed by the love of wisdom and the wisdom of
love."[11] It is a practical enterprise, one that reshapes how we engage with

ourselves, with others, and with the world more broadly. Philosophy, according to Yancy, questions both the present moment and the philosopher's own capacity to question, that is, philosophy is a question for itself. He claims that philosophers need a routine dose of reflection on just what it is they are doing when they actually do philosophy.

Yancy suggests that the philosopher ought to be a troublemaker, one who asks *how ought we to live* for surely the present state of the things is not the best of all possible worlds. Philosophy as an academic discipline is not removed from the possibility of being the object of criticism and being unsettled—perhaps being the epicenter of unsettling. Yancy writes:

> Philosophy as practiced in many universities . . . is ripe to have its inertial tendencies troubled. . . . One form of troublemaking in the field of philosophy involves removing the veneer that departments of philosophy are these respectful, engaging sites free of deep political and personal fights. . . . Many philosophical voices are marginalized and deemed ersatz vis-à-vis the dominant philosophical voice.[12]

A problem for philosophy is that it often divorces itself from our lived experience, that is, from the very *need* to be wise. Another is that what has become mainstream philosophy bends toward a desire for universality while ignoring particularity—in terms of both content and methodology as well as the philosopher's own subject position.

Yancy asks, "Have professional philosophers become prisoners of the philosopher as *homo academicus*, where they are simply entertained by semantic and conceptual games played within academic spaces, of ruthlessly philosophically trumping and politically controlling the views of others?"[13] One criticism of philosophy is that much of it deals with ideas devoid of any attachment to the real world. Put differently, philosophers have a tendency to keep their minds in the clouds for the body is often understood to diminish or even negate one's capacity for philosophizing. This is unfortunately true in terms of the content (that about which one philosophizes), the methodology (how one interprets and utilizes the content), and the philosopher's identity (the context from which one philosophizes). Many philosophers strive for a theory from nowhere, that is, decontextual theory or philosophy that makes one's biography and social positioning invisible as if it plays absolutely no role in how one engages with the world and with ideas. The trend toward *homo academicus* "is obfuscated through processes of normalization. This normalizing process—through canonical repetition, the crafting of syllabi, funding, socially constituted valorizations, and other institutionalizing processes—attempts to blur the reality that philosophizing is immanent and grounded within social and historical practices as opposed to founded upon a transcendental basis."[14] Good philosophy, according to dominative disciplinary practice, is allegedly philosophy done from a neutral, universalizable perspective; and the dominative canonical tendencies maintain this. However, mainstream philosophy's aim of universality manifests its bad faith since the reality is that our musings are always immanent to our quotidian existence with its interconnecting lines of interpersonal, institutional, and cultural influences. It masks its particularity as white, thereby allowing whiteness to pass as both normative and hidden and yet nonetheless dominative. Talk of race is assumed to be below philosophical considerations. White philosophers often think their faculty of reason is without influence of sociohistorical context; moreover, they think their whiteness is incidental to their personal identity. When the social conditions for whiteness impact philosophy but those conditions are bracketed in suspension, philosophy's whiteness is made invisible.

Consider the oft-cited Immanuel Kant, who is arguably the most important moral philosopher of the modern era. Despite his contributions to liberalism, cosmopolitanism, and universal human rights, Kant is undoubtedly the model philosopher of concealed whiteness. Since the early 1990s, however, scholars have been coming to terms with the extent to which his racism permeates through his works.[15] In the early and mid-twentieth century, Martin Heidegger was a *tour de force* of German philosophy but it is quite recently that his anti-semitism is taken seriously as a problematic component of his work. In the second half of the twentieth century, the overwhelming majority of philosophers disavowed such racist sentiment; and yet, they often remained silent regarding the racism in their midst. For instance, Paul Ricoeur, most known for his work in hermeneutics, published widely in value theory and political philosophy but never addressed the problem of racism.[16] The most famous political philosopher in recent anglophone philosophy, John Rawls, devoted only a handful of pages throughout his five major works to the problem of racism. I give these as a few examples of how philosophy tends to ignore the devastating effects racism has on the daily lives of the world's majority.

For Yancy, philosophy is multiple, and as such, it is better to speak of philosophies, always in the plural. Those philosophies that are radically critical, that ask about the common state of affairs, and that affirm the body as a site of knowledge, are the ones that ought to be pursued because they attempt to actually guide us in answering how one ought to live wisely. However, mainstream philosophy remains wedded to a way of thinking about and doing philosophy that is myopic and unilingual, that is, that there is only one true philosophical voice. This voice, this oracle voice, is totalizing insofar as it assumes particular phenomenon to be universal, conceptualizes about such phenomenon, and then proceeds to focus on the conceptualization more than the actual phenomenon. Unnerved and agitated by heterogeneous voices, the philosophical oracle voice makes itself the adjudicator of how best to delimit what properly counts as philosophy. It does this while simultaneously ignoring its own relation to those other heterogeneous voices. By judging itself as pure, it glosses over the extent to which philosophies are intertwined with others. Even the word and concept of "Sophia" [*philos*] or wisdom in "philosophy" comes from "*seba*" in Medu Neter. However, we still often hear that philosophy began in Greece stemming from a shift of *mythos* to *logos*, that is, from picture-thinking and superstition to reason and science.[17] This false narrative, which arguably arose in the eighteenth century, rests upon a rewriting of history that forgets, for example, that Pythagoras studied in Heliopolis, Memphis, and Thebes and that the giant Plato also studied in Heliopolis.[18] Why was the false narrative created? There are at least two likely answers. The first reason is the desire to assert and maintain the exceptionalism of the Western tradition. The second, which often overlaps with the first, is the denial to admit that Western culture has been influenced by Black philosophers in Africa. The philosophical oracle voice, Yancy claims, "is specious; it . . . elides its historicity, dutifully covering over its ideology of domination, power-lust, value-laden interests, and forms of institutional behavior that give material support to the perpetuation of the notion that what constitutes philosophy is determined by transcendental rules a priori."[19] Philosophies that do not fit into the false historical narrative and/or those that do not focus on abstracting, universalizing thought are portrayed as lacking rigor or as something like folk philosophy or dressed up religious mythology. This dominative nature of philosophy as a discipline protects the oracle's false narrative by counting Western philosophy (without influence from Africa) as the only real philosophy.

We can also think of the whiteness of philosophy in the literal sense that white philosophers feel at home in their discipline. The epidermal citationality of the human body codes members of various races differently. For whites, they will mostly be welcomed and assumed to be good philosophers. Sadly, the inverse is true for many People of Color, who are told "you don't belong here," "you're just not cut out for philosophy," or "what you do isn't really philosophy." People of Color know all too well how the philosophical oracle dictates what counts as philosophy and who belongs as a philosopher. Yancy suggests that we should "explore the ways in which White bodies are 'at home' within philosophy departments, philosophy conferences, and such mundane spaces as philosophy department lounges, and how that *feeling* of being at home is a function of an assemblage of philosophical practices enacted by White, typically male, bodies, bodies that have become reified as the paragon of philosophical performance."[20] Imagine a Latinx student in her third year of a doctoral program who returns to the department lounge at lunch time to collect all the books she brought to campus earlier that morning. Upon entering the lounge, a newly hired professor says:

"Hey, can you empty the trash cans in here? It'd probably best if you did it earlier in the day. Thanks."

She replies, "Hi, Prof. [white male], I'm a grad student in my third year."

"Oh, I'm sorry," he says. "I'm new to the department and just thought you were here to get the trash."

"Nah, I don't do trash. But, you should get to know some of the janitors. They're really sweet people," she responds.

"Yes, I should do that. I haven't seen them yet. Nice to meet you, though," he says as he leaves the lounge.

In the afternoon, the student sits in the professor's (white male's) class and listens as each student gives a short introduction. The Latinx student is not given the opportunity to introduce herself—not even to state her name. Once it is her turn, the professor says:

"Hi, again. Sorry about earlier. You just didn't look like a student. Thanks for taking this course. Ok, who's next?"

The white male professor's dysconscious racism is brought to the fore in several aspects.[21] First, his white gaze assumes that any Latinx person on campus must be a member of the staff and not faculty or graduate student. Notice that he has not actually met any of the janitorial staff, and yet he simply has already determined what status Latinx bodies occupy on campus. Furthermore, he has also already passed judgment that Latinx people cannot be graduate students. Later in class, he hastily tries to cover over his whiteness, and in doing so, he fails to let her speak. Her name, her story, her personhood remains unimportant to him.

I intend to avoid being reticent, so let me make the point as explicit as possible: too often our disciplines and classrooms are sites of white supremacy. For example, philosophers sometimes tend to think there is a philosophy *qua* philosophy that is universal and not bound by the particularity of identity, space, or time. Philosophy at its best, however, is "not simply about clarifying abstract ideas but about individuals who struggle in the flesh to make sense of their lives at an existentially deep and passionate level."[22]

In the next section, I want to describe Yancy's pedagogical posture as an example of how to cause trouble for, how to unsettle, the whiteness of philosophy. Cornel West describes Yancy as "one of the few distinguished public philosophers willing to get his hands dirty in the muck and mire of white supremacy in contemporary America."[23] Yancy does this with his consistent critique of the present whether he is teaching a class, giving a keynote address, or writing a book. Yancy claims that philosophy as a

penchant for conceptual abstraction, where the messiness of the real world is left behind as theory soars unencumbered. Imagine the impact on philosophy books and philosophy courses whose central foci deal with ethics, aesthetics, social and political philosophy, or even metaphysics, were they to begin with the reality that in white America there is this contemptible category that white people created called "nigger."[24]

Rather than begin with the abstract, we should, Yancy explains, begin with our everyday lived experience. What we say about race ontologically has consequences for how we behave racially, and how we live our racialized lives will influence how we philosophize about race. For philosophies to be at their best, we must speak truth to the power of the whitewashed world in which white supremacy strangles us all.

PEDAGOGICAL INTERVENTIONS

Although I am a specialist in philosophy, my hope is that teacher-scholars across the university can discern for themselves the extent to which my comments in this chapter regarding philosophy are apt for their disciples. Our resistance to the white normativity of educational spaces means in part that we "dialectically challenge and actually shape or transform the conceptual and normative spaces" established and sustained within mainstream philosophy.[25] Teacher-scholars, philosophers or otherwise, need to realize that what counts as a proper disciplinary topic or object of inquiry is not a neutral matter. Consider the position of the natural philosopher or scientist. The scientist carves up the world into measurable, quantifiable, and comparative entities. The scientist endeavors at freeing knowledge from the localized particularities of one's audience, that is, to account for the world in itself without bias, to provide a view from nowhere. However, in attempting this, the scientist already has imposed values on what object is to be investigated, to what extent it can be measured, and how it can be evaluated. Put differently, it is not the case that the evaluation occurs after the dissection as if the classificatory nature of the categories produced by sciences is neutral. Instead, the scientist already produces value in the act itself—first, in the actual observation, and second, in the observation statements that follow. Additionally, while focusing on one object of inquiry, the scientist ignores another. While one piece of data, one side of the story, is observed, other phenomena, other sides, are overlooked for the simple reason that all the data cannot be observed at once. The perceptions of what is seen and what is not seen are not given *a priori* by the objects themselves but are conditioned by a human decision. Likewise, the ruse of the philosophical oracle voice is that it assumes itself to be *a priori* and *sui generis*, despite it being created and maintained by a particular human decision.

How do we dialectically challenge our disciplinary decisions and pedagogical spaces? Inclusion of marginalized voices is not enough. There must be an explicit challenge to the history and norms that have governed philosophical practice. The starting point for this challenge is to show that philosophizing is always from a localized, particular position rather than from an Archimedean point from which everyone, regardless of gender, race, nationality, time, and place, can philosophize similarly. Let us return to our scientist. Observation involves much more than light making contact with one's retina; in other words, one's perception is also affected by one's disposition, biases, attention, intention, prior knowledge, and theoretical frameworks. All knowers come to have knowledge of reality through a mediator of sorts—a worldview, a theoretical framework. Theory-laden observations and the statements made from them, one might argue, result in an "observer's regress," that is, an endless set of presuppositions: theory T1 is based on observation O1, which presupposes T2, which is based on O2, which presupposes T3, and so on. If our observations are affected by our theories, then our observation statements can only be as solid or as certain as the theories they presuppose. Whether realizing it or not, the scientist or the philosopher observes and theorizes about the world like all human beings do—as a narrative self rooted in a cultural–historical context. René Descartes is illustrative in this regard.

In *Meditations on First Philosophy*, Descartes attempts to establish a ground for knowledge, that is, he seeks to answer how we come to know the things we claim to know. He begins by excluding all those things that he can doubt, including his own history, his own body, until he finds the one thing that he cannot doubt—that he is a doubting thing. This hyperbolic doubt results in the realization that he is fundamentally a thinking thing, for doubt is a form of thought. By displacing the body, he can claim to first and foremost be a mind. Of course, this is not to say that Descartes has no body or that he does not later acknowledge that his body is real. Rather, the problem lies in his starting point—thinking that he is, to borrow a phrase from Yancy, "an enclosed self-world unto itself."[26] He does not see "the self as facticity." It seems rather easy to methodologically push aside the body when his body is normative within his social matrix. Locked in his study with only his thoughts, he is unencumbered with caring for children, the sick, or the elderly. His inherited wealth affords him servants to look after the worries of physical existence. His Cartesian quest for certainty is a philosophical pursuit untethered from humanity, that is, from the concrete life in the streets affected by the vicissitudes of the world. The vast majority of the world's population would not pursue such a disembodied endeavor. Rather, they are well aware of how they are embodied since that embodiment conditions their identity and existence.

Once we grasp our embeddedness within a sociohistorical matrix, which we are shaped by discursive regimes, we can then consider fecund, transformative alternatives for pedagogical spaces. Critical pedagogy is not only about who teaches, what is read, and from what perspective. It is not only about experience. It is also about our epistemic lens, that is, how we interpret our experience. Part of what maintains the whiteness of philosophy is the normalizing process in which what topics or problems are discussed, what books are read, what assignments are meant to assess, how class time is managed, and so on work to the benefit of whites. In response, a transformative maneuver demands the acknowledgment that context matters. "Context," Yancy writes, "is fundamentally related to how we come to construct what a philosophical problem looks like. To forget this, it seems to me, nurtures the illusion that philosophers are 'pure' minds capable of standing nowhere."[27] Our thinking is always from somewhere and so too is our writing. The deployment of texts we discuss at conferences or teach in the classroom is value-laden and the vast majority of these will reflect the perceptual expectations of white philosophers. For example, if one were to survey popular textbooks used in ethics courses, one would likely find excerpts that discuss torture but not racist policing, terrorism but not xenophobia, global poverty but not white supremacist capitalism. What these textbooks tell us is which concerns are important and which are unimportant to everyday life. To love wisdom is a practical endeavor and our ethical concerns should arise out of our lived experience. To the point, these textbooks leave the impression that the oppression of People of Color does not merit our utmost attention. In other words, what we read is often the explicit or implicit reflection of the author's (or teacher's) own racialized experience. I once heard a senior colleague claim that he missed the "good old days" when America was close to "reaching its ideals" and only the best went to college, to which I asked for clarification. I replied with something sarcastic and raised concerns about antiblack racist policies and practices from loan discrimination to school segregation. His response vexed me: "Those things weren't part of my childhood. In fact, that stuff has been blown out of proportion." Notice that his racialized experience stood as representative of American life as a whole; his epistemic lens purported to be the only lens through which one ought to interpret reality.

When we teach, what is our aim? Are we truly investigating and reflecting upon reality as it is experienced by many, what sorts of people we wish to be, and upon what kinds of fellow humans we ought to be? For Yancy, we should generate *krisis*, that is, we should collaborate on creating spaces in which we, both teachers and students, must make a decision about what political imaginary we want to become reality. White students who honestly face a *krisis* will have to tarry with both "the sense of loss . . . that militates against centering whiteness in the form of a guilt-ridden and pitied white subject" and "the pain and suffering that people of color endure because of the effects of the historical sedimentation of white modes of being."[28] I facilitate a conversation with my students that engages them on multiple levels, namely, their understanding of the history of ideas (as well as practices and institutions), their current awareness of their own thrownness into a world already conditioned by race-thinking, and their imagination of a world otherwise. Thinking practically, we ought not be surprised if our students avoid discussing race. Like many of us, they try to keep a distance from conflict, particularly if that conflict involves self-examination and dealing with the mess we/they find. Rarely, if ever, will we find the white student who is a classical, overt racist, but frequently will we face the goodwill white student. Janine Jones claims that

> goodwill whites define racism simply as racial prejudice. By not understanding racism as a system of advantage based on race, the goodwill white avoids the considerable pain, guilt, and shame that might be elicited by a definition of racism that clarifies how she benefits from racism and perhaps serves as an active, intentional though unconscious, participant in it.[29]

By relegating racism only to the beliefs and/or actions of the overt racist, goodwill whites claim ignorance of their being implicated within a white normative, white supremacist society. To bring students to a point of decision, we need to help them think metaphilosophically about their own racial inheritance and how that affects them as well as others.

Rather than sanctuaries for whiteness, havens of the transcendental norm, our classrooms should be more like workshops. If we are successful with our aim, then white students will experience unsuturing, which is "a deeply embodied phenomenon that enables whites to come to terms with the realization that their embodied existence and embodied identities are always already inextricably linked to a larger white racist social integument or skin which envelops who and what they are."[30] This will not be a one-off event, not one decision that stands forever; rather, unsuturing requires renewal as well as vigilance to guard against the insidious return of whiteness as dominative.

Seeking to remove white denial, we will confront resistance since most students recognize racism as an individual matter rather a systemic one. It is tough for whites to chisel themselves out of the cemented falsity of whiteness. "The truth," Yancy writes, "is that by the time you realize that something has gone awry within our white racist polity, white racism has already etched its way into your psyche and become part of your very embodiment."[31] This is one reason Yancy calls us to fearless speech or *parrhesia*. Teacher-scholars need to courageously name whiteness wherever we encounter it before our students will hopefully realize their own encrusted, embodied embeddedness within white supremacy. Furthermore, students must accept the call to be vulnerable, to be open to the productive rupture of their sense of self-certainty. We should be aware that classrooms are already (epistemically) violent to People of Color, especially when they become victims of white denial. People of Color, Yancy explains, "confront whiteness in their every lives, not as an abstract concept but in the form of embodied [racism]."[32] White denial also impedes white students from coming to terms with the ubiquity of white supremacy or their privilege that arises from it. To risk being vulnerable with the hope of personal and communal growth, students must grasp their own historicity and contingency.

The practice of philosophy involves encouraging students to ask questions of the world and themselves that they have not asked before. White students are likely not to have analyzed their own racial embodiment with much depth. Yancy claims, "To encourage white people to understand how they benefit from structures of white racist power that are historically grounded, pervasive, subtle, and often invisible to them, is actually an encouragement to enlarge their consciousness and to see the world with greater clarity, especially in terms of its complexity."[33] We should not let education be solely about exposing students to the curriculum but about how to integrate embodied practices from the classroom into their daily lives. Students already enter having already participated in the world; they are already actors within a social framework. We ought to encourage them to tap into that lived experience in fecund, reflective ways.

PEDAGOGICAL MUSINGS

Education is not only about what we *think* but, more importantly, how we *live*. Yancy and I both desire for our "students to be gadflies, troublemakers, and fearless speakers (or *parrhesiastes*) when it comes to whiteness."[34] Let me conclude with a few brief points about pedagogy, which I hope will challenge us to think more deeply about how we frame our courses and how we flesh these out in classroom conversations.

• Listen to Multiple Voices

In *Black Feminist Thought*, Patricia Hill Collins claims that advocating for situated knowledge is not the same as advocating for relativism.[35] The latter treats all knowledge claims as equally valid. For Collins, however, one's position in the social matrix grants a particular perspective, and some perspectives give better insight into the phenomenon under investigation. "It is important,"

Yancy writes, "that one changes the medium itself—the way both philosophical discourse and philosophical performance are enacted."[36] Do our classrooms perform a genuine dialogue or do they merely offer a cacophony of synchronous monologues in which whiteness is not named or challenged?

- Reject Tokenism

We should not pride ourselves for including one diverse voice in the syllabus. And we should not allow "alternative philosophical voices [to be] treated as sideshow performances in philosophical exotica"; in other words, throwing in some "diversity" here and there in our courses is insufficient.[37] Alternative voices ought to subvert the normative assumptions and historical underpinnings of what counts as philosophy.

- Let Go of Our Masks

We are all works in progress. We need to model and be transparent about our own experience of race and racism. At the same time, we must accept that we are not the cause of students' progress and that our function is to encourage them to remove their own masks.

- Move From What *Is* the Case to What *Ought* to Be the Case

Does the education we provide help students better navigate the vicissitudes of life? Our embodied practices in the classroom should provide training for how to imagine and create a better future.

Chapter 10

The Courage to Be a Killjoy

George Yancy's Gift to Social Justice Educators

Barbara Applebaum

> Not everything that is faced can be changed, but nothing can be changed until it is faced.
>
> —James Baldwin

There is a shelf in my personal library exclusively designated for books authored, edited, or coedited by George Yancy—the books are packed so tightly that they barely fit. And I do not even own all of his books (I count twenty-three on his current website[1] and more to come). Along with the countless scholarly articles and book chapters he has written, the influential essays and provocative interviews that appeared in the *New York Times* philosophy column, "The Stone," not to mention presentations too numerous to reference here, Yancy's role as an erudite academic philosopher and as a prolific public intellectual is indisputable. It is not only the sheer quantity of his work that is striking but, more significantly, its quality, as will become apparent in what follows. As a white woman who teaches graduate courses to education students focusing on the ways in which whiteness/white supremacy impacts the lives of students through education, Yancy's scholarship has become an indispensable part of my pedagogical tool kit and also a vital aid in my own understanding of how whiteness impacts *what* I teach and *how* I teach.

In this chapter, I inquire: Why should social justice educators be interested in George Yancy's work? According to Özlem Sensoy and Robin DiAngelo, social justice educators "guide students in critical analysis of the presentation of mainstream knowledge as neutral, universal, and objective . . . guide students in critical self-reflection of their own socialization into structured relations of oppression and privilege . . . [and] guide students in developing the skills with which to see, analyze, and challenge relations of oppression and privilege."[2] One of the intractable challenges facing social justice educators involves balancing the needs and academic interests of all students but, most significantly, checking that the pedagogical needs of white students are not privileged and re-centered. Encouraging the systemically privileged to engage in learning about their complicity in maintaining systems of racial injustice, while at the same time also attending to the needs and academic interests of students of color, has been a difficulty that many social justice educators encounter.

George Yancy's scholarship can help social justice educators negotiate that challenge and form a basis for students to examine such important concepts as racial embodiment, racial battle fatigue, epistemic injustice, Black resistance, white denials, white fragility, and white complicity. Yancy's earlier projects, *Black Bodies, White Gazes: The Continuing Significance of Race*[3] and *Look, a White!: Philosophical Essays on Whiteness,*[4] will be my main focus. However, Yancy's book *Backlash: What Happens When We Talk Honestly about Racism in America*[5] will also be examined because it serves as a courageous model for dealing with the hostile response often launched at those who challenge whiteness/white supremacy. The book describes the personal costs of writing a fearless letter of love calling white people to critically engage with their whiteness. Borrowing a concept from Sara Ahmed,[6] I maintain that Yancy offers us an exemplar who has the courage to be a killjoy and offers educators "post-hope" in very trying political times.

Before I turn to those insights, I want to briefly preface this chapter with the unique type of philosopher I take Yancy to be. Yancy recognizes that whiteness is reproduced when only abstract argumentation is what counts as "doing philosophy." Traditional philosophical methods contribute to the invisibility of whiteness/white supremacy because race and other social markers are considered irrelevant to such theorizing. It is not only that most philosophers in the so-called West ignore the rich philosophical traditions of many parts of the world but also that traditional philosophical methods of inquiry have been obscurant. Along with other philosophers of race, Charles Mills,[7] who makes Blackness visible in traditional liberal theory, exposes the colorblindness of white-normed, Western philosophical inquiry. Building on Mills, Arnold Farr explains that "there is no white perspective (in philosophy) but only the universal, impartial, disinterested view from nowhere."[8] Yet whiteness/white supremacy, in fact, matters in the very problematic way the issue of race is considered in traditional philosophy because from the perspective of color-blind inquiry it becomes almost unimaginable to critically examine the white norms that influence the discipline and its methods of inquiry.

Yancy's inspiring and multifaceted theorizing makes these critiques concrete because he begins with the quotidian, the place of lived embodied experience that can be ignored when analyzed by an abstract, individualist, and ahistorical theoretical lens. Because racism is not only about a set of beliefs but is embedded in white habits or practices that whites can remain oblivious to, reasoned arguments must be complimented with "forms of expressive discourse that unsettle us, that make us uncomfortable with a daring frankness that pulls us even as it unnerves."[9] Yancy's writing demonstrates that in order to disrupt white habits and practices, philosophy must embrace the passionate. Being passionate is further expanded when Yancy advocates parrhesia or courageous speech that is not unmoved and personally risk-free but rather necessitates vulnerability and the willingness to stay in moments of discomfort. To study Black embodiment and white supremacy, philosophers must be willing to use fearless methods of inquiry.

Yancy's philosophy is passionately "real" in the sense that it starts from social reality as experienced by the systemically marginalized and also in that it is philosophy that can make a real difference. When philosophy ignores lived experience and is ahistorical, it becomes, as Michael Peters puts it, a site of bad faith and "is just as well dead, devoid of relevance, devoid of particularity, and escapist."[10] As one who was trained in philosophy, Yancy is a model of what I consider to be philosophy at its best.

UNDER THE WHITE GAZE: HOW DOES IT FEEL TO BE BLACK IN WHITE SPACES?

Like many who teach about racial injustice, I was searching for material for my graduate course that would assist me in exposing the ways that whiteness impacts my white students *and* my students of color when I came across Yancy's *Black Bodies, White Gazes*. In this book, Yancy exposes the relationship between the white gaze and Black embodiment. It is a project that reaches an audience of diverse racial positionalities. While refusing to reduce the Black body to the white gaze, Yancy articulates the *systematic* confiscation of the Black body by the white gaze, thus demonstrating how the white gaze is implicated in the continuing oppression of Black people. Yancy sheds light on what it feels like to be Black in white spaces—more specifically, to *become* Black via the white gaze. At the same time by focusing on the white gaze, this remarkable book also reveals what it means to be white, challenging white students to critique the myth of the "transcendental norm" of whiteness and to acknowledge their role in sustaining its invisibility.

Yancy offers a variety of rich illustrations of how the Black body is confiscated in the quotidian, everyday level of social interaction. The "elevator effect," for instance, describes what happens when Yancy's body enters an elevator occupied by a white woman who seemingly instinctively clutches her purse. Yancy explains that "the corporeal integrity of my Black body undergoes an onslaught as the white imaginary, which centuries of white hegemony have structured and shaped, ruminates over my dark flesh and vomits me out in a form not in accordance with how I see myself."[11] Regardless of what he is wearing or any of his own actions, he becomes "Black" flush with criminality, a predator to be feared, within the contours of her seeing him. Her "seeing," Yancy explains, is really a form of reading, whether she is aware of it or not.[12]

Yancy scrutinizes both sides of the coin—how the white gaze confiscates the corporal integrity of the Black body but also how the white body is "a prisoner of (its) own historically inherited imaginary and the habitual racist performances that have become invisible to (the white individual)."[13] In other words, the white gaze that constitutes the Black body also constitutes white being as innocent. As he puts it, "Not only does the white woman in the elevator ontologically freeze my 'dark' embodied identity but she also becomes ontologically frozen in her own embodied (white) identity. . . . Her performances reiterate the myth of the proverbial white victim at the hands of the Black predator."[14] Powerfully and succinctly, Yancy claims, "she performs her white body, ergo, I 'become' the predatory Black."[15] The emphasis on performativity underscores that "racist actions are habits of the body and not simply cognitively false beliefs."[16] Moreover, he exposes that racial interpellation is relational.

In a compelling articulation of white complicity, Yancy brings home the idea that even white students who believe they are antiracist can act "whitely" and, in doing so, are the "vehicle through which such practices get performed and sustained."[17] This is only one of the systematic and reiterative white practices that enact violence on Black bodies in ways that obscure their own production and simultaneously conceal the reproduction of white as good, pure, and innocent.

My students of color find that Yancy's work speaks to them. I can use Yancy's books and articles as a springboard to discuss concepts such as epistemic injustice,[18] and especially willful hermeneutical ignorance[19] that can lead to racial battle fatigue.[20] For example, Yancy critically examines numerous responses ("what if . . . ?") that he has received when he relates what happens to him in the elevator. While not shrinking into doubt,[21] he wonders how he might be mistaken in an interpretation of an experience that Black men collectively have experienced throughout time. He also recounts how a student responds with alacrity and derision to his analysis of the elevator effect with an arrogant, "Bullshit!" White students have discursive strategies at their disposal to dismiss, deny, and/or refuse to engage with what Yancy tells them and they employ them because the critique of whiteness implicates them in ways that threaten their racial innocence. Whites presume, as Yancy elucidates, that "when it comes to the complexity and depth of their own racism, they possess the capacity for absolute epistemic clarity and that the self is transparent, fully open to inspection."[22] This presumed sense of mastery inhibits the vulnerability that is required to be open to change.

My white students find Yancy helpful because he acknowledges that the challenge for white antiracism is the need to "(destabilize) the center while still remaining in it."[23] Yancy examines the reproduction of whiteness as "ambush" referring to the ways in which, even as whites consciously attempt to move against racism, they/we are suddenly ambushed by their whiteness. In other words, it refers to the insidious ways in which power is habitually enacted even by "good" white people who strive for racial justice. "To be white in America," Yancy states, "is to be always already implicated in structures of power."[24] There is "no place called 'innocence,'"[25] because there is no outside of power. That is why the undoing of whiteness must remain an ongoing process. Yancy advocates vigilance because, as long as white supremacy exists, there can be no such thing as a white antiracist who has "arrived." Disarticulating the white gaze, according to Yancy, involves a continuous effort on the part of whites to forge new ways of seeing, knowing, and being.[26] Yancy compels the white readers to move beyond the frameworks of meaning by which one traditionally interprets experience and to stay with the discomfort of doing so.

FLIPPING THE SCRIPT: RETURNING THE WHITE GAZE

In *Look, a White!*, a kind of sequel to *Black Bodies, White Gazes*, Yancy unflinchingly takes white people as the object to be examined rather than as the subject who examines. Like bell hooks,[27] who reveals whiteness as represented in the Black imagination, this relocation of the problem from the focus on people of color to the white person is meant to encourage white people to get a glimpse of themselves in the mirror of the Black gaze. By flipping the script, Yancy aims to name and mark whiteness so that whites can consider how they are the problem of racism—*especially* when they perceive themselves to be good and innocent. For "good" whites to see themselves as a problem is a first step in creating a transformative relationship to whiteness and new existential possibilities for being in the world.

Many of the cases that Yancy examines are personal and about his encounters as a Black professor in predominantly white university spaces. He addresses how "doing philosophy-in-Black" he is often read as an "angry Black professor" and how the descriptor "angry" is a form of dismissal.

> For him, I was simply angry, my judgment was clouded, and therefore my philosophical observations were nugatory. It was about *my* anger, *my* inability to discard cumbersome and misplaced (perhaps even fabricated) charged emotions

that for him were clearly the real problem. . . . In other words, "I see an angry black professor!" can be theorized as an instance of distancing whiteness from examination and critique, of safeguarding whiteness. Hence, "I see an angry black professor!" can be described as the deployment (whether consciously or unconsciously) or a white "distancing strategy [to] avoid being positioned as racist or implicated in systemic oppression."[28]

Most significantly, Yancy's analysis can help white students understand how distancing strategies[29] seem normal, everyday, and how the desire to evade, to escape, becomes rationalized. Further contextualizing and supplementing the discussion of this part of the book by assigning the work of Audre Lorde[30] and Sara Ahmed[31] on the anger of women of color can lead to engaging and stimulating discussions.

Yancy shares many of the pedagogical practices that he employs in the classroom to challenge white students to interrogate their feelings of comfort and security. Quoting from the work of Zeus Leonardo and Ronald Porter,[32] Yancy explains that "if we are truly interested in racial pedagogy, then we must become comfortable with the idea that for marginalized and oppressed minorities, there is no safe space. . . . Violence is already there."[33]

Consonant with his attempts to flip the script, Yancy underscores that the pedagogical push for "safe spaces" functions as a way to "suppress serious and probing questions that interrogate 'sacred' boundaries."[34] Yancy fearlessly acknowledges the turbulent nature of social justice pedagogy and how white discomfort can offer teachable moments. Yancy calls for dangerous spaces rather than safe spaces in order to inspire students to engage in parrhesia or fearless speech that requires vulnerability and the possibility of loss. As a white woman who has been socialized to avoid conflict, Yancy's counsel of staying in the moment of disturbance, especially when one desires to escape, has become a crucial guide to my pedagogy.

Yancy borrows from the work of Judith Butler[35] in order to facilitate our understanding of the type of subjectivity that can lead to the necessary characteristics for "doing whiteness differently." Butler contends that subjectivity is not a site of complete self-possession but rather a site of dispossession.[36] As Butler puts it, "My body is and is not mine."[37] Yancy employs Butler's notion of the opacity of the subject to explicate his notion of the embedded white racist that good white people refuse to concede. Acknowledging opacity can be a source of insight that can take the form "I don't know myself as I thought I had" or "I am other to myself despite my assumptions to the contrary."[38] This hints at some of the ways that white students can challenge racism because if whites grant that one is not the "ego-logical sovereign that governs its own meaning, definition and constitution,"[39] it might encourage them/us to develop the humility and vulnerability that paves the ground for fearless listening and learning.

Yancy proposes as crucial aspects of antiracist work that whites acknowledge the opacity of the embedded white racist and that whites "tarry" with the discomfort of contemplating one's complicity in racist structures. Yancy powerfully points to a move that is *too quick* to counter and that forfeits the possibility to learn. Instead, he entreats whites to *delay* the counter questions (the what ifs?) and stay in the moment of discomfort, uncertainty, and vulnerability long enough to hear what people of color are trying to tell them. In a discussion of microaggressions in his classroom, a Black student shares her painful experience of being labeled as "the Black girl" and a white student quickly adds that she understands the Black girl's experience because she lived in a neighborhood where she was referred to as the "white girl." Yancy underscores the swiftness of the white student's response and what it means.

> There was the alacrity, the rush. . . . However, this form of "identification" forced a conflation that both undermined the uniqueness of the black student's experience of what she was as an instance of white terror, and it obfuscated the specific power and privilege of the historical uniqueness of white racism. The white student placed under erasure the reality and gravitas of the black student's experience of whiteness as terror by shifting the discussion away from the black student's experience to *her own* (white) situation of being an object of insult in a black neighborhood. "I am just like you" also suggested that there is nothing special about being white (or black for that matter) in America, despite the fact that America is a country predicated on white privilege and white power.[40]

The white student could not hear what was being communicated because she too quickly re-centered her own experience. It is important to note that it is not that Yancy is rejecting the possibility of disagreement and critique. Rather, his point is to interrogate when white responses move too quickly ("the alacrity, the rush") and as a result diverts attention from and, indeed, conceals, what needs to be interrogated.

Tarrying with the embedded and opaque white racist self implies that while white bodies are vehicles of power, there is also the possibility of "doing whiteness differently" by welcoming difficult learning about one's limited vision and one's complicity in racism. Yancy insists that his aim is to get whites "not to rush past the question of accountability or responsibility."[41] Only by being willing to tarry with discomfort can whites "hear" the experiences of people of color and, consequently, work together to fight unjust systems that create and maintain suffering. Yancy's call for whites to stay in the moment of discomfort and not run away is, in and of itself, a first step to doing whiteness differently.

Social justice educators would do well to be interested in Yancy's work because of his efforts to illuminate what it means to be Black under the white gaze but also because of his unrelenting efforts to expose whiteness to white people. It goes without saying that George Yancy's emotionally provocative and intellectually stimulating scholarship has been an inspiration for me and that his work has been so vital to who I am as a white educator. There is one more way that Yancy's scholarship has been a model for my pedagogy that I want to conclude with in the final section.

THE COURAGE TO BE A KILLJOY: EDUCATION WITHOUT HOPE?

At the end of 2015, after he had conducted and published a series of important interviews on race in the *New York Times* online forum, "The Stone," with contemporary philosophers and public intellectuals, Yancy contributed what he refers to as a letter of love titled "Dear White America," presenting white people with a "gift" urging them to challenge the inherent whiteness that shapes their/our existence. In this letter of love, Yancy urges white people to listen with love, not "the Hollywood type of love, but the scary kind, the kind that risks not being reciprocated."[42] Quoting James Baldwin, Yancy contends it is the type of love that "takes off the masks that we fear we cannot live without and know that we cannot live within."[43]

As a way to model what he is asking white people to do, Yancy, daringly vulnerable, draws a parallel between his complicity in sexism and white people's complicity in racism. He is sexist, Yancy acknowledges, simply because he is a man who benefits from a patriarchal society even if this is not his intent. "This doesn't mean that I intentionally hate women,"[44] he explains. "It means that despite my best intentions, I perpetuate sexism every day of my life."[45] Yancy has learned to struggle to disrupt sexism every day in his life and cannot cease from doing so until systemic and structural patriarchy is eradicated. In displaying his vulnerability, he hoped that white people would be willing to do the same and acknowledge how whiteness is a way of being embodied and a way of being ("it is a lie that is so intimate that *it is you*"[46]) that has "a multitude of ways of hiding from the white view."[47] Racism is not only about neo-Nazis and the Alt-Right; racism is maintained and reproduced by all white people even when, especially when they believe they are "good."

The letter quickly went viral. The deluge of negative responses that he received lasted over a year. They were refusals of the gift, refusals to listen with love. These responses were not only hostile and vulgar but also viciously violent, attacking his intelligence and his character, and even threatening his life. Yancy explicates how the written words and phone messages he received "carry the vestiges of the bloody and brutal contexts in which they were animated."[48] *Backlash* is Yancy's attempt not only to make public the costs of fearless speech but also to once again engage "good white people" and help them/us to recognize the depth and pervasiveness of white supremacy, drawing attention to the ways in which their/our complicity maintains and upholds systemic racial injustice.

Attempting not to coddle his white readers but also wrestling with them to engage, Yancy acknowledges how disorienting and even painful it is to tarry with discomfort. Yet such discomfort is necessary for the development of new ways of being white that "move you to action, to fight for a world in which whiteness, your whiteness, ceases to violate me, Black people, and people of color."[49] After all he has experienced, Yancy continues to engage with white people adding that he "can't be a pessimist, because I'm alive . . . (even though) being alive feels like borrowed time."[50] In a number of interviews, Yancy grapples with hope versus pessimism but lands on the side of "post-hope or post-optimism that results in a realism that musters enough strength that says, 'We refuse to wait another day!'"[51]

Asking students to compare and contrast Yancy's last chapter in *Backlash* to Reni Eddo-Lodge's *Why I'm No Longer Talking to White People about Race*,[52] as well as with recent work in the area of epistemic injustice that addresses willful hermeneutical ignorance[53] and contributory injustice,[54] can bear interesting fruits. Willful hermeneutical ignorance involves marginalized resources that are readily available to the systemically privileged, but the latter refuse to give these resources uptake. It is a way that the dominantly situated dismiss epistemic resources that make sense of our social world. Dotson refers to this as to contributory injustice in which the framework of intelligibility that is derived from the gaze of the marginalized is denied admittance into dominant epistemic schemes. What does it mean to do social justice education in these contexts? Given Yancy's experience, what would he say?

Sara Ahmed, who also insists on using theory in an embodied way, critically examines the pejorative trope of "killjoy" that feminists are often labeled with and turns it into a sacred aspiration.[55] The killjoy is courageously willing to disrupt myths of happiness that reproduces femininity and compel women to "give up having a will of one's own."[56] In other words, a feminist is a killjoy because she makes people uncomfortable and challenges people to critically reflect on their investments in happiness and also critically reflect on their investments in comfort. A feminist killjoy is willing to acknowledge how models of happiness may depend on the oppression of others. To be a feminist, then, is to be willing to make trouble. As Ahmed explains, "To become feminist is to kill other people's joy, to get in the way of other people's investments."[57] Ahmed describes the killjoy as someone who is willing to point out injustices and take the risk of being blamed for the problem rather than blaming the injustices.

This latter point connects to one of the costs of being a killjoy. Ahmed exhorts us to inquire whether the feminist killjoy is the one who causes bad feelings or if she merely exposes the bad feeling that already exists but is concealed. She narrates a story about the family dinner table and voicing her disagreement with a problematic remark made by someone in her family. Instantly, the happy mood recedes and the atmosphere is drenched in silent bad feeling. But was it the killjoy who caused the bad feeling or was it the family member who made the remark that brought negativity into the room? Feminists are often attributed as the origin of bad feelings, as the ones who ruin the atmosphere, as if by exposing the problem one becomes the problem. Ahmed admonishes us to remember the real source of a problem. Most significantly, Ahmed explains that being a killjoy means to be willing to kill not only others' joy but also *one's own*, to be willing to challenge even our own comforts, our own investments in joy. George Yancy is a model of a killjoy who has endured the terrorizing costs of challenging white people with love and yet, with love, he continues to educate white people. In addition, he has been willing not only to kill the joys of others but also to critically examine his own positionality as a man.

Just like feminist philosophers and feminist philosophers of color have exposed the non-neutrality of philosophical inquiry and contributed to making philosophy more useful for exploring gender norms and the intersection of gender and race, philosophers of race, like Yancy, have revealed the whiteness of philosophy and compels philosophy to turn a critical eye on itself. As a philosophical killjoy, Yancy daringly and boldly challenges the racial innocence of philosophy. Moreover, he inspires philosophers to recognize that the empirical is significant for the theoretical.

Why should social justice educators be interested in George Yancy's work? If the aforementioned is not a sufficiently compelling answer, I quote from Cornel West's foreword to *Backlash* in which he describes Yancy as "one of the few distinguished public philosophers willing to get his hands dirty in the muck and mire of white supremacy in contemporary America."[58] I hope this chapter makes clear why Yancy's scholarship is an essential material for social justice educators.

Chapter 11

George Yancy's Embodied Critical Space of Antiracist Praxis

E. Lâle Demirtürk

George Yancy is a leading international scholar whose work provides a foundation not only for academics working on race across the United States but also for those of us working in non-Western social and cultural geographies. Yancy provides us with the conceptual tools to understand, to see through, and to fight against racial injustice on both a personal and institutional level. More than anyone else, George Yancy has worked to deconstruct Black lived experience, exposing how the binary logics of racism are reproduced through discursive practices that render the Black body a site of evil and criminality in the white imaginary. As a socially engaged philosopher, Yancy's major contribution has been to critically deconstruct the ideology of Whiteness and its impact on Black lived experience in order to help build a democratic social change in the United States.

In the following response I have chosen to focus on the ways in which Yancy's work has impacted my own scholarship and has guided me as a writer and as a teacher in Turkey over the years. Because Yancy's work speaks to his audience on many different levels—from the philosophical, to the structural, to the personal—I have tried to respond in kind. My hope is that in detailing the profound influence of Yancy's work on my own scholarship and thinking I will pay homage to the ways in which his work resonates, not only across racial boundaries but also across place.

As a literary critic, my work on the contemporary African American novel aims to conceptualize the normative invisibility of whiteness through the study of African American literary texts. In so doing, it draws together insights from across a range of disciplines, such as Critical Whiteness Studies, Critical Philosophy of Race, and African American literary studies. Since my central area of concern is the discursive practices of whiteness that affect Black characters in everyday social encounters, I have drawn on Yancy's work extensively in my critical analysis of literary fiction. In particular, I have utilized Yancy's conceptualization of how the ideology of whiteness works through white embodied discursive practices that affect the Black body. Yancy's theories and concepts in the area of Critical Philosophy of Race have helped me to think through what is at stake in interpersonal encounters in a racist context, while impressing upon me the significance of understanding the lived experience of Black people who are racialized by the white embodied gaze.

In this chapter, I discuss George Yancy's earlier and more recent work highlighting the configuration of whiteness as a transcendental norm, and the ways in which this configuration shapes the everyday embodied discursive practices of white people. In so doing, this chapter explores how Yancy's work has provided me as a scholar-teacher with an awareness of the ways in which lived experiences are shaped by a racial context in everyday life. Even though I am not working in the field of philosophy, Yancy's work has long been an integral part of my research for many different reasons. First, his work has helped me to understand how whiteness operates in invisible but insidious ways in shaping our social relations across the color line in everyday life. Second, Yancy situates his philosophical discourse on Whiteness in close relationship to the existing sociocultural context, offering his own embodied critical perspective as a Black man. Third, he exposes what it means to be Black in a society in which whiteness functions as "the transcendental norm,"[1] privileging whiteness and white people as ideal and virtuous while framing Black people as both deviant and criminal. Such a norm "reduces the Black body to a wretched particularity."[2] These insights culminate in Yancy's radical critique of whiteness operating as "a center from which one . . . makes sense of things, evaluates and judges, remains invisible while the discursive field of white power/knowledge continues to open up a social space of intelligibility in terms of which the black/white body appears."[3]

As a Turkish woman scholar who teaches undergraduate courses to students seeking to learn about how race shapes the social imaginary in the United States, Yancy's scholarship has been an invaluable resource that has helped me to see how whiteness impacts my own understanding of what I teach. Yancy's work has helped me to conceptualize Black lived experience, and to appreciate the ways in which racial structures of power are embodied in the real social world, much like their counterparts in the novels I discuss in my work. Yancy's work has also helped me to begin class discussions about race-related topics with my undergraduate students in Turkey. Even though they do not share the same experiences as Black Americans, they make an effort to understand not only how present social relations in the United States are shaped by the ideology of whiteness but also the need to become "fearless speakers . . . when it comes to whiteness."[4]

WHITENESS AS THE TRANSCENDENTAL NORM AND CRITICAL REFLECTIONS

When I first began doing serious research in Critical Whiteness Studies, I, a Turkish scholar, was intrigued by George Yancy's comparison of the dehumanization and racialization of Iraqi male prisoners with that of Black people in American society, in his introduction to *White on White/Black on Black*. He described "a prisoner with a leash around his neck like a dog" as a way of talking about the dehumanization of Iraqi prisoners in close affinity with how Black people have been treated within white supremacist American society: "I found myself bombarded with thoughts of the racist historical processes of 'Niggerization' . . . that Blacks in North America have undergone."[5] That moment of reading an African American philosopher describe how the ideology of whiteness positioned "us" Middle-Easterners, racialized as people of color (sometimes even in spite of our white skin) began shaping my critical perspective in my own research on African American novels. It helped me to understand the broader damaging impacts of whiteness on the lived experiences of all of us across the globe who are deemed people of color by a white gaze. As I continued learning from Yancy's books, book chapters, articles, and interviews over the years, I continued to grapple with his insight into how "whiteness implicates (even a white anti-racist) in a structural white power system from which [s/he is] able to gain so many privileges."[6] Analyzing this white power structure, Yancy explains how the white police officers who killed Amadou Diallo, for instance, "acted replete with 'knowledge' about the black body as criminal, as rapacious, as a problem."[7] Finally, in his article on Toni Morrison's *The Bluest Eye*, Yancy opened my eyes to how I could examine a black character—that is, Pecola, whose self-destructive conception of her Black body as ugly demonstrates the ways in which a Black person can be impacted and injured by the power structure of whiteness. The emotional process of a young Black child's internalization of the destructive and unfulfillable desire to be white, Yancy argues, locates her as "a product of the power/knowledge nexus of whiteness. . . . Within the context of Morrison's *The Bluest Eye*, whiteness is a value code represented as constituting universal beauty. Pecola's body is negatively marked, shaped, and disciplined within a (*generative*) white normative semiotic field."[8] Insights such as these have enabled me to appreciate the ways in which African American novels offer a discourse of critique regarding the ideology of whiteness in their depictions of interracial social encounters.

Becoming familiar with Yancy's work has helped me to sharpen my ability to see through racist practices, even those performed unconsciously by, according to Yancy, "good white people."[9] In his phenomenal book *Black Bodies, White Gazes*, George Yancy argues that, since slavery in the United

States, "the Black body has been historically marked, disciplined, and scripted and materially, psychologically, and morally invested in to ensure . . . white supremacy."[10] In other words, the brutal enslavement, lynching, and rape of Black bodies have shaped a historical and social context that testifies to "the insidious nature of whiteness,"[11] a nature that continues to manifest through different forms of oppression and racism in contemporary everyday life. Yancy explains how the white gaze produces a surveilled social space in which the "*Black body* has been confiscated."[12] The meaning of Yancy's blackness has been shaped by the white gaze, "a *structured* way of 'seeing' mediated by racist norms and values, which interpellates the Black as that which is epistemologically and ontologically 'given.'"[13] The white gaze is informed by the white imaginary, which violates the humanity of Yancy's Black body by viewing it through "the medium of historically structured forms of 'knowledge' that regard it as an object of suspicion."[14] Unlike those Black bodies "confiscated from Africa," his own body, Yancy explains, "is confiscated within social spaces of meaning construction and social spaces of transversal interaction that are buttressed by a racist value-laden episteme."[15]

This concept is further explored in Yancy's description of the "elevator effect," where he finds himself alone in an elevator with a white woman, a situation that makes her nervous. The elevator is a socially shared space where the white woman demonstrates through uncomfortable bodily comportment her unease at finding herself alone with a Black man; she clutches her purse to protect herself while avoiding direct eye contact. To her, Yancy's Black body represents a criminal threat rather than a human being with a dynamic subjectivity, reminding him that he can never be free of "the historical power of the white gaze, a perspective that carries the weight of white racist history and everyday encounters of spoken and unspoken anti-Black racism."[16] For Yancy, the elevator is a microsocial space which mimics "the larger social macrocosm of problems in Black and white," as the white woman's embodied white imaginary constitutes his "Blackness *as* evil."[17] He sees her as "a prisoner of her own historically inherited imaginary and the habitual racist performances that have become invisible to her."[18] As Yancy explains, the white woman is not necessarily aware of the racial schema informing her action or that "she has come to see herself as pure, civilized, innocent, and an easy victim of untamed Black men."[19]

The white embodied gaze in the elevator is "shaped through the power of whiteness as the transcendental norm," which perceives Yancy's Black body "as problematic and morally flawed." He emphasizes that the white woman needs to understand that racism is not an abstraction; she needs to understand that she herself is "the *vehicle* through which such practices get performed and sustained."[20] The woman's embodied white gaze, situated within the context of racial power relations, produces material effects on Yancy's body, leading to his self-perception as a kind of "phantom," who lives "between the interstices of my physical, phenotypically dark body and the white woman's gesticulatory performances."[21] The elevator scene shows us that the ideology of whiteness continues to shape everyday life and to generate material effects in the social world, as Yancy continues in an antiblack North American society "to *live* my body in Black within a culture where Blackness is still overdetermined by myths and presuppositions that fix my body as a site of danger."[22]

However, there is still hope for Black resistance in undoing whiteness: In a context where Black bodies suffer epistemic distortion and discursive erasure, Black resistance involves an affirmation of "the existential and ontological force of having a perspective, a subjectivity." In other words, the individual act of Black resistance is a moment of questioning "the philosophical anthropological assumptions of white racism, assumptions that deny the reality and complexity of Black self-determination, self-reflexivity, and interiority."[23] For Yancy to see himself beyond the white imaginary requires the affirmation of his subjectivity as an excess of the discursive confines of that imaginary, embracing "a form of Black humanity that has been denied."[24]

Reading *Black Bodies, White Gazes*, I came to see the ways in which whiteness directly impacts racialized Black bodies. Yancy explains that the Black body is "confiscated within social spaces of meaning construction"[25] simply because the spatiality of the white imaginary defines everyday social encounters. The spatiality of whiteness in urban spaces refers not only to discursive but also to physical and social practices of racial divisiveness. In my own work I have applied Yancy's concept of spatial nonbelonging, in the context of Black bodies operating in urban spaces, to understand how the Black characters in the novels I studied were subject to tense interactions with white people which fueled conflict both in and beyond the inner city. In this way, Yancy's phenomenological study of the Black body and his reflections on his own lived experiences with white people helped me to "know" Black characters in their interracial encounters. George Yancy's perception of the distorted view of the Black body as criminal vis-à-vis the white imaginary has helped me to deconstruct urban encounters between white racist characters and black urban residents. His work has enabled me to study the ways in which the Black counter-gaze in the face of a white imaginary is situated within the context of its lived experience, invoking dynamic, multiple, and complex Black subjectivities. The individual acts of Black resistance in performing Blackness otherwise are indicative of a self-narrative excess that exists beyond the normative constraints of the white imaginary. In all my research over the years, Yancy has recurrently opened new avenues of thinking that have profoundly influenced my intellectual journey. The discursive positioning of the Black body vis-à-vis the white imaginary in *Black Bodies,*

White Gazes continues to inspire and to challenge me, as do his insights in many other works, some of which are mentioned later.

In *Look, a White!*, for instance, Yancy explores how the Black body as inscribed in the white imaginary causes white people to feel vulnerable to danger, whereas the impact of being read as suspicious affects the Black man or woman who inevitably bears "an anterior guilt," for the meaning of his or her blackness is always linked to having done "something wrong."[26] Yancy suggests that Black people can subvert the white gaze and, in "flipping the script," can effectively render whiteness visible. This literal or figurative enunciation—"Look, a White!"[27]—can open new, antiracist spaces of recognition for white people, provided they are willing to face "the problem of whiteness."[28] Only then, through self-reflexivity, will they be better able to diagnose their complicity in "systemic racism."[29] As Yancy suggests, when they are forced to negotiate the "problem of whiteness," white people will have the opportunity to face their racist assumptions. In this respect, the insights of people of color will be "necessary to the project of [white people's] critically thinking through whiteness, because they are the ones who confront whiteness in their everyday life."[30] "Flipping the script," then, is an act of marking whiteness from the vantage point of Black people: "Black people and people of color thus strive to disarticulate the link between whiteness and the assumption of just being human, to create a critical slippage."[31]

What Yancy points to, here, as the need to value the discursive "cracks" in whiteness drove me to think more deeply about the need for white people to challenge the white imaginary through learning from Black people's experiential knowledge of whites. This challenge opens up the discursive space of possibility to disrupt whiteness by redefining the social reality as a site of normative privilege and power simply because whiteness "as an embedded set of social practices . . . render white people complicit in larger social practices of white racism."[32] While Yancy is aware of the embedded and psychically opaque dimensions of whiteness, he believes that the more white people become aware of how their whiteness impacts Black people and try to change their ways of thinking and doing whiteness, the more the embodied practices of the white imaginary can be importantly subverted and transformed. If white people attempt "to suspend their normative racist assumptions and look at their whiteness through the eyes of people of color they can contribute to social transformation."[33] There is hope that white people can use their privilege and power to challenge institutional racism in the social structures of the society, which reproduce themselves through interpersonal encounters in everyday life.

In his article "White Gazes: What It Feels Like to Be an Essence," Yancy expands on this possibility, arguing that white people need moments of breakdown to be encouraged to leave their comfort zones. White people, then, need more honest encounters with Black people in order "to be put into crisis vis-à-vis their whiteness."[34] Here too, Yancy explores the ways in which white people's sense of safety is produced through the "false construction" of the Black body as always already criminal within the structure of the white imaginary. The white construction of this false binary speaks to racial Manichean logics, since the white "fabricated space of safety" is contingent on "the false construction of the Black body as dangerous."[35] Paradoxically, white people render themselves deeply *dependent* upon Blackness for their construction of self at the same time as they wall themselves off against the possibility of living within the domain of shared, relational humanity. Hence, Yancy considers racial embodiment "within the context of white everyday power or hegemony," drawing attention to the ways in which Black lived experience "is dialectically linked to an account of whiteness and how whites construct Black bodies, how the latter are experienced as problematic bodies, as problem people."[36] As a result, constructed as an object "within the context of white anti-Black racism, Blacks were/are reduced to their bodies, bodies without subjectivity."[37]

This affective argument has enabled me to comprehend why interracial social interactions have taken a particular form in different scenes within the various novels that I have studied, both in my own work and with my students in the classroom. Reading Yancy's books over and over again for the classes I teach has impressed upon me the value and urgency of engaged thinking with others. His theorizing and discussions of his own personal experiences as a Black scholar with white individuals have helped me gain insight into the emotional and psychic impacts of racism, and the importance of developing a critical Black subjectivity.

THE CRITIQUE OF EVERYDAY LIFE AND POLICE KILLINGS

Yancy's direct, immediate responses to the current issues of racism demonstrate that he is an engaged public intellectual ready to take action in the wake of continued state-sanctioned violence against Black men, women, and children. This is a scholar who knows "how to break into the present" and "how to intervene in the present as opposed to merely submitting to it."[38] George Yancy's work has given me new ways of understanding how the everyday habits of whiteness are embedded in the increased police killings of predominantly unarmed Black men. These habits shape how Black bodies are read from the beginning as criminal and threatening, demonstrating that "White *gazing* is a violent process."[39] White people engage in "habituated embodied white racist practices," which are reinforced within everyday social

spaces and "further supported by deeply ingrained and sedimented historical, institutional structures."[40] In "The Violent Weight of Whiteness," Yancy
points to the ongoing existence of "many daily manifestations of black male
racialized trauma that whites fail or refuse to see."[41] One need only remember that the white police killings of predominantly Black unarmed men and
women caused by racial profiling are events that cannot be isolated from the
historical construction of Blackness in North America. These acts of murder
uncover the everyday violent practices of whiteness, revealing racist sensibilities intensified by "the distorted racist imago of the Black body in the white
imaginary, [as] sites of violence."[42] Black bodies are killed by white police
officers (and civilians) not because they pose a real threat but because they
are "by virtue of [their] Blackness, always already about to commit or cause
[physical violence]."[43] Given the history of Blackness in white-dominant
American society, the police killings of unarmed Black men mark "a form
of violence exercised through the corporeal and spatial policing of the Black
body."[44] Since whiteness functions as "corporeal entitlement to spatiality,"[45]
white police officers experience their autonomy by way of killing Black
people, whose very appearance in public space is already perceived as illicit.
The Black body in the white imaginary represents a criminal who has to be
"erased" from the public space, for the Black body is an intruder, "invading"
white spaces and hence disposable.

The white normative criminalization of racialized Black bodies, or what
Marcus Bell calls "the criminalization of blackness," is "both a habit of mind
and an institutional practice": "In contemporary US society, there are few
racial stereotypes that are more powerful and more pervasive than that of
the criminal black man."[46] This discursive criminalization of Blackness both
reinforces and expresses the assumption of Black bodies "not belonging"
in social space, while justifying the policing of such bodies. George Yancy
interprets these violent acts of targeting Black male bodies as demonstrating
the power that racial scripting holds over the Black male body as a site of
criminality. In his view, Black men are killed because they are conceptualized
and perceived as always already guilty through "the white racist historical
sedimentation of the white imago of the black body as inherently and unconsciously violent and cruel."[47] The discursive construction of the Black body is
fixed through "white gazes and white bodily forms of comportment."[48]

We are now living in the era of Trump, a president who has relied upon
the white/black binary as the basis of a racist public discourse that affects all
people of color, whose presence and problems he has swept under the rug
as the foundation of his presidential housekeeping. Even though, as George
Yancy's work convincingly demonstrates, American society has always been
terrorized by whiteness, we are still dumbfounded and haunted by the fact
that *overt racism* and a neo–Jim Crow white racist imaginary have been voted

into the U.S. presidency, not only embodied but also embraced wholeheart-edly by Donald Trump. Yancy sees the kinds of racial insults dispensed by Donald Trump online as his way of establishing and legitimizing even social media "as a site for harassing others."[49] Here, Yancy quotes Henry A. Giroux, who rightfully suggests that Trump's ideology of whiteness has lent increas-ing visibility to various white supremacist groups, "who have turned their hate-filled discourse into a weaponized element of political culture."[50] In fact, Trump, in "exemplifying white male dominance," comes to represent what Joe R. Feagin and Kimberley Ducey call "the *elite-white-male dominance system*," the "small ruling class [that] holds exceptional social rank and privi-leges, [enjoying] . . . more power than non-elite members of society."[51]

George Yancy's recent book *Backlash* effectively shows how white supremacy functions in the current moment. The book is based on Yancy's previously published letter, "Dear White America," which drew the uncon-trollable rage of white racist Americans who unabashedly responded with letters containing racist slurs and death threats, many using the n-word. These letters were written by those white people who were apparently perfectly at home with their racist values and views, until this sense of comfort was dis-rupted by Yancy's address. These threatening and insulting letters in reaction to Yancy's call for an antiracist society demonstrate the violent entitlement of the white imaginary embodied and activated by Donald Trump. Some of the letters written by white people were not simply insulting but actually con-tained threats to *kill* Yancy, demonstrating a movement from insidious covert racism to overt white supremacist violence. Such a response constituted an act of "*white terror*"[52] that did not only reduce Yancy to a mere Black body but also revealed the positioning of his Black body within the white imagi-nary, "the pervasive reality of pain experienced by Black people under white supremacy and their excruciating awareness of the ways of whiteness."[53] This incident powerfully demonstrates that the reproduction of discursive practices of whiteness has direct implications and material consequences for a Black person's life. The current conjuncture of white police killings of Black people in public has come to define twenty-first-century America as a "Trumpoc-racy,"[54] and no longer a democracy, although we must acknowledge that such practices were part of the deep fabric of North American society, long before the trumping of antiblackness made its way as ideological currency into the White House.

Yancy, one of the leading public intellectuals and philosophers in North America today, is seriously involved in what can be called "engaged activism for social change,"[55] taking part in antiracist praxis through both his publi-cations and his public talks and interviews. Yancy's response to the present conjuncture comes full circle with *Backlash*, for his articulation of his cou-rageous and ethical confrontation with white racists as an embodied Black scholar is important in helping those of us who follow his work to understand the real, lived costs of being a Black "renegade philosopher" in the academy. *Backlash* is the most recent and effective proof that George Yancy is running against danger, rather than running away from it. This is not because he is fearless. Rather, Yancy's consciousness of his vulnerability to the embodied violence of whiteness provides Yancy with a strong sense of fortitude and resistance that empowers him to be and remain human in the face of white dehumanization of Black people. In a racist world, Yancy shows us that being a Black antiracist renegade philosopher requires turning written work into antiracist praxis. His colossal work as a public intellectual has shown me that philosophy and literature, politics and action must go hand in hand.

Yancy's work challenges the comfortable, neoliberal belief that American society has become "postracial" through refusing to reduce white racism to individual prejudice or cultural misunderstanding. Instead, Yancy focuses on the white institutional and embodied racism, which has to change in order to end white supremacy. He is clear that while this racism may manifest through individual and sometimes unconscious embodied action, it neither begins nor ends with the individual. Yancy argues that the seeming invisibility of white racial thinking that goes "unmarked" has to be rendered visible if we are to "undo" it in order to change society for the better. Here Yancy is enacting what José Medina calls "epistemic resistance" to the "epistemic vices"[56] of white racist people. One such epistemic vice is white arrogance. While Yancy invites white racist people to explore the deadly costs of their habitual comfort zone vis-à-vis the Black body, he calls for the recognition of Black resistance "as epistemic virtue," rather than "as epistemic vice." Yancy knows that what is involved in resistance to white supremacy is the larger concern of "transforming a social imaginary."[57]

In his work, George Yancy has focused on the need for white individuals to risk vulnerability in seeking to know the world beyond the limits of their white gazes. This will involve, Yancy tells us, a willingness to become "un-sutured." To become "un-sutured," for Yancy, means to reopen and to confront a psychic wound that has been covered over. For white people, this means relinquishing one's sense of certainty and self-possession in order to come to terms with one's dependence on the larger social and historical structures of race. Yancy writes, "Un-suturing is a deeply embodied phenomenon that enables whites to come to terms with the realization that their embodied existence and embodied identities are always already inextricably linked to a larger white racist social integument." In order to engage in this kind of unsuturing, Yancy argues, white people will need to learn to practice self-criticality, so that they might begin to "challenge whiteness as the transcendental norm that actually conditions their perception of themselves as not needing to undo anything at all."[58] In *Black Bodies, White Gazes*, Yancy explains that being a white antiracist ally is a highly complicated struggle that involves "a self-reflexive moment of realization that people of color don't owe white people anything," as well as readiness for a moment of "suspension of self-certainty, arrogance, fear, and other-blaming" in order to strive for "a counter-hailing for anti-racist action."[59] I absolutely agree with Yancy's deconstruction of how even unconscious "habits of whiteness"[60] can safeguard white embodied lives at the expense of Black lives, because white people are inevitably invested in the systemic privileges they live by. Yancy suggests that it is possible for whites to become allies, so long as they learn to risk their normative values in moments of self-reflexivity in order to engage in the ongoing process of undoing their whiteness. In a very recent coedited book titled *Buddhism and Whiteness: Critical Reflections*, Yancy explains that it is imperative for white people to learn to love both themselves and people of color. In the introduction to the book, he writes: "If whiteness is a covered-over wound, then one must un-suture as an act of loving kindness and touch that wound. Indeed, mindfully, one must embrace that wound."[61]

Yancy's argument that white individuals' discriminatory practices are in fact socially structured and cannot be thought of in isolation from institutional racism is significant, while not excluding the hope to be found in new avenues for white American allies to engage in antiracist praxis. These "positive" instantiations of white progressive acts of fighting personal and institutional forms of racism can serve as positive role models for other white people, who can strive to locate material and discursive nonviolence, rather than violence, as the basis for a new configuration of white subjectivity and white institutional life. In addition, white people, Black people, people of color—indeed, all communities in American society—certainly need a broader sense of coalition if they are to make change possible, paving the way for the construction of new relations between the state and its racialized Black citizens.

George Yancy's decisive influence on my projects and classes is ongoing. His work continues to help me develop my critical perspective on the political implications of changing society at large. In addition, it is interesting to see how Yancy's theoretical framework, informed by his phenomenological explorations of Black subjectivity, fits neatly into the current conjuncture of ongoing activist struggles against white supremacy in Trump's America. George Yancy's work can help us all to better understand what is at stake in those white embodied discursive practices that seriously jeopardize the possibility of "undoing" the white governance of Black bodies in everyday life.

Part Four

RACE, WHITENESS, AND PHILOSOPHY

Chapter 12

Philosophy, Race, and Social Practices in George Yancy's Scholarship

Clarence S. Johnson

A central organizing theme in George Yancy's scholarship is the problematic nature of race and racial issues in general but with a specific focus on the United States. Historically, race discourse commenced in seventeenth-century science in which racial categories were created and structured in a hierarchy, with whites at the apex and, in descending order, Blacks at the base mediated by other racial groups.[1] On a superficial level, race was synonymous with color, in which whiteness was considered the ideal color of humans and blackness a degenerate color. However, on a substantive level, race (and racial categorization) entailed the supposed possession of certain inherent psychological, aesthetic, and moral attributes that were considered essential to, and correlated with, the various colors. Thus, for example, whiteness was considered the ideal human color and, as a necessary correlate, whiteness entailed (having) inherent superior intelligence, aesthetic pleasantness, and positive moral characteristics. By contrast, Blackness was deemed a degenerate color, and its instantiation in (question beggingly) quasi-cognitive entities entailed that such entities suffered from an inherent cognitive deficiency, were aesthetically unpleasant and inherently morally deficient. In sum, in the context of racial categorization, humanity was perfectly instantiated in whites and least instantiated in Blacks.[2]

This hierarchical structuring of racial categories has had severe social consequences universally, including in the United States, in light of this country's history with the enslavement of Africans that led to the creation of African Americans as an ethnic group. One of the unsavory consequences of this hierarchical racial caste system in the United States is that it largely accounts for the social inequities, in the form of white privilege and Black disadvantage, that permeate the institutional structures of the society. White privilege is the acquisition and conferring of benefits on a person who is white because of his or her white pigmentation and Black disadvantage is the denial of benefits to a person who is Black on account of the same—his or her black pigmentation. George Lipsitz has provided a thorough documentation and analysis of this racial distributive dynamic in his remarkable study, *The Possessive Investment in Whiteness*. This racial/social dynamic in the United States argues against the supposed egalitarian, meritocratic principle to which the society rhetorically lays claims.[3]

In focusing on this phenomenon of race as a central organizing feature of his scholarship, then, George Yancy calls attention to the social injustice that pervades the society whose victims, in light of this racial dynamic, are people of color. Of course, Yancy's focus on this issue is unsettling for some whites, as is clear from some of the hostile and even threatening responses Yancy has received on this score. (I take up this issue later.) However, as I show, such responses are to be seen as forms of resistance to Yancy's overarching aim, which is to hold up a mirror to the society as a whole, through the world of scholarship, thereby to facilitate a conversation about, and confront, this social reality itself and the injustice that it feeds. In other words, such responses manifest a reluctance by some whites to confront the reality of the injustice in which they participate wittingly or unwittingly. In light of this fact, then, my proposed aim in this study is to elaborate a few of the contours of Yancy's engagement with this issue of white racism in the United States and bring out the impact of his engagement with this issue on my own thinking on race and social injustice. To that end, I single out for special consideration what I regard as two of Yancy's most poignant discussions, namely, "The Elevator Effect" and "Whiteness as Ambush," both taken from his book *Black Bodies, White Gazes*.[4] Using these works as a springboard, I highlight the effect of Yancy's discussion on my own scholarship on race, and in doing so I draw attention to Yancy's challenge to white America in his recent "Dear White America."[5] Noting the hostile and inhospitable responses he has received to this challenge as emblematic of a deep-seated antiblack racial animus in the very interstices of the society at large, I proceed to question Yancy's optimistic outlook that he proffers as a resolution to the problematic nature of racism in the United States.

RACIAL DYNAMIC IN CLOSE PROXIMITY

In the tradition of luminary Black liberation philosophers, theologians and social activists such as W. E. B. Du Bois, Frederick Douglass, Sojourner Truth, Ida B. Wells-Barnett, Martin Delany, Marcus Garvey, Malcolm X, Martin Luther King Jr., Toni Morrison, bell hooks, Cornel West, and others, whose views address questions of social justice in the United States, Yancy's

"The Elevator Effect" and "Whiteness as Ambush" take on this issue of social justice by grounding it on the racial and sociocultural politics that are endemic to the nation. Although autobiographical, "The Elevator Effect" is an engaging, penetrating, illustrative analysis of an encounter between the protagonist, a well-educated, middle-class Black male (Yancy) and a nondescript white female in the confined space of an elevator. Of note, the white female was petrified and felt threatened by the mere fact of being ("trapped") in an elevator with the Black male, while the Black male felt uncomfortable, anxious, and even angry about the fact that he was mechanically being read by the white female as an object of fear, terror, and danger by virtue of his race and not seen as any other human being worthy of respect. The Black male, in other words, was merely a script that the white woman read and interpreted in a particular way consistent with whites' sociocultural conditioning of what blackness signifies, namely, fear, threat, and danger. More generally, then, the elevator encounter between the Black male and the white female is a synecdoche of the racial/social dynamics in the larger society of which the elevator, the space of the encounter, is symbolic of the larger polity itself, the United States, and the two subjects represent the two races in binary opposition. It should be noted, however, that the protagonist's experience is not peculiar. Richard A. Jones reminds us of this fact in his review of Yancy's *Black Bodies, White Gazes*. Says Jones:

> We've all been there. . . . Black men in the presence of white women in elevators (and elsewhere) try to make themselves less threatening by moving as far away as possible, not making eye contact, and trying not to appear as "rapists." Yet in acting out these externalized self-infantilizing scripts, while white women act out clutching their purses—black bodies self-interpellate themselves into racially essentialized and un-changing historicized concrete others. Yancy has it just right. We can all identify with this scenario.[6]

The point Yancy tries to make through the elevator encounter is that racism is not simply a function of false beliefs that whites have come to hold and of which they can very easily be disabused by providing them with correct beliefs. Rather, at least at the psychological level, racism is a deeply held set of beliefs that whites have come to acquire over a sustained period of time, and it exists cognitively at the subconscious level, despite claims to the contrary that some whites may affirm, and then manifests itself somatically in their actions.[7] Yancy later illustrates this point in noting an admission by a self-avowed white antiracist Tim Wise who, despite his antiracist views, caught himself questioning the intellectual capability and competence of two Black pilots at the controls of a Boeing 737 Wise had boarded. To his credit, another, and a more powerful, example Tim Wise offers is of his own grandmother's use of the n-word. A staunch antiracist most of her life,

Wise's grandmother had well taught her children and grandchildren to be antiracists like herself. At old age, however, she unfortunately got afflicted with Alzheimer's disease in consequence of which, among other things, she lost all memory of her former self. (As is well known, loss of memory and of one's personal identity are among the debilitating effects of the disease.) Wise reports that his grandmother could not recognize her loved ones nor even recognize a glass of water. "But she could recognize a nigger," Wise tells us, and "she began to call her nurses 'niggers.'"[8]

A final example Yancy gives of how racism exists at the level of the sub-conscious is of a white Jewish woman, Jane Lazarre, who has interracial sons. Lazarre had intervened when one of her sons' friends was being racially harassed. Shocked and angered, Lazarre described the incident as "unbeliev-able!" to which one of her sons angrily responded that such harassment was part of his/their own regular experience. The point here is that Jane Lazarre, being white, did not (and could not) know of the type of experiences of her biracial/Black sons. Her lived reality as a white person was very different from that of her sons and their Black friends. Citing these examples, Yancy goes on to point out that both Tim Wise and Jane Lazarre were "ambushed" by their own internalized racism, one that lurked in the subconscious. We can say the same of Wise's grandmother even despite the fact of her memory loss.

SIGNIFICANCE OF THE FOREGOING ILLUSTRATIONS

Yancy uses the foregoing illustrations to show that racist forms of behavior are overt or covert expressions of an internalized psychological phenomenon, in the form of certain tendencies and dispositions, that whites have been conditioned to acquire over generations through systemic (read institutional) structures that predate the individuals and systematic (read methodical) edu-cation in false representations of blackness—what Yancy calls "white lies." To the white mind, Blacks are deterministically represented as objects of fear and danger that must be dealt with most forcefully even if not brutally. Yancy articulates this phenomenon in the thesis that the Black (male) body is marked and confiscated as an object of fear and danger, and the Black male thus becomes a candidate for forceful and brutalized treatment by law enforcement, for institutional exclusion from societal mainstream through long-term incarceration, and as an object to be discarded or expunged if not contained. The many recent extrajudicial racial killings of young Black males attest to this last point.[9]

No doubt, this state of affairs poses a very grave existential problem for Blacks, especially young Black men, for short of ridding themselves of their phenotype, particularly their pigmentation that visibly announces their presence, which means eradicating themselves existentially, it would seem that Blacks would have to accept racial denigration as a fact of their existence. However, Yancy does not accept this state of affairs about the supposed problematic nature of blackness, and hence of the fabricated existential threat Black men supposedly pose to white women and to white society in general. Instead, he suggests, correctly, that it is whites who have the problem, not Blacks who are the victims of white internalized racism. Just as Blacks have been *deterministically represented in white minds* as objects of fear, however, the white mind too has been *deterministically constructed to experience* the world in white racist ways. As Yancy puts it,

> [The] white self is *prereflectively constituted* through various racial and racist discursive regimes, the sedimentation of experience shapes perceptions of, and mediates embodied transactions with, the social world in ways that reinforce the social order of things as normative and stable. *Hence the white racial and racist actions and discourse of others are anterior to it.* In this sense, then it is more accurate to talk about the white self as always already given as whitely, for it has already "gotten done," as it were, by whiteness.[10]

With this in mind, Yancy then suggests that it is whites who have the burden to engage in a deliberate self-conscious effort to deprogram themselves and to undo the ways they have been conditioned socioculturally, dispositionally, and otherwise, to experience and interpret blackness as they do. In other words, it is for whites to reconstruct themselves, at least psychologically, to acquire a contrary set of dispositions and hence somatic reactions to real or imaginary presence of Blacks/blackness. Whether or not such deprogramming and reconstructive enterprise makes sense, or is even possible, in such a deterministic framework is an issue I take up later. For now, I wish to note that Yancy advances this reconstructive project as a solution to white racism in the second essay, "Whiteness as Ambush" where, among other things, he responds to a series of objections from some audience members to whom he had given a lecture on the elevator encounter. Among reactions to his presentation, as he reports, is a particularly noteworthy one-word dismissive and vitriolic characterization by a white female student: "Bullshit!"[11] In other words, according to this student, Yancy's elaboration of whiteness and racism in the white self and society is "bullshit." Note, however, that by her reaction the student blatantly manifested white privilege in that she had arrogated to herself the authority to declare and pronounce as false or unreal, and thus as unworthy of any serious consideration, *a type of experience she could never have* by virtue of her race. One sees similar profanity-laced inhospitable and vitriolic responses to Yancy's "Dear White America."[12] The letter, in essence, is a request to white America (1) to take an introspective look at itself to acknowledge and confront its racism; (2) to be honest with itself and not try to avoid/evade its racism and the pain its racism causes Black people; and (3) to recognize the humanity of Black people and to love rather than hate Black people.[13] Let me just mention a few of the hostile responses that I found particularly noteworthy.

One reaction to "Dear White America" is a blatant *ad hominem* against Yancy by describing him as "another uppity Nigger" and deriding his intellectual capacity and membership in the academy, saying, "Calling a Nigger a professor is like calling White Black and Wet Dry."[14] In other words, to this white racist, the terms "nigger" and "professor" cannot be collocated any more than can "round" and "square" because they are mutually exclusive. In tandem with this racist reaction is another: "The concept of there being an intellectual Negro is a joke."[15] Notice that both of these reactions, though aimed at Yancy, apply to all of us who are Black professors. A third reaction takes aim at former President Obama by calling him "[The] Nigger in the white house" and deriding him as "a usurper of the office"—meaning that Obama's presidency was illegitimate.[16] I will say more about Obama's presidency—or at least some very prominent institutional reactions to it—in a later section.

Responses of this kind are unquestionably forms of bad faith, and Yancy says as much. In this context, bad faith occurs when some whites invoke their perspectival viewpoint, sometimes benign, but sometimes outright malicious as in the responses earlier, to reject/invalidate, downplay or minimize the experiences of victims of white racism. And by doing so those whites, especially those who see themselves as nonracists or antiracists, evade or deny responsibility for their own witting or unwitting participation in the oppressive structures and practices of white racism and how white racism transacts itself and is implicated in their daily lives.[17] Notwithstanding his acknowledgment of such bad faith, however, Yancy goes on to argue that all is not lost and that white racism can be dismantled.[18] But can it? In order to answer this question, let me first bring out what I consider a tension in Yancy's two conceptions of whiteness and racism.

TENSION IN YANCY'S TWO CONCEPTIONS OF WHITENESS AND RACISM

Yancy's discussion of white racism from his repertoire, but particularly from the two essays under consideration, is part of a larger, ongoing debate among some contemporary philosophers about how to address the problem of white racism in society. Two dominant positions on this issue are Racial/Social Realism and Racial Eliminativism. Racial/Social Realism holds that race is a social reality that needs to be acknowledged *and retained* in order to advance the cause of social justice and to attain social equality among the various groups in the polity. On this view, acknowledging the reality of race, particularly its impact on society, will enable whites to come to terms with white privilege and hence with the unequal distribution of social benefits and burdens that derive from such racial privileging. Confronted with this reality of race and the social inequity it engenders, it is believed that whites will become empathetic with the victims of white racism, and this empathy will make whites amenable to the idea of redistributive measures along racial lines to advance social justice. One redistributive measure would be race-based affirmative action programs as a remedy to the racial injustice that Blacks and people of color generally continue to experience. Advocates of this position include Lucius Outlaw, David B. Wilkins, Naomi Zack, and Bill Lawson.[19]

Racial Eliminativism, by contrast, advances the view that the concept of race is a socially constructed fiction that was established in the seventeenth century arguably to legitimate European conquest and domination of people of color and to validate the social degradation and oppression of the dominated and conquered. As a socially constructed fiction, therefore, this concept (and racial categories as such) can and ought to be eliminated as a prolegomenon to discussions of social justice and social equality. Put otherwise, Racial Eliminativism calls for the delegitimization of the concept of race and racial categories as a first and necessary step in the pursuit of social justice. And it does so by arguing that racial categories themselves are, to adapt an expression of William James's, "alters to unknown gods."[20] These categories were established as scientific taxonomies and have since been worshipped as philosophical and scientific ideals (read idols). Yet these ideals are manifestly false gods or give an inaccurate representation/account of reality even as they have doggedly been embraced by society. By ridding us of these ideals, then, we will be denying them any substantive content and meaning, and so provide the grounds to dismantling the distributive paradigm of white privilege and Black/Other disadvantage that is anchored to them. By doing so, we will advance the cause of social justice and equality. Proponents of this position include Charles Mills, Amy Guttman, and myself.[21]

Yancy makes a powerful case for Racial/Social Realism. In the essays in question and elsewhere, he elaborates how and why racism is so intractable and pernicious.[22] Recall that, on my reading, Yancy ontologizes whiteness and racism within a deterministic framework in which whiteness, and with it racist perceptions, beliefs, and actions seem to be effects of antecedent factors over which individuals seem to have absolutely no control. I now will characterize this viewpoint as a metaphysical conception of whiteness and racism. Perhaps a hyperbolic way of representing this metaphysical position is to say that whiteness and racism are, like some forms of cancer, acquired diseases that derive from antecedent factors *beyond the individual and over which the individual has absolutely no control, even regardless of what the individual might think.* Moreover, these diseases infect the entire soul, metastasize throughout the psyche, together with the institutions in the society, and then consciously and/or unconsciously manifest themselves somatically, including verbally, in practice. On this view, it would follow that racist thinking and actions are necessary. By this I mean that, considering any white person one encounters, one would be justified in believing that the person is racist even in the face of any *apparent* countervailing evidence to the contrary. And this belief would be justified in light of the following considerations: (1) the very metaphysical basis of whiteness and white racism such that an individual can be racist without manifesting racist behavior, and this fact allows for the individual to be "ambushed" by his or her internalized racism; (2) the fact of white socialization into racist beliefs and practices since birth, without the individual's input and even before the individual begins to think for himself or herself; and (3) the institutional structures within which whiteness and racism are embedded and so can reproduce and sustain their hegemony. This is how I understand Yancy's metaphysical conception of whiteness and racism, or the position to which I believe the logic of his argument commits him.

True, Yancy offers another, and even antithetical, view of whiteness and racism to the metaphysical/necessitarian just presented. The other position, which I now will call the contingency thesis, is that racist beliefs, thinking and actions are contingent, a result of merely particular accidental practices that have infected and affected white psyche in such a way that whites react as they do to their own very fabricated conception of blackness. As Yancy himself says elsewhere,

> I am arguing that there is nothing intrinsically problematic about one's white phenotypic constitution. White racist supremacy is not a natural property that inheres within the skin of those classified as white; it does not result from an innate, genotypic disposition. There is indeed a contingent relationship between having "white skin" and being a white racist.[23]

Obviously, these two theses on whiteness and racism are clearly at odds, and so warrant an explanation for such an incoherence in Yancy's overall position. A logical explanation for these conflicting positions, at least in my view, is that Yancy is struggling to capture the ubiquity and intransigence of whiteness and racism in society and at the same time is unwilling to capitulate to it. So in his endeavor to account for the pervasiveness of the phenomenon of whiteness and racism he uses a metaphysical language but whose logic entails consequences that are at variance with his positive endeavor, his aspiration to combat the phenomenon. It is this positive endeavor that leads him to advance the contingency thesis with the explicit declaration that racism can be undone. And along these lines, he makes use of rhetoric that harmonizes with his practice. I speak of Yancy's rhetoric because he now can at least speak of *conceptually* dismantling racism. And in terms of practice, we know that Yancy works with, and positively approves, the views of antiracist whites (e.g., Tim Wise, Peggy MacIntosh, Stephanie Wildman, and others) even as those whites, *by hypothesis*, are racists in virtue of whiteness. Only by so reading Yancy can one account for the incoherence in his overall position. But even on such a generous reading, I submit that given the entrenched nature of whiteness and racism, including white continual self-conscious remaking of the self, the disruptive activity of which Yancy speaks is tantamount to a near Sisyphean ordeal, predestined to fail. I say this in light of Yancy's very own characterization of what it is to be white: "To be white in America is to be always already implicated in structures of power, which complicates what it means to be a white ally. . . . For even as whites fight on behalf of people of color, that is engage in acts that bind them to people of color, *there is also a sense in which whites simultaneously 'bind to' structures of power.*"[24] This suggests that, like it or not, whites cannot extricate themselves from the stranglehold of whiteness, and hence from the iron-clad grip of racism. Elsewhere, in speaking of what he calls white academics' hypocrisy in distinguishing between white ways of being (reality) and white appearing (appearance), Yancy says the following:

> It is important not to overlook the real possibility that there are some white scholars, despite the fact that they engage in, and devote their academic careers to, critical studies of race/whiteness, who *self-consciously* engage in acts of white power maintenance, acts of overt racist nastiness, and forms of institutional control that silence and marginalize the voices of black scholars and scholars of color.[25]

In sum, if my reading of Yancy is sound, then the metaphysical conception of whiteness and racism trumps the existential. And granted this view, one is left to wonder if Yancy is not simply deluded or engaged in wishful thinking in entertaining the idea that whiteness can be dismantled through a continual disruptive process. To do that would involve disentangling the complex web-like link between whiteness and power, or the iron-clad grip of the power of whiteness over the white self, and this, so far as I can see, is an impossible feat, given the environment within which the white self and all therein about him or her are constituted. Added to this, the involuntary but compulsive identity-participation (or what existentialists would characterize as "thrownness") of the white self within what seems to me a ubiquitous, almost ethereal, power structure of the society, would nullify any agency the individual may think he or she has to exercise or engage in disruptive activity. An appropriate analogy here is the white European newcomer/outsider into the colony in Albert Memmi's *The Colonizer and the Colonized*. The newcomer/ outsider, upon entering the colonial space, immediately and necessarily acquires as an inheritance or a natural birthright the privileges appertaining to colonial life. As Memmi puts it, the newcomer cannot free himself from "this halo of prestige (read privilege) which crowns him."[26] In this connection, says Memmi, the colonial—whom he defines as the European without privileges in the colony—"does not exist, because it is not up to the European in the colonies to remain a colonial, even if he had so intended."[27] Another way to express Memmi's point is that the newcomer/outsider into the colonial space necessarily ceases to be an outsider because he or she gets absorbed or sucked into the environment by the overpowering operational forces therein even in spite of himself or herself and whether he or she likes it or not. In such an environment, then, as in a white racist environment too, the conception of the self as an agent with the capacity to alter the environment and its content would seem to be a myth. Of course, the white antiracist in the United States would be *psychologically determined* to imagine and/or believe that he or she could undo whiteness and racism. But, again, if the environment within which he or she functions and the states of affairs therein are as I have represented them—that is, overpowering, overwhelming, and deterministic—then such a belief too cannot but be an article of faith, a mere wishful thinking!

To reiterate my overall position, there is an acute tension between what I have called Yancy's metaphysical/necessitarian conception of whiteness and racism, on the one hand, and what I have characterized as his existential/ contingency conception, on the other hand. If my reading of Yancy is correct, then granted the metaphysical account, with its necessitarian import, whites cannot but be racists even in spite of themselves. On the other hand, given the existential conception, with its contingency thesis, whiteness and racism can be undone by continuous disruptive activities of victims of racism and their antiracist (racist) allies. I have already registered my doubt about the efficacy of the existential conception.

YANCY'S METAPHYSICAL CONCEPTION ON MY THINKING

Having made the case for racial eliminativism, I confess that Yancy's metaphysical account has convinced me to rethink my original eliminativist position as somewhat naïve and impracticable, given how racism has infected the institutional structures and social fabric, including the body politic, of the entire society. This insight allows me now to question not only Yancy's own optimistic view, grounded in his existentialist outlook that racism can be dismantled, but also my own earlier entertained optimism.[28] And I suspect that it is the forcefulness of the metaphysical account that induces the young white male student of whom Yancy himself speaks to capitulate to racism saying "since racism is so powerful, . . . we [whites] just might as well be racists."[29] Actually, what the student should have said in light of his appreciation of the force of the argument is, "Given the power of racism we whites cannot not be racists." And he would have been more accurate than the way he phrases his position because his current phraseology implies a choice. However, it is precisely the negation of choice that the metaphysical account entails. In any case, this shows all the more that Yancy's metaphysical account strongly argues against the optimism that he articulates through his existential account.

No doubt, Yancy will attempt to resolve the conflict between both accounts in favor of the existential to ensure that his optimism is meaningful. At least, the erosion, if not complete dismantling, of white supremacy and racism is something for which to hope. Still, in my view, the entrenched nature of whiteness and racism in the institutional and social fabric/topography of the society would render unrealistic and impracticable such an endeavor. I am saying, in other words, that the evidence that Yancy himself has adduced to account for the entrenched nature of whiteness and racism in society is much more powerful and intransigent than he is willing to admit or accept. Like a hydra, whiteness (with racism) has a way of rearing its ugly head at various times and places *especially when white power appears to be threatened.* This was exactly what happened with the election of Barack Obama to the presidency of the United States in 2008. We not only witnessed an unabashed, bold, and open resurgence of whiteness and racism, but we also witnessed (and still are witnessing) the mainstreaming of extremist racist groups whose rallying cry is to "take back our country." This rallying cry, however, has not been limited to extremist groups. We have also heard its echo in the major halls and corridors of power in the nation as I now proceed to show.

CONTRA YANCY'S OPTIMISM: THE PRESIDENCY, WHITENESS, AND RACIAL HATRED OF OBAMA

No leading political figure in the contemporary United States experienced as much racial animus as President Obama. This is because, while it was seductive of some to think that with the election of Obama to the presidency the United States was on the verge of a postracial society, thereby being a shining light to the rest of the world, that delusion came crashing to the ground even before Obama took office. As reported by Mark Potok of the *Southern Poverty Law Center*, even before the presidential campaign between John McCain and Obama was over, "racial rage, clearly driven by fear of a black man in the White House, began to break out around the country. Effigies of Obama appeared hanging from nooses on university campuses. Angry supporters of John McCain and [his vice presidential nominee] Sarah Palin shouted 'Kill him!' at a campaign rally and even screamed 'nigger' at a black cameraman, telling him 'Sit down, boy!'"[30] Potok goes on to note that, after Obama got elected, there were millions of whites who were "deeply upset over his victory for reasons that [were] fundamentally racial."[31] Obama's victory precipitated talk of "race war" by some neo-Nazis. One Klan leader, Thom Robb of Arkansas, used Obama's election to predict a race war between Blacks and whites, the latter of whom Robb saw as "the rightful owners and leaders of this country."[32]

In Congress, the Republicans launched a well-orchestrated plan to throttle and strangle any policy initiatives Obama had. According to Asmat Khan of PBS, on the night of Obama's inauguration as the forty-fourth president of the United States, a group of Republican senators and congressmen held a secret meeting to strategize on a plan to ensure that the president-elect fail. They included Senators Jim DeMint, Jon Kyl, and Tom Coburn, and Congressmen Eric Cantor, Kevin McCarthy, and Paul Ryan.[33] Continuing, Khan reports that after three hours of strategizing, "they [the group] decided they needed to fight Obama on everything."[34] This Republican obstructionist strategy carried over into the 2010 midterm elections that propelled the Republicans to gaining control of both Houses of Congress. But even prior to the 2010 midterms, and in anticipation of a Republican victory at the polls, Senator Mitch McConnell had already begun to lay down what may aptly be characterized as inauspicious conditions under which the Republicans claimed they would work with the president. In an interview with the *National Journal* on October 23, 2010, McConnell is reported to have said that if the Republicans won the midterm elections, then they [the Republicans] would say to their supporters: "Those of you who helped us make this a good day, you need to go out and help us finish the job." Asked what he meant by "the job" to be finished, he replied: "The single most important thing we want to achieve is for President Obama to be a one-term president."[35] Yes, McConnell also said that he did not want the president to fail; rather, he wanted the president "to change." But it is clearly implied in his declaration that he meant, unless the president did what the Republicans wanted him to do, and on their terms, they would all but guarantee his failure through obstructionism.

Similar to McConnell, John Boehner, who subsequently became the Speaker of the House after the Republicans won the 2010 midterm elections, is reported to have said that they [the House Republicans] planned to do any and everything to thwart Obama's agenda. As he put it, "We're going to do everything—and I mean everything we can do—to kill it [i.e., Obama's agenda], stop it, slow it down, whatever we can."[36] In short, Boehner, like

McConnell, not only wanted the first Black president to fail, but he planned to ensure that Obama would fail.

I submit that all of this is clear evidence of bad faith, arguably rooted in antiblack racism. I say this because in political contests between rival parties, in this case the Republicans and Democrats, after an election is over and the results are decided, both parties usually come together, if only for a short time, to work for the good of the nation. The media have dubbed this "temporary truce period," traditionally the first hundred days after the ruling party takes office, the honeymoon period for the new administration. In terms of the presidency, this is the period the incoming president is given time to begin to implement his policy goals for the nation. The Republicans did not allow Obama such a honeymoon. Their obstructionist strategies were hatched even before he took office and were implemented right from the start of his occupancy of the Oval Office.

Finally, consider former Speaker of the House Newt Gingrich who, in the NPR program "Morning Edition," on January 17, 2012, disparagingly referred to President Obama as "the food stamp president." Gingrich made this disparaging reference as a candidate for the Republican presidential ticket when he set out to offer his policy prescription for the nation, and to contrast his policy proposal from that of President Obama, the Democratic incumbent. Alluding to his days as Speaker of the House, Gingrich then said the following: "Over here you have a policy which, with Reagan and me as Speaker, created millions of jobs—it's called paychecks. Over here you have the most successful food stamp president in American history, Barack Obama."[37] By all measures, Gingrich's deprecating characterization of the first Black president of the nation is nothing short of racist in that he deliberately used racially coded language that stereotypes Blacks as inherently lazy and dependent on the public purse through welfare and food stamps, and of Obama therefore as chief of, and deliverer for, the inherently lazy and dependent. What this means, in effect, is that the respect that is normally accorded to the holder of the highest office in the land was not accorded to Obama. Instead, Gingrich showed blatant disrespect to, indeed utter contempt for, Obama. But the question is "Why?" And the response, as Carol Anderson puts it in her book *White Rage*,[38] is that Obama "had the audacity to become president."[39] On my view, this was nothing but unabashed, undiluted, and unsanitized racism from a one-time holder of the third-highest position of political power and authority in the nation.

On the practical/social front, Obama's ascent into the Oval Office, whether coincidentally or causally, saw an *intensification* of blatant violence against Black people, but especially young Black males, too numerous to catalogue here and about which Yancy himself has written. Remember Trayvon Martin, Eric Garner, Tamir Rice, and others. This is the all-too-familiar violence by law enforcement and white vigilantes that even precipitated the inauguration of the Black Lives Matter movement and demands for racial justice.[40] It is in the context of the extrajudicial killings of, and violence against, young Black males that I want to read the aforementioned horrific responses and more to Yancy's charitable "gift" to white America in "Dear White America." More importantly, and for my present purpose, it is against this catalogue of violence and threats even to Yancy himself that I question Yancy's optimism that all is not lost, and that white racism can be dismantled. The evidence is overwhelming that white racism has not only permeated the interstices of society, but that it also has enamored many whites to see themselves as custodians of the *status quo*—that is, of white dominance—with *de facto* license to accost, challenge, profile, or even interrogate any Black person as they deem fit. We are all too familiar with reports of white people calling the police on Black people as the latter go about the mundane and innocuous business of living: driving while Black, barbecuing in a public park while Black, shopping while Black, and so on. Even as I write this chapter there is a news video/report by Katherine Hignett from *Newsweek* titled "Young Boy Begs Father not to Call 911 on Black Man for 'Trespassing.'"[41] The video/report was of a Black man, Wesly Michel, a software engineer, who had gone to meet a friend with special needs at a building in San Francisco. While Michel was waiting for the friend at the lobby of the building, he was accosted by a white man who then promptly accused him of trespassing. The man asked Michel to leave the building and threatened to call the police. It was in response to this threat that the man's son started begging his father not to call the police, saying, "Daddy don't, don't, don't." When the man proceeded to dial his phone, Michel then began to record the encounter on his own cell phone and notified the man he was doing so. In speaking with the police over his phone, the man said Michel "appears to be African American" and later added that Michel had failed to properly identify himself.

All of this brings me back to Yancy and the elevator encounter with which I started. Black people are made to be on the defensive in all such encounters: They are to justify their presence in elevators and buildings; to justify their presence in particular (presumptively white) neighborhoods; to justify themselves as they go about their regular normal business of living; and, yes, to justify their worthiness of being in the Oval Office! Given these existential realities of blackness, or what it means to be black in the United States, on what basis can anyone realistically be optimistic that whiteness can be undone? Inasmuch as I hate to harken back to Du Bois, whether Black people like it or not, they (we) have been etched in the white imagination as a problem. We should not fail to note that Donald Trump's 2016 election victory was owing to, among other things, his appeal to strong white nationalist sentiments and white fear of loss of power and the advantages that derive thereof. This appeal to white racial insecurities and potential loss of power and benefits was incepted by the Republicans during Reconstruction and nurtured through Nixon's Southern Strategy.[42] As Anderson states:

> Trump tapped into an increasingly powerful conservative base that had been nurtured for decades on the Southern Strategy's politics of anti-black resentment. Similar to George Wallace's run for the presidency in 1968, Trump's supporters bristled at the thought that public policies would provide any help to African Americans and were certain that blacks were getting much more than they deserved from the government while the "average American" (*read white*) was getting much less. The message was clear: They weren't deserving and weren't really Americans.[43]

And Trump has continued to stoke white racial fears in preparation for his 2020 reelection bid by alleging that there had been voter fraud in the 2016 elections; in particular, that the Democratic Party recruited undocumented immigrants and felons to vote. In response to this allegation, and in preparation for the 2020 elections, therefore, his administration has enacted policies that target for deportation Mexicans and Hispanic minority group members presumed to be illegal immigrants. Not to mention the draconian measure of separating children from their parents as a deterrent to curtail illegal immigration that even some Republicans deem cruel and inhumane. These are undoubtedly strategies and policies geared toward preserving the hegemony of whiteness and white power to which, in the minds of some whites, Obama's election as president so visibly, palpably, and symbolically was a grievous threat. Trump's election to the office of the presidency, therefore, is a reassertion of white power, dominance, and place in the racial hierarchy. Keeping this in mind, I close with the following fitting words of sociologist Tressie McMillan Cottom: "Whiteness defends itself. Against change, against progress, against hope, against black dignity, against black lives, against reason, against truth, against facts, against native claims, and against its own laws and customs."[44]

Chapter 13

Disrupting Whiteness

The Productive Disturbance of George Yancy's Work on White Identity and the White Gaze

Stephen Brookfield

In life, the best moments are those of productive disturbance. When settled understandings are called into question, we are invited into the possibility of growth, change, and increased self-awareness. In my own case, the most significant learning I've experienced has resulted from times when I have been challenged to reappraise the accuracy and validity of my assumptions. This is why I'm always drawn to writers who disturb me. I love to encounter a thinker who shows me the world through a very different lens, thereby turning the familiar into something strange. This is why I find George Yancy's work on race so helpful. He presents me with an analysis of my white identity that I would prefer not to read but *have* to read. He gives me a gift that part of me thinks I don't need because, after all (I tell myself), I try to work in antiracist ways. So I must be one of the good guys, right? His gift of productive disruption stops me in my tracks whenever I start to feel too comfortable about my own moral correctness.

In 1943, the English poet Robert Graves and his collaborator Alan Hodge coauthored a book titled *The Reader over Your Shoulder*.[1] The book's proposition was simple; as an author you should imagine that there are people in the room with you looking over your shoulder as you write. Graves and Hodge argued that keeping the identity of these individuals in mind as you composed your prose would help you write more clearly, directly, and simply. You would be writing for your audience as much as for yourself.

As a writer I have always found this advice enormously helpful. Some of the people I imagine looking over my shoulder are Graves and Hodge themselves, along with George Orwell. When I begin to indulge myself in what I think are pleasingly lyrical turns of phrase I imagine these three saying, "come off it, Stephen, who are you trying to impress?" I will shamefacedly admit that the people I imagined looking over my shoulder as I climbed the academic ladder at Columbia to become a full tenured professor at Teachers College were the unknown future members of my tenure committee. It was only after gaining tenure that I could call Graves, Hodge, and Orwell back into the room. So much of my pre-tenure writing was bloated, an attempt to prove how much I'd read, my theoretical acumen, and the extent of my vocabulary. It is only since tenure that I've felt free to write simply and directly.

When I write about race, George Yancy is one of the people peering over my shoulder. He is a supportive and loving presence, encouraging me to be honest and to take the risk to acknowledge the white supremacy that moves within me. I rely and depend mostly on his rigorous criticality. Whenever I veer toward the self-congratulatory, whenever I feel the temptation to show off my "wokeness," I hear him saying, "Do you really want to say *that* Stephen?" Because Yancy's writing is so meticulously honest in its self-appraisal, I feel called on to try and match the same openness to critique he embodies. Reading his analysis of the white gaze and the power embodied in holding a white identity means that I am constantly stopped in my tracks as I'm about to propose some "truth" about whiteness. He reminds me that writing about race is a serious business and helps me understand that whatever words I compose are always going to be funneled through the white supremacist worldview that structures who I am. But stopping me from writing them is the last thing he would want to do. The generosity of spirit that moved him to write "Dear White America" as a Christmas gift to whites invites me into self-reflection.[2] But equally he reminds me that glibness about race is a mortal sin and that any responses, proposals, or conclusions I advance are always going to be inchoate, always partial.

One thing I take from Yancy's analysis in *Look, a White!*; *White on White/ Black on Black*; *What White Looks Like*; and *Black Bodies, White Gazes* is a better understanding of how the white supremacist ideology I've been brought up in is just too deeply embedded in me to shake.[3] Ever since I was old enough to perceive how the world worked, I've assimilated a set of paradigmatic assumptions that have seemed to me to represent such obvious, common sense realities that I've regarded them as tacit, empirical truth rather than assumptions. Chief among these are that leadership is white, intelligence is white, objectivity is white, rationality is white, political legitimacy is white, history is white, and logic is white.

These assumptions comprise the essence of white supremacy. Why do whites seem to end up in leadership positions making decisions for everyone else? Because, according to white supremacy, whites have a greater facility for thinking clearly and objectively about what comprises the common good and how that should be achieved. According to this logic, it would seem to make natural sense for them to be leaders. I also grew up accepting patriarchy. Not only did I accept that most leaders should be white, I also thought of them as obviously male. Just as I never questioned that whites should be in leadership positions because of their intelligence and rationality, so I never challenged the notion that men's supposed clarity and greater objectivity meant their decisions were to be trusted over those of women who were more likely to be swayed by emotion, particularly compassion. I was an excellent little student of the white patriarchy so clearly described by Rebecca Traister.[4]

Of course, critical theory has illuminated for me how ideological manipulation works, and on a purely rational level I've been aware of white supremacy as the ideological bulwark of permanent racism. Over the years, I've done all the "right" things to show my antiracist identity. I've marched against apartheid and the treatment of undocumented people; I've joined antiracist coalitions and been to antiracist conferences. I've tried to support colleagues and students of color by leveraging my white privilege whenever possible. But I still see the identity of a "good white person"[5] claiming its self-congratulatory hold on me. It's so easy to fall into thinking that now I'm one of the good guys who's rid himself of racist conditioning so that therefore my work is done. I have to remind myself constantly that racial awareness is something I can opt into or out of as I wish; the complete opposite of the reality experienced by people of color.

How Yancy has productively disturbed my thinking about race is by his insistence on locating the racism within me, by bringing home to me the way my body—as well as my actions and words—embody a supposedly superior white identity. When I read his work I'm unable to escape the uncomfortable truth of how I benefit from whiteness, how white supremacy is ideologically sedimented in me; the way it's evident in my emotional responses, baked into my synapses, embedded in my DNA. Yancy's work has helped me to face the visceral, preconscious nature of my white racism. I count on him to disrupt me, to disassemble me, to force me to face personal realities I would much rather avoid, and to require me to examine how I am going to commit myself to the future.

FIRST ACQUAINTANCE: *AFRICAN-AMERICAN PHILOSOPHERS*

I am a relative latecomer to a serious engagement with questions of racial identity and white supremacy. It was not until I entered my fifties and had the great good fortune to team teach with two African American colleagues—Scipio Colin Jr. III and Elizabeth Peterson—that questions of race began to loom large for me. That collaboration eventually resulted in an edited handbook on race and adult education, but up to that time, I was emblematic of a classic white consciousness.[6] I regarded race as something that only people of color exhibited and something that I could choose not to deal with unless I wished to. It was Scipio Colin Jr. III who introduced me to Leonard Harris's classic anthology of African American philosophy, *Philosophy Born of Struggle* and, in tracking down more of Harris's work, I came across an interview with him in Yancy's 1998 book of seventeen interviews with African American philosophers.[7] This is where I first encountered Yancy.

African-American Philosophers was an important book for me. Along with the Harris anthology, I was beginning to get a glimpse of the diversity of a philosophical terrain that I knew little about. Also, as someone who has only ever taken one undergraduate course in philosophy (it was in political philosophy which led to a lifelong engagement with critical theory), I am always hesitant as I approach philosophical treatises. Lacking training in, or familiarity with, philosophical terminology has meant that most of my attempts to read independently in that area have ended in a frustrating sigh of disappointment. I would usually feel that I was not smart enough to breathe in the rarified air of philosophical scholarship. But *African-American Philosophers* was a series of conversations and that drew me to it. Whenever I struggle with dense philosophically inclined prose, I always try to find a book of interviews or conversations with the philosopher concerned. This is how I managed to get into Foucault and Habermas.[8]

African-American Philosophers was also an important building block for a manuscript I was starting to write on critical theory.[9] Two of the philosophers Yancy interviewed for his book—Angela Davis and Lucius T. Outlaw Jr.—had been students of Herbert Marcuse, a philosopher I first encountered as a student in 1968 and someone I was profiling in what would become *The Power of Critical Theory*.[10] In Yancy's conversation with Angela Davis, she describes Marcuse and James Baldwin as two important mentors "who helped me to conceptualize a relationship between theory and practice, a challenge that I continue to struggle with today."[11] One of the things that most impresses me about Yancy's work is his exploration of this relationship, seen in books such as *On Race* and *Pursuing Trayvon Martin*.[12]

In Yancy's interview with Lucius T. Outlaw Jr., Outlaw describes being impressed and inspired by Marcuse, calling his work "provocative, interesting and insightful." Outlaw also comments of Marcuse that "it was the nature of the rhythm of his logic and writing that I found also attractive."[13] Incidentally, this is the exact opposite of my own experience of reading Marcuse! He makes me feel like I'm a complete impostor as I plough through his prose feeling like I'm missing 99.9 percent of what he's saying.

But despite my difficulties as a reader, Marcuse has been a very important figure to me. I have been struck by his theory of aesthetics and his belief that the most revolutionary break with reality has its roots in the experience of estrangement produced by artistic engagement. I have also felt that his small essay on repressive tolerance[14] gave me a wonderfully accurate analytical tool to understand how universities and other institutions appear to embrace change while simultaneously working to neuter any serious threat to their legitimacy.

Marcuse's influence was brought home to me a couple of decades ago during a class I was teaching. I was talking about his idea of repressive tolerance, and about how the contemporary emphasis on diversity could be interpreted as an example of the dominant culture's ability to seem to be opening itself up to dissenting views and different perspectives, when in fact it was subtly reasserting its control over public discourse. When we took a break, an African American woman who was a veteran of the civil rights movement still actively engaged in antiracist education came up to me. "Marcuse was a beautiful man," she said. "As soon as you mentioned his name I knew I could trust you."

One of the reasons I am interested in Marcuse is because, of all those associated with the Frankfurt School tradition, he placed race at the center of his analysis. He placed significant hope in extraparliamentary direct action by the most disenfranchised members of society, supporting the Black Power movement as a "far more subversive universe of discourse" than the Hippie movement. In the language of Black militants, particularly their claiming of soul—in "in its essence lily-white ever since Plato"—and their declaration that "Black is beautiful," Marcuse detected "the ingression of the aesthetic into the political."[15] Black Power represented "a systematic linguistic rebellion, which smashes the ideological context in which the words are employed and defined, and places them in the opposite context—negation of the established one. Thus, the blacks 'take over' some of the most sublime and sublimated concepts of Western civilization, desublimate them and redefine them."[16]

The interviews with Angela Davis and Lucius T. Outlaw Jr. (and also with Cornel West) in *African-American Philosophers* confirmed my decision to profile Marcuse in *The Power of Critical Theory*.[17] They provided me with some useful analytical leads and helped propel my intellectual project to link critical theory to a race-based analysis of the ideological dominance of white supremacy. Subsequently I published a piece in the *Harvard Educational Review*, which, following the lead of Lucius T. Outlaw Jr., investigated how critical theory could be racialized in the interests of African Americans.[18] For a white male, this was a perilous enterprise, but I took heart from the open-ended nature of the questioning Yancy exercised in *African-American Philosophers*.[19] He seemed so open to multiple perspectives that I felt as long as my piece was meticulously researched, and as long as I never purported to speak for any of the thinkers I was exploring, I could avoid the worst excesses of exploitation and colonization that happens when white thinkers "explain" black thought.

A DEEPENING ENGAGEMENT WITH WHITENESS

One of the things I enjoyed most about the interviews in *African-American Philosophers* was the disturbingly provocative nature of the questions that Yancy posed. Although the focus of the book was, quite legitimately, on the different philosophers profiled, the nature of Yancy's questioning meant that his voice—probing and productively disorienting—was strongly evident throughout.[20] That voice has continued to disturb me in a wonderfully productive way for twenty years. His work on white and black gazes, and his project of illuminating the nature of whiteness, has been particularly troublesome in the best way possible. I am always most drawn to philosophers and activists who mess my life up, who unsettle my worked out assumptions and worldview. Yancy has done me the favor of repeatedly sending me back to square one in terms of my comprehension of white identity. I am particularly grateful for his sustained, multiyear interrogation of whiteness. Most work on whiteness is executed by white scholars and, while that is undeniably valuable, an analysis informed by the embodied African American experience is enormously helpful. As whites, we can never really know what it's like to have a white gaze permanently settled on us, but scholars of color can force us to be more self-aware of how we exert that gaze on those we regard as the "other."

Yancy's work on whiteness is complex, passionate, and, for a White adult educator like me, productively jarring. He writes elegantly with an enviable knack of interweaving striking stories of personal experience into philosophical analysis. When I read him, I have so many turned down pages, notes in the margin and underlined sections that I know I've been in a real engagement. What I most appreciate is his repeated naming of how "the opaque, white racist self" pervades Whites' identities. In the very last paragraph of *Look, a White!* he captures what for me has been a truth about myself: "Being a white antiracist and yet being racist are not mutually exclusive. Rather, being a white antiracist racist signifies tremendous tension and paradox but not logical or existential futility."[21] I will always benefit from the unearned privileges and blindness embedded in the racist institutions and structures I move through each day. And I will never lose entirely the racist perspectives, intuitive judgments, and embedded filters I have learned all too well and that are "insidiously operating as the level of simply being bodily in the world as white."[22] But I need to move forward with antiracist work even knowing the flawed and contradictory nature of that project.

The overall intent of Yancy's work on whiteness is to name the enduring reality of white racism. In *Look, a White!* he describes being "interviewed" by a White professor of philosophy. The so-called interview turns into an uninterrupted effort by the professor

> to present himself as "pure," as a "good white," who was above the fray of racism and lived beyond the trappings of race matters. He used my presence, my hour, as a space for white self-confession and self-glorification, . . . desiring that I spend my time bearing witness to his "white purity," so that I could state emphatically and unequivocally that he was one of the "good guys."[23]

That passage hit uncomfortably close to home for me. I was forced to ask myself how many times have I done this, and how did it make my colleagues of color feel? How, in my search for approval, have I marginalized colleagues by refocusing attention on myself?

One of the great strengths of Yancy's work for me is how it constantly yanks me back from the realm of academic analysis to questions of daily conduct. Just as I'm becoming comfortable with a critical theory focus on structures and ideology, Yancy introduces a powerful personal example that concretizes this analysis and makes me ask disturbing questions of myself. This is particularly so in an analysis of bell hooks's transgressive pedagogy. Yancy's examples of classroom moments when students burst into tears when discussing race, and the awkwardness this induces, were vividly recognizable. He writes of "silence in the room, a sort of awkwardness of not knowing what to do next," arguing that "this awkwardness is indicative of pedagogical success, not failure." Pedagogically, allowing silence to linger "functions as a teachable moment (where) all of us present might feel the weight of the moment."[24]

Pondering uncomfortable, emotionally charged outbursts is, for Yancy, "fearless listening" in which people live with important discomfort. He argues, along with hooks, that foregrounding race makes classrooms necessarily unsafe, dangerous spaces. He regards his classrooms as dangerous, "because they demand so much at the level of personal integrity, honesty, and exposure while not sacrificing critical engagement."[25] And these demands are just as present for teachers who are called on to disclose their own contradictions, knowing all the while that "to engage one's identity and being-in-the-world through the *passionate* deployment of critical interrogation can cause suffering, great disappointment, and creative vertigo."[26]

One of the things I have most struggled with over the years is the notion, derived from enlightenment philosophy, that progress toward a kind of perfection is a natural dynamic. I have conducted my fifty years of teaching on the assumption that with the passage of time I will become more skilled at dealing with contradiction and living with inevitable ambiguity. In *Just Mercy*, Bryan Stevenson writes that for transformation around racial injustice to occur, we must all learn to embrace the discomfort of talking across difference about racially charged issues and of becoming self-reflective regarding our own learned racism.[27] For white people, entering into difficult conversations that emerge around race invariably involves the temptation offered by the white fragility to preserve white emotional equanimity.[28] The reason that many race-based discussions veer off into cries from participants to be "respected" by each other is because being treated respectfully is equated with not being upset, not being challenged, and not being called out. When your whole being is focused on preserving your identity and self-concept as a good white person, and your emotional synapses are screaming "keep me safe!" then embracing discomfort is completely counterintuitive. Yet, as Stevenson argues, it is at the moment when you are feeling most threatened that the potential for the greatest learning is often present.[29]

Yancy's work has deepened my understanding of, and steeled my determination to navigate, the emotionally turbulent nature of any effort to ask teachers and learners to challenge dominant ideologies and interrogate settled practices around race. He asks (very pertinently for me), "When did anger and the simultaneous truthful disclosure of pain and suffering become incompatible?"[30] I have to say that the most memorable moments of my teaching career have all been suffused with emotion. And the kind of fearless, unsafe listening to passionate declarations of hurt, including denunciations of my own actions, is something that will never become routine or habitual for me. But I find Yancy's work so deeply grounded in identifiable experiences and felt emotions that there is a comfort of recognition.

His analysis has also helped prompt a paradigmatic shift in how I view success in antiracist teaching. Now I realize that before I take an initial step into any room in which I'm working I need to do some important internal mental calibration. I want to do good work and believe passionately in the importance of what I'm striving to do. I'm not immune to media depictions of successful teachers (from *Goodbye Mr. Chips* to *Dead Poets Society* and *Dangerous Minds* to *The Great Debaters*) that feature charismatic individuals who bring transformative changes in their students' lives. The linear progress of increasing perfectionism that's so much a part of white epistemology also has its hold on me. I always expect improvement, a smoothing out of difficulties I'm encountering. The institutional evaluations and performance appraisals I am subjected to invariably measure my effectiveness on a continuum of improvement and there is the expectation as each year goes by that I'll get "better" at teaching about race.

Working within this framework of continuous quality improvement, it's easy to go into an event designed to help people recognize whiteness assuming that success will be represented by ever larger numbers of people telling you how the racial blinders have been lifted from their eyes and how they now see whiteness and white supremacy in every corner of their lives. I've privately yearned for "Kumbaya" moments of racial healing when people put their arms around each other and sing "We Shall Overcome." So before I meet with any group I have to give myself a stern talking to and tell myself, "that ain't gonna happen."

Yancy has helped me understand that what should count as success is leaving a session with some evidence that people are ready to continue a conversation. I expect a lot of confusion, push back, and some expressions of outright hostility. I anticipate long, awkward, uncomfortable silences, crying, and angry outbursts and expect to feel like a complete novice. I tell myself that if I'm defining "going well" by things adhering to the white epistemological norm of staying calm, keeping things on an even keel, and not letting things "get out of control" through the expression of strong emotions, then I'm destined to fail. So I have tried to reframe the indicators of what I used to think of as failure as actually representing success. I accept there will be periods of noncommunication along the way as people need time to process the starkly different realities they hear from others in a group or from myself as facilitator. But if, at the end of a session, people are still open to talking further, then for me the event has exceeded expectations.

FACING BACKLASH

A couple of years ago I was having dinner with a woman friend who had spent a career of forty years engaged in literacy work in New York's Harlem and Washington Heights. She is white and has worked almost entirely with people of color who love her for her humor, spirit, and warmth, but mostly for her tireless advocacy on their behalf. She won't put up with any bullshit and woe betide any Gotham administrator who creates a bureaucratic obstacle to block her students trying to realize their potential.

Over dinner she told me she had been to a workshop on racism and that the first thing the workshop facilitators did was to ask every white person in the room to stand up and take turns saying, "I am a racist." As she recounted this event, her voice shook with anger. She couldn't believe that her four decades of antiracist endeavors had been discounted by these facilitator—strangers who didn't know anything about her. I'm guessing that the intent of the facilitators was to convey the message that we are all implicated in a racist system and that we have all learned racist instincts and impulses. But my friend was so profoundly insulted that she left the workshop immediately.

I thought about this event, and so many others that have happened to me, as I read Yancy's *Backlash: What Happens When We Talk Honestly about Racism in America*.[31] The book recounts the fallout from a December 2015 op-ed piece he wrote for the *New York Times* philosophy column, "The Stone." Titled "Dear White America," the piece was framed as a gift inviting whites to consider their often unacknowledged collusion in a white supremacist system. But for Yancy it was the start of a vicious and sustained assault unleashed on him that continues to this day. Death threats became common, and being called (all from one voicemail) "a fucking racist . . . a piece of shit destroying the youth of this country . . . a fucking smug nigger . . . a fucking animal" is now his new normal.[32]

In his words, his "physiology registered the wounds. Mood swings. Irritability. Trepidation. Disgust. Anger. Nausea."[33] *Backlash* expands on why he wrote the original letter and allows him to explore more fully the nature of contemporary racism. It chronicles the vitriol directed at him via emails, letters, and voicemails, and on various websites. To anyone proclaiming the arrival of a postracial world, *Backlash* stands as the starkest possible rebuttal. It illustrates how President Trump's nativist signals have clearly legitimized white supremacy to emerge full blown into our national discourse.

Most white readers will, I suspect, be struck most powerfully by the cruelty that Yancy endured. For a professional philosopher to communicate such deep rawness and suffering is, quite simply, astounding. Philosophy sometimes privileges language games but *Backlash* vibrates with visceral feeling and emotion. Pain leaps from its pages along with righteous anger and an agonizing cry for relief. There is simply no contemporary book on race by a professional philosopher written with this level of directness and emotional candor. But what does this book mean for Whites like myself and my woman friend quoted earlier, who can never walk in Yancy's shoes but who are committed to antiracist work?

As I have argued already, as a white man I always look to Yancy to profoundly, but productively, disturb me. In his own terms, I need him to wound me, to unsuture my *de facto* view of myself as a good white person on the right side of history. Whenever I start to get too comfortable with thinking I've got a handle on white supremacy, I count on him to be my Paul Robeson, Angela Davis, or W. E. B. Du Bois. As he figuratively peers over my shoulder to see what I'm writing, I expect to hear him saying, "Come off it, Stephen, are you kidding me? *That's* why you think you've escaped racism?"

Backlash uncompromisingly calls on whites to do one of the most difficult things we can do—to acknowledge being racist as an unvarnished empirical fact. It asks us to recognize how we are caught within a racist system that we benefit from. Whether or not we are righteously committed to working in antiracist ways is beside the point. There is no contradiction in Whites working as antiracist leaders, activists, teachers, or citizens and their being racist. This is because racism is *not* the process of individually demeaning or diminishing others, "a site of individual acts of meanness" rather, it's being "implicated in a complex web of racist power relationships, . . . heteronomous webs of white practices to which you, as a white, are linked both as a beneficiary and as co-contributor to such practices."[34] Since my whiteness constantly benefits me, and since that benefit accrues to me because I'm defined in relation to the stigma of blackness, I am a racist. I don't go about hurling racial epithets but I am "embedded in a pre-existing social matrix of white power" that gives me advantages of which I have only an occasional awareness. To feel safe is my norm, to be "systemically *racially* marked for death" is Yancy's.[35]

Because I grew up intellectually as a critical theorist, I agree that I am systemically formed. I don't think I—Stephen Brookfield—constitute a monological, atomistic, discrete identity. I'm in history and culture and I'm fluid. Who I am is in large part a function of ideological manipulation. I've grown up surrounded with, and formed by, some very powerful ideologies. These include racism, patriarchy, heterosexism, capitalism, and militarism. These belief systems, and the practices and systems in which they're embedded, construct my normal. I've spent a lot of time teaching against racism but, as Yancy argues, that doesn't mean I'm not a racist. I have internalized racist stereotypes at such a deeply visceral, preconscious level that I will never lose them.

Take my instinctive reaction to blackness, especially to black maleness. Blackness screams a complex and contradictory mess of signals to me. In my youth, it was "coolness," mostly because of music and cricket (I grew up in England). In my adulthood, it's been "danger," something animalistic, uncontrollable, and profoundly threatening. I feel an instinctive tightening of my body when I encounter a group of black men. This is beyond reason, deeply sedimented, learned, and transmitted over several decades of media and cultural representations of blackness as violence. My physiology changes as I drive through a mostly black area and I hear a panicked voice inside my head saying "whatever happens, please don't let my car stall." I find myself locking the doors, checking my surroundings and preparing for confrontation.

My conscious thinking process is remarkably weak when placed against these impulses and feelings. I can tell myself "there's your white supremacist conditioning kicking in again" and steel my cognitive warriors to fire their arrows of reason into this oncoming tsunami of emotion. But reasoning doesn't mean much in the face of white supremacist ideological conditioning. Just as with the clinical depression and anxiety that I suffer from, admonitions to "snap out of it" or "stop being so irrational" are mostly powerless. With my depression and anxiety, the doctor can prescribe medication that makes a big difference and keeps me stable. If only someone could write me a prescription to combat the white supremacist ideology embedded in my cultural DNA.

So I am fine (well, maybe not fine, I still desperately want to plead for absolution and forgiveness even as I speak it out loud) with saying I am racist. But this is not true for my woman friend. Even though she has a white racial identity in a white supremacist world, she resents being called racist and feels her life in antiracist work proves that she's not. I meet many white friends, colleagues, and students who feel the same. What do I say to them?

Well, I'll start off by talking about how I've noticed my own learned racism framing my perception of a current event, or how I caught myself in a microaggression earlier that day. There is such shame in the word "racist," such power to humiliate, that I'm wary of beginning a conversation by asking that white friends and colleagues declare themselves racist. Instead, I need to "normalize" racism, to show that because most whites are constantly immersed in racist conditioning, it would be strange if they *didn't* have learned racist impulses, instincts, and perspectives lurking within them. So I need to show first how racism is embedded in my worldview and how I enact racism. I need to earn the right to ask them to consider their own racist identity by first exploring mine. The kind of public modeling that Yancy has done around his own sexism has been an important example of how I might do the same around my racism.

Does a preparatory modeling of one's own racism pay too much respect to white fragility, to the alarm and subsequent retreat from confrontation that stops so many whites from looking squarely at their own racism? I go back and forth on this question. My teacher voice says, "You have to start where people are. Starting with your own agenda without having built a connection to their world is self-indulgent. Get over making yourself feel righteous and take the time to know them." My activist voice replies, "Here you go again, copping out and backing off from necessary danger. Don't be so cowardly— tell it like it is."

Depending on the day, either one of these voices triumphs. But I am helped by the distinction offered by Myles Horton,[36] the social activist who formed the Highlander Folk School in Tennessee that played such a crucial role in the civil rights movement. Myles would say that if your agenda is an educational one and you want to foster learning, you have no option but to start where people are. You need to understand their experiences and worldviews. However, if your agenda is immediate social change and you're fighting against a powerful enemy, you often have no choice other than direct confrontation. You don't have the luxury of time and space needed to bring people into a radical new worldview. You need to drop bombs of dissonance and create crises that explode settled perspectives and disrupt power.

The last part of *Backlash* explores what whites can do in terms of searching honestly for the learned racism and privilege at the heart of their identity.[37] This is hard, given that bearing witness to the kind of racist terrorism chronicled in the book typically prompts whites to show solidarity with people of color. We want to tell them that not all whites are their enemy and that they can count on some of us for support. Speaking for myself, I know that part of me desperately wants the approval of people of color. I want to be told I'm one of the good guys who's exempted from blanket condemnations of white racism. I want to be reassured that I'm an exception and to feel a flush of self-aggrandizing pleasure when saying to myself, "you know what, my mother was right, I *am* a good person."[38]

One of the hardest lessons I have learned as a white person, and therefore as a representative (in the eyes of people of color) of white supremacy, is that I must expect to be mistrusted. I must also anticipate white colleagues accusing me of politically correct reverse racism. When this happens, I need to remember that this is *not* a sign that somehow I'm failing; it happens to every white person in this work. So I tell colleagues getting involved in anti-racist teaching or other activism for the first time that, for different reasons, they should be prepared to be called a racist both by people of color and by Whites. It comes with the territory.

I remember in the early 1990s teaching a class in which the only student of color in the room declared, "I will never trust a White person." Yancy's analysis of the effects of the white gaze and white constructions of blackness help explain why that's the case. I responded to that student by saying, "That's completely understandable, I don't see why you would." But the white majority in the group were shocked and demoralized by his comment and spent a lot of time and energy trying to convince him that they were humane, enlightened, and worthy of his trust. Yancy helps me see that completely valid suspicion, skepticism, and hostility will inevitably accompany any white person's attempt to work alongside people of color in an antiracist effort. This is no comment on you personally. It's a comment on how the history of white supremacy has conditioned people of color to expect whites always to pursue their own self-interest and bolster their own power.

Yancy teaches me that the judgment of whether or not you are an ally to people of color is completely in their hands. You should never expect to be told that you are one and shouldn't get hung up on gauging your antiracist virtue by whether or not you receive that designation. Of course, if you *do* hear that term applied to you by people of color, you should take it as a sincere recognition that you're doing something important and worthwhile. And, for a moment, it's fine to be proud of yourself. We all need moments of recognition and affirmation to keep our energy up for the tough stuff.

But repeat after me: *never declare yourself an ally*. No matter how strongly you are committed to that identity, keep it private. A White person saying "I'm your ally" comes across as condescending and inauthentic. You don't become an ally by saying that you are. You become one by consistently showing up in support of people of color. You become one by losing something. Instead of worrying about getting approval for being heroically antiracist, you should be putting yourself on the line. You should be risking institutional condemnation by doing and saying the things that people of color will suffer even more harshly for doing and saying. Your job is to lose friends, colleagues, money, employment, perks, and prestige by calling out white supremacy in yourself and other Whites and then not to have anyone notice or thank you for it.

CONCLUSION

I expect, rely, and depend on Yancy to keep upending my worldview. His role as a public intellectual has been inspiring and I know he will keep crossing the boundary between the ivory tower and civil society to pose difficult questions regarding the enduring significance of race. As the permanent racial fissures embedded in this apparently "postracial" United States become ever clearer, we will need truth tellers who are unafraid to disturb and provoke us on what it means to be white. Yancy's body of work does this for us as we move into the third decade of the new millennium, and we will be all the better for it.

Chapter 14

Hopeless Whiteness and the Philosophical and Pedagogical Task

Anthony Paul Smith

"You leave us with *no* hope."[1] This is the response George Yancy received from a white male professor after a public lecture by Yancy where he analyzed whiteness and white racism. Challenging exactly who is included in this white professor's "us," Yancy testifies to the power of hope found in the Black tradition and used to protect and fight back against the nefarious and death-dealing effects of white supremacist, antiblack racism. Yancy recognizes that the hope desired by this white professor is of a different kind. In some sense, it represents the hopelessness of whites to take responsibility for their position within a violent society. For white educators it represents the hopeless lack of responsibility taken for examining how that whiteness functions in the classroom.

What might happen if we—the *we* implicated in the words earlier—begin to undertake the philosophical task of analyzing whiteness without hope? What would our pedagogy—complicated and doomed to failure by that whiteness—look like if we nevertheless did that work without hope? Could we live in such infidelity? That is, though this will need explanation, what would happen if we undertook this task under the conditions set for it by the demand for Black freedom?

Frank B. Wilderson III describes this demand for Black freedom as "hyperbolic":

For the Black, freedom is an ontological, rather than experiential, question. There is no philosophically credible way to attach an experiential, a contingent, rider onto the notion of freedom when one considers the Black—such as freedom from gender or economic oppression, the kind of contingent riders rightfully place on the non-Black when thinking freedom. Rather, the riders that one could place on Black freedom would be hyperbolic—though no less true—and ultimately untenable: freedom from the world, freedom from Humanity, freedom from everyone (including one's Black self).[2]

How might white educators teach if they were to take seriously such a demand? The hyperbolic negativity, the hopelessness, manifest for so many whites in this demand provokes so much anxiety. This anxiety is present only because those who are sick with the desire to be good and to be innocent confuse the refusal of some experiential freedom with a demand that can be answered with some form of compromise located in the white supremacist, antiblack world.[3] Jared Sexton describes the analytical position of this negativity when he describes how such a call is heard by Black men when given by Black feminism: "What complicates this ethical call immediately is not simply that it is impossible . . . but rather that it is strictly *unanswerable*."[4] What would it mean to give up on goodness and innocence as white people who still take responsibility for hearing this ethical demand for Black freedom?

This chapter explores these questions by way of and in homage to the philosophical work of George Yancy, the attendant pedagogical reflections and practices he details in his work, and what might follow from it. The chapter begins with an overview of elements of Yancy's philosophical work with the goal of demonstrating the analytical power of that work. This section examines the social ontology of *bodies* and *gazes* that Yancy outlines before turning to summarize how that ontology plays out in pedagogical practice. Sad affects, like that of hopelessness, are necessary and good for white subjects to undergo in this practice. Therefore, I offer an analysis of white shame as a supplement to Yancy's work, before turning to a reflection on how white shame might be used positively in a pedagogical setting.

It is common for white scholars to spend some time laying out the confessional boundaries of their work when engaging in questions related to race and racism. So common is this practice that one can find it mocked in memes and posts scattered across social media. The temptation to such confession arises out of the anxiety of being seen as white and in the desire to be a "good white" with recognition as such.[5] I offer no such confession here; I take it as given that taking responsibility for one's social position as white means giving up on the very innocence hoped for through confession. Though it must be recognized that such a meta-move is open to further traps of narcissism or the re-centering of whites. Yancy marks the different practices of theory by white and Black subjects powerfully:

> Whites who deploy theory in the service of fighting against white racism must caution against the seduction of white narcissism, the recentering of whiteness, even if it is the object of critical reflection, and, hence, the process of

sequestration from the real world of weeping, suffering, and traumatized Black bodies impacted by the operations of white power. As antiracist whites continue to make mistakes and continue to falter in the face of institutional interpellation and habituated racist reflexes, tomorrow, a Black body will be murdered as it innocently reaches for its wallet. The sheer weight of this reality mocks the patience of theory.[6]

I locate my position as a white subject not because it deserves recognition or sympathy but because the analytical method detailed here makes it necessary and contextualizes why whiteness is the focus of this chapter. Any critical analysis of whiteness must be subject to the excessive demands of Black freedom if it is to move beyond critique to abolition. The process of abolishing whiteness and the social ontology it underpins requires eroding whiteness as an identity by subjecting it to a critique (that might be described as *hysterical* for its refusal to be satisfied with the reform of whiteness) as part of a multifaceted struggle against the white supremacist, antiblack world order.[7]

The analysis of whiteness is only a useful tool when it is part of a broader project of abolishing the connection of whiteness with powers.[8] It requires that one consider whiteness using the philosophical and theoretical tools developed largely by Black thinkers and undertake a serious course of study in the debates and works collected under the banner of Black Studies, knowing that one—if they are a white subject—cannot make a home there and that such homelessness is a gift in the struggle against the traps of one's own white self. Perhaps, at the end of the world, when the hyperbolic demands of Black freedom have found their proper expression, which may indeed be a kind of cacophonous and joyful silence, we will all be free from the very terms of value. Until then we must take up this work without hope of winning or success.

ELEMENTS OF THE PHILOSOPHY OF GEORGE YANCY: THEORY AND PRACTICE

Bodies and Gazes; Or, Some Elements of the Social Ontology of Race

Over the course of Yancy's prolific philosophical career, he has reoriented our thinking about race generally and whiteness in particular. While important philosophical work has been done and continues to be done on the "being (or nonbeing) of blackness," the fundamental concern of Yancy's theoretical work is to hold a mirror to the white gaze so that *that* subject may begin to see himself or herself as a problem.[9] Yancy's work tells us something about blackness, but specifically about blackness within the constructed social ontology of the white gaze. As that gaze is both constitutive and constituted by white antiblack racism, the understanding of blackness that emerges there is always with blackness and Black subjects as a negative term, the negation of which allows for the securing of the being of whiteness. The white self secures his existence in the world by not being nonbeing, the negative, the abject, or, in Yancy's preferred terms, the Other. But by making whiteness a problem, by calling attention to the position of a subject as white, Yancy disrupts the coherence of that subject, the smooth movement of that white subject through the world. This aspect of his work might be described as "Critical White Studies," but not in the sense that the majority of the canon in the humanities might be thought of as a kind of unacknowledged white (male) studies. Here the canon of mostly straight, white men is not studied, but the question suddenly comes, "What is the white?" When the question is asked with a white subject present, then the experience is suddenly one of being seen, being caught in a gaze that is not one's own. One is now not a subject, the one who gazes, but an object, a body, caught up in the gaze of another.

Yancy's investigation of race in general and whiteness in particular is carried out with a sophisticated philosophical framework. Reading his work is an encounter with a philosophy in action, not a discourse about philosophy or the works of other philosophical thinkers. The clarity of his writing and analyses can obscure the philosophical tools being used and framework being deployed. Yancy also does not position himself within any particular philosophical school or tradition and borrows freely from American pragmatism and existential phenomenology as well as from thinkers who have been positioned outside the philosophical establishment in the United States, like Judith Butler. In this section, I will trace a few of the elements of Yancy's philosophy, focusing specifically on elements important for what I term the "social ontology of race" in his work.

One of the most powerful ways that Yancy is able to turn whiteness into a problem is through his analysis of the White/Black relationship. This relationship is scalable and can be located between two people or all the way up to the level of society. This scalable relationship is the site of the social ontology of race that undergirds each level of relationality. In simple terms, the existence of a subject as white or black is not given "naturally" but is given through a social construction. There is no White/Black relationship between two individuals outside of a social sphere where the two lived bodies come to be White or Black through recognition. In the White/Black relation, there are bodies and there are gazes; these are the fundamental parts of Yancy's social ontology.

In this way, Yancy's analysis of the White/Black relation in *Black Bodies, White Gazes* mirrors Frantz Fanon's own in *Black Skin, White Masks*.[10] Fanon is moved to declare that there is to be found no positive ontology of the

Black individual or person to be found within the history of philosophy and so turns to the lived experiences of bodies and gazes in the world in order to give attention to the negative ontology found there. In following this method Yancy focuses his attention and ours upon the ways that bodies are placed in social space and the way that such positioning allows for movement through that space or cuts off such movement. In biology, this is the classic meaning of the term "lifeform." The space that a species is able to take up within an environment gives form to the life that can be lived by that species and the individual creatures that make it up.

Yancy shows us that the body is the material through which race is lived and that the social relation, conditioned hegemonically by the white gaze, is the condition for that lived experience, a kind of pressure at varying intensities upon the two bodies. He writes, "Within this context, 'seeing' is not merely a private and isolated performance but the repetition of a collective performative gazing, the reproduction of the weight of a racist oracular epistemic order sustained by 'a culturally and structurally racist society.'"[11] The bodies come to be particularly racialized subjects through this white gaze; the bodies come to have meaning and value through their placement by this gaze. This is shown throughout Yancy's numerous analyses of seemingly quotidian moments, from the riding of an elevator by a Black man and a white woman, to the Black teenager walking down the street and hearing the present absence of the white subject in the clicking of the car lock, to his own reflections of being a Black professor in a classroom populated mostly by white students.

By starting with bodies and gazes both Fanon and Yancy turn us to what is before us. Theirs is not a philosophy of ideas applied to the lived realities around us, but a philosophy that begins with those lived realities and fearlessly questions how they are structured. This is important for readers of Yancy's work to note, especially for those who want to take its lessons into the classroom or apply them generally. If Yancy began with just the gaze, then he would be forced to begin with philosophical discourse, with what is *said* to be. Since what is said about Black people—even when it is said with a particularly nefarious form of silence—is always ontologically negative, this would be to begin a game that is fixed from the start and which the Black subject is destined to lose. The gaze gives meaning and value to the body, but the body exists before that gaze and in some sense escapes it. Within the white gaze the Black subject is placed under a kind of erasure, but those who are Black experience their power and vitality in the lived experience of being a body. By insisting that the being of white subjects or Black subjects is constituted not by truth or eternal ideas or any "natural" reality but by gazes looking at bodies, Yancy disrupts that gaze. With this gap between the body and the gaze Yancy introduces the unsettling (for the white) and potentially liberatory (for the Black) experience of *decoherence*. It is true that "whiteness . . . is a master of concealment," but in turning the gaze upon the white body and making it seen *as white* the startling reality of that body's finitude and porousness emerges.[12] Where the white gaze directed outward offered coherence, the gaze turned back toward the white body brings shame.

Anxious Subjects; Or, the Intersection of Theory and Practice

The quotidian scenes that make up the material for Yancy's analysis often describe experiences of guilt or shame, or generally sad affects, on the part of white students or colleagues. At one point, Yancy is even accused by a white woman philosopher of wanting to bring tears to the eyes of white people.[13] Yancy's philosophical work does evoke affects in those who engage with it, and the emotional response that manifests often is in my experience one of rejection or confession, especially, I would risk the wager, among many white students and readers.

Yancy's own creation of a "space of vulnerability" in the classroom and in his writing is part of his mode of analysis. The aim is to understand the nature of our racialized selves in a white supremacist, antiblack world and not to demand confessions that all too often function to "ease the conscience of whites."[14] This theoretical project is thoroughly philosophical, but Yancy understands that the way it elicits emotional responses marks it as quite different from projects concerned with the ontology of numbers. The material being analyzed matters because *we* are the material, along with the social world that we live in. As he says, "Discussions involving the ontology of numbers, while I imagine can get very passionate, do not implicate the self in the same way discussions around race and racism do. The self is not similarly exposed, made potentially vulnerable."[15] When white subjects are made to recognize themselves as racial subjects in a mirrored relational way to how Black subjects have historically been recognized, they are then subject to the same experience of decoherence that marks blackness within the antiblack social ontology of whiteness. By "mirrored relational way," I do not intend to suggest anything like an equality of experience between white and Black subjects. In being made to see themselves as white through Yancy's critical apparatus, the white subject experiences this self-seeing only very locally, without the attendant systems of power and domination that further make up the antiblack world. This "white double-consciousness" is affected through a split between how we/they see themselves and how we/they imagine themselves to be seen by the other.[16] To note the important difference between true double-consciousness, which is one part of a wider antiblack apparatus of power, and white experience of this effect, we should think of the "mirroring" as a kind of *pale* reflection of the real violence experienced by Black subjects. Yancy's mode of analysis invites those white subjects who wish to use it to reflect upon themselves and their own positionality within lived experience, quite literally to reflect upon their bodies not only as they interact in time and space with other bodies but also as they are named by the gazes that form the system of recognition and give form to an unevenly shared social life.

Such an experience produces anxiety. In terms of the classroom space, such anxiety is the affective mood of the space for vulnerability, a literally unsafe space. In the fostering of anxious subjects (lived bodies) through being faced with the anxiety-producing subject of race (which for white subjects means confronting whiteness as such), Yancy actually levels the playing field. For Black students in majority-white classrooms, most often with white professors, there are no such safe spaces. He quotes Zeus Leonardo and Ronald K. Porter to this effect: "Violence is already there."[17] Through the practice of recognizing that violence and being subject to a much less intensive version of it (the white who sees themselves as white is not subject to social death), the white subject is forced, through their theoretical practice, to begin to see how their own position within the social ontology is predicated upon that violence.

This is how Yancy's notion of the "ambush" plays out as a positive pedagogical moment.[18] In the intersection of theory and practice, we find the subject under the refined critical gaze directed toward whiteness. When undertaking a philosophical analysis of whiteness and the racist world that is co-constituted by antiblack white/black social ontology, one's subject position is fully present and cannot be simply ignored. The subject, wherever they are positioned, is part of the analysis itself. For example, it is through the ambush that it is revealed "how the white self is other to itself."[19]

EXCURSUS ON WHITE SHAME

Yancy is correct that "*thankfulness* ought to be the attendant attitude as one is ambushed."[20] Yet, pedagogically, this intersection of theory and practice requires some thought to be given to how such thankfulness might be evoked when so often the reaction is one of defense, sometimes violently lashing out as the coherence of one's white self is threatened through being subject to the gaze. To move toward this positive pedagogical moment of thankfulness, we must return first to the sad affects that appear to emerge for white subjects when they encounter this work, namely guilt and shame. Again, Yancy's work invites his readers to a mode of analysis and not confession. That analysis, for white readers, requires a turning to their attendant whiteness that carries with it sad affects. When a white subject feels guilty or shameful, the point is not to find relief from that feeling, but to turn fearlessly toward it, to "tarry with the embedded and opaque white racist self," as Yancy's final chapter of *Look, a White!* has it. In this section, I will analyze white guilt and white shame from within the social ontology of bodies and gazes outlined by Yancy and then discuss how I have come to use it in framing a specific kind of pedagogical practice.

People often shut down when confronted by the demand to live ethically within a world where ideal ethical living is impossible at a basic, foundational level. Even though the problems are structural, their effects are lived by individual people in social relations with others. When confronted by that problem, the individuals rightly sees themselves as part of the problem, either as one who benefits or even propagates the problem or as the one who suffers directly under it. For those in both positions, there are ample examples in everyday life of people needing to repress the affects that emerge through the analysis of the problem.

Consider a heterosexual romantic relationship between a cis-gendered man and woman. However loving and supportive the partners try to make their life together, that relationship is still structured and pressurized by patriarchal norms, capitalist demands on life, heteronormative framings of happiness, compulsory notions of monogamy and ownership, and a host of other social relations that actively attack the possibility of a love that transcends those structures. Queer relationships, though having the virtue of historically pushing back against these framings more antagonistically and offering alien ways of being together, have to face their own set of structural constraints. For, in our homes, regardless of who inhabits them, all the problems of nature and culture meet, all the problems of politics and ethics coalesce, and though we navigate them the best we can, we are but bound to failure. The failure of our society and culture.[21]

Now such an experience of failure is even more obvious within the relationship between a white person and a Black person. When confronted with the unavoidable ethical failure of such a relationship, the white subject reacts with the need to break the gaze, to not be seen as white. Specifically not to be seen as white within the social ontology where the cohesiveness of whiteness is only guaranteed through the incoherence of blackness, where being is only secured through not being nonbeing, where one's identity is secured through a form of violence against Black subjects and bodies that is so pervasive as to recede into the background.[22] One such reaction is to identify this affect as guilt so that they may dispose of it. White guilt, the response goes, would necessitate that the individual white person had done some specific ethical wrongdoing. Calling to mind Yancy's analyses of these lived experiences throughout his work, the individual white person might say, "Sure, I've said the n-word now and then while singing along to my favorite song, or maybe I've clutched my purse in the elevator, but more because I fear men than because I fear Black men in particular." "However," they continue, "no one in my family ever owned slaves and I have never been rude or abusive to anyone because of the color of their skin. Therefore, this guilt you are trying to make me bear is something I am not guilty of."

In this constant declaration of innocence from white guilt, a more powerful affect is being repressed and denied: white shame. It is common enough in pop psychological publications and media to find the difference between guilt and shame marked this way: guilt is about some real or imagined harm I have done, an individual or discrete harmful act, and shame is about what someone is, that they are the kind of person who could do something harmful. This pop psychological notion further can be filled out by looking to the existentialist understanding found in Sartre and developed by the environmental theorist William R. Jordan III, where shame is located at the very level of being recognized as a self. As Sartre writes, "Shame . . . is the recognition of the fact that I *am* indeed that object which the Other is looking at and judging."[23] In seeing ourselves through how the Other sees us, we see one truth of who we are, we see ourselves as objects in the world and therefore not as free, transcendent subjects, but as positioned within social ontology.[24] By virtue of being embedded within that social ontology, we are by definition not that free, transcendent subject we may in bad faith believe ourselves to be.

Both guilt and shame manifest from the experience of some limit or failing on the part of the body that experiences them. But we may refine the difference between the two affects by noting that, in this register, guilt indices a debt that we are responsible for and that might be repaid, whereas shame indices our "natural, radical, existential dependency" and so a debt that we are not responsible for in any meaningful sense and are unable to repay.[25] Guilt is about individual acts and when people talk about justice in the usual way this is often what they mean. Justice, in this sense, is about correcting relationships, balancing the scales, or even restoring what has been damaged. Shame is an affect that gets at something more intransigent about our existence. Individual acts may be part of our shame, but the brokenness here is manifest at the very condition for "our" existence, according to Sartre and Jordan.

Both guilt and shame emerge from within some kind of relation and a form of debt found there. The way in which one is not "responsible" for the debt incurred in shame is easier to see when it is considered at the ecological level, where it is most important for Jordan's work. That is, shame is bound up in the network of interdependent relations that make up a food web. Jordan laconically remarks, "This involves, quite simply, eating—or being eaten by—other members of the community. Such a relationship is obviously deeply problematic."[26] For all living bodies to continue living, other bodies must be destroyed and killed. Even vegetarians, despite the more ethical nature of their relationship to other animals, do not escape this reality. While there is, to my mind, a qualitative difference between most animals and most plants, there are also the deaths caused by industrial farming, destruction of ecosystems that unevenly impact other animals, and pollution that impacts negatively more impoverished humans (a difference in human worth that is usually tied to racial and gender differences). The killing of anything so that one may live evokes shame because it forces us to see that there is something essentially rend open within the very fabric of existence itself. Existence requires an act which is violent (the killing of an animal, in this example) in order for an act that is good (continuing to live). Following Yancy, we may say that the order of being is unsutured itself and this fissure is given affective attention in our shame.

Some readers may feel concern and suspicion about the seeming naturalist paradigm I have described here and its fit with the essentially constructed nature of the white supremacist, antiblack racist social ontology of Yancy's work. Those readers would be correct if ecological thinking was understood to fit such a naturalistic philosophical framework, whereas I instead understand nature to be an essentially plastic and perverse reality that immanently is inseparable from what we would normally think of as culture (and vice versa). Consequently, I do not accept that "natural" is another name for "good," or even that appeals to nature provide any kind of ground for ethics.[27] At the level of individual acts (or in terms of guilt), the shame that is present in the ecosystem relationship of killing and eating is distinct from the white shame that I claim should emerge when the white body is taken as such (i.e. as a white body) through the gaze that is redirected towards him. But what is important here is the precise way white shame manifests at the level of the white subject's very existence. The individual person who eats likely had nothing to do with the killing of the animal or farming of the plant they are ingesting, yet they are objectively a part of that relation of exchange and dependent upon it. White shame is isomorphic in that the existence of a body that lives in the world as a white subject—the very existence lived through me every day—is predicated on the genocide of indigenous peoples and the enslavement and afterlife of that social death for bodies that live as Black. The white subject only exists as white because of the abject role constituted relationally as the Black body. Even at the brute empirical level of economic conditions, the wealth of white Americans and other Westerners are directly tied to the primitive accumulation gained through the labor of enslaved Black people. As Yancy writes, "Because white racism is so incredibly rooted in the fabric of white America, there is no place called 'innocence.'"[28] This is what the gaze reveals to the white subject when one is made to recognize their white self, especially when that white self is experienced as other to itself.[29]

Sartre and Jordan's easy use of the plural pronoun "we" and the plural possessive pronoun "our" suggests a universalism that the concept of white shame rejects. While all human bodies may be caught up in the unsutured nature of being, as within an ecosystem relationship, those bodies experience that relatedness in uneven ways owing to the racialized social ontology of white supremacist antiblackness. The shame a white subject may feel when they recognize their own recognition within the gaze is different from the shame one may feel when they see their finitude and dependency to the violence of eating. Yet, while there is no way to continue living without eating, the white subject also sees no possibility for their continued existence as a white subject within the social ontology as constructed in the white supremacist, antiblack world. While one's body (if one is a white subject) is not predicated on that exclusion, one's identity as a white subject with all its attendant relative privileges is, even if one did not choose to be thrown as a white subject into a world. The very existence of white people is predicated on the (mis)recognition of Black men and women who inhabit the world with those subjects. Therefore, the abolition of whiteness is the apocalyptic demand to destroy the present state of things.

Yancy writes that when white subjects are subject to the critical gaze there is often an acting-out rooted in a desire to be seen as singular and not white.[30] Such a desire is understandable and no doubt mirrors, albeit *palely* again, the desire that Black subjects have to be seen as singular and not subject to the negative and death-dealing effects of their subject position. Yet there is no escape from these subject positions, save the end of the (white, antiblack) world.

ATTENDING TO SHAME

Shame is a more adequate affect to the hyperbolic demand for Black freedom than hope or guilt. Both hope and guilt suggest that there is some way to definitively answer the demand for Black freedom; both suggest that there are actions that can be taken which might right the scales or bring out some change that would balance the White/Black relation of our white supremacist, antiblack social ontology. Shame, located at the level of being or existence itself, is affectively immanent to the brokenness of bodies and the seemingly intractable nature of the white gaze. There appears to be no total escape from the white gaze and even when that gaze is deployed in a critical manner back toward white people it still repeats certain logics of the white world. The desire not to be white, while surfacing largely as a defense reaction, witnesses to a certain negativity, a sense that whiteness and the world it co-constitutes need to be abolished. At the same time, in the interim, everyone feels the need to survive and that requires a kind of objective collusion with the state of things.

Yancy often speaks from his own position as a Black male professor teaching in majority-white classrooms. Yet the vast majority of the Western professoriate is made up of white professors. There is something shameful about being a white professor. The modern university has always been a bastion of white supremacy and antiblackness. It is in the works of scholars that the racial social ontology was given scientific status and in classrooms where the tools of racial governmentality were passed to mostly white students.[31] Today, as the neoliberal consensus continues to erode what Wendy Brown calls the *demos*, inclusive of public and private universities, our very means for survival are provided for by the increasingly unsustainable debts taken on by students, an increasing number of whom are not white and so are not guaranteed the same modes of access that white graduates are guaranteed.[32] In the United States, as demographics continue to shift and the country heads toward a majority nonwhite population (where white people will make up less than 50 percent of the population, though still likely the largest demographic group), the demographics of many universities are also beginning to change. My current institution reflects this reality and like many other small, private, liberal arts universities, it is largely dependent upon student tuition dollars. While the faculty are nearly 90 percent white and the institution undoubtedly is hegemonically white, oscilates year to year between majority white and majority nonwhite.

The demand to decolonize the curriculum and to incorporate analyses of race (as well as gender, sexuality, and class) into our courses takes on a different meaning in those classrooms where the majority of students are not white, but where the professor is. Questions of race cannot be siloed off but should be part of any serious class that looks at questions of ethics or, as in my field, religious practices and beliefs. Yet the white professor who takes this seriously and has critically examined their own whiteness, when standing before a class of bodies caught and made subjects within the social ontology, is sure to feel the anxiety and shame of that critical gaze. When it is said that "violence is already there" in the classroom, for many of our students, our white bodies are the embodiment of that violence. There should be shame in that recognition.

Jordan says that modern society is particularly adept at turning away and running from shame or tries to address that shame through mastery. When what is called for is attention to the reality that evokes such shame.[33] For the white educator I think this means recognition that there will never be an adequate pedagogy, that the work in your classroom will never be done. It also requires a serious and focused course of study in the Black tradition of scholarship and thought as it relates to your field with the understanding that this is not ours. That there is no cohesive "we." It is a painful experience to see something beautiful like the tradition of Black thought and know that you cannot participate fully, though again palely and without any analogue to the pain that has called forth the power of the Black tradition. Your necessary engagement with the Black tradition should not win you accolades or elicit anger when the labor you undertake is not recognized. To attend to shame means to recognize the finitude and limitations of ourselves in the face of the work that is to be done here.

When Yancy writes about subverting white academic spaces, he does so in dialogue with the pedagogical works of bell hooks. For hooks, every student and educator is on a quest for wholeness.[34] From the perspective of shame, however, such a quest is always doomed to failure. From within the differential social ontology of the White/Black, there is never any cohesion, there is never a rootedness that might give us a self we can identify as truly "I." In this vein, Jared Sexton says that the deracination of Black subjects witnesses to the possibility of a universal deracination and a figure of the unsovereign.[35] When a white professor opens themselves up to the unsuturing powers of the gaze of their Black students, they are forced to attend pedagogically to the task of teaching as a deracinated, unsutured body. In placing themselves under the condition of Black thought, a thought at the end of the world, they have to begin the arduous and unending task of disarticulating teaching from white power.[36] This is a call, an unanswerable one, to teach shamed face.

Afterword

As I thought and rethought about how I might begin to engage the space of this afterword, there is one word that emerged over and over again: *Thankfulness*. Being thankful presupposes the concept of a species dependency; it says that I am not alone, a solipsistic consciousness. Thankfulness, as I am using it, is a robust form of recognition, pregnant with sociality, and richly filled with *kenosis*—a self-emptying of any illusions that my voice, my work, my attempt to come to terms with the meaning of human suffering, in all of its modalities, is generated *ex nihilo*. The truth of this interconnectedness, this social ontological contiguity, this shared space of corporeal entanglement, was made evident to me as I read through all the contributions—from the foreword and the introduction to the contributed chapters. The self-narrative that I construct, the story that I tell myself, the critical voice that I try to hone, the insights that I attempt to generate and forge, well, all of these, are limited and shaped by a form of active meaning-making that is always already part of a larger discursive field, linked to a concatenation of ideas that have their own historical situatedness and background assumptions and are mediated by multiple voices. So, as I read through the critically rich material within this text, the *lie* of absolute epistemic mastery and self-transparency and the other lie that takes the form of the "god trick," which is to presuppose that I can theorize or philosophize from nowhere, were brought to the fore. While it is true that I'm aware of these lies, it is not always the case that I experience them with such gravity and salience. As I read each of the contributions, there was that sense of coming to see myself/my work anew, coming to recognize some aspect of how my philosophical voice, which is never a "pure voice," prized open another way of seeing the world or some issue, and coming to appreciate how my philosophical voice is both mine and yet not mine. Again, this speaks to our dependency, a form of radical and generative precarity.

Hence, *giving thanks*, being *thankful*, would not make much sense were it the case that I was born from the head of a god, fully formed—complete, whole. My thankfulness recognizes the ontology of my limits, but it also appreciates the vulnerability that this entails. And while it is true that vulnerability can and will lead to moments of wounding, vulnerability also functions as the condition for healing, being heard, creating spaces and openings for being thankful. Indeed, in the very act of giving thanks, I recognize the not-me, the other who has given of themselves, a gesture which their vulnerability makes possible. So, when I read through the contributions, I immediately recognized my limits through the alterity of the contributors, and through their words that spoke to me and will continue to speak to me.

I want to thank the editors, Kimberley Ducey, Clevis Headley, and Joe R. Feagin. I can say with a fair amount of certainty that this text is Kimberley's brainchild. And for that, I am honored. Her outpouring of generosity is indicative of the theme of thankfulness, and it is profoundly mutual. When she communicated to me that she would put together this text, I was deeply humbled. Kimberley's disposition has always been one of thankfulness, joy, and appreciation, of showing an abundance of indebtedness to my work. Given that she is a brilliant sociologist, and such a genuine, caring, and generous person, I don't take her indebtedness for granted. I take it as a beautiful acknowledgment that affirms my philosophical value, my contributions to this world. I am also thankful for the editors' framing of my work as improvisatory, my writing as an act of embodied courage, and how my thinking breaks with institutional "stasis of thought and imagination." From scholar Robert Farris Thompson, the editors deploy the theme of "flashes of the spirit" to characterize my philosophical and meta-philosophical work. Counter-semiotically, vis-à-vis whiteness, they argue that "Yancy's opuses represent a continuous discursive manifestation of pulses of light." Given the disruptive and constructive spirit of my work, which is inseparable from the historical and conceptual synergy of Blackness or from the resistant and productive spirit of Africana philosophical thought—with its "pulses of *light*"—here is a case where there is the inverse of the semiotic hegemony and exclusionary logics of whiteness as "purity," "spotless," "cleanliness," and "enlightenment."

While Kimberley courageously initiated this text, Clevis Headley and Joe R. Feagin, both brilliant scholars, gave of themselves to support its conceptual contours and materialization. Clevis is one of the most critically engaging contemporary philosophers that I know, and he is so much more. His interdisciplinary fund of philosophical knowledge is astonishing. Whether its Africana philosophy, analytic philosophy, philosophy of language, or critical philosophy of race, Clevis's conceptual acuity is inviable. His generosity and friendship are appreciated. He has always been there for me when asked. His critically engaging commentary over the years on my work has always been charitable, synthetic, and demanding. His thoughts on my work have very often revealed to me aspects of my work that I've missed. In short, he is a critical voice that I would say functions as a witness, especially within the context of locating the historical and philosophical importance of my work and identity within Africana or African American philosophy and existential phenomenological philosophy of existence. Joe, the sociologist and critical theorist of structural systemic white racism who, as far as I'm concerned, has no contemporary equal, is one of those academic legends that I read about before coming to know him. Joe is a scholar who has not been seduced by academic elitism. Indeed, he finds it anathema to intellectual and scholarly integrity. I would even say that he sees academic elitism, especially given the whiteness and maleness that typically underwrites it, as ethically wanting, a bastion of neoliberal debauchery tied to corrupt forms of marketization and racial capitalist hegemony. Joe is humble, giving, and a powerhouse of critical knowledge production; he has named the problem—whiteness and its violent logics and governmentality vis-à-vis the United States and the world. The editors' collectively written introduction speaks *to me* and *about me*, and yet the introduction functions as a form of invitation, a gesture, to see myself from a perspective that is not of my own making—an elsewhere—which again raises the issue of alterity and thankfulness.

I am also incredibly humbled by the generous and philosophically substantial foreword written by Judith Butler. The foreword gives an account of my work and my embodied identity in ways that recognize me, that honor me as a person of integrity and a philosopher of passion. There is a generative and profoundly appreciable sense of having been seen and yet constituted by a narrative telling and sharing that is not mine, but Judith's. I found myself silently saying: "Yes! She sees me. Yes! That's what I'm trying to do." Judith not only sees what I also understand as the love of philosophy coming through in my work, but she also sees how I, as she says, "[experiment] with the essay form." Judith wagers that my leaving academia temporarily and my engagement with Black culture through the medium of journalism, which I see as an important moment in my life to experiment with the essay form, was indispensable in terms of leading to a "keener sense of intimate and respectful love." I feel compelled to quote Judith in full:

> All this he brought forward into philosophy, expanding its terms, its forms, and its public audience. The journalism never fell away, and the philosophy is, as it were, all over the public writings: the questions, the demonstration of what it is to be unknowing and self-reflective, the effort to discern meaning, even ultimate meaning, in the field of Black cultural production, the openness to other worlds, but also, the public solicitation: think with me, come closer.

Judith's wager is not just faithful to my life, but cuts at the very core of an inchoate aspect of myself—an opacity—that nevertheless can be said to have enabled a self-narration with greater clarity, which never means total transparency. She writes: "His writing is organized by a keen sense of address. He is called upon to call upon us, and with every piece there is a question: now, who will take this up? Sometimes these writings are fierce challenges, but always a mode of address: he is speaking and writing to us." What do I make of the description of being "called upon to call upon us?" Well, again, there is one response: thankfulness. Judith locates a passionate striving in my work, a yearning that is profoundly located at the site of a complex intercorporeality. Judith also locates that yearning, that "keen sense of address," within the space of a fragile theological hope that longs for, and that hungers for, something *more*.

It is a deep sense of gratitude that I give to Judith Butler, and to my mentor, the late James G. Spady, and to a Black historical tradition that has never not been courageous in its call for something more, something truer than empty promises and vacuous symbols. Telescoping two of my articles, "Dear God" and "Dear White America," Judith discerns and names something that is deeply significant to me, something that, if death comes tomorrow, I will leave still treasuring. I suffer. I am philosopher who weeps. I feel my complicity with forms of evil which I mourn. I don't know why I am here, why we are here, in this cosmos. This makes me mourn. Children are brutally murdered. I ache because I feel as if I have failed them. I have for many years now, beginning when I was about seventeen years old, genuinely desired an original relationship with God, an appeal that acknowledges the risk that there is no God at all. It's not an epistemological desire fused with arrogance. Rather, as Judith describes my entreaty, it is because I suffer, we suffer, we are forlorn. There is nothing that tells me *a priori* that such an original relationship is impossible. After all, I have *never* been here before. None of us have. This thing call "being" is our first time. And it is so incredibly short. In "Dear White America," I was also seeking an original relationship. Instead of silence from a "hidden God" (*Deus Absconditus*), all was revealed in an onslaught of racist vitriol: Nigger, Nigger, Nigger, Nigger. Yet that is the price of a gift given in mode of vulnerability. At the core of each of those letters, their salutations were not mere rhetorical devices, but indicative of a longing, a gesture of risk. Judith recognizes these modes of address within my work. As Judith says, I am asking: "Is anyone listening? Is anyone reading? The essays show their pain and their longing, making a bid for relationality on the basis of vulnerability." If what I do is "a passionate form of philosophizing," as Judith notes, then it is trying to rethink philosophy, to embody philosophical practice as an address, an address shaped not simply by *Logos* but by *Sarx*, a mode of address directed to the other, especially the suffering persons of embodied *flesh*. It is an address directed to those who refuse to see those who suffer, to those who refuse to honor the vulnerability and precarity of others through a process of "grieving" that consists only in a mode of static emotionality, *noblesse oblige*, or ethical heroism, which remains all about the hero. My aim is a mode of address that motivates the removal of that knee, an address that encourages the swallowing of those words (or the spitting out of those words) of hatred and xenophobia. It is a mode of address that envisions self-emptying and unsuturing in the presence of those whose lives have not been deemed grievable. I am thankful that Judith tarries within that space of vulnerability, which is really a mode of being, *our inescapable* mode of being, and where she desires to "think with me, come closer."

Each of the contributors within this book attempts to "think with me, come closer." As I read through the chapters, there were these heightened affective moments where I wrote in the margins: "Thank you!" To be thankful, within this context, speaks to an important way in which I conceptualize the ethical weight of knowledge production. Writing is a socially grounded activity. It invites readers to tarry with our work, to see themselves (or not) reflected in our work, to encourage them to reach within and beyond themselves. I have always found the process of writing to be ethically daunting, a profound act of risk-taking. I am often faced with a sense of uncertainty, unease, of having inadvertently misled someone. This not only speaks to the importance of making sure that we think with as much clarity as possible as we write, but it also speaks to our care for the other, the reader, the responsibility that comes with communication, persuasion, truth-telling, and trustworthiness. The chapters within this book function, *inter alia*, to create a textual space of shared epistemic responsibility and a commitment to truth-telling as best we can. This raises again the importance of our limits and dependency.

Each chapter, to do it justice, would require an extensive response beyond the purview of this afterword. Ryan J. Johnson (a white male) and Biko Mandela Gray (a Black male) have written an engaging chapter that moves with a dialectic of tension that resists resolution. My sense is that this mimics what I theorize as the binary structure of whiteness. In this case, as they make clear, the Black body as a problem is thrown forward, an obstacle to its own emergence. There is also the sense of the Black body being confiscated and having a distorted meaning projected upon it. Being an obstacle to one's own Black being is not ahistorical, but profoundly historical. By marking whiteness as "blemish," the authors refuse to leave whiteness unmarked, as "innocent," especially as this "blemish" creates the very conditions for the sociogenic production of Black persons as problems. What is experimentally rich about this chapter is the core of a deep and yet phenomenologically fruitful contradiction—the Black body (Biko) speaks. Rather than reinscribing the binary assumption that whiteness (Ryan) does theory and Blackness (Biko) can only provide experience, the dialectic is richer as Biko's voice speaks from the interior "non-being" of Blackness, while leaving us to determine if his voice is indicative of "freedom" or still trapped within the consumptive logics of whiteness. It is Biko's voice, along with the demands of my interrogations of whiteness that begin to trouble Ryan's whiteness. In this way, Ryan tarries with his whiteness, its antiblack structural and lived dimensions. Both authors thematize the importance of whiteness to risk its embodied habits, privilege, and hegemony through risk, vulnerability, and unsuturing. What is also fascinating is that even as Biko understands the power of the white gaze, he resists, though he understands that this risk can amplify freedom and yet can lead to his death—physical and psychological. Think here of George Floyd or the fact that Black bodies are deemed fungible. Yet Blackness seems to emerge as a demand—"See me white man!" Of course, therein lies the death of whiteness as it needs the Black body to appear in its own (white) image. Whiteness wants to touch without being touched, which is a denial of its dependency. More specifically, we are all interdependent and we are all touching. This follows from what I call an ontology of no edges. *That* is who we are. We are haptic, intercorporeal. What we want to do is to disrupt those specifically *historical processes* that unethically, deleteriously, and mortally intensify that touching. Our vulnerability is just who we are—beautifully so and yet dangerously so. Our vulnerability is not a problem *simpliciter*. What we need is an insurgency vis-à-vis the problematic material conditions, and the socially constitutive and historically normative assumptions and practices (*for which we are responsible*) that violently mediate how we respond to the collective fact of our vulnerability.

Selihom Andarge, Nicholas Aranda, Josie Brady, Tricia Charfauros, Kelley Coakley, Becky Vartabedian, and Regi Worles have written a chapter that illustrates the beauty of an engaged pedagogy where the hierarchy of student-professor is troubled to create a space for mutual unsuturing. This multiauthored chapter critically engages the concept of lived experience or *Erlebnis*, and what I've theorized as tarrying, which avoids the immediacy of seeking "solutions." In other words, tarrying troubles a mode of temporality that moves with alacrity to discern "formulaic resolutions" vis-à-vis the complexity of whiteness. Tarrying troubles fictions of self-transparency and self-mastery and asks white people to dig deeper, to remain in the pain of newly discovered layers of opacity, bad faith, and obfuscation. Tarrying doesn't function as a leisurely or laidback moment for monastic meditation. Tarrying *is* doing the complex work of troubling whiteness *in medias res*, and it *is* the pain of self-interrogation in the thick of antiblack social injustices caused by whiteness. Tarrying is that space of painful unsuturing. It is agonizing in its continual revelatory potential. The authors powerfully compare how I understand tarrying with an Arendtian conception of thinking. One of the many crucial philosophical insights that is concretely enacted and demonstrated within this chapter is the shared understanding that each voice is situated within history, a history that is saturated with all its pain and suffering. In this way, each of the contributors speak from a site of situated embodiment and contextual facticity, which unabashedly mark their complicity in the pain of others. Improvisatorially, each voice articulates how my work (and my visit at their school, Regis University) created a dangerous space, a space that named white complicity, and delineated parrhesia as a continuous project that belies quick and easy definitive solutions and does the work of hegemonic disruption without being seduced by the logics of arrival.

Bill Bywater is unflinching. He invites us into his life, a life shaped by whiteness. We get a sense of his trajectory—from the overt racism shown by his father (e.g., the use of the n-word) to the fact that he began teaching about race in the 1970s. I have always admired Bill's courageous speech. As a reader of my work, for which I'm grateful, he not only understands what I'm saying, but he attempts to embody it, while risking the ways in which the phenomenon of white ambushing unsettles an "uncomplicated" conception of the white antiracist. As he argues, "If you are oppressed, I am an oppressor." In this way, Bill rethinks my emphasis upon the gift not as a singular moment of acceptance but as a recurrence, a life-project. As a philosophical pragmatist, who also engages critical whiteness studies and critical philosophy of race, Bill is more aware than most of the insidious nature of white racist habits. When such habits are framed through a critical phenomenology, Bill understands the work to be done, and he *does the work*.

Kathy Glass is a force to be reckoned with. As a parrhesiastes, Kathy's work on Black women's affectivity is brilliant. Undergirding and argued throughout her chapter is the importance of what she calls "structures of feeling." Kathy's emphasis here made me think about the ways in which it is necessary to rethink such "structures of feeling" that occlude forms of necessary white antiracism. She links this impetus for change to the power of Black agency and the deployment of counter-gazes, and counter-hegemonic voices that speak courageously in the tradition of Black "back talk." Kathy is generous in her analysis. She reads my voice in conjunction with Frederick Douglass's "What to the Slave Is the Fourth of July?" How does one deal with that comparison? I'm honored, though I fully realize one can *never* be a Frederick Douglass. We owe Douglass for his courage, given the existentially tumultuous conditions under which he lived. Kathy forces me to ask: "What to the Black Is Contemporary America?" There are times when I echo Douglass: "This America is *yours*. It has always been for you, white America, not *mine*, and not *for me*." Yet isn't this what white America must hear, and mustn't it hear it, as Douglass would say, in the *severest language* that we can command. Locating my voice within a jeremiad tradition, one that speaks with lamentation and mourning, Kathy historically grounds my voice within a rich discursive tradition as far back as Maria W. Stewart. Kathy's use of "structures of feeling" powerfully runs in multiple directions. For me, I am often moved by an overwhelming structure of affectivity that is difficult to contain, especially in the face of so much evil. Yet we want the heaviness of this affectivity to create a white double consciousness where white people internalize ethically motivated structures that effectively help in the undoing of whiteness. Thank you, Kathy.

Tom Sparrow opens his chapter by troubling the very concept of the Black body as "superhuman." He's aware of how any discourse regarding the Black body as "superhuman" plays into various racist stereotypes. Yet I get Tom's meaning. He wants to locate what drives me to "talk back" against whiteness in its various permutations. Tom says, "Yancy must be tired." I once heard bell hooks say that being tired is a privilege after a young Black female student mentioned that she is tired of fighting against antiblack racism. I agree with bell and I understand Tom's point. It is important that Black people fight to stay alive. And we are indeed tired, sick of it. However, it's also important that Black people are not construed as "moral gods," capable of taking whatever is thrown at them. We are fully human, racially vulnerable, and tired, what Tom refers to as "existential fatigue." Tom defines me as an existentialist, with which I agree, though one who is engaged in an existential phenomenological mode of theorizing within and about *lived* Blackness. I am also an existentialist who is a *hopeful* theist with important Christian sensibilities that emphasize the infinite value of the least of these, one who weeps in the presence of so much pain and catastrophe. In this way, I share Cornel West's construal of hope, which is not the same as optimism. Racialized as Black, existence unfolds as a site of racialized terror. For me, I see no end to antiblack horror, which has important implications for thinking about Black existence in the mode of fugitivity. That is, Black facticity in relationship to a possible future of Black freedom may not be possible until the end of "the world." Picking up on Tom's emphasis on the insomniac, this is what I want for white people. I want them to lose sleep over their white racist complicity, their feigned innocence. This is where Tom's chapter pushes white people, pushes himself. He writes, "When Yancy speaks of the necessity of the death of white supremacy, he is speaking directly to me." This raises one of the most important themes within existentialism: responsibility. Tom has brought us full circle.

Daniel C. Blight focuses on the theme of "seeing." As a distinguished British scholar who grapples with theorizing photography, his contribution delineates my emphasis, which I get from the inimitable James Baldwin, on showing white people what they would prefer not to see: Themselves. Daniel provides a powerful narrative of how he, being educated in the United Kingdom, internalized the lie of whiteness, a form of whiteness underwritten by an historical hegemonic white empire. He analytically brings to our attention, or brings into focus, the idea that whiteness doesn't see Blackness. Pulling from the work of Elizabeth Davis, Daniel brilliantly locates "seeing" within its historical setting and illustrates how "seeing" is shaped through various power relations. By making this point, Daniel makes us attentive to the socially constructed ways in which "sight" undergoes a frequently unacknowledged historical formation. This point, when read through Daniel's unsuturing, speaks to his own whiteness. He links his professional identity as a photographer to the fact that he didn't see race, his whiteness, and yet he doesn't, as he says, offer this disclosure "up as a bullshit white epiphany." That is the language of white parrhesia! Daniel doesn't mince words, as he also rejects the symbol of the "white hero." His tarrying is embodied and frank, especially where he argues that his whiteness is a "colonial leech," which speaks to what I see as the logics of white consumption or white racist parasitism. Daniel has brought attention to our collective need to undo, to shatter, violent modes of white ocular-centricity that are structured by white hegemonic conditions that epistemically and normatively underwrite white visuality itself.

Boram Jeong speaks from a site of embodied racialization. Boram deploys the insights of critical phenomenology as a conceptual framework through which to tarry with the pain and suffering of anti-Asian and anti-Asian American racism. As "the Yellow body," Boram explores the paradoxical nature of its seen invisibility or its seen absence. Pulling from my work regarding the white gaze and how it "sees" that which is absent, a paradox that Lewis Gordon has also explored in phenomenologically engaging ways, Boram's chapter speaks powerfully to what we have witnessed regarding the contemporary forms of cowardly and vicious attacks against racialized Yellow bodies. Boram argues that the white gaze is by no means passive or receptive but actively constructs that which is "seen" or "unseen." She names this perceptual distortion a "perceptual dysfunction." Yet Boram avoids conflating the ways in which Black bodies and Yellow bodies have been confiscated. On this score, Boram distinguishes between the "exaggeration" of the Black body versus the "belittlement" of the Yellow body. The image in the white imaginary differs, but the lived experience of dehumanization overlaps. Boram brilliantly theorizes the racial spatialization and temporalization of Yellow bodies through the white gaze. The Yellow body in the United States, according to white perceptual logics, has no place in which it can claim legitimacy. The Yellow body is always already spatially temporary. It can be excluded and interned if judged necessary by the power of whiteness. In this way, the Yellow body lives on the precipice of a sudden spatial deracination. Temporally, the Yellow body is always already "not here," but removed—"ancient," "oriental," "primitive," beyond the "enlightenment" and reach of modernity. Boram, of course, knows that she is *not* a problem; it is whiteness that is the problem.

H. A. Nethery IV moves the reader into the heart of important questions regarding whiteness as a site of hegemonic usurpation through its colonial logics. Nethery is a hip-hop head and a professional white philosopher. It's important to note, though, that he does not make a distinction between the "real work" of philosophy and the "non-philosophical" world of hip-hop culture and rap music. Philosophy is always already embodied within hip-hop culture and rap music. In fact, rap music tarries within those nonideal spaces where death and dying take place, where a niggah has to be cognizant of his social ontological surroundings, where Black folk find it hard to breathe because whiteness has created conditions for Black social death, and where Black people epistemically, because of their racialized location, understand what W. E. B. Du Bois calls the "entrails" of whiteness. Nethery understands the epistemic disruptive dimensions that can lead to a form of white double consciousness. He offers a powerful and convincing argument. He sees rap lyrics, not all of them, as a species of parrhesia, a form of truth-telling that he sees as a gift. In "Dear White America," I offered white people a gift. Nethery sees rap music as creating an unsuturing, a dehiscence, in relationship to what I refer to as the opacity of whiteness. Insightfully, and especially in terms of its intersubjective generativity, he calls this disruptive phenomenon a process of "experiencing-with the artist." This process has no white colonial desire to claim Black experience, even as it avoids forms of racial essentialism. Rap music, like James Baldwin, holds up a disagreeable mirror to white people. Through an engaging analysis of rap lyrics, Nethery articulates rap music as a space of/for tarrying, a space which encourages white people to pull off their masks and to radicalize the unsuturing of their whiteness.

Mark William Westmoreland's chapter tarries within the space of critical pedagogy and insightfully integrates not just how I *conceptualize* creating "unsafe" spaces within the classroom but also how I embody that pedagogy through courageous speech and the importance of mutual unsuturing as a space for creating trust and, thereby, risk. Mark emphasizes the importance of the quotidian, bridging the "bifurcation" between the extramural and the intramural. More radically, he argues that students are always already being-in-the-world and so bring to those academic spaces a host of experiences that can be explored "in fecund, reflective ways." Deploying how I've conceptualized whiteness as the transcendental norm, Mark sees its psychological and material manifestations within pedagogical practices and metaphilosophical assumptions that inform and underwrite philosophical practices. Naming whiteness in these ways requires, as Mark argues, being a pedagogical gadfly, a troublemaker that questions white intelligibility. He recognizes that white-ness is not something from which he is disconnected. Rather, he understands his own project of speaking courageously as inclusive, where he is the subject of that critical discourse, and where he emphasizes *krisis* (or crisis) as a criti-cal juncture for generating a turning point, a point of generative disorienta-tion. Mark is as much committed to unsuturing his own whiteness as he is committed to unsuturing the whiteness of his students and our shared field of philosophy, perhaps the whitest of the humanities.

Barbara Applebaum is a scholar whose work on whiteness, critical peda-gogy, and complicity has played an important and conceptually robust role in shaping my own thinking. I am indebted to her pedagogical praxis. So, I am incredibly humbled when she says, "Yancy's scholarship has become an indispensable part of my pedagogical tool kit and also a vital aid in my own understanding of how whiteness impacts *what* I teach and *how* I teach." Barbara is a skillful, epistemically astute, and critically engaged educator. She is aware of the insidious nature of whiteness and thereby understands the necessity of being vigilant to guard against its re-centering (consciously or unconsciously). Barbara situates my philosophical work within the quo-tidian, which is a place where the messiness of life happens. As an example of what has become known as my famous "elevator effect," Barbara locates an engaged description of how whiteness operates within the everyday. Like Judith Butler, Barbara locates ways in which I use forms of expressive discourse and suffering as a mode of address. I was excited to read that my work especially speaks to Barbara's students of color. That she uses my work as a philosophical link to the work of Miranda Fricker (epistemic injustice) and Kristie Dotson (willful hermeneutical ignorance), speaks to Barbara breadth of philosophical knowledge and her critical capacity to synthesize a range of philosophical ideas and find important overlap. I must say that I was especially excited to read Barbara's use of Sara Ahmed's conception of the "killjoy." Barbara explains that a killjoy is one who is ready "to kill not only others' joy but also *one's own*, to be willing to challenge even our own com-forts, our own investments in joy." I embrace that label with humility. Barbara knows that it is not some apolitically aesthetic, self-congratulatory title that marks "academic eminence." I recall that some academic scholars said to me that they were envious that their names had not appeared on *The Professor Watchlist*, which was founded by a conservative youth group. Yet there is no real pleasure to be gained from being surveilled. My continuous invitation that white people unsuture comes at a price, one that is vile and filled with ugly white racist epithets. Then again, Barbara's use of the concept of killjoy captures so much more of profound significance: I, too, must unsuture; I, too, must remove my own masks. I, too, must come to terms with how my joy and my comforts are predicated upon the oppression, the profound sadness, and deep discomfort—even violence or death—of others. That knowledge is a gift even as we would rather refuse it.

E. Lâle Demirtürk is a prolific Turkish scholar and literary critic whose work on African American literary studies is critically engaging. Lâle insightfully engages my work on the insidious (etymologically, "ambushing") nature of whiteness; indeed, she embraces the significance of my exemplification of embodied philosophy of existence (in my written work and in my pedagogical practice), and she also adopts and further theorizes my understanding of whiteness as the transcendental norm, inclusive of my take on white privilege, and my contention that whiteness is a binary structure. I am envious, in the best possible way, of Lâle's fund of knowledge regarding African American literature. She is brilliant at providing philosophically informed exegetical analyses of fictional texts. In this way, the deployment of my work within such a context reflects back to me its inherent interdisciplinary and de-disciplinary assumptions. In her chapter, Lâle traces how my work has impacted her work. Taking me back to earlier formulations and instantiations of my work is a journey that reveals how my work on whiteness and embodied racialization impacts scholars, as Lâle says, "working in non-Western social and cultural geographies." I suspect that whiteness, given its global reach, has effectively communicated to the world the image of the "terrifying nigger." In this way, despite the non-Western social and cultural geographies, there is a stable and shared antiblack imaginary. In my introduction to my edited book *White on White/Black on Black* (2005), I wrote about the dehumanizing practices that were taking place at Abu Ghraib Prison. My objective was to demonstrate that the hypersexualization of Iraqi prisoners there was not new to Black people in the United States, that the white imaginary has a long history of racialized sexual obsessiveness. Lâle shares that it was reading my description of how the Iraqi prisoners were treated according to the ideology and fictional distortions of whiteness that she came to see "how the ideology of whiteness positioned 'us' Middle-Easterners, racialized as people of color (sometimes even in spite of our white skin)." She shares that it was then that her critical perspective began in terms of her own research on African American novels. Lâle's chapter is rich in terms of exploring central themes of my work: the white gaze, the confiscation of the meaning of Black bodies, the importance of the counter-Black gaze, the power of naming whiteness and flipping the script, quotidian forms of racialize trauma, that is, everyday encounters with antiblack racism (e.g., the elevator effect), the importance of mindfulness and vigilance (through my attempt to create a textual space where practitioners of Buddhism are placed in conversation with whiteness), my work on forms of frank speech and the formation of "dangerous" classrooms, and my articulation of what it means to undergo forms of white racist backlash as a Black philosopher in the United States who dared to ask white people to think about their racism. I am thankful to Lâle's generous coverage of so many aspects of my philosophical corpus.

Clarence Sholé Johnson opens his analytically engaging chapter by noting the emergence of race discourse in seventeenth-century science. While I agree with Clarence, one might argue for a "proto-racial" semiotics whereby "Blackness" was identified with that which is "evil," "cruel," "demonic," and "immoral." "Blackness," in short, even prior to an explicit taxonomy of "racial types," had deep axiological implications. Indeed, within this symbolic ordering, "whiteness" was identified with "virtue," "goodness," and the "angelic." The point here is that there is an earlier and strong Manichaean influence vis-à-vis color differentiations, most typically along a Black/white binary divide. It would have been fairly easy to construe those normative terms as having deeper/fixed epidermal implications for certain hued bodies. For the most part, Clarence focuses his philosophical attention on two central motifs in my work that have received much philosophical commentary—what has been called the "elevator effect" and my theorization of whiteness as ambush. Clarence is correct where he says that in the elevator analysis, I don't construe racism as simply a set of false beliefs. My argument is that the white woman in the elevator performs racism through certain modes of bodily comportment. This is important as I don't want to reduce white racism to the space of the doxastic, or to those white persons who hold explicit white racist projects. Through a phenomenological lens, I'm interested in how the white woman has learned-to-be-in-the-world "whitely," as Marilyn Frye might say. I'm interested in how she carries her racism in her body, in her muscles, and in terms of her corporeal occupation within the space of the elevator. Indeed, I am interested in how the space within the elevator itself is always already white and how it thereby functions as a site of white affordance. Clearly, I think that the white woman has a problem that she fails or refuses to see as her problem. Her problem, though, is part of a larger systemic white problem in America. Hence, Clarence is correct to see the elevator effect as a synecdoche.

Clarence argues, however, that I place the burden on white people "to engage in a deliberate self-conscious effort to deprogram themselves." While I do place the burden on white people, as Black people cannot play the role of "super-moral heroes," I also argue against the claim that white people have the absolute capacity, as if through a sheer act of voluntarism, to "acquire a contrary set of dispositions" that will offset their negative (antiblack) somatic responses to Black bodies. Sure, white people can challenge their racist somatic habits, but I also argue (in *Look, a White!*) that white people are dispossessed through what I call their white racist opacity, that is, white people cannot know the limits of their own racism, and that white racist images, affects, and stereotypes have been etched into their unconscious. This is why the phenomenon of ambush is so important to how I think about whiteness. The ambush experience signifies psychic modes of white racist opacity that have been internalized and cannot be substantially addressed through a simple act of introspection. Moreover, I ague that white people are *embedded* within white racist structures of institutional, material, and historical forces that ensure processes of interpellation and complicity and that belie acts of autonomy as sufficient for them to extricate themselves completely from such processes. Given this, I'm critical of racially rehabilitative projects vis-à-vis white people. This doesn't mean that *all* white people are part of the Ku Klux Klan, but it does mean that whiteness within a systemically white racist America, with its long history of white racist inculcation and embodied habitual encrustation, requires more than rehabilitation, which implies a species of restoration. Whiteness is beyond restoration, meaning to make firm again. My sense is that whiteness requires complete dismantlement. However, because of its entrenched hegemony and psychic needs, especially in relationship to the Black body, whiteness will continue to exert and maintain its violent existence. Indeed, even a rehabilitated whiteness doesn't mean that the structural hegemony of whiteness will be magically eradicated or that white racist opacity will somehow mysteriously dehisce.

Misleading here is where Clarence says that "Yancy ontologizes whiteness and racism within a deterministic framework." I see whiteness as constituting a *social* ontology that is contingent and global. Moreover, I don't argue that white people have "absolutely no control" over their racism. This framework confuses how I see whiteness as constitutive, but not deterministic. While it is true that I think that white people can be racists *"even regardless of what the individual might think"* (Clarence's words), this does not mean that I hold a deterministic view, a term that is too strong and that comes with all sorts of metaphysical assumptions. That white people can be racists regardless of what they think follows from what I've argued about white opacity and white systemic racism. Again, though, there isn't anything deterministic about this view, unless one holds that ambush implies a certain determinism. But it doesn't. It reveals aspects of how white people are *constituted*—not determined. While I enjoyed Clarence's discussion about racial eliminativism, I don't have much to say about it as it isn't my philosophical project. Nevertheless, there is nothing *prima facie* true regarding the elimination of categories of race that would *ipso facto* eliminate antiblack animus. Clarence argues that I hold two incompatible conceptions of white racism: a deterministic view and a contingent view. If in fact I held these two positions, I think that Clarence would be correct. However, my view that whiteness is opaque/unconscious and systemic/structurally embedded is completely consistent with my view that there is nothing *intrinsically* problematic about white phenotypic constitution or that white racism is not a natural property that *inheres* in white skin. I can hold my view about white opacity and systemic white racism while also arguing that there is a *contingent* (historical) relationship between having "white skin" and being a "white racist." To have white skin and to be a racist is not *analytically* true. To have white skin and to be a racist is not *deterministically* true, but to have white skin *is* to be privileged within a social structure of white hegemony, a social order that has shaped what white people "see" vis-à-vis Black bodies. Within this context, as white, one is privileged and perpetuates (intentionally or unintentionally) antiblack racism and racialized social injustice. To be shaped by/constituted by is not synonymous with being *determined* by.

"Determinism" connotes a nomological relationship. Even intransience qua durability doesn't imply determinism. W. E. B. Du Bois argued that the eradication of racism will require a "long siege" and he eventually abandoned his earlier Enlightenment approach to racism because of its insidiousness. However, neither of these facts means that he held a deterministic alternative view regarding racism. In my later work, I am not as optimistic as Clarence suggests. The history of whiteness leaves me pessimistic, which I see as a species of racial realism that says that whiteness is here to stay, and that antiblack racism is inextricably linked to the struts of the foundations of this white hegemonic nation. From what we have witnessed under Trump, I am more convinced than ever that whiteness is consumptive; it can absorb what is thrown at it. I agree with Clarence, and have argued elsewhere, that whiteness is a Hydra-like monster. Hence, when it comes to optimism or the dismantlement of whiteness, I agree with Clarence where he writes about the "entrenched nature of whiteness and racism in the institutional and social fabric/topography" of the United States. This was the message that I tried to communicate in "Dear White America." The overwhelmingly racist vitriolic response belied any substantial sense of optimism. My gift to white America was to name the problem: *Whiteness!*

Stephen Brookfield's chapter insightfully captures what he sees as the productive disturbance of my work. Stephen communicates that same sense of profound discomfort that Barbara Applebaum raised through her use of the concept of "killjoy." He writes that I present him "with an analysis of [his] identity that [he] would prefer not to read." Reading Stephen's chapter provides an engaging lens through which a white prominent and critically engaging antiracist scholar refuses to retreat from the complexity, subtly, and insidiousness of whiteness. At every turn, Stephen rethinks and troubled the definitiveness of arrival, which is that chimerical place where progressive and liberal whites think that they have achieved. You know them. They often seem to gloat in their "wokeness." They are now free of antiblack racist assumptions, affects, and images. They have been freed from embodied racist habits that have been installed and shaped by centuries of white expectations. They have cognitively penetrated the opacity of their white racist unconscious. They somehow exist "outside" of the institutional and material white racist forces and structures that are American as Apple Pie. They might be white, but, hey, they're just human—individuals, atomic, neoliberal. Stephen deploys a powerful metaphor of having someone look over his shoulder as he risks being seduced by the illusion of having washed himself clean of the stains of white supremacy. It is a powerful metaphor as it captures the idea that white self-narration vis-à-vis giving an account of one's "anti-racism" cannot be trusted. It is Stephen's honesty, his unsuturing, his hesitancy, and his constantly being stopped in his steps, that I see as loving gestures that signify what is at stake. And what is at stake is nothing less than the murder of George Floyd. That is the weight that Stephen carries; it is the weight of the complexity of white complicity. He writes, "When I write about race, George Yancy is one of the people peering over my shoulder." Like Stephen, I am attracted to thinkers/writers who force moments of self-recognition that leave their disturbance forever. Those moments constitute sites of "productive jarring," as Stephen says. Or as Stephen says, I am drawn "to philosophers and activists who mess my life up." Being "messed up" is not about an epistemic oversight. Rather, it about disorientation, cognitive, and phenomenological destabilization, where a previous form of being-comfortably-in-the-world collapses through the recognition of a deeper truth about one's identity, one's ethical self-certainty, and one's sense of wholeness. That deeper truth for Stephen is the way in which white supremacy is "ideologically sedimented in [him]; the way it's evident in [his] emotional responses, baked into [his] synapses, embedded in [his] DNA." I feel this way about my own conscious and unconscious sexism and the rigid assumptions that I assign to gender roles. I must be yanked back "from the realm of academic analysis to questions of daily conduct." To be white and to read Stephen's chapter comes with a cost—the cost of relinquishing the illusion that your whiteness does not render you complicit with white supremacy and thereby antiblack racism. Accepting this is what it looks like to mess up your life. And, by the way, it also means that you, as a white person, "must expect to be mistrusted" by people of color. So, with Stephen, I would encourage you to go ahead—mess up your life!

Anthony Paul Smith opens his chapter with a powerful question regarding white hope, which is really a form of white evasion. He wonders what pedagogy would look like if the collective we of whiteness undertook to engage whiteness without hope. He asks, "What would happen if we undertook this task under the conditions set for it by the demand for Black freedom?" My response to that question is that "the world" as we know it, that is, the white world that has been historically constructed, would collapse. I say this because white hope is governed by a set of temporal logics. It says everything will be fine, just be patient. Yet Black pain and suffering mocks that sense of time. It is always too late. So, once white people dismantle a conception of hope that favors their power, this would mean an end to their nation-building. Perhaps this is consistent with Anthony's quote from Frank Wilderson III, where he describes freedom for Black people as ontological as opposed to experiential, which sounds more like a temporary, punctate moment of reprieve. Anthony's chapter is undergirded by a racial realism that is a challenge to white "innocence." My sense is that white hope, for Anthony, functions as a solipsistic bubble that actually obscures the gravity of white racist complexity and complicity that I have discussed throughout my body of work on whiteness. While I credit Stephen Brookfield as being more than aware of the trappings of the white confessional voice, Anthony's point is, nevertheless, poignant. His frankness regarding his social position as white belies any attempt to claim innocence that is entailed, in this case, through white confession. Anthony sees any talk of white abolition to be inextricably linked to the demands vis-à-vis Blackness that exist outside the operational logics of whiteness, which means that whiteness must be disarticulated not only from the white imaginary or from white libidinal investments in the Black body, but whiteness must become *powerless*. There are profound lines of argumentation that Anthony's chapter embodies. One such argument is where he says that whiteness (or a white subject) cannot make a home within Black Studies, "and that such homelessness is a gift." I have been recently thinking about whiteness and homelessness and so I'm delighted that Anthony raises it here. Part of being at home is the problem. The consumptive logics of whiteness would rather consume the entire earth. In this sense, whiteness is homicidal and suicidal. There is no Levinasian "face" that issues or signifies the command—"Do not kill me"—that whiteness respects. Everything falls under white consumption. Indeed, whiteness will eat itself to stay alive. Of course, at the moment there are just too many Black bodies yet to consume, which suggests, paradoxically, that the Black body is both disposable and yet necessary for whiteness. Anthony is correct that my work attempts to disrupt the coherence of the white subject and the machinations that help to support it. Anthony does a wonderful job of theorizing my work at the site of the transactional, where racial embodiment is troubled or advantaged in relationship to institutional, material, and phenomenological vectors. He uses the term "lifeform" that speaks to this powerful interrelationship. I am thankful for his Fanonian reference to my work on race as that which begins with existence, not an abstract ontology. He is correct that I want whiteness to undergo what he calls "decoherence." More radically, I would say that whiteness needs to unsuture, fall apart. But to fall apart, whiteness must lose its identity and sense of "safety." And it is Blackness (as the *not* of whiteness) that keeps whiteness safe. Our collective objective, then, is to make whiteness choke. To choke on the illusions and lies that have been projected onto Blackness. If this is true, then at the core of whiteness is a deep lie. Given Anthony's engaging work on the distinction between guilt and shame, I wonder if the latter would apply once white people face what they have never really faced: an abyss.

Taken together, these deeply engaging contributions tarry with important aspects of my work. As they amplify and critically explore my work, I also feel a deeper sense of commitment to speak with the love of wisdom and the wisdom of love, recognizing, of course, that this is a continuous existential project, not a *fait accompli*. The contributions within this text communicate the work that lies ahead, which will require tremendous effort and risk, which means that it will be dangerous work. Yet isn't this what love looks like when embodied on behalf of (or, even better, in conjunction with) those who suffer, especially as one will need to confront those hegemonic forces that don't give a damn about their suffering? Who says that love isn't dangerous, requires effort, and involves risk? Love is this and so much more. *George Yancy: A Critical Introduction* is a text that exemplifies Baldwin's emphasis upon a love that isn't cheap or infantile, but a form of courage that is prepared to take off masks, to see ourselves as we are, and to stop running for safety. Within this context, "safety" is a mode of mummification, stasis, and mimesis, while "unsafety" faces the horror, the complicity, and the social evil that continues to exist. "Unsafety" is what unsuturing looks like. It is a site of dehiscence, a bursting forth. For white people, being unsafe is, counterintuitively, existentially, and social ontologically fecund; it is the key to a form of humanity that is no longer defined by whiteness, that is not trapped by the seductions of white nostalgia and preservation, or where there is the myopic desire to make themselves "great again." There is no real life there. There is only death and dying through a narcissistic form of racial idolatry, a lie that refuses to look into the void that it is.

George Yancy

Notes

INTRODUCTION

1. Robert Farris Thompson, *Flash of the Spirit: African & Afro-American Art & Philosophy*. (New York: Vintage Books, 1984), xiii.

2. Bryan W. Van Norden, *Taking Back Philosophy: A Multicultural Manifesto* (New York: Columbia University Press, 2017), 30.

3. Ibid., 16.

4. David Walker, "Walker's Appeal, in Four Articles; Together with a Preamble, to the Coloured Citizens of the World, but in Particular, and Very Expressly, to Those of the United States of America, Written in Boston, State of Massachusetts, September 28, 1829: Electronic Edition," Documenting the American South, University of North Carolina at Chapel Hill: Academic Affairs Library, UNC-CH, 2001, https://docsouth.unc.edu/nc/walker/walker.html.

5. Ibid., 85–86 (Walker's punctuation).

6. George Yancy, *Backlash: What Happens When We Talk Honestly about Racism in America* (Lanham, MD: Rowman & Littlefield, 2018).

7. Miranda Fricker, *Epistemic Injustice: Power and the Ethics of Knowing* (Oxford: Oxford University Press, 2007).

8. Nick Nesbitt, *Caribbean Critique: Antillean Critical Theory from Toussaint to Glissant* (Liverpool: Liverpool University Press, 2013), xi.

CHAPTER 1

1. See "Watch Stokely Carmichael's Best Response to the Most Stupid Question Ever." https://www.youtube.com/watch?v=HvksaM7rRX0.

2. George Yancy, "Should I Give Up on White People?" *New York Times*, "The Stone," April 16, 2018. https://www.nytimes.com/2018/04/16/opinion/white-racism-threats.html.

3. Martin Heidegger, *Being and Time*, translated by John MacQuarrie and Edward Robinson (New York: HarperCollins, 1952).

4. Emmanuel Levinas, *Totality and Infinity: An Essay on Exteriority*, translated by Alphonso Lingis (Pittsburgh, PA: Duquesne University Press, 1969), 21.

5. W. E. B. Du Bois, *The Souls of Black Folk* (London: Penguin Classics, 2018), 1.

6. George Yancy, *Backlash: What Happens When We Talk Honestly about Racism in America* (Lanham, MD: Rowman & Littlefield, 2018), 90.

7. George Yancy, *Look, a White!: Philosophical Essays on Whiteness* (Philadelphia, PA: Temple University Press, 2012), 1–2, quoting from Frantz Fanon, *Black Skin, White Masks*, translated by Richard Philcox (New York: Grove Press, 2008), 91.

8. Yancy, *Look, a White!*, 1.

9. Louis Althusser, "Ideology and Ideological State Apparatus," in *Lenin and Philosophy and Other Essays*, 117–121 (New York: Monthly Review Press, 2001). First published in 1970. https://www.marxists.org/reference/archive/althusser/1970/ideology.htm.

10. Yancy, *Look, a White!*, 2.

11. See https://www.etymonline.com/word/leisure.

12. Ibid.

13. George Yancy, "Elevators, Social Spaces and Racism: A Philosophical Analysis." *Philosophy and Social Criticism* 34, no. 8 (2008): 844.

14. Yancy, *Look, a White!*, 2.

15. Yancy, *Backlash*, 11.

16. Ibid., 27.

17. Ibid., 28.

18. Lewis Gordon, *Existentia Africana: Understanding Africana Existential Thought* (New York: Routledge, 2000), 33.

19. Ibid., 33.

20. Ibid.

21. Ibid.

22. Hortense J. Spillers, "Mama's Baby, Papa's Maybe: An American Grammar Book." *Diacritics* 17, no. 2 (1987): 64.

23. Ibid.

24. Yancy, "Elevators, Social Spaces and Racism," 844.

25. Yancy, *Look, a White!*, 1.

26. See Foucault's *The Order of Things* for stuff on etymology as a way in which man "writes himself." See the section "Derivations," 287. (Search Perseus project for "problem" and "blemish" for poets using these terms. Look for them existing, in culture, near each other, despite etymological differences.)

27. Yancy, *Backlash*, 90.

28. Ibid., 92.

29. Jean Hyppolite, *Genesis and Structure of Hegel's* Phenomenology of Spirit (Evanston, IL: Northwestern University Press, 1979), 173.

30. Georg Wilhelm Friedrich Hegel, *Phenomenology of Spirit*, translated by A. V. Miller (New York: Oxford University Press, 1977), 12.

31. Ibid., 18–19.

32. Hyppolite, *Genesis and Structure of Hegel's* Phenomenology of Spirit, 166.

33. Shannon Sullivan, *Revealing Whiteness* (Bloomington: Indiana University Press, 2006), 10.

34. Yancy, *Backlash*, 79.

35. Shannon Sullivan, *Good White People* (Albany: SUNY Press, 2014).

36. Ibid., 79.

37. Ibid.

38. Ibid., 78.

39. Ibid., 89.

40. Ibid., 92.

41. Ibid., 30.

42. Calvin L. Warren, *Ontological Terror: Blackness, Nihilism, and Emancipation* (Durham, NC: Duke University Press, 2018), 171.

CHAPTER 2

1. George Yancy, "Introduction: Philosophy and the Situated Narrative Self," in *The Philosophical I: Personal Reflections on Life in Philosophy*, edited by George Yancy, ix (Lanham, MD: Rowman & Littlefield, 2002).

2. Ibid., x.

3. Regis is not unique in this regard. The *Chronicle of Higher Education* developed a "running roundup" of what they termed "campus-climate incidents" on U.S. campuses following the 2016 election and through 2017. The roundup of November and December 2016 events is available at https://www.chronicle.com/blogs/ticker/heres-a-rundown-of-the-latest-campus-climate-incidents-since-trumps-election/115553; the January–March 2017 list is available at https://www.chronicle.com/blogs/ticker/heres-a-roundup-of-the-latest-campus-climate-incidents-early-in-the-trump-presidency/117219. Dan Bauman offers an analysis of campus-climate incidents in relation to the 2016 election in "After 2016 Election, Campus Hate Crimes Seemed to Jump."

4. Tim Wise, "Challenging the Culture of Cruelty: Understanding and Defeating Race and Class Inequality in America." November 8, 2017. Video Recording. Regis University, Denver, CO.

5. Martin Jay, *Songs of Experience: Modern American and European Variations on a Universal Theme* (Berkeley: University of California Press, 2005), 11.

6. Ibid.

7. John Arthos, "'To Be Alive When Something Happens': Retrieving Dilthey's *Erlebnis.*" *Janus Head: An Interdisciplinary Journal* 3, no. 1 (spring 2000).

8. Jay, *Songs of Experience*, 11.

9. George Yancy, "Walking While Black in the 'White Gaze.'" *New York Times*, "The Stone," September 1, 2013. https://opinionator.blogs.nytimes.com/2013/09/01/walking-while-black-in-the-white-gaze/.

10. Arthos, "'To Be Alive When Something Happens'," 3.

11. George Yancy, "Black Bodies, White Gazes: The Risk of Seeing Differently." Presentation, Regis University, Denver, CO, 2018.

12. George Yancy, "Looking at Whiteness: Tarrying with the Embedded and Opaque White Racist Self," in *Look, a White!: Philosophical Essays on Whiteness*, 153 (Philadelphia, PA: Temple University Press, 2012).

13. Cf. Yancy, "Walking While Black in the 'White Gaze.'"

14. Robin DiAngelo names this phenomenon "white fragility," while Cheryl E. Matias labels it "white emotionality." See Robin DiAngelo, *White Fragility: Why It's So Hard for White People to Talk about Racism* (Boston, MA: Beacon Press, 2018); Cheryl E. Matias and Ricky Lee Allen, "Loving Whiteness to Death, 2013: Sadomasochism, Emotionality, and the Possibility of Humanizing Love." *Berkeley Review of Education* 4, no. 2 (2013).

15. Yancy, "Looking at Whiteness," 152.

16. Pauline Oliveros, "The Difference between Hearing and Listening." *TEDxIndianapolis*. November 12, 2015. Video. https://www.youtube.com/watch?v=_QHfOuRrJB8.

17. George Yancy, "White Gazes: What It Feels Like to Be an Essence," in *Living Alterities: Phenomenology, Embodiment, and Race*, edited by Emily S. Lee, 46 (Albany: SUNY Press, 2014).

18. George Yancy, *Backlash: What Happens When We Talk Honestly about Racism in America* (Lanham, MD: Rowman & Littlefield, 2018), 119.

19. Hannah Arendt, "Thinking and Moral Considerations," in *Responsibility and Judgment*, edited by Jerome Kohn, 159 (New York: Schocken Books, 2003).

20. Ibid., 160.

21. Ibid.

22. Ibid.

23. Ibid., 164.

24. Yancy, "Looking at Whiteness," 169.

25. Arendt, "Thinking and Moral Considerations," 176.

26. Cf. Yancy, "White Gazes," 62ff.

27. It should be noted that these things are not all identical—nuance is required in this context.

CHAPTER 3

1. John Dewey, "Creative Democracy—the Task before Us," in *The Later Works of John Dewey*, edited by J. A. Boydston, 14, 224–230 (Carbondale: Southern Illinois University Press, 1989).

2. bell hooks, *Feminist Theory: From Margin to Center* (Boston, MA: South End Press, 1984).

3. Ta-Nehisi Coates, *Between the World and Me* (New York: Spiegel & Grau, 2015).

4. Ibid., 149.

5. Charles W. Mills, *The Racial Contract* (Ithaca, NY: Cornell University Press, 1997).

6. Bill Bywater and Zach Piso, "Neuropragmatism and Apprenticeship," in *Neuroscience, Neurophilosophy and Pragmatism: Brains at Work with the World*, edited by Tibor Solymosi and John R. Shook, 185–214 (London: Palgrave Macmillan, 2014); Bill Bywater, "Becoming a Deweyan Apprentice: A Struggle against White Supremacy," in *The Role of the Arts in Learning: Cultivating Landscapes of Democracy*, edited by Jay Michael Hanes and Eleanor Wiseman, 19–35 (New York: Routledge, 2018).

7. Coates, *Between the World and Me*.

8. George Yancy, *Look, a White!: Philosophical Essays on Whiteness* (Philadelphia, PA: Temple University Press, 2012), 137.

9. Judith Butler, *Giving an Account of Oneself* (New York: Fordham University Press, 2005), 125–127.

10. John R. Shook and Tibor Solymosi, *Pragmatist Neurophilosophy: American Philosophy and the Brain* (London: Bloomsbury, 2014); Tibor Solymosi and John R. Shook, *Neuroscience, Neurophilosophy and Pragmatism: Brains at Work with the World* (London: Palgrave Macmillan, 2014); Butler, *Giving an Account of Oneself*.

11. Ibid., 20.

12. Ibid., 33.

13. George Yancy, *Black Bodies, White Gazes: The Continuing Significance of Race* (Lanham, MD: Rowman & Littlefield, 2008), 229.

14. Yancy gives the rant in full in ibid., 231.

15. Ibid., 232.

16. Ibid., 233.

17. Ibid., 232 (italics in original).

18. Ibid., 240–241 (italics in original).

19. Ibid., 240.

20. George Yancy, *Backlash: What Happens When We Talk Honestly about Racism in America* (Lanham, MD: Rowman & Littlefield, 2018), 11, 13.

21. Yancy, *Look, a White!*, 5–11.

22. Ibid., 5.

23. Ibid., 6.

24. George Yancy, "Dear White America." *New York Times*, "The Stone," December 24, 2015. https://opinionator.blogs.nytimes.com/2015/12/24/dear-white-america/

25. Yancy, *Backlash*, 122–124.

26. Ibid., 67.

27. Yancy, *Look, a White!*, 54, 57, 60.

28. Ibid., 78.

29. Yancy, *Backlash*, 78, 111.

30. Ibid., 90.

31. Ibid.

32. Ibid., 101.

33. Ibid., 102.

34. John Dewey, "Reconstruction in Philosophy," in *The Middle Works of John Dewey*, edited by J. A. Boydston, 12, 181 (Carbondale: Southern Illinois University Press, 1985).

35. John Dewey, "The Need for a Recovery of Philosophy," in *The Middle Works of John Dewey*, edited by J. A. Boydston, 10, 3–48 (Carbondale: Southern Illinois University Press, 1985).

36. Ibid.

37. Ibid.

38. Barbara Applebaum, *Being White, Being Good: White Complicity, White Moral Responsibility, and Social Justice Pedagogy* (Lanham, MD: Rowman & Littlefield, 2010); Yancy, *Look, a White!* and *Backlash*.

39. John Dewey, "Democracy and Education," in *The Middle Works of John Dewey*, edited by J. A. Boydston, 9, 54–55 (Carbondale: Southern Illinois University Press, 1985).

40. Yancy, *Look, a White!*, 85.

41. Ibid., 82–105.

42. Ibid., 84–85.

43. Walter Rodney, *How Europe Underdeveloped Africa* (Washington, DC: Howard University Press, 1974); H. L. T. Quan, *Growth against Democracy: Savage Developmentalism in the Modern World* (Lanham, MD: Lexington Books, 2012).

44. Yancy, *Backlash*, 118.

45. Ibid., 118.

46. Ibid., 100.

47. Ibid., 111.

CHAPTER 4

1. George Yancy, *Look, a White!: Philosophical Essays on Whiteness* (Philadelphia, PA: Temple University Press, 2012), 8.

2. Frederick Douglass, "From 'What to the Slave Is the Fourth of July?': An Address Delivered in Rochester, New York, on 5 July 1852," in *The Norton Anthology of African American Literature*, edited by Henry L. Gates Jr. and Nellie Y. McKay, 462–473 (New York: W. W. Norton & Company, 2004).

3. Stuart Hall, "Race, Articulation and Societies Structured in Dominance by Race," in *Black British Cultural Studies: A Reader*, edited by Houston A. Baker Jr., Manthia Diawara, and Ruth H. Lindeborg, 16–60 (Chicago, IL: University of Chicago Press, 1996).

4. Yancy, *Look, a White!*, 8.

5. Ibid.

6. Douglass's rhetorical approach closely resembles that of the jeremiad, as Bernard Bell has noted. See Bernard Bell, "The African-American Jeremiad and Frederick Douglass's Fourth of July 1852 Speech," In *The Fourth of July: Political Oratory and Literary Reactions, 1776–1876*, edited by Paul Goetsch and Gerd Hurm, 139–153 (Tübingen: Gunter Narr Verlag, 1992). While Yancy's argument is not rooted in the Christian tradition, it nonetheless coincides with the jeremiad as it critiques and warns the oppressor, describing the myriad consequences of their racism.

7. Valerie Cooper, "Maria Stewart's Attitudes toward Race and Nation," in *Word, Like Fire: Maria Stewart, the Bible, and the Rights of African Americans*, edited by Valerie Cooper, 163 (Charlottesville: University of Virginia Press, 2011).

8. Ibid.

9. Wilson J. Moses, *Black Messiahs and Uncle Toms: Social and Literary Manipulations of a Religious Myth*. Rev. ed. (University Park: Pennsylvania State University Press, 1993), 30–31.

10. The speech took place on July 5 because July 4 fell on a Sunday.

11. For full biographical information, see "Frederick Douglass: 1818–1895," 385–387. In *The Norton Anthology of African American Literature*, edited by Henry L. Gates Jr. and Nellie Y. McKay, New York: W. W. Norton & Company, 2004.

12. To avoid slave catchers who were eager to return him to slavery, Douglass embarked on a lecture tour in England after publishing his *Narrative* in 1845. He returned to the United States in 1847 and soon started his own paper, *The North Star*.

13. Douglass, "From 'What to the Slave Is the Fourth of July?'" 462.

14. Ibid. (Emphasis added)

15. Sarah Meer, "Douglass as Orator and Editor," in *The Cambridge Companion to Frederick Douglass*, edited by Maurice S. Lee, 5 (Cambridge: Cambridge University Press, 2009). Citations refer to the ProQuest version (https://search.proquest.com/doc view/2138007671?accountid=10610).

16. Douglass, "From 'What to the Slave Is the Fourth of July?'" 467.

17. Ibid., 468.

18. Eduardo Cadava. "The Monstrosity of Human Rights." *PMLA* 121, no. 5 (2006): 1558–1565.

19. Douglass, "From 'What to the Slave Is the Fourth of July?'" 468.

20. Paul Taylor, "Silence and Sympathy," in *What White Looks Like: African-American Philosophers on the Whiteness Question*, edited by George Yancy, 229 (New York: Routledge, 2004). Here, Taylor expands on Marilyn Frye's phrase "seeing whitely."

21. Douglass, "From 'What to the Slave Is the Fourth of July?'" 468.

22. Ibid.

23. Ibid.

24. Ibid.

25. Elsewhere in his speech, Douglass forthrightly alludes to the Founding Fathers' hypocrisy, as they critiqued England's "oppression" of the colonies while endorsing slavery. Specifically, he writes, "The point from which I am compelled to view them is not, certainly, the most favorable; and yet I cannot contemplate their great deeds with less than admiration" (ibid., 465).

26. Douglass, "From 'What to the Slave Is the Fourth of July?'" 463 (emphasis added).

27. Ibid., 463, 464.

28. Ibid., 463.

29. Ibid., 464.

30. Ibid., 463.

31. Ibid., 468.

32. Ibid., 468–469.

33. Ibid., 472.

34. Frederick Douglass, "Narrative of the Life of Frederick Douglass, an American Slave," in *The Norton Anthology of African American Literature*, edited by Henry L. Gates Jr. and Nellie Y. McKay, 448–452 (New York: W. W. Norton & Company, 2004).

35. Douglass, "From 'What to the Slave Is the Fourth of July?'" 472.

36. Ibid.

37. Moses, *Black Messiahs and Uncle Toms*, 31.

38. See https://americainclass.org/what-to-the-slave-is-the-fourth-of-july/.

39. Ibid.

40. Bell, "The African-American Jeremiad and Frederick Douglass's Fourth of July 1852 Speech," 152.

41. Hall, "Race, Articulation and Societies Structured in Dominance by Race," 16.

42. George Yancy, "Dear White America." *New York Times*, "The Stone," December 24, 2015. https://opinionator.blogs.nytimes.com/2015/12/24/dear-white-america/.

43. Ibid.

44. Ibid.

45. Ibid.

46. Ibid.

47. Ibid.

48. Ibid.

49. Ibid.

50. Ibid.

51. Ibid.

52. Yancy, *Look, a White!* 10.

53. Yancy, "Dear White America."

54. Ibid.

55. Ibid.

56. Ibid.

57. Ibid.

58. Ibid.

59. Ibid.

60. Ibid.

61. Ibid.

62. Ibid.

63. Scott Jaschik, "Backlash." *Inside Higher Ed*, April 24, 2018. https://www.insidehighered.com/news/2018/04/24/author-discusses-new-book-how-americans-respond-discussions-race

64. Yancy, "Dear White America."

65. Jaschik, "Backlash."

66. George Yancy, *Backlash: What Happens When We Talk Honestly about Racism in America* (Lanham, MD: Rowman & Littlefield, 2018).

67. See Marilyn Richardson, *Maria W. Stewart, America's First Black Woman Political Writer: Essays and Speeches* (Bloomington: Indiana University Press, 1987) and Michelle Obama, *Becoming* (New York: Crown Publishing Group, 2018).

68. Helpful in my thinking are Pribram and Harding, who write: "Here, structure of feeling is equated with the experiential results of living within a specific social and cultural context, particularly those results affectively experienced. A distinction is drawn between the knowledge that can be derived from an era's institutions and social structures versus an understanding of its relations of experience. . . . Structure of feeling deals 'not only with the public ideals but with their omissions and consequences, as lived,' . . . that is, something that exists beyond or in addition to the articulated beliefs and values of a specific society or social group" (Deidre E. Pribram and Jennifer Harding, "The Power of Feeling: Locating Emotions in Culture." *Faculty Works: Communications* 5, no. 4 (2002)).

CHAPTER 5

1. Thomas Jefferson, "Query XIV (The Laws of Virginia: Slavery, the Natural Endowments of the Black Race, Education)," in *The Essential Jefferson*, edited by Jean M. Yarbrough, 115 (Indianapolis: Hackett, 2006).

2. George Yancy, *Backlash: What Happens When We Talk Honestly about Racism in America* (Lanham, MD: Rowman & Littlefield, 2018), 2.

3. On the existential situation, see Simone de Beauvoir, *The Second Sex*, translated by Constance Borde and Sheila Malovany-Chevallier (New York: Vintage Books, 2011).

4. S. Kay Toombs, "The Lived Experience of Disability." *Human Studies* 18, no. 1 (1995): 9–23.

5. I borrow the phrase "minority body" from Elizabeth Barnes, *The Minority Body: A Theory of Disability* (Oxford: Oxford University Press, 2016).

6. Toombs, "The Lived Experience of Disability," 15.

7. Ibid.

8. Ibid.

9. Ibid., 16.

10. Ibid. Toombs cites Maurice Merleau-Ponty, *Phenomenology of Perception*, translated by Colin Smith (London: Routledge and Kegan Paul, 1962), 150.

11. On whiteness as an orientation and as disorienting for nonwhite bodies, see Sara Ahmed, "A Phenomenology of Whiteness." *Feminist Theory* 8, no. 2 (2007): 152–155.

12. Ralph Ellison, *Invisible Man* (New York: Vintage Books, 1947), 4–5.

13. Yancy, *Backlash*, 44. On the fatigue induced by resentment toward invisibility, see Yancy, *Black Bodies, White Gazes*, 75–79.

14. Yancy, *Backlash*, 18.

15. Ibid., 9.

16. In "White Gazes: What It Feels Like to Be an Essence," Yancy, following Sartre and Fanon, demonstrates how the white gaze always already operates to objectify the Black body and to supersede the meaning of its lived experience under white supremacy. The white gaze prefigures, and therefore always already knows, the meaning of Blackness. Consequently, Black bodies are reduced to brute beings in themselves

(essences), rather than free beings for themselves (agents), to use the Sartrean language. While it may be the case that, for white bodies, "existence precedes essence," for Black bodies, the pragmatic truth is that "essence precedes lived experience."

17. Simone de Beauvoir, The Ethics of Ambiguity, translated by Bernard Frechtman (New York: Citadel Press, 1976), 46.

18. Yancy, *Backlash*, 9. The phrase "zone of nonbeing" is from Frantz Fanon, *Black Skin, White Masks*, translated by Richard Philcox (New York: Grove Press, 2008), xii. See also Lewis Gordon, "Through the Zone of Nonbeing: A Reading of *Black Skin, White Masks* in Celebration of Fanon's Eightieth Birthday." *The C. L. R. James Journal* 11, no. 1 (2005): 1–43.

19. Fanon, *Black Skin, White Masks*, xii.

20. Yancy's Fanonian text *Look, a White!* is dedicated to reversing this process of negation, of objectification and reduction, but it self-consciously and precisely dismisses the serious attitude that inspired it. Consequently, Yancy's analyses of whiteness avoid the existential pitfall of bad faith. This, it seems to me, is the critical point that too many readers of "Dear White America" miss. This oversight, willful or not, fuels their outrage and vitriol. There is, I sense, a touch of irony in many of Yancy's texts. This irony works subtly to undo the seriousness of his criticism ("serious" is used here to denote an existential attitude diagnosed by Beauvoir in *The Ethics of Ambiguity*), while at the same time retaining the sincerity of his criticism. Irony, we learn from Socrates, is not the negation of sincerity; it is parasitic upon sincerity. Yancy is often working in the Socratic mode, it seems to me, both inside the classroom and outside in the agora. It is no surprise that his white interlocutors and white students reply to his critique of whiteness like so many rebuffed characters in the Platonic dialogues and to their own detriment.

21. Ahmed, "A Phenomenology of Whiteness," 161, 160.

22. George Yancy, *Black Bodies, White Gazes: The Continuing Significance of Race* (Lanham, MD: Rowman & Littlefield, 2008), 76.

23. Yancy, *Backlash*, 4.

24. Yancy, *Black Bodies, White Gazes*, 1.

25. Ibid., 110.

26. Yancy, *Backlash*, 56.

27. For an extended analysis of the fragility and vulnerability of the human condition, see Todd May, *A Fragile Life: Accepting Our Vulnerability* (Chicago, IL: University of Chicago Press, 2017).

28. Yancy, *Backlash*, 58.

29. Georg Wilhelm Friedrich Hegel, *Phenomenology of Spirit*, translated by A. V. Miller (New York: Oxford University Press, 1977), 111–119.

30. Yancy, *Backlash*, 58.

31. For an account of Douglass as an existentialist, see Lewis Gordon, *Exisentia Africana: Understanding Africana Existential Thought* (New York: Routledge, 2000), chapter 3, and Yancy, *Black Bodies, White Gazes*, chapter 5.

32. Yancy, *Backlash*, 58.

33. Yancy, *Black Bodies, White Gazes*, 239. See also Terrance MacMullan, *Habits of Whiteness: A Pragmatist Reconstruction* (Bloomington: Indiana University Press, 2009).

34. Yancy, *Black Bodies, White Gazes*, 238.

35. Ibid., 239.

36. "While existential conversion is not sufficient for undoing the various ways in which whiteness reasserts power and privilege, it functions as a necessary critical process in terms of exposing the contingency and historicity of whiteness, and challenging and troubling its ideological constitution as absolute and permanent" (Yancy, *Black Bodies, White Gazes*, 242).

37. Ibid., 244.

CHAPTER 6

1. In his letter, "Dear White America," Yancy offers his writing as a gift to white people.

2. Alastair Bonnett, *White Identities: Historical and International Perspectives* (London: Prentice Hall, 2000).

3. Kalpana Seshadri-Crooks, *Desiring Whiteness: A Lacanian Analysis of Race* (London: Routledge, 2000), 459.

4. W. E. B. Du Bois, *The Souls of Black Folk* (London: Penguin Classics, 2018).

5. George Yancy, *Look, a White!: Philosophical Essays on Whiteness* (Philadelphia, PA: Temple University Press, 2012).

6. Jason Arday and Heidi Safia Mirza, *Dismantling Race in Higher Education: Racism, Whiteness and Decolonising the Academy* (London: Palgrave Macmillan, 2018), 140.

7. George Yancy, "Introduction: Framing the Problem," in *Christology and Whiteness: What Would Jesus Do?*, edited by George Yancy, 3 (New York: Routledge, 2012).

8. Yancy, *Look, a White!*, 4.

9. Andrea Mubi Brighenti, *Visibility in Social Theory and Social Research* (New York: Palgrave Macmillan, 2010), 30.

10. George Yancy, *Black Bodies, White Gazes: The Continuing Significance of Race in America*, 2nd ed. (London: Rowman & Littlefield, 2017), 106.

11. Ibid., 107.

12. Ibid.

13. Ibid., 4.

14. Hans Belting, *An Anthropology of Images: Picture, Medium, Body* (Princeton, NJ: Princeton University Press, 2011), 22.

15. Shawn O. Utsey and Carol A. Gurnat, "White Racial Identity Attitudes and the Ego Defense Mechanisms Used by White Counselor Trainees in Racially Provocative Counseling Situations." *Journal of Counselling and Development* 80, no. 4 (2011): 475–483.

16. Yancy, *Black Bodies, White Gazes*, 4.

17. Ibid.

18. Karl R. Wallace, *Francis Bacon on the Nature of Man* (Champaign: University of Illinois Press, 1967), 58.

19. Elizabeth Davis, "Structures of Seeing: Blindness, Race and Gender in Visual Culture." *The Senses and Society* 14, no. 1 (2019): 73.

20. Ibid.

21. Yancy, *Black Bodies, White Gazes*, 107.

22. Seshadri-Crooks, *Desiring Whiteness*, 183.

23. Ken McMullen, *Ghost Dance*. London: Channel 4 Films, 1983

24. Jacques Derrida, "White Mythology: Metaphor in the Text of Philosophy." *New Literary History* 6, no. 1 (1974): 11.

25. Ludwig Wittgenstein, *Tractatus Logico-Philosophicus* (Oxford: Routledge, 2001), 82.

26. John Berger, *Ways of Seeing* (London: Penguin Books, 1972), 6.

27. Yancy, *Black Bodies, White Gazes*, 6.

28. Yancy, "Introduction: Framing the Problem," 2.

29. Ibid., 5.

30. Martin Bernal, *Black Athena: The Afroasiatic Roots of Classical Civilization* (London: Vintage Books, 1991).

31. Yancy, "Symbolic White Death," in *The Image of White-ness: Contemporary Photography and Racialization*, edited by Daniel C. Blight, 194 (London: SPBH Editions in Collaboration with Art on the Underground, 2019).

32. Yancy, "Introduction: Framing the Problem," 6.

33. Nell Irvin Painter, *The History of White People* (New York: W. W. Norton & Company, 2010), 326.

34. Yancy, "Introduction: Framing the Problem," 4.

35. Richard Dyer, *White: Essays on Race and Culture*, 2nd ed. (London: Routledge, 2017), 40.

36. Yancy, "Symbolic White Death," 192.

37. Ibid., 198.

38. Julia Dolan, Sara Krajewski, and Sarah Elizabeth Lewis, "Unbranded: A Century of White Women, 1915–2015," in *Hank Willis Thomas: All Things Being Equal*, edited by Lesley A. Martin, 114 (New York: Aperture, 2018).

39. Yancy, "Symbolic White Death," 198.

40. Ibid.

41. Ibid., 199.

42. Thomas Kjeller Johansen, *Plato's Natural Philosophy: A Study of the Timaeus-Critias* (Cambridge: Cambridge University Press, 2004).

43. Nickolas Pappas, "Autochthony in Plato's Menexenus." *Philosophical Inquiry* 34, nos. 1–2 (2011): 66–80.

44. Dyer, *White*, 208.

45. Yancy, "Symbolic White Death," 199.

46. Ibid.

47. Barbara Applebaum, "Critical Whiteness Studies," in *Oxford Research Encyclopedia of Education* (Oxford: Oxford University Press, 2016).

48. Yancy, "Symbolic White Death," 199.

49. Ibid., 200.

50. Ibid., 196.

CHAPTER 7

1. I'd like to thank Chad Shomura, Tania Islas Weinstein, Sarah Tyson and Fred Evans for their comments on drafts of this chapter.

2. George Yancy, *Black Bodies, White Gazes: The Continuing Significance of Race* (Lanham, MD: Rowman & Littlefield, 2008), 43 (emphasis added; hereafter *BBWG*).

3. Ibid., 21.

4. Ibid., 68.

5. Judith Butler, "Endangered/Endangering: In Schematic Racism and White Paranoia," in *Reading Rodney King, Reading Urban Uprising*, edited by Robert Gooding-Williams, 16 (New York: Routledge, 1993).

6. Ralph Ellison, *Invisible Man* (New York: Vintage Books, 1947), 7.

7. Yancy, *BBWG*, 69.

8. Ibid., 17.

9. George Yancy, *Look, a White! : Philosophical Essays on Whiteness* (Philadelphia, PA: Temple University Press, 2012), 116–117.

10. Crispin Sartwell, *Act Like You Know: African-American Autobiography and White Identity* (Chicago, IL: University of Chicago Press, 1998), 6.

11. Alia Al-Saji, "A Phenomenology of Hesitation: Interrupting Racializing Habits of Seeing," in *Living Alterities: Phenomenology, Embodiment, and Race*, edited by Emily S. Lee, 133–172 (Albany: SUNY Press, 2014).

12. I use the term "Yellow bodies" instead of Asian American bodies here, following Anne Anlin Cheng; in *Ornamentalism*, Cheng proposes to use the term "yellow woman" in her analysis of Asiatic femininity that focuses "not on the real Asian or Asian American woman but instead on the very real formation of her ghost in Euro-American culture: the yellow woman" (Anne Anlin Cheng, *Ornamentalism* [New York: Oxford University Press, 2019], xii).

13. Yancy, *BBWG*, 68.

14. Aimé Césaire, *Discourse on Colonialism* (New York: Monthly Review Press, 2000), 42.

15. Sabrina Tavernise and Richard A. Oppel Jr., "Spit On, Yelled At, Attacked: Chinese Americans Fear for Their Safety." *New York Times*, March 23, 2020. https://www.nytimes.com/2020/03/23/us/chinese-coronavirus-racist-attacks.html.

16. *BBC News*, "Coronavirus: French Asians Hit Back at Racism with 'I'm Not a Virus.'" January 29, 2020. https://www.bbc.com/news/world-europe-51294305.

17. George Yancy, "Whiteness and the Return of the Black Body." *The Journal of Speculative Philosophy* 19, no. 4 (2005): 221.

18. Johannes Fabian, *Time and the Other: How Anthropology Makes Its Object* (New York: Columbia University Press, 1983).

19. Quoted in Stuart Creighton Miller, "An East Coast Perspective to Chinese Exclusion, 1852–1882." *The Historian* 33, no. 2 (February 1971): 190.

20. Cathy Park Hong, *Minor Feelings: An Asian American Reckoning* (New York: One World, 2020), 7.

21. Butler, "Endangered/Endangering," 16.

22. Ibid., 22.

23. Anti-Defamation League, "Reports of Anti-Asian Assaults, Harassment and Hate Crimes Rise as Coronavirus Spreads." *ADL blog*, June 18, 2020. https://www.adl.org/blog/reports-of-anti-asian-assaults-harassment-and-hate-crimes-rise-as-coronavirus-spreads; Gianluca Mezzofiore, "A White Woman Called Police on Black People Barbecuing." *CNN*, May 22, 2018. https://www.cnn.com/2018/05/22/us/white-woman-black-people-oakland-bbq-trnd/index.html; *New York Times*, "Amy Cooper Faces Charges after Calling Police on Black Bird-Watcher." July 6, 2020. https://www.nytimes.com/2020/07/06/nyregion/amy-cooper-false-report-charge.html.

24. Charles W. Mills, *The Racial Contract* (Ithaca, NY: Cornell University Press, 1997), 18.

25. Yancy, *Look, a White!*, 110.

26. Sara Ahmed, "A Phenomenology of Whiteness." *Feminist Theory* 8, no. 2 (2007): 149–168.

27. Ellison, *Invisible Man*, 7.

28. Yancy, *BBWG*, 69.

29. Mills, *The Racial Contract*, 18.

CHAPTER 8

1. Kendrick Lamar, *good kid, m.A.A.d city*. Interscope Records, 2012.

2. As a white man, it is not right for me to use or write the n-word in any form. As such, the word will be rendered as "n****" when directly quoted and "the n-word" when outside of direct quotations.

3. Stereo Williams, "Kendrick Lamar, Black Language and What White Fans Don't Get about the N-Word." *Billboard*, May 24, 2008. https://www.billboard.com/articles/columns/hip-hop/8457834/kendrick-lamar-n-word-white-fans.

4. Real Time with Bill Maher, June 9, 2017.

5. Joel Rudinow, "Race, Ethnicity, Expressive Authenticity: Can White People Sing the Blues." *The Journal of Aesthetics and Art Criticism* 52, no. 1 (1994): 132.

6. George Yancy, *Backlash: What Happens When We Talk Honestly about Racism in America* (Lanham, MD: Rowman & Littlefield, 2018), 34.

7. Harry A. Nethery, "Philosophy as a Practice of Suffering: An Interview with George Yancy." *Philosophia Africana: Analysis of Philosophy and Issues in Africa and the Black Diaspora* 19, no. 1 (2020): 64–79.

8. There is also a sense in which this project argues that hip-hop engages in a "phenomenology of traumatization in virtue of being specifically Black in an anti-Black world (which does not exclude other bodies of color) that can also take us in a different direction, one that theorizes specific forms of Black trauma that don't occur for white people" (George Yancy, *Black Bodies, White Gazes: The Continuing Significance of Race in America*, 2nd ed. (New York: Rowman & Littlefield, 2017), 66).

9. Vince Staples, *Summertime '06*. Released June 30, 2015. Def Jam Recordings, 2015.

10. Yancy, *Black Bodies, White Gazes*, xv.

11. Ibid.

12. For an excellent history of hip-hop culture, please see Jeff Chang, *Can't Stop, Won't Stop: A History of the Hip-Hop Generation* (New York: St. Martin's Press, 2005).

13. George Yancy, *Look, a White! : Philosophical Essays on Whiteness* (Philadelphia, PA: Temple University Press, 2012), 12.

14. Yancy, *Black Bodies, White Gazes*, 231.

15. Yancy, *Look, a White!*, 107.

16. It is my hope that, in this way, I can avoid making the mistake of (1) "reducing Black people to experience" and (2) "making whites the oracular interpretive voices of Black experience" (Yancy, *Black Bodies, White Gazes*, 52).

17. Jay-Z, *Decoded*. New York: Spiegel & Grau, 2011.

18. For more, please see my essay "Jay-Z, Phenomenology, and Hip-Hop," in which I develop a tripartite phenomenological structure of rap music (beat/music/flow), such that it draws the listener in to *experience-with* the artist.

19. For an extended phenomenological analysis of the white gaze, please see my "Husserl and Racism as the Level of Passive Synthesis."

20. Jay-Z, *Decoded*, 293.

21. Ibid.

22. Ibid., 296.

23. From the Netflix series *Rapture* (Clarke et al., *Rapture*. 2018. https://www.netflix.com/ca/title/80145087).

24. Jay-Z, *Decoded*, 293.

25. Ibid., 261.

26. Ibid., 239.

27. Ibid., 240.

28. Yancy, *Black Bodies, White Gazes*, 5.

29. Ibid., 17.

30. Ibid., 59.

31. Ibid., 18.

32. Ibid., 61.

33. Du Bois, *The Souls of Black Folks* (New York: Dover Thrift Edition, 1994), 2.

34. Ibid.

35. Yancy, *Black Bodies, White Gazes*, 31.

36. Muddy Waters also deeply influenced the Rolling Stones, and had a song entitled "Rollin' Stone." In this sense, Vince is also pointing to what jazz critic Amari Baraka called "the great American music robbery."

37. "Chopper" is slang for "gun," but a chopper can also be a knife. And, a knife is a utensil, like chopsticks.

38. Yancy, *Black Bodies, White Gazes*, 23.

39. Ibid., 26.

40. Michel Martin and Scott Greenstone, "Vince Staples: 'We Live in A Space Where Your Name Isn't Enough.'" *NPR*, April 2, 2017. https://www.npr.org/2017/04/02/522236735/vince-staples-we-live-in-a-space-where-your-name-isnt-enough.

41. Yancy, *Look, a White!*, 110.

42. Ibid., 111.

43. Ibid., 118.

44. Yancy, *Backlash*, 25.

45. Ibid., 3.

46. Ibid., 55. In his song "Sunshine," the rapper Pusha-T tells us "America, you need a miracle / Beyond spiritual / I need a realer view / I hold a mirror to it." That is, white America cannot see itself for what it is and thus we need Pusha-T to show us what is really happening and who we really are.

47. Yancy, *Backlash*, 55.

48. Yancy, *Look, a White!*, 5.

49. George Yancy, "Tarrying Together." *Educational Philosophy and Theory* 47, no. 1 (2015): 26.

50. Yancy, *Black Bodies, White Gazes*, 231.

51. Alia Al-Saji, "A Phenomenology of Hesitation: Interrupting Racializing Habits of Seeing," in *Living Alterities: Phenomenology, Embodiment, and Race*, edited by Emily S. Lee, 147 (Albany: SUNY Press, 2014).

52. Yancy, "Tarrying Together," 26.

53. Kendrick purposefully censors the name here, rather than invent a new one.

54. Vince Staples, *FM!* Released November 2, 2018. Def Jam Recordings, 2018.

55. To be "strapped" is to carry a weapon.

56. Denzel Curry, "SPEEDBOAT." Track 6 on *ZUU*. Released May 31, 2019. Loma Vista Recordings, 2019.

57. Murs, "P T S D." Track 5 on *Have a Nice Life*. Released May 18, 2015. Strange Music Inc., 2015.

58. Deebo is a character from the film *Friday* (F. Gray, *Friday* [Los Angeles, CA: New Line Cinema, 1995]).

CHAPTER 9

1. George Yancy, *Black Bodies, White Gazes: The Continuing Significance of Race in America*, 2nd ed. (New York: Rowman & Littlefield, 2017), xxxvii, 3.

2. For a succinct and perhaps the seminal text in thinking about white ignorance, see Charles Mills, "White Ignorance," in *Race and Epistemologies of Ignorance*, edited by Shannon Sullivan and Nancy Tuana, 11–38 (Albany: SUNY Press, 2007).

3. Yancy, *Black Bodies, White Gazes*, 245.

4. George Yancy, *Backlash: What Happens When We Talk Honestly about Racism in America* (Lanham, MD: Rowman & Littlefield, 2018), 25.

5. Yancy, *Black Bodies, White Gazes*, 245.

6. See Orlando Patterson, *Slavery and Social Death: A Comparative Study* (Cambridge, MA: Harvard University Press, 1982).

7. George Yancy, "Introduction: Fragments of a Social Ontology of Whiteness," in *What White Looks Like: African-American Philosophers on the Whiteness Question*, edited by George Yancy, 12 (New York: Routledge, 2004).

8. Patricia J. Williams, *Seeing a Color-Blind Future: The Paradox of Race* (New York: Farrar, Straus and Giroux, 1997), 27.

9. See John L. Jackson Jr., *Racial Paranoia: The Unintended Consequences of Political Correctness* (New York: Basic Civitas, 2008); Carol Anderson, *White Rage: The Unspoken Truth of Our Racial Divide* (New York: Bloomsbury, 2016); and Robin DiAngelo, *White Fragility: Why It's So Hard for White People to Talk about Racism* (Boston, MA: Beacon Press, 2018).

10. George Yancy, *What White Looks Like: African-American Philosophers on the Whiteness Question* (New York: Routledge, 2004), 10.

11. George Yancy, "Introduction: Framing the Problem," in *Christology and Whiteness: What Would Jesus Do?*, edited by George Yancy, 7 (New York: Routledge, 2012).

12. George Yancy, "No Philosophical Oracle Voices," in *Philosophy in Multiple Voices*, edited by George Yancy, 6 (Lanham, MD: Rowman & Littlefield, 2007).

13. George Yancy, "Introduction: Philosophy and the Situated Narrative Self," in *The Philosophical I: Personal Reflections on Life in Philosophy*, edited by George Yancy, xvi (Lanham, MD: Rowman & Littlefield, 2002).

14. Yancy, "No Philosophical Oracle Voices," 7.

15. See Jon M. Mikkelsen, Kant and the Concept of Race*: Late Eighteenth-Century Writings*, translated and edited by Jon M. Mikkelsen (Albany: SUNY Press, 2013); Peter K. J. Park, *Africa, Asia, and the History of Philosophy: Racism in the Formation of the Philosophical Canon, 1780–1830* (Albany: SUNY Press, 2013); and Andrew Valls, Race and Racism in Modern Philosophy, edited by Andrew Valls (Ithaca, NY: Cornell University Press, 2005).

16. To my knowledge, the only place where Paul Ricoeur discusses race is in the interview "France/United States: Two Incomparable Histories," in *Critique and Conviction: Conversations with François Azouvi and Marc de Launay*. Translated by Kathleen Blamey, 41–67 (New York: Columbia University Press, 1998).

17. For arguments favoring the view that Greek philosophy was highly influenced by African philosophy, see Cheikh Anta Diop, *The African Origin of Civilization: Myth or Reality*, translated by Mercer Cook (Chicago, IL: Lawrence Hill Books, 1974), and George G. M. James, *Stolen Legacy: Greek Philosophy is Stolen Egyptian Philosophy* (New York: Philosophical Library, 1954).

18. The false narrative of Greek philosophical uniqueness likely originated with Christoph Meiners (1747–1810).

19. Yancy, "No Philosophical Oracle Voices," 8.

20. George Yancy, "White Crisis and the Value of Losing One's Way," in *Exploring Race in Predominantly White Classrooms: Scholars of Color Reflect*, edited by George Yancy and Maria del Guadalupe Davidson, 5 (New York: Routledge, 2014).

21. See Joyce E. King, "Dysconscious Racism: Ideology, Identity, and the Mis-education of Teachers." *The Journal of Negro Education* 60, no. 2 (1991): 133–146.

22. George Yancy, *Look, a White!: Philosophical Essays on Whiteness* (Philadelphia, PA: Temple University Press, 2012), 163.

23. Cornel West, "Foreword: The End of White Innocence," in *Backlash: What Happens When We Talk Honestly about Racism in America*, George Yancy, vii (Lanham, MD: Rowman & Littlefield, 2018).

24. Yancy, *Backlash*, 3.

25. Yancy, "No Philosophical Oracle Voices," 9.

26. Yancy, "Philosophy and the Situated Narrative Self," xxii.

27. Ibid., xii.

28. George Yancy, "Introduction: Un-Sutured," in *White Self-Criticality beyond Anti-racism: How Does It Feel to Be a White Problem?* edited by George Yancy, xv (Lanham, MD: Lexington Books, 2015).

29. Janine Jones, "The Impairment of Empathy in Goodwill Whites for African Americans," in *What White Looks Like: African-American Philosophers on the Whiteness Question*, edited by George Yancy, 69 (New York: Routledge, 2004).

30. Yancy, "Introduction: Un-Sutured," xvii.

31. Yancy, *Backlash*, 62.

32. Yancy, *Look, a White!*, 7.

33. Yancy, *Backlash*, 67.

34. Yancy, *Look, a White!*, 136.

35. See especially part 3 of Patricia Hill Collins, *Black Feminist Thought: Knowledge, Consciousness, and the Politics of Empowerment* (New York: Routledge, 1991).

36. Yancy, *Look, a White!*, 58.

37. Yancy, "No Philosophical Oracle Voices," 10.

CHAPTER 10

1. See http://www.georgeyancy.com/books.html (accessed October 27, 2020).

2. Özlem Sensoy and Robin DiAngelo, "Respect Differences? Challenging the Common Guidelines in Social Justice Education." *Democracy and Education* 22, no. 2 (2014): 2–3.

3. George Yancy, *Black Bodies, White Gazes: The Continuing Significance of Race* (Lanham, MD: Rowman & Littlefield, 2008) (citations refer to the 2008 edition).

4. George Yancy, *Look, a White!: Philosophical Essays on Whiteness* (Philadelphia, PA: Temple University Press, 2012).

5. George Yancy, *Backlash: What Happens When We Talk Honestly about Racism in America* (Lanham, MD: Rowman & Littlefield, 2018).

6. Sara Ahmed, *Living a Feminist Life* (Durham, NC: Duke University Press, 2017).

7. Charles Mills, *Blackness Visible: Essays on Philosophy and Race* (Ithaca, NY: Cornell University Press, 1998).

8. Arnold Farr, "Whiteness Visible: Enlightenment Racism and the Structure of Racialized Consciousness," in *What White Looks Like: African-American*

Philosophers on the Whiteness Question, edited by George Yancy, 154 (New York: Routledge, 2004).

9. Yancy, *Look, a White!*, 30.

10. Michael A. Peters, "White Philosophy in/of American." *Linguistic and Philosophical Investigations* 10 (2011): 150.

11. Yancy, *Black Bodies, White Gazes*, 2.

12. Ibid., 22.

13. Ibid., 19.

14. Ibid.

15. Ibid., 23.

16. Ibid., 24.

17. Ibid., 22.

18. Miranda Fricker, *Epistemic Injustice: Power and the Ethics of Knowing* (Oxford: Oxford University Press, 2007).

19. Kristie Dotson, "A Cautionary Tale: On Limiting Epistemic Oppression." *Frontiers: A Journal of Women Studies* 33, no. 1 (2012): 24–47; Gaile Pohlhaus Jr., "Relational Knowing and Epistemic Injustice: Toward a Theory of Willful Hermeneutical Ignorance." *Hypatia* 27, no. 4 (2012): 715–735.

20. William A. Smith, Tara J. Yosso, and Daniel G. Solórzan, "Challenging Racial Battle Fatigue on Historically White Campuses: A Critical Race Examination of Race-Related Stress," in *Faculty of Color: Teaching in Predominately White Colleges and Universities*, edited by Christine Stanley, 299–327 (Bolton, MA: Anker Publishing, 2006).

21. Saba Fatima, "On the Edge of Knowing: Microaggressions and Epistemic Uncertainty as a Woman of Color," in *Surviving Sexism in Academia: Feminist Strategies for Leadership*, edited by Kirsti Cole and Holly Hassel, 147–154 (New York: Routledge, 2017).

22. Yancy, *Look, a White!*, 168.

23. Yancy, *Black Bodies, White Gazes*, 237.

24. Ibid., 235.

25. Ibid., 233.

26. Ibid., xxiii.

27. bell hooks, *Black Looks: Race and Representation* (Boston, MA: South End Press, 1992).

28. Yancy, *Look, a White!*, 153.

29. Kim Case and Annette Hemmings, "Distancing Strategies: White Women Preservice Teachers and Antiracist Curriculum." *Urban Education* 40, no. 6 (2005): 606–626.

30. Audre Lorde, *Sister Outsider: Essays and Speeches* (Freedom, CA: The Crossing Press, 1984).

31. Sara Ahmed, "Embodying Diversity: Problems and Paradoxes for Black Feminists." *Race Ethnicity and Education* 12, no. 1 (2009): 41–52.

32. Zeus Leonardo and Ronald Porter, "Pedagogy of Fear: Toward a Fanonian Theory of 'Safety' in Race Dialogue." *Race Ethnicity, and Education* 13, no. 2 (2010): 139–157.

33. Ibid., 149, quoted in Yancy, *Look, a White!*, 58.

34. Yancy, *Look, a White!*, 130.

35. Judith Butler, *Undoing Gender* (New York: Routledge, 2004).

36. Yancy, *Look, a White!*, 130.

37. Butler, *Undoing Gender*, 21.

38. Yancy, *Look, a White!*, 170.

39. Ibid., 165.

40. Ibid., 160.

41. Ibid., 167.

42. Yancy, *Backlash*, 19.

43. Ibid., 23.

44. Ibid., 20.

45. Ibid.

46. Ibid., 115.

47. Ibid., 28.

48. Ibid., 44–45.

49. Ibid., 118.

50. Ibid., 101.

51. George Yancy and Maria del Guadalupe Davidson, "Thinking about Race, History, and Identity: An Interview with George Yancy." *The Western Journal of Black Studies* 40, no. 1 (2016): 11.

52. Reni Eddo-Lodge, *Why I'm No Longer Talking to White People about Race* (London: Bloomsbury, 2018).

53. Pohlhaus Jr., "Relational Knowing and Epistemic Injustice."

54. Dotson, "A Cautionary Tale."

55. Ahmed, *Living a Feminist Life.*

56. Ibid., 62.

57. Ibid., 65.

58. Cornel West, "Foreword: The End of White Innocence," in *Backlash: What Happens When We Talk Honestly about Racism in America*, George Yancy, vii (Lanham, MD: Rowman & Littlefield, 2018).

CHAPTER 11

1. George Yancy, *Black Bodies, White Gazes: The Continuing Significance of Race* (Lanham, MD: Rowman & Littlefield, 2008), xxii.

2. George Yancy, "White Embodied Gazing, the Black Body as Disgust, and the Aesthetics of Un-Suturing," in *Body Aesthetics*, edited by Sherri Irvin, 245 (New York: Oxford University Press, 2016).

3. George Yancy, "Introduction: Fragments of a Social Ontology of Whiteness," in *What White Looks Like: African-American Philosophers on the Whiteness Question*, edited by George Yancy, 10 (New York: Routledge, 2004).

4. George Yancy, *Look, a White! : Philosophical Essays on Whiteness* (Philadelphia, PA: Temple University Press, 2012), 136.

5. George Yancy, "Introduction," in *White on White/Black on Black*, edited by George Yancy, 10 (Lanham, MD: Rowman & Littlefield, 2005).

6. George Yancy, "Introduction: Fragments of a Social Ontology of Whiteness," 3.

7. Ibid., 8.

8. George Yancy, "A Foucauldian (Genealogical) Reading of Whiteness: The Production of the Black Body/Self and the Racial Deformation of Pecola Breedlove in Toni Morrison's *The Bluest Eye*," in *What White Looks Like: African-American Philosophers on the Whiteness Question*, edited by George Yancy, 109, 122 (New York: Routledge, 2004).

9. Barbara Applebaum, *Being White, Being Good: White Complicity, White Moral Responsibility, and Social Justice Pedagogy* (Lanham, MD: Rowman & Littlefield, 2010), 33.

10. Yancy, *Black Bodies, White Gazes*, 1.

11. Ibid., xv.

12. Ibid., 2.

13. George Yancy, "White Gazes: What It Feels Like to Be an Essence," in *Living Alterities: Phenomenology, Embodiment, and Race*, edited by Emily S. Lee, 51 (Albany: SUNY Press, 2014).

14. Yancy, *Black Bodies, White Gazes*, 3.

15. Ibid., 4.

16. Ibid., 5.

17. Ibid., 8, 9.

18. Ibid., 19.

19. Ibid.

20. Ibid., 21, 22.

21. Ibid., 23.

22. Ibid., 59.

23. Ibid., 112.

24. Ibid., 121.

25. Ibid., 4.

26. Yancy, *Look, a White!*, 2.

27. George Yancy explains what he means by his title, *Look, a White!*, to reexamine Frantz Fanon's poignant study of how a white boy in public points him out to his mother, "Look, a Negro!" (Yancy, *Look, a White!*, 5).

28. Ibid., 6.

29. In *Elite White Men Ruling*, Joe R. Feagin and Kimberley Ducey explain that they use the term "systemic racism" to mean "these well-institutionalized patterns of subordinate and dominant social positions and roles, respectively, for people of color and whites in a white-dominated hierarchical society." They argue that the term includes many factors, including "the many racial prejudices, stereotypes, images, ideologies, emotions, interpretations, and narratives that constitute the dominant *white racial frame* (white world-view) that rationalizes and implements everyday racial oppression" (Joe R. Feagin and Kimberley Ducey, *Elite White Men Ruling: Who, What, When, Where, and How* [New York: Routledge, 2017], 34).

30. Yancy, *Look, a White!*, 7.

31. Ibid.

32. Ibid., 11.

33. Ibid., 69.

34. Yancy, "White Gazes," 62.

35. Ibid., 49.

36. Ibid., 69.

37. Ibid., 52.

38. David Scott, *Stuart Hall's Voice: Intimations of an Ethics of Receptive Generosity* (Durham, NC: Duke University Press, 2017), 83.

39. Yancy, "White Embodied Gazing," 244, 243.

40. Ibid., 257.

41. George Yancy, "The Violent Weight of Whiteness: The Existential and Psychic Price Paid by Black Male Bodies," in *The Oxford Handbook of Philosophy and Race*, edited by Naomi Zack, 587 (Oxford: Oxford University Press, 2017).

42. Yancy, "White Embodied Gazing," 246.

43. Ibid., 249.

44. Ibid., 250.

45. Shannon Sullivan, "The Racialization of Space: Toward a Phenomenological Account of Raced and Antiracist Spatiality," in *The Problems of Resistance: Studies in Alternate Political Cultures*. Vol. 2 of *Radical Philosophy Today*, edited by Steve Martinot and Joy James, 94 (Amherst, NY: Humanity Books, 2001).

46. Marcus Bell, "Criminalization of Blackness: Systemic Racism and the Reproduction of Racial Inequality in the U.S. Criminal Justice System," in *Systemic Racism: Making Liberty, Justice, and Democracy Real*, edited by Ruth Thompson-Miller and Kimberley Ducey, 166, 175 (New York: Palgrave Macmillan, 2017).

47. Yancy, "The Violent Weight of Whiteness," 590.

48. Ibid., 596.

49. George Yancy, "Introduction: *Dangerous Conversations*," in *On Race*, edited by George Yancy, 4 (New York: Oxford University Press, 2017).

50. Giroux, quoted in ibid.

51. Feagin and Ducey write: "The central problem of the 21st century is elite white men. They long ago created what we term the *elite-white-male dominance system*, a complex and oppressive system central to most western societies that now affects much of the planet. This small elite rules actively, undemocratically, and globally, yet remains largely invisible to the billions of people it routinely dominates. In the US case . . . few people outside the top rank of this powerful elite or its immediate subordinates can name more than a tiny number of the mostly white men at the pinnacle of major US institutions" (Feagin and Ducey, *Elite White Men Ruling*, 1).

52. George Yancy, *Backlash: What Happens When We Talk Honestly about Racism in America* (Lanham, MD: Rowman & Littlefield, 2018), 45.

53. Ibid., 89.

54. David Frum, *Trumpocracy: The Corruption of the American Republic* (New York: HarperCollins, 2018), 65.

55. Aldon D. Morris, *The Scholar Denied: W. E. B. Du Bois and the Birth of Modern Sociology* (Oakland: University of California Press, 2015), 221.

56. José Medina, *The Epistemology of Resistance: Gender and Racial Oppression, Epistemic Injustice, and Resistant Imaginations* (New York: Oxford University Press, 2013), 3, 51.

57. Ibid., 56, 249.

58. George Yancy, "Introduction: Un-Sutured," in *White Self-Criticality beyond Anti-Racism: How Does It Feel to Be a White Problem?*, edited by George Yancy, xi, xiii, xvii (Lanham, MD: Lexington Books, 2015).

59. Yancy, *Black Bodies, White Gazes*, 237, 241.

60. Terrance MacMullan, *Habits of Whiteness: A Pragmatist Reconstruction* (Bloomington: Indiana University Press, 2009), 5.

61. Emily McRae and George Yancy, "Introduction," in *Buddhism and Whiteness: Critical Reflections*, xx (Lanham, MD: Lexington Books, 2019).

CHAPTER 12

1. Léon Poliakov, *The Aryan Myth: A History of Racist and Nationalist Ideas in Europe*, translated by Edmund Howard (New York: Basic Books, 1974), particularly chapters 7–9; and Emmanuel Eze, *Race and the Enlightenment* (Cambridge, MA: Blackwell Publishers, 1997).

2. Clarence Sholé Johnson, "(Re)Conceptualizing Blackness and Making Race Obsolescent," in *White on White/Black on Black*, edited by George Yancy, 173–202 (Lanham, MD: Rowman & Littlefield, 2005).

3. George Lipsitz, *The Possessive Investment in Whiteness: How White People Profit from Identity Politics* (Philadelphia, PA: Temple University Press, 2016).

4. Yancy, *Black Bodies, White Gazes: The Continuing Significance of Race* (Lanham, MD: Rowman & Littlefield, 2008) (hereafter *BBWG*).

5. This essay was originally published in the *New York Times* in 2015 (George Yancy, "Dear White America." *New York Times*, "The Stone," December 24, 2015. https://opinionator.blogs.nytimes.com/2015/12/24/dear-white-america/) and was later reprinted in George Yancy, *Backlash: What Happens When We Talk Honestly about Racism in America* (Lanham, MD: Rowman & Littlefield, 2018). All references are to the reprinted version.

6. Richard Jones, "Black Bodies, White Gazes." *Radical Philosophy Review* 13, no. 1 (2010): 70.

7. Yancy seems also to account for the existence of racism as an ontological feature of whiteness which, if so, would entail that every white person by default is racist. I take up this issue later.

8. Yancy, *BBWG*, 230–231.

9. See, e.g., Naomi Zack, *White Privilege and Black Rights* (Lanham, MD: Rowman & Littlefield, 2015); Clarence Sholé Johnson, "Cornel West, American Pragmatism and the Post-Obama Racial/Social Dynamics," in *The Oxford Handbook of Philosophy and Race*, edited by Naomi Zack (Oxford: Oxford University Press, 2017); Yancy, *Backlash*, 45–46; George Yancy, *What White Looks Like:*

African-American Philosophers on the Whiteness Question (New York: Routledge, 2004), 6; Yancy, *BBWG*.

10. Ibid., 233 (emphases added).

11. Ibid., 227.

12. Yancy, *Backlash*.

13. Yancy, "Dear White America."

14. Yancy, *Backlash*.

15. Ibid., 29.

16. Ibid.

17. See also Yancy, *What White Looks Like*, chapter 1, especially pages 4–6.

18. Yancy, *BBWG*, 231.

19. See Lucius Outlaw, *On Race and Philosophy* (New York: Routledge, 1996), particularly chapter 6; David Wilkins, "Introduction: The Context of Race," in *Color Conscious: The Political Morality of Race*, edited by Kwame Anthony Appiah and Amy Guttman, 21–24 (Princeton, NJ: Princeton University Press, 1998); Naomi Zack, *Thinking about Race* (Belmont, CA: Wadsworth, 1998), chapter 2; Naomi Zack, "Ideal, Nonideal and Empirical Theories of Social Justice: The Need for Applicative Justice in Addressing Injustice," in *The Oxford Handbook of Philosophy and Race* (Oxford: Oxford University Press, 2017); and Bill E. Lawson, "Moral Discourse and Slavery," in *Between Slavery and Freedom: Philosophy and American Slavery*, edited by Howard McGary and Bill E. Lawson, chapter 5 (Bloomington: Indiana University Press, 1992). I have examined the views of Outlaw, Wilkins, and Zack in my "(Re) Conceptualizing Blackness and Making Race Obsolescent" in Yancy 2005, 183–193. And I have also briefly examined Lawson's view in my *Cornel West & Philosophy* (New York, Routledge, 2003), 141–143.

20. See William James, "The Dilemma of Determinism," in *The Writings of William James*, edited by John J. McDermott, 589 (Chicago, IL: University of Chicago Press, 1977).

21. See Charles W. Mills, *The Racial Contract* (Ithaca, NY: Cornell University Press, 1997); Amy Guttman, "Responding to Racial Injustice," in *Color Conscious: The Political Morality of Race*, edited by Kwame Anthony Appiah and Amy Guttman, 163–178 (Princeton, NJ: Princeton University Press, 1996); and Johnson, "(Re) Conceptualizing Blackness and Making Race Obsolescent," chapter 8.

22. See, e.g., Yancy, *What White Looks Like*.

23. George Yancy, "Elevators, Social Spaces and Racism: A Philosophical Analysis." *Philosophy and Social Criticism* 34, no. 8 (2008): 849 (emphasis in original).

24. Yancy, *BBWG*, 235–236 (emphasis added). See also Yancy, *What White Looks Like*, 1–15.

25. George Yancy, *Look, a White!: Philosophical Essays on Whiteness* (Philadelphia, PA: Temple University Press, 2012), 26–27 (emphasis in original).

26. Albert Memmi, *The Colonizer and the Colonized* (Boston, MA: Beacon Press, 1965), 20.

27. Ibid., 17.

28. Johnson, "(Re)Conceptualizing Blackness and Making Race Obsolescent."

29. Yancy, *BBWG*.

30. Mark Potok, "The Radical Right's Reaction to the Election of Barack Obama," *Southern Poverty Law Center*, 1, November 30, 2008. https://www.splcenter.org/fighting-hate/intelligence-report/2008/radical-right's-reaction-election-barack-obama.

31. Ibid., 2.

32. Ibid., 2.

33. Frontline, "Inside Obama's Presidency." *PBS*, January 15, 2013. https://www.pbs.org/video/frontline-inside-obama-presidency/

34. Ibid.

35. Glenn Kessler, "When Did McConnell Say He Wanted to Make Obama a 'One-Term President'?" *Washington Post*, September 25, 2012. https://www.washingtonpost.com/blogs/fact-checker/post/when-did-mcconnell-say-he-wanted-to-make-obama-a-one-term-president/2012/09/24/79fd5cd8-0696-11e2-afff-d6c7f20a83bf_blog.html; Robert Farley, "President Barack Obama claims Mitch McConnell Says His Main Goal Is for the GOP to Regain the White House." *Politifact*, October 30, 2010. https://www.politifact.com/factchecks/2010/oct/30/barack-obama/president-barack-obama-claims-mitch-mcconnell-says/; Ewen MacAskill, "Democrats Condemn GOP's Plot to Obstruct Obama as 'Appalling and Sad.'" *Guardian*, April 26, 2012. https://www.theguardian.com/world/2012/apr/26/democrats-gop-plot-obstruct-obama.

36. Andy Barr, "The GOP's No-Compromise Pledge." *Politico*, October 28, 2010. https://www.politico.com/story/2010/10/the-gops-no-compromise-pledge-044311.

37. Debbie Elliott, "'Food Stamp President': Race Code, Or Just Politics." *NPR*, "Morning Edition," January 17, 2012. https://www.npr.org/2012/01/17/145312069/newts-food-stamp-president-racial-or-just-politics.

38. Carol Anderson, *White Rage: The Unspoken Truth of Our Racial Divide* (New York: Bloomsbury, 2016).

39. Ibid.

40. See, e.g., Zack, *White Privilege and Black Rights*, and even media reports about Cornel West's protest march in Ferguson, Missouri, following the shooting of Michael Brown by police officer Darren Wilson.

41. Katherine Hignett, "Young Boy Begs Father Not to Call 911 on Black Man for 'Trespassing.'" *Newsweek*, July 9, 2019. https://www.newsweek.com/man-calls-police-black-man-phone-boy-son-racism-1448276.

42. Anderson, *White Rage*, 169–174.

43. Ibid., 169 (emphasis added).

44. Quoted in ibid., 172.

CHAPTER 13

1. Robert Graves and Alan Hodge, *The Reader over Your Shoulder: A Handbook for Writers of English Prose* (New York: Seven Stories Press, 1943).

2. George Yancy, "Dear White America." *New York Times*, "The Stone," December 24, 2015. https://opinionator.blogs.nytimes.com/2015/12/24/dear-white-america/.

3. George Yancy, *Look, a White!: Philosophical Essays on Whiteness* (Philadelphia, PA: Temple University Press, 2012); *White on White/Black on Black* (Lanham, MD: Rowman & Littlefield, 2005); *What White Looks Like: African-American Philosophers on the Whiteness Question* (New York: Routledge, 2004); and *Black Bodies, White Gazes: The Continuing Significance of Race* (Lanham, MD: Rowman & Littlefield, 2008).

4. Rebecca Traister, *Good and Mad: The Revolutionary Power of Women's Anger* (New York: Simon & Schuster, 2018).

5. Shannon Sullivan, *Good White People: The Problem with Middle-Class White Anti-Racism* (Albany: SUNY Press, 2014).

6. Vanessa Sheared, Juanita Johnson-Bailey, Scipio A. J. Colin III, Elizabeth Peterson, and Stephen D. Brookfield, eds., *Handbook of Race and Adult Education: A Resource for Dialogue on Racism* (San Francisco, CA: Jossey-Bass, 2010).

7. Leonard Harris, *Philosophy Born of Struggle: Anthology of African-American Philosophy from 1917* (Dubuque, IA: Kendall/Hunt, 1983).

8. George Yancy, *African-American Philosophers: 17 Conversations* (New York: Routledge, 1998); Michel Foucault, *Power/Knowledge: Selected Interviews and Other Writings, 1972–1977* (New York: Pantheon Books, 1980); Jürgen Habermas, *Autonomy and Solidarity: Interviews with Jurgen Habermas* (London: Verso, 1992).

9. Yancy, *African-American Philosophers*.

10. Stephen Brookfield, "Racializing the Discourse of Adult Education." *Harvard Educational Review* 73, no. 4 (2003): 497–523.

11. Angela Y. Davis, "Angela Y. Davis," in *African-American Philosophers: 17 Conversations*, edited by George Yancy, 20 (New York: Routledge, 1998).

12. George Yancy, *On Race* (New York: Oxford University Press, 2017), and George Yancy and Janine Jones, *Pursuing Trayvon Martin: Historical Contexts and Contemporary Manifestations of Racial Dynamics* (Lanham, MD: Lexington Books, 2013).

13. Lucius. T. Outlaw Jr., "Lucius T. Outlaw," in *African-American Philosophers: 17 Conversations*, edited by George Yancy, 321 (New York: Routledge, 1998).

14. Herbert Marcuse, "Repressive Tolerance," in *A Critique of Pure Tolerance*, edited by Robert Paul Wolff, Barrington Moore Jr, and Herbert Marcuse (Boston, MA: Beacon Press, 1965).

15. Ibid., 35–36.

16. Ibid., 35.

17. Brookfield, "Racializing the Discourse of Adult Education"; Yancy, *African-American Philosophers*.

18. Brookfield, "Racializing the Discourse of Adult Education."

19. Yancy, *African-American Philosophers*.

20. Ibid.

21. Yancy, *Look, a White!*, 173–75.

22. Ibid., 21.

23. Ibid., 18.

24. Ibid., 59.

25. Ibid., 71, 132.

26. Ibid., 80.

27. Bryan Stevenson, *Just Mercy: A Story of Justice and Redemption* (New York: Random House, 2014).

28. Robin DiAngelo, *White Fragility: Why It's So Hard for White People to Talk about Racism* (Boston, MA: Beacon Press, 2018).

29. Stevenson, *Just Mercy*.

30. Yancy, *Look, a White!*, 153.

31. George Yancy, *Backlash: What Happens When We Talk Honestly about Racism in America* (Lanham, MD: Rowman & Littlefield, 2018).

32. Yancy, "Dear White America"; *Backlash*, 36–37.

33. Ibid., 45.

34. Ibid., 74–75.

35. Ibid., 76, 102.

36. Myles Horton, *The Long Haul: An Autobiography* (New York: Doubleday, 1990).

37. Yancy, *Backlash*.

38. Ibid.

CHAPTER 14

1. Yancy, *Look, a White!: Philosophical Essays on Whiteness* (Philadelphia, PA: Temple University Press, 2012), 154 (hereafter *LAW*).

2. Frank B. Wilderson III, *Red, White, & Black: Cinema and the Structure of U.S. Antagonisms* (Durham, NC: Duke University Press, 2010), 22.

3. Throughout this chapter, I use the term "world." This term does not refer to the physical earth that we share but is a philosophical term largely calling on the tradition of phenomenology, but also referencing the use of the term as found in Wilderson, Aimé Césaire, Frantz Fanon, and Édouard Glissant. In these philosophical systems, the world is the name for the background against which meaning is secured for whatever is in that world. Thus, calls to "end the world" are not calls for the apocalyptic destruction of the earth but calls for abolition of a particular kind of seeing and living, a particular embodied gaze dependent upon that background and for the devaluing of (white, antiblack) worldly values.

4. Jared Sexton, *Black Men, Black Feminism: Lucifer's Nocturne* (New York: Palgrave Macmillan, 2018), 55.

5. Yancy analyses this desire throughout his work. If one is unable to escape being seen as white or if the differential identity of whiteness is going to continue with all its attendant powers and privileges, then to be a "good white" is to be "already positioned beyond the muck and mire of contemporary forms of white racism" such that this white person "has already come to terms with his or her racist past" (Yancy, *LAW*, 157).

6. George Yancy, *Black Bodies, White Gazes: The Continuing Significance of Race in America*, 2nd ed. (New York: Rowman & Littlefield, 2017), 220 (hereafter *BBWG*).

7. The hysteric is a figure whose role takes on a particularly salient political feature in the Lacanian interpretation of psychoanalysis. Lacan's "four discourses" begin

with discourse of the master, then the university, then the hysteric, and finally the analyst. Marika Rose summarizes the political nature of the hysteric's discourse: "The real possibility of transformation begins to emerge with the hysteric's discourse. This is the discourse of protest, of refusal, of the divided subject who refuses the existing narrative or the present order of things . . . whereas the master's discourse and the university discourse operate according to the logic of the masculine exception, the hysteric's discourse is feminine in its refusal of any narratives of harmony and completion, in its relentless assertion of the non-all" (Marika Rose, *A Theology of Failure: Žižek against Christian Innocence* (New York: Fordham University Press, 2019), 165).

8. Yancy makes this point in *BBWG*, 229. It echoes, in a certain sense, Kwame Ture's famous description of racism as a matter of political power and not simply about individual bias or prejudices.

9. On the recent discussion and debate about the ontology of blackness, see Christina Sharpe, *In the Wake: On Blackness and Being* (Durham, NC: Duke University Press, 2016); Calvin L. Warren, *Ontological Terror: Blackness, Nihilism, and Emancipation* (Durham, NC: Duke University Press, 2018); Wilderson, *Red, White, & Black*; Jared Sexton, "Afro-Pessimism: The Unclear Word." *Rhizomes: Cultural Studies in Emerging Knowledge* 29, nos. 4–5 (2016): 583–597; David Marriott, *Whither Fanon? : Studies in the Blackness of Being* (Stanford, CA: Stanford University Press, 2018); and the three volumes of Fred Moten's (*consent not to be a single being*) project *Black and Blur* (Durham, NC: Duke University Press, 2017), *Stolen Life* (Durham, NC: Duke University Press, 2018), and *The Universal Machine* (Durham, NC: Duke University Press, 2018). The early debate between Moten and Wilderson regarding the meaning of social death for Black subjects post-slavery has been addressed and arguably resolved by Sexton in his "The Social Life of Social Death: On Afro-Pessimism and Black Optimism" (*InTensions Journal* 5 (Fall/Winter 2011). https://www.yorku.ca/intent/issue5/articles/pdfs/jaredsextonarticle.pdf). This is but a sampling of some of the recent literature. The philosophical work being undertaken in these texts and the ones they build with and off is some of the most important and exciting work going on in philosophy and critical theory today, even as that work is undertaken largely outside philosophy departments.

10. See Frantz Fanon, *Black Skin, White Masks*, translated by Richard Philcox (New York: Grove Press, 2008), chapter 5. In his biography of Fanon, David Macey notes that Yancy's work in particular makes use of Fanon's work to analyze the social ontology of race in America. See David Macey, *Frantz Fanon: A Biography* (New York: Verso, 2012), 58.

11. Yancy, *BBWG*, 224.
12. Ibid., 219.
13. Yancy, *LAW*, 58.
14. Yancy, *BBWG*, 228. See also Yancy, *LAW*, 159.
15. Yancy, *BBWG*, 219.
16. Yancy describes "white double-consciousness" in *BBWG*, 231.
17. Yancy, *LAW*, 58.
18. Yancy, *BBWG*, chapter 7.
19. Ibid., 232.

20. Ibid.

21. I am indebted to the analysis of failure and its relationship to anxiety and innocence outlined by Marika Rose in *A Theology of Failure* here and throughout the chapter.

22. For a nuanced philosophical investigation of the securing of relationality as such through the creation of nonbeing, see Daniel Coluciello Barber, "The Creation of Non-Being." *Rhizomes: Cultural Studies in Emerging Knowledge* 29 (2016). doi:10.20415/rhiz/029.e10.

23. Jean-Paul Sartre, *Being and Nothingness, a Phenomenological Essay on Ontology*, translated by Hazel E. Barnes (New York: Washington Square Press, 1984), 350.

24. This summary is found in William R. Jordan's account of Cheryl Foster's reading of Sartre, though heavily modified. See William R. Jordan III, *The Sunflower Forest: Ecological Restoration and the New Communion with Nature* (Berkeley: University of California Press, 2003), 48.

25. Jordan, *The Sunflower Forest*, 47.

26. Ibid., 56.

27. For a further elucidation of this, see my *A Non-Philosophical Theory of Nature: Ecologies of Thought* (New York: Palgrave Macmillan, 2013).

28. Yancy, *BBWG*, 223.

29. Ibid., 232. See also Yancy, *LAW*, 169, where Yancy develops this idea further.

30. Yancy, *LAW*, 75.

31. See the genealogy and philosophical analysis of the intertwined nature of philosophical pedagogy and racial governmentality in Denise Ferreira da Silva, *Toward a Global Idea of Race* (Minneapolis: University of Minnesota Press, 2007).

32. See Wendy Brown, *Undoing the Demos: Neoliberalism's Stealth Revolution* (New York: Zone Books, 2015), chapter 6.

33. Jordan, *The Sunflower Forest*, 47.

34. Yancy, *LAW*, 55–56.

35. Sexton, "The *Vel* of Slavery: Tracking the Figure of the Unsovereign." *Critical Sociology* 42 (2014): 583–597.

36. This disarticulation is what Yancy proscribes as the task for whites (Yancy, *BBWG*, 229).

Bibliography

INTRODUCTION

Fricker, Miranda. *Epistemic Injustice: Power and the Ethics of Knowing*. Oxford: Oxford University Press, 2007.

Nesbitt, Nick. *Caribbean Critique: Antillean Critical Theory from Toussaint to Glissant*. Liverpool: Liverpool University Press, 2013.

Thompson, Robert Farris. *Flash of the Spirit: African & Afro-American Art & Philosophy*. New York: Vintage Books, 1984.

Van Norden, Bryan W. *Taking Back Philosophy: A Multicultural Manifesto*. New York: Columbia University Press, 2017.

Walker, David. "Walker's Appeal, in Four Articles; Together with a Preamble, to the Coloured Citizens of the World, but in Particular, and Very Expressly, to Those of the United States of America, Written in Boston, State of Massachusetts, September 28, 1829: Electronic Edition." Documenting the American South, University of North Carolina at Chapel Hill: Academic Affairs Library, UNC-CH, 2001, https://docsouth.unc.edu/nc/walker/walker.html.

Yancy, George. *Backlash: What Happens When We Talk Honestly about Racism in America*. Lanham, MD: Rowman & Littlefield, 2018.

CHAPTER 1

Althusser, Louis. "Ideology and Ideological State Apparatus." In *Lenin and Philosophy and Other Essays*, 117–121. New York: Monthly Review Press, 2001. First published in 1970. https://www.marxists.org/reference/archive/althusser/1970/ideology.htm.

Du Bois, W. E. B. *The Souls of Black Folk*. London: Penguin Classics, 2018.

Fanon, Frantz. *Black Skin, White Masks*. Translated by Richard Philcox. New York: Grove Press, 2008.

Foucault, Michel. *The Order of Things*. New York: Routledge, 2002.

Gordon, Lewis. *Existentia Africana: Understanding Africana Existential Thought*. New York: Routledge, 2000.

Hegel, Georg Wilhelm Friedrich. *Phenomenology of Spirit*. Translated by A. V. Miller. New York: Oxford University Press, 1977.

Heidegger, Martin. *Being and Time*. Translated by John MacQuarrie and Edward Robinson. New York: HarperCollins, 1952.

Hyppolite, Jean. *Genesis and Structure of Hegel's* Phenomenology of Spirit. Evanston, IL: Northwestern University Press, 1979.

Levinas, Emmanuel. *Totality and Infinity: An Essay on Exteriority*. Translated by Alphonso Lingis. Pittsburgh, PA: Duquesne University Press, 1969.

Spillers, Hortense J. "Mama's Baby, Papa's Maybe: An American Grammar Book." *Diacritics* 17, no. 2 (1987): 64–81.

Sullivan, Shannon. *Good White People*. Albany: SUNY Press, 2014.

———. *Revealing Whiteness*. Bloomington: Indiana University Press, 2006.

Warren, Calvin L. *Ontological Terror: Blackness, Nihilism, and Emancipation*. Durham, NC: Duke University Press, 2018.

Yancy, George. *Backlash: What Happens When We Talk Honestly about Racism in America*. Lanham, MD: Rowman & Littlefield, 2018.

———. "Elevators, Social Spaces and Racism: A Philosophical Analysis." *Philosophy and Social Criticism* 34, no. 8 (2008): 843–876.

———. *Look, a White!: Philosophical Essays on Whiteness*. Philadelphia, PA: Temple University Press, 2012.

———. "Should I Give Up on White People?" *New York Times*, "The Stone," April 16, 2018. https://www.nytimes.com/2018/04/16/opinion/white-racism-threats.html.

CHAPTER 2

Arendt, Hannah. "Thinking and Moral Considerations." In *Responsibility and Judgment*, edited by Jerome Kohn, 159–189. New York: Schocken Books, 2003.

Arthos, John. "'To Be Alive When Something Happens': Retrieving Dilthey's *Erlebnis*." *Janus Head: An Interdisciplinary Journal* 3, no. 1 (spring 2000). http://janushead.org/wp-content/uploads/2020/07/John-Arthos.pdf.

Bauman, Dan. "After 2016 Election, Campus Hate Crimes Seemed to Jump. Here's What the Data Tell Us." *Chronicle of Higher Education*, February 16, 2018. https://www.chronicle.com/article/After-2016-Election-Campus/242577.

DiAngelo, Robin. *White Fragility: Why It's So Hard for White People to Talk about Racism*. Boston, MA: Beacon Press, 2018.

Jay, Martin. *Songs of Experience: Modern American and European Variations on a Universal Theme*. Berkeley: University of California Press, 2005.

Matias, Cheryl E. and Ricky Lee Allen. "Loving Whiteness to Death: Sadomasochism, Emotionality, and the Possibility of Humanizing Love." *Berkeley Review of Education* 4, no. 2 (2013): 285–309.

Oliveros, Pauline. "The Difference between Hearing and Listening." *TEDxIndianapolis*. November 12, 2015. Video. https://www.youtube.com/watch?v=_QHfOuRrJB8.

Wise, Tim. "Challenging the Culture of Cruelty: Understanding and Defeating Race and Class Inequality in America." November 8, 2017. Video Recording. Regis University, Denver, CO.

Yancy, George. *Backlash: What Happens When We Talk Honestly about Racism in America*. Lanham, MD: Rowman & Littlefield, 2018.

———. "Black Bodies, White Gazes: The Risk of Seeing Differently." Presentation, Regis University, Denver, CO, 2018.

———. "Introduction: Philosophy and the Situated Narrative Self." In *The Philosophical I: Personal Reflections on Life in Philosophy*, edited by George Yancy, ix–xxix. Lanham, MD: Rowman & Littlefield, 2002.

———. "Looking at Whiteness: Tarrying with the Embedded and Opaque White Racist Self." In *Look, a White!: Philosophical Essays on Whiteness*. Philadelphia, PA: Temple University Press, 2012.

———. "Walking While Black in the 'White Gaze.'" *New York Times*, "The Stone," September 1, 2013. https://opinionator.blogs.nytimes.com/2013/09/01/walking-while-black-in-the-white-gaze/.

———. "White Gazes: What It Feels Like to Be an Essence." In *Living Alterities: Phenomenology, Embodiment, and Race*, edited by Emily S. Lee, 43–64. Albany: SUNY Press, 2014.

CHAPTER 3

Applebaum, Barbara. *Being White, Being Good: White Complicity, White Moral Responsibility, and Social Justice Pedagogy*. Lanham, MD: Rowman & Littlefield, 2010.

Butler, Judith. *Giving an Account of Oneself*. New York: Fordham University Press, 2005.

Bywater, Bill. "Becoming a Deweyan Apprentice: A Struggle against White Supremacy." In *The Role of the Arts in Learning: Cultivating Landscapes of Democracy*, edited by Jay Michael Hanes and Eleanor Wiseman, 19–35. New York: Routledge, 2018.

Bywater, Bill and Zach Piso. "Neuropragmatism and Apprenticeship: A Model for Education." In *Neuroscience, Neurophilosophy and Pragmatism: Brains at Work with the World*, edited by Tibor Solymosi and John R. Shook, 185–214. London: Palgrave Macmillan, 2014.

Coates, Ta-Nehisi. *Between the World and Me*. New York: Spiegel & Grau, 2015.

Dewey, John. "Creative Democracy—the Task before Us." In *The Later Works of John Dewey*, edited by J. A. Boydston, 14, 224–230. Carbondale: Southern Illinois University Press, 1989. First published in *John Dewey and the Promise of America*, Progressive Education Booklet No. 14, 12–17. Columbus, OH: American Education Press, 1939, from an address read by Horace M. Kallen at the dinner in honor of Dewey in New York City on October 20, 1939.

————. "Democracy and Education." In *The Middle Works of John Dewey*, edited by J. A. Boydston, 9. Carbondale: Southern Illinois University Press, 1985. First published in 1916.

————. "The Need for a Recovery of Philosophy." In *The Middle Works of John Dewey*, edited by J. A. Boydston, 10, 3–48. Carbondale: Southern Illinois University Press, 1985. First published in 1917.

————. "Reconstruction in Philosophy." In *The Middle Works of John Dewey*, edited by J. A. Boydston, 12, 77–202. Carbondale: Southern Illinois University Press, 1985. First published in 1920.

hooks, bell. *Feminist Theory: From Margin to Center*. Boston, MA: South End Press, 1984.

Mills, Charles W. *The Racial Contract*. Ithaca, NY: Cornell University Press, 1997.

Quan, H. L. T. *Growth against Democracy: Savage Developmentalism in the Modern World*. Lanham, MD: Lexington Books, 2012.

Rodney, Walter. *How Europe Underdeveloped Africa*. Washington, DC: Howard University Press, 1974.

Shook, John R. and Tibor Solymosi, eds. *Pragmatist Neurophilosophy: American Philosophy and the Brain*. London: Bloomsbury, 2014.

Solymosi, Tibor and John R. Shook, eds. *Neuroscience, Neurophilosophy and Pragmatism: Brains at Work with the World*. London: Palgrave Macmillan, 2014.

Yancy, George. *Backlash: What Happens When We Talk Honestly about Racism in America*. Lanham, MD: Rowman & Littlefield, 2018.

————. *Black Bodies, White Gazes: The Continuing Significance of Race*. Lanham, MD: Rowman & Littlefield, 2008.

————. "Dear White America." *New York Times*, "The Stone," December 24, 2015. https://opinionator.blogs.nytimes.com/2015/12/24/dear-white-america/.

————. *Look, a White!: Philosophical Essays on Whiteness*. Philadelphia, PA: Temple University Press, 2012.

CHAPTER 4

Bell, Bernard. "The African-American Jeremiad and Frederick Douglass's Fourth of July 1852 Speech." In *The Fourth of July: Political Oratory and Literary Reactions, 1776–1876*, edited by Paul Goetsch and Gerd Hurm, 139–153. Tübingen: Gunter Narr Verlag, 1992.

Cadava, Eduardo. "The Monstrosity of Human Rights." *PMLA* 121, no. 5 (2006): 1558–1565.

Cooper, Valerie. "Maria Stewart's Attitudes toward Race and Nation." In *Word, Like Fire: Maria Stewart, the Bible, and the Rights of African Americans*, edited by Valerie Cooper, 153–174. Charlottesville: University of Virginia Press, 2011.

Douglass, Frederick. "From 'What to the Slave Is the Fourth of July?': An Address Delivered in Rochester, New York, on 5 July 1852." In *The Norton Anthology of African American Literature*, edited by Henry L. Gates Jr. and Nellie Y. McKay, 462–473. New York: W. W. Norton & Company, 2004.

———. "Narrative of the Life of Frederick Douglass, an American Slave." In *The Norton Anthology of African American Literature*, edited by Henry L. Gates Jr. and Nellie Y. McKay, 448–452. New York: W. W. Norton & Company, 2004.

Hall, Stuart. "Race, Articulation and Societies Structured in Dominance by Race." In *Black British Cultural Studies: A Reader*, edited by Houston A. Baker Jr., Manthia Diawara, and Ruth H. Lindeborg, 16–60. Chicago, IL: University of Chicago Press, 1996.

Jaschik, Scott. "Backlash." *Inside Higher Ed*, April 24, 2018. https://www.insidehigh-ered.com/news/2018/04/24/author-discusses-new-book-how-americans-respond-discussions-race.

Jennifer Harding and Deidre E. Pribram "The power of feeling: Locating emotions in culture." *European Journal of Cultural Studies*. 2002; 5(4): 407–426. doi:10.1177/1364942002005004294.

Meer, Sarah. "Douglass as Orator and Editor." In *The Cambridge Companion to Frederick Douglass*, edited by Maurice S. Lee, 46–59. Cambridge: Cambridge University Press, 2009.

Moses, Wilson J. *Black Messiahs and Uncle Toms: Social and Literary Manipulations of a Religious Myth*. Rev. ed. University Park: Pennsylvania State University Press, 1993.

Obama, Michelle. *Becoming*. New York: Crown Publishing Group, 2018.

Richardson, Marilyn. *Maria W. Stewart, America's First Black Woman Political Writer: Essays and Speeches*. Bloomington: Indiana University Press, 1987.

Taylor, Paul. "Silence and Sympathy." In *What White Looks Like: African-American Philosophers on the Whiteness Question*, edited by George Yancy, 227–242. New York: Routledge, 2004.

Yancy, George. *Backlash: What Happens When We Talk Honestly about Racism in America*. Lanham, MD: Rowman & Littlefield, 2018.

———. "Dear White America." *New York Times*, "The Stone," December 24, 2015. https://opinionator.blogs.nytimes.com/2015/12/24/dear-white-america/.

———. *Look, a White!: Philosophical Essays on Whiteness*. Philadelphia, PA: Temple University Press, 2012.

CHAPTER 5

Ahmed, Sara. "A Phenomenology of Whiteness." *Feminist Theory* 8, no. 2 (2007): 152–155.

Barnes, Elizabeth. *The Minority Body: A Theory of Disability*. Oxford: Oxford University Press, 2016.

Beauvoir, Simone de. *The Ethics of Ambiguity*. Translated by Bernard Frechtman. New York: Citadel Press, 1976.

———. *The Second Sex*. Translated by Constance Borde and Sheila Malovany-Chevallier. New York: Vintage Books, 2011.

Ellison, Ralph. *Invisible Man*. New York: Vintage Books, 1947.

Fanon, Frantz. *Black Skin, White Masks*. Translated by Richard Philcox. New York: Grove Press, 2008.

Gordon, Lewis. *Exisentia Africana: Understanding Africana Existential Thought*. New York: Routledge, 2000.

———. "Through the Zone of Nonbeing: A Reading of *Black Skin, White Masks* in Celebration of Fanon's Eightieth Birthday." *The C. L. R. James Journal* 11, no. 1 (2005): 1–43.

Hegel, Georg Wilhelm Friedrich. *Phenomenology of Spirit*. Translated by A. V. Miller. New York: Oxford University Press, 1977.

Jefferson, Thomas. "Query XIV (The Laws of Virginia: Slavery, the Natural Endowments of the Black Race, Education)." In *The Essential Jefferson*, edited by Jean M. Yarbrough, 109–124. Indianapolis: Hackett, 2006.

MacMullan, Terrance. *Habits of Whiteness: A Pragmatist Reconstruction*. Bloomington: Indiana University Press, 2009.

May, Todd. *A Fragile Life: Accepting Our Vulnerability*. Chicago, IL: University of Chicago Press, 2017.

Merleau-Ponty, Maurice. *Phenomenology of Perception*. Translated by Colin Smith. London: Routledge and Kegan Paul, 1962.

Toombs, S. Kay. "The Lived Experience of Disability." *Human Studies* 18, no. 1 (1995): 9–23.

Yancy, George. *Backlash: What Happens When We Talk Honestly about Racism in America*. Lanham, MD: Rowman & Littlefield, 2018.

———. *Black Bodies, White Gazes: The Continuing Significance of Race*. Lanham, MD: Rowman & Littlefield, 2008.

———. "Dear White America." *New York Times*, "The Stone," December 24, 2015. https://opinionator.blogs.nytimes.com/2015/12/24/dear-white-america/.

———. *Look, a White!: Philosophical Essays on Whiteness*. Philadelphia: Temple University Press, 2012.

———. "White Gazes: What It Feels Like to Be an Essence." In *Living Alterities: Phenomenology, Embodiment, and Race*, edited by Emily S. Lee. Albany: State University of New York Press, 2014.

CHAPTER 6

Applebaum, Barbara. "Critical Whiteness Studies." In *Oxford Research Encyclopedia of Education*. Oxford: Oxford University Press, 2016.

Arday, Jason and Heidi Safia Mirza. *Dismantling Race in Higher Education: Racism, Whiteness and Decolonising the Academy*. London: Palgrave Macmillan, 2018.

Belting, Hans. *An Anthropology of Images: Picture, Medium, Body*. Princeton, NJ: Princeton University Press, 2011.

Berger, John. *Ways of Seeing*. London: Penguin Books, 1972.

Bernal, Martin. *Black Athena: The Afroasiatic Roots of Classical Civilization*. London: Vintage Books, 1991.

Bonnett, Alastair. *White Identities: Historical and International Perspectives*. London: Prentice Hall, 2000.

Brighenti, Andrea Mubi. *Visibility in Social Theory and Social Research*. New York: Palgrave Macmillan, 2010.

Davis, Elizabeth. "Structures of Seeing: Blindness, Race and Gender in Visual Culture." *The Senses and Society* 14, no. 1 (2019): 63–80.

Derrida, Jacques. "White Mythology: Metaphor in the Text of Philosophy." *New Literary History* 6, no. 1 (1974): 5–74.

Dolan, Julia, Sara Krajewski, and Sarah Elizabeth Lewis. "Unbranded: A Century of White Women, 1915–2015." In *Hank Willis Thomas: All Things Being Equal*, edited by Lesley A. Martin, 114. New York: Aperture, 2018.

Du Bois, W. E. B. *The Souls of Black Folk*. London: Penguin Classics, 2018.

Dyer, Richard. *White: Essays on Race and Culture*. 2nd ed. London: Routledge, 2017.

Johansen, Thomas Kjeller. *Plato's Natural Philosophy: A Study of the Timaeus-Critias*. Cambridge: Cambridge University Press, 2004.

McMullen, Ken. *Ghost Dance*. London: Channel 4 Films, 1983.

Painter, Nell Irvin. *The History of White People*. New York: W. W. Norton & Company, 2010.

Pappas, Nickolas. "Autochthony in Plato's Menexenus." *Philosophical Inquiry* 34, nos. 1–2 (2011): 66–80.

Seshadri-Crooks, Kalpana. *Desiring Whiteness: A Lacanian Analysis of Race*. London: Routledge, 2000.

Utsey, Shawn O. and Carol A. Gernat. "White Racial Identity Attitudes and the Ego Defense Mechanisms Used by White Counselor Trainees in Racially Provocative Counseling Situations." *Journal of Counselling and Development* 80, no. 4 (2011): 475–483.

Wallace, Karl R. *Francis Bacon on the Nature of Man*. Champaign: University of Illinois Press, 1967.

Wittgenstein, Ludwig. *Tractatus Logico-Philosophicus*. Oxford: Routledge, 2001. First published in 1922.

Yancy, George. *Black Bodies, White Gazes: The Continuing Significance of Race in America*. 2nd ed. London: Rowman & Littlefield, 2017.

———. "Dear White America." *New York Times*, "The Stone," December 24, 2015. https://opinionator.blogs.nytimes.com/2015/12/24/dear-white-america/.

———. "Introduction: Framing the Problem." In *Christology and Whiteness: What Would Jesus Do?*, edited by George Yancy, 1–18. New York: Routledge, 2012.

———. *Look, a White!: Philosophical Essays on Whiteness*. Philadelphia, PA: Temple University Press, 2012.

———. "Symbolic White Death." In *The Image of White-ness: Contemporary Photography and Racialization*, edited by Daniel C. Blight, 194. London: SPBH Editions in Collaboration with Art on the Underground, 2019.

CHAPTER 7

Ahmed, Sara. "A Phenomenology of Whiteness." *Feminist Theory* 8, no. 2 (2007): 149–168.

Al-Saji, Alia. "A Phenomenology of Hesitation: Interrupting Racializing Habits of Seeing." In *Living Alterities: Phenomenology, Embodiment, and Race*, edited by Emily S. Lee, 133–172. Albany: SUNY Press, 2014.

Anti-Defamation League, "Reports of Anti-Asian Assaults, Harassment and Hate Crimes Rise as Coronavirus Spreads." *ADL blog*, June 18, 2020. https://www.adl.org/blog/reports-of-anti-asian-assaults-harassment-and-hate-crimes-rise-as-coronavirus-spreads.

BBC News. "Coronavirus: French Asians Hit Back at Racism with 'I'm Not a Virus.'" January 29, 2020. https://www.bbc.com/news/world-europe-51294305.

Butler, Judith. "Endangered/Endangering: In Schematic Racism and White Paranoia." In *Reading Rodney King, Reading Urban Uprising*, edited by Robert Gooding-Williams, 15–22. New York: Routledge, 1993.

Césaire, Aimé. *Discourse on Colonialism*. New York: Monthly Review Press, 2000.

Cheng, Anne Anlin. *Ornamentalism*. New York: Oxford University Press, 2019.

Ellison, Ralph. *Invisible Man*. New York: Vintage Books, 1947.

Fabian, Johannes. *Time and the Other: How Anthropology Makes Its Object*. New York: Columbia University Press, 1983.

Hong, Cathy Park. *Minor Feelings: An Asian American Reckoning*. New York: One World, 2020.

Mezzofiore, Gianluca. "A White Woman Called Police on Black People Barbecuing." *CNN*, May 22, 2018. https://www.cnn.com/2018/05/22/us/white-woman-black-people-oakland-bbq-trnd/index.html.

Miller, Stuart Creighton. "An East Coast Perspective to Chinese Exclusion, 1852–1882." *The Historian* 33, no. 2 (February 1971): 183–201.

Mills, Charles W. *The Racial Contract*. Ithaca, NY: Cornell University Press, 1997.

New York Times. "Amy Cooper Faces Charges after Calling Police on Black Bird-Watcher." July 6, 2020. https://www.nytimes.com/2020/07/06/nyregion/amy-cooper-false-report-charge.html.

Sartwell, Crispin. *Act Like You Know: African-American Autobiography and White Identity*. Chicago, IL: University of Chicago Press, 1998.

Tavernise, Sabrina and Richard A. Oppel Jr. "Spit On, Yelled At, Attacked: Chinese Americans Fear for Their Safety." *New York Times*, March 23, 2020. https://www.nytimes.com/2020/03/23/us/chinese-coronavirus-racist-attacks.html.

Yancy, George. *Black Bodies, White Gazes: The Continuing Significance of Race*. Lanham, MD: Rowman & Littlefield, 2008.

———. *Look, a White!: Philosophical Essays on Whiteness*. Philadelphia, PA: Temple University Press, 2012.

———. "Whiteness and the Return of the Black Body." *The Journal of Speculative Philosophy* 19, no. 4 (2005): 215–241.

CHAPTER 8

Al-Saji, Alia. "A Phenomenology of Hesitation: Interrupting Racializing Habits of Seeing." In *Living Alterities: Phenomenology, Embodiment, and Race*, edited by Emily S. Lee, 133–172. Albany: SUNY Press, 2014.

Chang, Jeff. *Can't Stop, Won't Stop: A History of the Hip-Hop Generation*. New York: St. Martin's Press, 2005.

Clarke, Marcus A., Steven Caple Jr., Geeta Gandbhir, Sacha Jenkins, Gabriel Noble, and Ben Selkow, dirs. *Rapture*. 2018. https://www.netflix.com/ca/title/80145087.

Curry, Denzel. "SPEEDBOAT." Track 6 on *ZUU*. Released May 31, 2019. Loma Vista Recordings, 2019, digital streaming.

Du Bois, W. E. B. *The Souls of Black Folks*. New York: Dover Thrift Edition, 1994.

Gray, F. Gary, dir. *Friday*. Los Angeles, CA: New Line Cinema, 1995.

Jay-Z. *Decoded*. New York: Spiegel & Grau, 2011.

Lamar, Kendrick. *good kid, m.A.A.d city*. Interscope Records, 2012.

Martin, Michel and Scott Greenstone. "Vince Staples: 'We Live in A Space Where Your Name Isn't Enough.'" *NPR*, April 2, 2017. https://www.npr.org/2017/04/02/522236735/vince-staples-we-live-in-a-space-where-your-name-isnt-enough.

Nethery, Harry A. "Husserl and Racism as the Level of Passive Synthesis." *Journal of the British Society for Phenomenology* 49, no. 4 (2018): 280–290.

———. "Jay-Z, Phenomenology, and Hip-Hop." *APA Newsletter on Philosophy and the Black Experience* 11, no. 1 (2011): 23–28.

Muddy Waters. *Rollin' Stone*. Recorded February 1950. Chess Record Corp, Shellac.

Murs. "P T S D." Track 5 on *Have a Nice Life*. Released May 18, 2015. Strange Music Inc., 2015.

Nethery, Harry A. "Philosophy as a Practice of Suffering: An Interview with George Yancy." *Philosophia Africana: Analysis of Philosophy and Issues in Africa and the Black Diaspora* 19, no. 1 (2020): 64–79.

Pusha-T. "Sunshine." Released December 2015. Track 10 on *King Push—Darkest Before Dawn: The Prelude*. Def Jam Recordings, 2015, compact disc.

Rudinow, Joel. "Race, Ethnicity, Expressive Authenticity: Can White People Sing the Blues." *The Journal of Aesthetics and Art Criticism* 52, no. 1 (1994): 127–137.

Staples, Vince. *FM!* Released November 2, 2018. Def Jam Recordings, 2018.

———. *Summertime '06*. Released June 30, 2015. Def Jam Recordings, 2015, compact disc.

Williams, Stereo. "Kendrick Lamar, Black Language and What White Fans Don't Get about the N-Word." *Billboard*, May 24, 2008. https://www.billboard.com/articles/columns/hip-hop/8457834/kendrick-lamar-n-word-white-fans.

Yancy, George. *Backlash: What Happens When We Talk Honestly about Racism in America*. Lanham, MD: Rowman & Littlefield, 2018.

———. *Black Bodies, White Gazes: The Continuing Significance of Race in America*. 2nd ed. New York: Rowman & Littlefield, 2017.

———. *Look, a White!: Philosophical Essays on Whiteness*. Philadelphia, PA: Temple University Press, 2012.

———. "Tarrying Together." *Educational Philosophy and Theory* 47, no. 1 (2015): 26–35.

CHAPTER 9

Anderson, Carol. *White Rage: The Unspoken Truth of Our Racial Divide*. New York: Bloomsbury, 2016.

DiAngelo, Robin. *White Fragility: Why It's So Hard for White People to Talk about Racism*. Boston, MA: Beacon Press, 2018.

Diop, Cheikh Anta. *The African Origin of Civilization: Myth or Reality*. Translated by Mercer Cook. Chicago, IL: Lawrence Hill Books, 1974.

Hill Collins, Patricia. *Black Feminist Thought: Knowledge, Consciousness, and the Politics of Empowerment*. New York: Routledge, 1991.

Jackson, John L. Jr., *Racial Paranoia: The Unintended Consequences of Political Correctness*. New York: Basic Civitas, 2008.

James, George G. M. *Stolen Legacy: Greek Philosophy is Stolen Egyptian Philosophy*. New York: Philosophical Library, 1954.

Jones, Janine. "The Impairment of Empathy in Goodwill Whites for African Americans." In *What White Looks Like: African-American Philosophers on the Whiteness Question*, edited by George Yancy, 65–86. New York: Routledge, 2004.

King, Joyce E. "Dysconscious Racism: Ideology, Identity, and the Miseducation of Teachers." *The Journal of Negro Education* 60, no. 2 (1991): 133–146.

Mikkelsen, Jon M. *Kant and the Concept of Race: Late Eighteenth-Century Writings*. Translated and edited by Jon M. Mikkelsen. Albany: SUNY Press, 2013.

Mills, Charles. "White Ignorance." In *Race and Epistemologies of Ignorance*, edited by Shannon Sullivan and Nancy Tuana, 11–38. Albany: SUNY Press, 2007.

Park, Peter K. J. *Africa, Asia, and the History of Philosophy: Racism in the Formation of the Philosophical Canon, 1780–1830*. Albany: SUNY Press, 2013.

Patterson, Orlando. *Slavery and Social Death: A Comparative Study*. Cambridge, MA: Harvard University Press, 1982.

Ricoeur, Paul. "France/United States: Two Incomparable Histories." In *Critique and Conviction: Conversations with François Azouvi and Marc de Launay*. Translated by Kathleen Blamey, 41–67. New York: Columbia University Press, 1998.

Valls, Andrew. *Race and Racism in Modern Philosophy*. Edited by Andrew Valls. Ithaca, NY: Cornell University Press, 2005.

West, Cornel. "Foreword: The End of White Innocence." In *Backlash: What Happens When We Talk Honestly about Racism in America*, George Yancy, vii–viii. Lanham, MD: Rowman & Littlefield, 2018.

Williams, Patricia J. *Seeing a Color-Blind Future: The Paradox of Race*. New York: Farrar, Straus and Giroux, 1997.

Yancy, George. *Backlash: What Happens When We Talk Honestly about Racism in America*. Lanham, MD: Rowman & Littlefield, 2018.

———. *Black Bodies, White Gazes: The Continuing Significance of Race in America*. 2nd ed. New York: Rowman & Littlefield, 2017.

———. "Introduction: Fragments of a Social Ontology of Whiteness." In *What White Looks Like: African-American Philosophers on the Whiteness Question*, edited by George Yancy, 1–23. New York: Routledge, 2004.

———. "Introduction: Framing the Problem." In *Christology and Whiteness: What Would Jesus Do?*, edited by George Yancy, 1–18. New York: Routledge, 2012.

———. "Introduction: Philosophy and the Situated Narrative Self." In *The Philosophical I: Personal Reflections on Life in Philosophy*, edited by George Yancy, ix–xxix. Lanham, MD: Rowman & Littlefield, 2002.

———. "Introduction: Un-Sutured." In *White Self-Criticality beyond Anti-racism: How Does It Feel to Be a White Problem?* edited by George Yancy, xi–xxvii. Lanham, MD: Lexington Books, 2015.

———. *Look, a White!: Philosophical Essays on Whiteness*. Philadelphia, PA: Temple University Press, 2012.

———. "No Philosophical Oracle Voices." In *Philosophy in Multiple Voices*, edited by George Yancy, 11–19. Lanham, MD: Rowman & Littlefield, 2007.

———. *What White Looks Like: African-American Philosophers on the Whiteness Question*. New York: Routledge, 2004.

———. "White Crisis and the Value of Losing One's Way." In *Exploring Race in Predominantly White Classrooms: Scholars of Color Reflect*, edited by George Yancy and Maria del Guadalupe Davidson, 1–16. New York: Routledge, 2014.

CHAPTER 10

Ahmed, Sara. "Embodying Diversity: Problems and Paradoxes for Black Feminists." *Race Ethnicity and Education* 12, no. 1 (2009): 41–52.

———. *Living a Feminist Life*. Durham, NC: Duke University Press, 2017.

Butler, Judith. *Undoing Gender*. New York: Routledge, 2004.

Case, Kim and Annette Hemmings. "Distancing Strategies: White Women Preservice Teachers and Antiracist Curriculum." *Urban Education* 40, no. 6 (2005): 606–626.

Dotson, Kristie. "A Cautionary Tale: On Limiting Epistemic Oppression." *Frontiers: A Journal of Women Studies* 33, no. 1 (2012): 24–47.

Eddo-Lodge, Reni. *Why I'm No Longer Talking to White People about Race*. London: Bloomsbury, 2018.

Farr, Arnold. "Whiteness Visible: Enlightenment Racism and the Structure of Racialized Consciousness." In *What White Looks Like: African-American Philosophers on the Whiteness Question*, edited by George Yancy, 143–158. New York: Routledge, 2004.

Fatima, Saba. "On the Edge of Knowing: Microaggressions and Epistemic Uncertainty as a Woman of Color." In *Surviving Sexism in Academia: Feminist Strategies for Leadership*, edited by Kirsti Cole and Holly Hassel, 147–154. New York: Routledge, 2017.

Fricker, Miranda. *Epistemic Injustice: Power and the Ethics of Knowing*. Oxford: Oxford University Press, 2007.

hooks, bell. *Black Looks: Race and Representation*. Boston, MA: South End Press, 1992.

Leonardo, Zeus and Ronald Porter. "Pedagogy of Fear: Toward a Fanonian Theory of 'Safety' in Race Dialogue." *Race Ethnicity, and Education* 13, no. 2 (2010): 139–157.

Lorde, Audre. *Sister Outsider: Essays and Speeches*. Freedom, CA: The Crossing Press, 1984.

Mills, Charles. *Blackness Visible: Essays on Philosophy and Race*. Ithaca, NY: Cornell University Press, 1998.

Peters, Michael A. "White Philosophy in/of American." *Linguistic and Philosophical Investigations* 10 (2011): 144–154. http://www.pragmatismtoday.eu/summer2011/Peters.pdf.

Pohlhaus Jr., Gaile. "Relational Knowing and Epistemic Injustice: Toward a Theory of Willful Hermeneutical Ignorance." *Hypatia* 27, no. 4 (2012): 715–735.

Sensoy, Özlem and Robin DiAngelo. "Respect Differences? Challenging the Common Guidelines in Social Justice Education." *Democracy and Education* 22, no. 2 (2014): 2–3.

Smith, William A., Tara J. Yosso, and Daniel G. Solórzan. "Challenging Racial Battle Fatigue on Historically White Campuses: A Critical Race Examination of Race-Related Stress." In *Faculty of Color: Teaching in Predominately White Colleges and Universities*, edited by Christine Stanley, 299–327. Bolton, MA: Anker Publishing, 2006.

West, Cornel. "Foreword: The End of White Innocence." In *Backlash: What Happens When We Talk Honestly about Racism in America*, George Yancy, vii–viii. Lanham, MD: Rowman & Littlefield, 2018.

Yancy, George. *Backlash: What Happens When We Talk Honestly about Racism in America*. Lanham, MD: Rowman & Littlefield, 2018.

———. *Black Bodies, White Gazes: The Continuing Significance of Race*. Lanham, MD: Rowman & Littlefield, 2008.

———. *Black Bodies, White Gazes: The Continuing Significance of Race in America*. 2nd ed. New York: Rowman & Littlefield, 2017.

———. *Look, a White!: Philosophical Essays on Whiteness*. Philadelphia, PA: Temple University Press, 2012.

Yancy, George and Maria del Guadalupe Davidson. "Thinking about Race, History, and Identity: An Interview with George Yancy." *The Western Journal of Black Studies* 40, no. 1 (2016): 3–13.

CHAPTER 11

Applebaum, Barbara. *Being White, Being Good: White Complicity, White Moral Responsibility, and Social Justice Pedagogy*. Lanham, MD: Rowman & Littlefield, 2010.

Bell, Marcus. "Criminalization of Blackness: Systemic Racism and the Reproduction of Racial Inequality in the U.S. Criminal Justice System." In *Systemic Racism: Making Liberty, Justice, and Democracy Real*, edited by Ruth Thompson-Miller and Kimberley Ducey, 163–183. New York: Palgrave Macmillan, 2017.

Feagin, Joe R. and Kimberley Ducey. *Elite White Men Ruling: Who, What, When, Where, and How*. New York: Routledge, 2017.

Frum, David. *Trumpocracy: The Corruption of the American Republic*. New York: HarperCollins, 2018.

MacMullan, Terrance. *Habits of Whiteness: A Pragmatist Reconstruction*. Bloomington: Indiana University Press, 2009.

McRae, Emily and George Yancy, eds. "Introduction." In *Buddhism and Whiteness: Critical Reflections*, xv–xxi. Lanham, MD: Lexington Books, 2019.

Medina, José. *The Epistemology of Resistance: Gender and Racial Oppression, Epistemic Injustice, and Resistant Imaginations*. New York: Oxford University Press, 2013.

Morris, Aldon D. *The Scholar Denied: W. E. B. Du Bois and the Birth of Modern Sociology*. Oakland: University of California Press, 2015.

Scott, David. *Stuart Hall's Voice: Intimations of an Ethics of Receptive Generosity*. Durham, NC: Duke University Press, 2017.

Sullivan, Shannon. "The Racialization of Space: Toward a Phenomenological Account of Raced and Antiracist Spatiality." In *The Problems of Resistance: Studies in Alternate Political Cultures*. Vol. 2 of *Radical Philosophy Today*, edited by Steve Martinot and Joy James, 86–104. Amherst, NY: Humanity Books, 2001.

Yancy, George. *Backlash: What Happens When We Talk Honestly about Racism in America*. Lanham, MD: Rowman & Littlefield, 2018.

———. *Black Bodies, White Gazes: The Continuing Significance of Race*. Lanham, MD: Rowman & Littlefield, 2008.

———. "A Foucauldian (Genealogical) Reading of Whiteness: The Production of the Black Body/Self and the Racial Deformation of Pecola Breedlove in Toni Morrison's *The Bluest Eye*." In *What White Looks Like: African-American Philosophers on the Whiteness Question*, edited by George Yancy, 107–142. New York: Routledge, 2004.

———. "Introduction." In *White on White/Black on Black*, edited by George Yancy, 1–14. Lanham, MD: Rowman & Littlefield, 2005.

———. "Introduction: Dangerous Conversations." In *On Race*, edited by George Yancy, 1–11. New York: Oxford University Press, 2017.

———. "Introduction: Fragments of a Social Ontology of Whiteness." In *What White Looks Like: African-American Philosophers on the Whiteness Question*, edited by George Yancy, 1–23. New York: Routledge, 2004.

———. "Introduction: Un-Sutured." In *White Self-Criticality beyond Anti-Racism: How Does It Feel to Be a White Problem?*, edited by George Yancy, xi–xxvii. Lanham, MD: Lexington Books, 2015.

———. *Look, a White!: Philosophical Essays on Whiteness*. Philadelphia, PA: Temple University Press, 2012.

———. "The Violent Weight of Whiteness: The Existential and Psychic Price Paid by Black Male Bodies." In *The Oxford Handbook of Philosophy and Race*, edited by Naomi Zack, 587–597. Oxford: Oxford University Press, 2017.

———. "White Embodied Gazing, the Black Body as Disgust, and the Aesthetics of Un-Suturing." In *Body Aesthetics*, edited by Sherri Irvin, 243–260. New York: Oxford University Press, 2016.

———. "White Gazes: What It Feels Like to Be an Essence." In *Living Alterities: Phenomenology, Embodiment, and Race*, edited by Emily S. Lee, 43–64. Albany: SUNY Press, 2014.

CHAPTER 12

Anderson, Carol. *White Rage: The Unspoken Truth of Our Racial Divide*. New York: Bloomsbury, 2016.

Barr, Andy. "The GOP's No-Compromise Pledge." *Politico*, October 28, 2010. https://www.politico.com/story/2010/10/the-gops-no-compromise-pledge-044311.

Elliott, Debbie. "'Food Stamp President': Race Code, Or Just Politics." *NPR*, "Morning Edition," January 17, 2012. https://www.npr.org/2012/01/17/145312069/newts-food-stamp-president-racial-or-just-politics.

Eze, Emmanuel. *Race and the Enlightenment*. Cambridge, MA: Blackwell Publishers, 1997.

Farley, Robert. "President Barack Obama claims Mitch McConnell Says His Main Goal Is for the GOP to Regain the White House." *Politifact*, October 30, 2010. https://www.politifact.com/factchecks/2010/oct/30/barack-obama/president-barack-obama-claims-mitch-mcconnell-says/.

Frontline. "Inside Obama's Presidency." *PBS*, January 15, 2013. https://www.pbs.org/video/frontline-inside-obama-presidency/.

Guttman, Amy. "Responding to Racial Injustice." In *Color Conscious: The Political Morality of Race*, edited by Kwame Anthony Appiah and Amy Guttman, 106–178. Princeton, NJ: Princeton University Press, 1996.

Hignett, Katherine. "Young Boy Begs Father Not to Call 911 on Black Man for 'Trespassing.'" *Newsweek*, July 9, 2019. https://www.newsweek.com/man-calls-police-black-man-phone-boy-son-racism-1448276.

James, William. "The Dilemma of Determinism." In *The Writings of William James*, edited by John J. McDermott, 589. Chicago, IL: University of Chicago Press, 1977.

Johnson, Clarence Sholé. "Cornel West, American Pragmatism and the Post-Obama Racial/Social Dynamics." In *The Oxford Handbook of Philosophy and Race*, edited by Naomi Zack, 214–224. Oxford: Oxford University Press, 2017.

———. *Cornel West & Philosophy*. New York, Routledge, 2003.

———. "(Re)Conceptualizing Blackness and Making Race Obsolescent." In *White on White/Black on Black*, edited by George Yancy, 173–202. Lanham, MD: Rowman & Littlefield, 2005.

Jones, Richard. "Black Bodies, White Gazes." *Radical Philosophy Review* 13, no. 1 (2010): 69–75.

Kessler, Glenn. "When Did McConnell Say He Wanted to Make Obama a 'One-Term President'?" *Washington Post*, September 25, 2012. https://www.washingtonpost.com/blogs/fact-checker/post/when-did-mcconnell-say-he-wanted-to-make-obama-a-one-term-president/2012/09/24/79fd5cd8-0696-11e2-afff-d6c7f20a83bf_blog.html.

Lawson, Bill E. "Moral Discourse and Slavery." In *Between Slavery and Freedom: Philosophy and American Slavery*, edited by Howard McGary and Bill E. Lawson, 71–89. Bloomington: Indiana University Press, 1992.

Lipsitz, George. *The Possessive Investment in Whiteness: How White People Profit from Identity Politics*. Philadelphia, PA: Temple University Press, 2016.

MacAskill, Ewen. "Democrats Condemn GOP's Plot to Obstruct Obama as 'Appalling and Sad.'" *Guardian*, April 26, 2012. https://www.theguardian.com/world/2012/apr/26/democrats-gop-plot-obstruct-obama.

Memmi, Albert. *The Colonizer and the Colonized*. Boston, MA: Beacon Press, 1965.

Mills, Charles W. *The Racial Contract*. Ithaca, NY: Cornell University Press, 1997.

Outlaw, Lucius. *On Race and Philosophy*. New York: Routledge, 1996.

Poliakov, Léon. *The Aryan Myth: A History of Racist and Nationalist Ideas in Europe*. Translated by Edmund Howard. New York: Basic Books, 1974.

Potok, Mark. "The Radical Right's Reaction to the Election of Barack Obama." *Southern Poverty Law Center*, November 30, 2008. https://www.splcenter.org/fighting-hate/intelligence-report/2008/radical-right's-reaction-election-barack-obama.

Wilkins, David. "Introduction: The Context of Race." In *Color Conscious: The Political Morality of Race*, edited by Kwame Anthony Appiah and Amy Guttman, 3–29. Princeton, NJ: Princeton University Press, 1998.

Yancy, George. *Backlash: What Happens When We Talk Honestly about Racism in America*. Lanham, MD: Rowman & Littlefield, 2018.

———. *Black Bodies, White Gazes: The Continuing Significance of Race*. Lanham, MD: Rowman & Littlefield, 2008.

———. "Dear White America." *New York Times*, "The Stone," December 24, 2015. https://opinionator.blogs.nytimes.com/2015/12/24/dear-white-america/.

———. "Elevators, Social Spaces and Racism: A Philosophical Analysis." *Philosophy and Social Criticism* 34, no. 8 (2008): 843–876.

———. *Look, a White!: Philosophical Essays on Whiteness*. Philadelphia, PA: Temple University Press, 2012.

———. *What White Looks Like: African-American Philosophers on the Whiteness Question*. New York: Routledge, 2004.

Zack, Naomi, ed. "Ideal, Nonideal and Empirical Theories of Social Justice: The Need for Applicative Justice in Addressing Injustice." In *The Oxford Handbook of Philosophy and Race*. Oxford: Oxford University Press, 548–559, 2017.

———. *Thinking about Race*. Belmont, CA: Wadsworth, 1998.

———. *White Privilege and Black Rights*. Lanham, MD: Rowman & Littlefield, 2015.

CHAPTER 13

Brookfield, Stephen. "Racializing the Discourse of Adult Education." *Harvard Educational Review* 73, no. 4 (2003): 497–523.

Davis, Angela Y. "Angela Y. Davis." In *African-American Philosophers: 17 Conversations*, edited by George Yancy, 13–30. New York: Routledge, 1998.

DiAngelo, Robin. *White Fragility: Why It's So Hard for White People to Talk about Racism*. Boston, MA: Beacon Press, 2018.

Foucault, Michel. *Power/Knowledge: Selected Interviews and Other Writings, 1972–1977*. New York: Pantheon Books, 1980.

Graves, Robert and Alan Hodge. *The Reader over Your Shoulder: A Handbook for Writers of English Prose*. New York: Seven Stories Press, 1943.

Habermas, Jürgen. *Autonomy and Solidarity: Interviews with Jurgen Habermas*. London: Verso, 1992.

Harris, Leonard. *Philosophy Born of Struggle: Anthology of African-American Philosophy from 1917*. Dubuque, IA: Kendall/Hunt, 1983.

Horton, Myles. *The Long Haul: An Autobiography*. New York: Doubleday, 1990.

Marcuse, Herbert. *An Essay on Liberation*. Boston, MA: Beacon Press, 81–123, 1969.

———. "Repressive Tolerance." In *A Critique of Pure Tolerance*, edited by Robert Paul Wolff, Barrington Moore Jr, and Herbert Marcuse. Boston, MA: Beacon Press, 1965.

Outlaw, Lucius. T. Jr. "Lucius T. Outlaw." In *African-American Philosophers: 17 Conversations*, edited by George Yancy, 307–326. New York: Routledge, 1998.

Sheared, Vanessa, Juanita Johnson-Bailey, Scipio A. J. Colin III, Elizabeth Peterson, and Stephen D. Brookfield, eds. *Handbook of Race and Adult Education: A Resource for Dialogue on Racism*. San Francisco, CA: Jossey-Bass, 2010.

Stevenson, Bryan. *Just Mercy: A Story of Justice and Redemption*. New York: Random House, 2014.

Sullivan, Shannon. *Good White People: The Problem with Middle-Class White Anti-Racism*. Albany: SUNY Press, 2014.

Traister, Rebecca. *Good and Mad: The Revolutionary Power of Women's Anger*. New York: Simon & Schuster, 2018.

Yancy, George. *African-American Philosophers: 17 Conversations*. New York: Routledge, 1998.

———. *Backlash: What Happens When We Talk Honestly about Racism in America*. Lanham, MD: Rowman & Littlefield, 2018.

———. *Black Bodies, White Gazes: The Continuing Significance of Race*. Lanham, MD: Rowman & Littlefield, 2008.

———. "Dear White America." *New York Times*, "The Stone," December 24, 2015. https://opinionator.blogs.nytimes.com/2015/12/24/dear-white-america/.

———. *Look, a White!: Philosophical Essays on Whiteness*. Philadelphia, PA: Temple University Press, 2012.

———. *On Race*. New York: Oxford University Press, 2017.

———. *What White Looks Like: African-American Philosophers on the Whiteness Question*. New York: Routledge, 2004.

———. *White on White/Black on Black*. Lanham, MD: Rowman & Littlefield, 2005.

Yancy, George and Janine Jones. *Pursuing Trayvon Martin: Historical Contexts and Contemporary Manifestations of Racial Dynamics*. Lanham, MD: Lexington Books, 2013.

CHAPTER 14

Barber, Daniel Coluciello. "The Creation of Non-Being." *Rhizomes: Cultural Studies in Emerging Knowledge* 29 (2016): 1–23. doi:10.20415/rhiz/029.e10.

Brown, Wendy. *Undoing the Demos: Neoliberalism's Stealth Revolution*. New York: Zone Books, 2015.

Fanon, Frantz. *Black Skin, White Masks*. Translated by Richard Philcox. New York: Grove Press, 2008.

Jordan, William R. III. *The Sunflower Forest: Ecological Restoration and the New Communion with Nature*. Berkeley: University of California Press, 2003.

Macey, David. *Frantz Fanon: A Biography*. New York: Verso, 2012.

Marriott, David. *Whither Fanon?: Studies in the Blackness of Being*. Stanford, CA: Stanford University Press, 2018.

Moten, Fred. *Black and Blur*. Durham, NC: Duke University Press, 2017.

———. *Stolen Life*. Durham, NC: Duke University Press, 2018.

———. *The Universal Machine*. Durham, NC: Duke University Press, 2018.

Rose, Marika. *A Theology of Failure: Žižek against Christian Innocence*. New York: Fordham University Press, 2019.

Sartre, Jean-Paul. *Being and Nothingness, a Phenomenological Essay on Ontology*. Translated by Hazel E. Barnes. New York: Washington Square Press, 1984.

Sexton, Jared. "Afro-Pessimism: The Unclear Word." *Rhizomes: Cultural Studies in Emerging Knowledge* 29, nos. 4–5 (2016): 583–597.

———. *Black Men, Black Feminism: Lucifer's Nocturne*. New York: Palgrave Macmillan, 2018.

———. "The Social Life of Social Death: On Afro-Pessimism and Black Optimism." *InTensions Journal* 5 (Fall/Winter 2011) pp. 1–47. https://www.yorku.ca/intent/issue5/articles/pdfs/jaredsextonarticle.pdf.

———. "The *Vel* of Slavery: Tracking the Figure of the Unsovereign." *Critical Sociology* 42 (2014): 583–597.

Sharpe, Christina. *In the Wake: On Blackness and Being*. Durham, NC: Duke University Press, 2016.

Silva, Denise Ferreira da. *Toward a Global Idea of Race*. Minneapolis: University of Minnesota Press, 2007.

Smith, Anthony. *A Non-Philosophical Theory of Nature: Ecologies of Thought*. New York: Palgrave Macmillan, 2013.

Warren, Calvin L. *Ontological Terror: Blackness, Nihilism, and Emancipation*. Durham, NC: Duke University Press, 2018.

Wilderson, Frank B. III. *Red, White, & Black: Cinema and the Structure of U.S. Antagonisms*. Durham, NC: Duke University Press, 2010.

Yancy, George. *Black Bodies, White Gazes: The Continuing Significance of Race in America*. 2nd ed. New York: Rowman & Littlefield, 2017.

———. *Look, a White!: Philosophical Essays on Whiteness*. Philadelphia, PA: Temple University Press, 2012.

Index

281

About the Contributors

Selihom Andarge is a graduate of Regis University in Denver, Colorado, with degrees in peace and justice studies and communication.

Dr. Barbara Applebaum is professor of cultural foundations of education at Syracuse University in Syracuse, New York, whose training is in philosophy of education but whose work and teaching are interdisciplinary in nature. Her academic research focuses on the ways in which whiteness is reproduced through education, especially in the guise of good intentions and, more specifically, within the context of social justice pedagogy. Among the journals in which her publications appear are *Hypatia*, *Philosophy of Education*, *Race, Ethnicity and Education*, and *Educational Theory*. Her recent work addresses such topics as the non-performativity of white virtue signaling, challenging the comfort of white willful ignorance, a critique of implicit bias training on college campuses, and when comforting white discomfort is a form of complicity. Her book *Being White/Being Good: White Complicity, Responsibility and Social Justice Education* (2010) examines the meaning of white complicity, its ethical and epistemological assumptions, and offers recommendations for how white complicity can be named and disrupted.

Nicholas Aranda is a graduate of Regis University in Denver Colorado, with degrees in philosophy and peace and justice studies.

Daniel C. Blight is lecturer (assistant professor) in critical and historical studies in photography at the University of Brighton, United Kingdom, and a PhD student in sociology at Goldsmiths, University of London. His first edited book is *The Image of Whiteness: Contemporary Photography and Racialization* (2019). Blight's writing has been published by *1000 Words*, *The*

Guardian, *Philosophy of Photography*, *Photoworks*, *Vogue*, Manchester Art Gallery, UCL Art Museum, Art Museum of Estonia, FOMU Belgium, and the Australian Centre for Photography. He has been a visiting lecturer at institutions such as Royal Academy of Art The Hague, Royal College of Art, University of Oxford, and Yale University.

Josie Brady is a graduate of Regis University in Denver, Colorado, with degrees in politics and peace and justice studies.

Dr. Stephen Brookfield is distinguished scholar at Antioch University and also adjunct professor at Teachers College, Columbia University. Over a fifty-year career, his overall project has been to help people learn to think critically about the dominant ideologies they have internalized and to explore how these can be challenged. To that end he has written, cowritten, or edited twenty books on methodologies of critical thinking, discussion and dialog, critical reflection, leadership, critical theory, and the exploration of power dynamics, particularly around racial identity and white supremacy. His latest book (coauthored with Mary Hess) is titled *Becoming a White Antiracist* (2021).

Dr. Bill Bywater is emeritus professor of philosophy at Allegheny College in Meadville, Pennsylvania. His work on apprenticeship as central to democracy as a way of life and to education for democracy can be found in *Kettering Review* volume 29, number 1, and in the edited volumes *Neuroscience, Neurophilosophy and Pragmatism*, *The Role of the Arts in Learning*, and *Educating for Critical Consciousness*.

Tricia Charfauros is a graduate of Regis University in Denver, Colorado, with degrees in psychology and philosophy.

Kelley Coakley is a graduate of Regis University in Denver, Colorado, with degrees in philosophy and neuroscience.

Dr. E. Lâle Demirtürk is professor of American literature in the Department of American Culture and Literature at Bilkent University in Turkey. Her work appears in such publications as *College Literature*, *Southern Literary Journal*, *Melus*, *CLA Journal*, and *Mississippi Quarterly*. Her books include *The Contemporary African American Novel* (2012), *The Twenty-first Century African American Novel and the Critique of Whiteness in Everyday Life* (2016), *African American Novels in the Black Lives Matter Era* (2019), and *America as the Global(izing) Threat in the 21st Century* (2020) (in Turkish).

Dr. Kathy Glass is professor of English at Duquesne University in Pittsburgh, Pennsylvania, where she teaches African American literature and Black feminist critical theory. She is the author of *Politics and Affect in Black Women's Fiction* (2018) and *Courting Communities: Black Female Nationalism and Syncre-nationalism in the Nineteenth-Century North* (2006). Her work on gender, race, spirituality, and pedagogy also appears in numerous journal articles and book chapters.

Dr. Biko Mandela Gray is assistant professor of religion at Syracuse University in Syracuse, New York. He writes and thinks about the relationship between race, religion, and subjectivity, particularly as it relates to questions of embodiment and ethics. He has coedited (with Stephen C. Finley and Lori Latrice Martin) a volume titled *The Religion of White Rage: Religious Fervor, White Workers and the Myth of Black Racial Progress* (2020), and his manuscript *Black Life Matter* is forthcoming. He has published multiple articles and books chapters, including "Embodiment and Black Religion: Rethinking the Body in African American Religious Experience," *Equinox* (2017); and (with Stephen C. Finley) "God Is a White Racist: Immanent Atheism as a Religious Response to Black Lives Matter and Antiblack State-Sanctioned Violence," *Journal of Africana Religions* (2015).

Dr. Boram Jeong is assistant professor of philosophy at the University of Colorado in Denver, Colorado. Her research focuses on the intersection of the formation of political subjectivity and theories of temporality. She is currently working on a book project called *Capitalism and Melancholia* that examines the temporality of debt and the production of subjects in capitalism, and an article on colonial temporality that reconstructs the "newness" of the New Women in colonial Korea as a temporal resistance against colonial-Western modernity from a decolonial feminist perspective.

Dr. Clarence S. Johnson is professor of philosophy at Middle Tennessee State University in Murfreesboro, Tennessee. In addition to his book *Cornel West and Philosophy* (2002), Johnson's works have appeared in major scholarly journals such as *The Journal of Social Philosophy*, *Social Philosophy Today*, *The Journal of Philosophical Research*, *DIALOGUE: Canadian Philosophical Review*, *Metaphilosophy*, *The Southern Journal of Philosophy*, *The Southwest Philosophy Review*, and *The Journal of Thought*. He has also contributed chapters to a number of books and entries in *The Encyclopedia of Global Bioethics* (edited by Henk ten Have) and a forthcoming *Encyclopedia of African Religions and Philosophy* (edited by V. Y. Mudimbe).

Dr. Ryan J. Johnson is assistant professor of philosophy at Elon University in Elon, North Carolina. His work includes include two monographs: *The Deleuze-Lucretius Encounter* (2017) and *Deleuze, A Stoic* (2020). He has also edited three volumes: *The Movement of Nothingness* (2012), *Contemporary Encounters with Ancient Metaphysics* (2018), and *Nietzsche and Epicurus* (2020). Dr. Johnson's work also includes many journal articles and book chapters. A monograph on *Hegel and Black Thought*, as well as an edited volume on *Ancient Practice* are forthcoming. Johnson has earned multiple awards and fellowships, such as a John William Miller Society Fellowship, a National Endowment for the Humanities Summer Stipend, an Archie K. Davis Fellowship, *Deutscher Akademischer Austauschdienst/German Academic Exchange Service*, and more.

Dr. Harry A. Nethery is assistant professor of philosophy at Florida Southern College in Lakeland, Florida. He graduated with a BA in philosophy from Humboldt State University in 2003, MA in philosophy from the University of Memphis in 2005, and PhD in philosophy from Duquesne University in 2013. His dissertation, titled *The Companions: Husserl and Foucault on the Subject*, was written under the direction of Dr. Lanei Rodemeyer and is an attempt to create a new form of critical phenomenology through a dialogue between Edmund Husserl and Michel Foucault. Nethery's areas of specialization are critical theories of race, the philosophy of time, and contemporary continental philosophy. His most recent publication, "Husserl and Racism at the Level of Passive Synthesis" in the *Journal of the British Society for Phenomenology*, investigates the production of a racialized world within the experience of white people through an application of Husserl's analyses of passive synthesis to George Yancy's famous elevator example. In addition, Nethery has given numerous presentations in both Europe and North America on the topics of Husserl, Foucault, and critical theories of race. Currently, Nethery is working on a book-length project that argues for hip-hop as a source of philosophical insight.

Dr. Anthony Paul Smith is associate professor in the Department of Religion and Theology at La Salle University in Philadelphia, Pennsylvania. He publishes widely in philosophy, religious studies, and the environmental humanities. Among his publications are *Laruelle: A Stranger Thought* (2016) and *A Non-Philosophical Theory of Nature: Ecologies of Thought* (2013). He is currently completing a book project on theodicy as philosophical form titled *To Justify the World* and a translation of Malcom Ferdinand's *Decolonial Ecology: Thinking from the Caribbean World* (2021).

Dr. Tom Sparrow is associate professor of philosophy at Slippery Rock University in Slippery Rock, Pennsylvania, where his research is situated at the intersection of embodiment, phenomenology, and aesthetics. He is the author or editor of seven books, including *The Alphonso Lingis Reader* (2018), *Plastic Bodies* (2015), and *The End of Phenomenology* (2014). He has published nearly twenty book chapters and articles, some of which have appeared in *Philosophy Today*, *Epoché: A Journal for the History of Philosophy*, *IJFAB: International Journal of Feminist Approaches to Bioethics*, and *The Nordic Journal of Aesthetics*.

Dr. Becky Vartabedian is associate professor of philosophy at Regis University in Denver, Colorado. Dr. Vartabedian specializes in contemporary continental philosophy and maintains research and teaching interests in phenomenology's intersection with feminist, critical race, and queer theories.

Dr. Mark William Westmoreland is lecturer of philosophy at Ocean County College in Ocean County, New Jersey. He is coeditor, with Andrea J. Pitts, of *Beyond Bergson: Examining Race and Colonialism through the Writings of Henri Bergson* (2019). His most recent work includes "White Supremacy: The Present is Prologue" in *Perspectives on Global Development and Technology*, "The Racial Oracle Has a History" in *Teaching Race in Perilous Times* (2021), and "Bergson, Colonialism, and Race" in *Interpreting Bergson: Critical Essays* (2019). His other works have appeared in *Educational Philosophy and Theory*, *Journal of French and Francophone Philosophy*, *Kritike*, *Palgrave MacMillan*, *Phaenex: Journal of Existential and Phenomenological Theory and Culture*, and *SUNY Press*.

Regi Worles is a graduate of Regis University in Denver, Colorado, and is presently a community activator at Metrocaring, Denver, Colorado's frontline antihunger organization.

About the Editors

Dr. Kimberley Ducey is associate professor of sociology at the University of Winnipeg in Winnipeg, Manitoba. Her work appears in such publications as *Animal Oppression*, the *Handbook of Public Criminologies*, the *Cambridge Handbook of Sociology*, and the *Handbook of the Sociology of Racial and Ethnic Relations*. Her books include *Revealing Britain's Systemic Racism: The Case of Meghan Markle and the Royal Family* (2021, with J. Feagin), *Racist America* (4th ed., 2018, with J. Feagin), *Elite White Men Ruling* (2017, with J. Feagin), and *Liberation Sociology* (3rd ed., 2014, with J. Feagin and H. Vera). Previously, Dr. Ducey coedited *Systemic Racism Theory: Making Liberty, Justice, and Democracy Real* (2017, with R. Thompson-Miller).

Dr. Clevis Headley is associate professor of philosophy at Florida Atlantic University in Boca Raton, Florida. He specializes in Africana philosophy, critical race theory, epistemology, analytic philosophy, philosophy of language, and philosophy of mathematics. He has made considerable contributions to these fields through publications in such journals as *Semiotica*, *Man and World: International Philosophical Journal*, *Diogenes*, *Shibboleths: A Journal of Comparative Theory*, *Philosophia Africana*, and the *Journal for Social Philosophy*, in addition to contributing chapters to numerous books in his areas of specialization. Previously, Dr. Headley coedited two books, *Shifting the Geography of Reason* (2007) and *Haiti and the Americas* (2013). In addition to being an active member of many philosophical organizations, Dr. Headley was the cofounder (with Lewis Gordon and Paget Henry) of the Caribbean Philosophical Association. He has presented numerous papers for such conferences as the American Philosophical Association and the International Society for the Study of African Philosophy, and he has given invited lectures at the University of Memphis, the University of the West Indies, the

University of Oslo, and Rhodes University in Grahamstown (South Africa). In November 2017, Dr. Headley had the honor of presenting the keynote address at the sixty-third annual conference of the Florida Philosophical Association.

Dr. Joe R. Feagin is distinguished professor and Ella C. McFadden Professor in Sociology at Texas A & M University in College Station, Texas. He has done much internationally recognized research on U.S. racism, sexism, and political economy issues. He has written or cowritten seventy-four scholarly books and 200-plus scholarly articles in his social science areas. His books include *Systemic Racism* (2006); *White Party, White Government* (2012); *Latinos Facing Racism* (2014, with J. Cobas); *How Blacks Built America* (2015); *Elite White Men Ruling* (2017, with K. Ducey); *Racist America* (4th ed., 2019, with K. Ducey); *Rethinking Diversity Frameworks in Higher Education* (2020, with E. Chun); and *The White Racial Frame* (3rd ed., 2020). He is the recipient of a 2012 Soka Gakkai International-USA Social Justice Award, the 2013 American Association for Affirmative Action's Arthur Fletcher Lifetime Achievement Award, and three major American Sociological Association awards: W. E. B. Du Bois Career of Distinguished Scholarship Award, the Cox-Johnson-Frazier Award (for research in the African American scholarly tradition), and the Public Understanding of Sociology Award. He was the 1999–2000 president of the American Sociological Association.

CPSIA information can be obtained
at www.ICGtesting.com
Printed in the USA
BVHW042015181021
619081BV00014B/9